JESUS, THE JEWS, AND THE END OF THE AGE

WHAT THE BIBLE PREDICTS ABOUT THE END TIMES

DR. BROCK D. HOLLETT

B.S. ED., M.DIV., D.O.

Jesus, the Jews, and the End of the Age

FIRST EDITION 2023

Copyright 2023 Brock D. Hollett

Book designed by Mark Karis

Illustrations by Travis Bennett and Tom Quinlan. Used by permission.

Edited by Geoffrey Stone

Unless otherwise indicated, most Scripture quotations are from the New King James Version (NKJV) of the Bible.

ISBN: 9780988931633

FOR INFORMATION CONTACT

Brock D. Hollett

brockhollett@yahoo.com

Printed in the United States of America by

IngramSpark

ingramspark.com

(855) 997-7275

Dedicated to my dear friend Reggie Kelly

Thank you for helping me to properly understand Bible prophecy.

CONTENTS

1

THE SPIRIT OF PROPHECY

THE GOD OF ISRAEL does nothing without first revealing His secret to His servants the prophets (Amos 3:7). The major events of history, at least those which pertain to the redemption, are foretold by His prophets. Once the Lord's people come to understand these previously hidden mysteries, they become revealed secrets (Isa. 48:6). The prophet Moses declared, "The secret things belong to the Lord our God, but those things which are revealed belong to us and to our children forever" (Deut. 29:29; cf. Prov. 29:18). The mysteries which the prophets revealed to the nation of Israel have become the inheritance of all God's elect, those who trust in the Jewish Messiah—Jesus Christ.

One function of a prophet is to predict future events. Many biblical prophecies, such as those regarding the suffering, death, and resurrection of the Messiah, have already been fulfilled.[1] The Lord spoke through the prophet Isaiah, saying, "Behold, the former things have come to pass, and new things I declare; before they spring forth I tell you of them" (Isa. 42:9). By giving messages through His prophets, God declares "the end from the beginning, and from ancient times things that are not yet done" (Isa. 46:10; cf. Isa. 41:21-24, 26; 48:6). Jesus proclaimed, "I am the Alpha and the Omega, the Beginning and the End, the First and the Last" (Rev. 22:13; cf. Rev. 1:8, 11, 17; 2:8).

One of the purposes for Christ coming to earth was to fulfill the law of Moses and the Prophets (Matt. 5:17). He promised, "Assuredly, I say to you, till heaven and earth pass away, one jot or one tittle will by no means pass from the law till all is fulfilled" (Matt. 5:18). Every stroke of the prophets' pens must precisely and without exception come to pass. The apostle Peter provided the reason for this inerrancy: "No prophecy of Scripture is of any private interpretation, for prophecy never came by the will of man, but holy men of God spoke as they were moved by the Holy Spirit" (2 Pet. 1:20-21). As such, both the giving and the reception of the Scriptures are from God.

The God of heaven reveals mysteries, even deep secrets, to His prophets (Dan. 2:22, 28-29, 47). To illustrate, the second chapter of the book of Daniel relates that King Nebuchadnezzar of Babylon experienced a terrifying, prophetic dream which none of his wise men or astrologers could decipher. The king threatened to execute them but the prophet Daniel petitioned the Lord that He might make known the dream's contents and its interpretation. The Lord revealed "this secret," the dream's meaning, to the prophet in a night vision (Dan. 2:18-19, 28-30; cf. Dan. 4:9). Daniel praised the Lord with the following blessing:

> Blessed be the name of God forever and ever. . . . And He changes
> the times and the seasons; He removes kings and raises up kings; He

---

[1] For a detailed analysis of many of these prophecies, see *Moshiach Now* by Tzemach David (pen name for Brock D. Hollett).

gives wisdom to the wise and knowledge to those who have understanding. He reveals deep and secret things; He knows what is in the darkness, and light dwells with Him. I thank You and praise You, O God of my fathers; You have given me wisdom and might and have now made known to me what we asked of You. (Dan. 2:20, 21-23)

The Spirit of God within Daniel gave him divine wisdom, enabling him to understand prophetic visions and dreams and their interpretations (Dan. 4:9; 5:11). Because of the grace given to him, the prophet displayed "an excellent spirit, knowledge, understanding, interpreting dreams, solving riddles, and explaining enigmas" (Dan. 5:12). This is the nature of a true prophet. The greatness of the prophetic Spirit within Moses brought him to exclaim, "Oh, that all the Lord's people were prophets and that the Lord would put His Spirit upon them!" (Num. 11:29).

God continues to reveal prophetic messages to His servants, and He will reveal many more mysteries in their proper season. Christ taught His disciples about this work of the Holy Spirit:

I still have many things to say to you, but you cannot bear them now. However, when He, the Spirit of truth, has come, He will guide you into all truth; for He will not speak on His own authority, but whatever He hears He will speak; and He will tell you things to come. He will glorify Me, for He will take of what is Mine and declare it to you. (John 16:12-14)

The Spirit of truth, who searches "the deep things of God," has revealed a knowledge of future events to His Church (1 Cor. 2:10). The Son of God testified that the Spirit would continue to reveal many things to come, but only when we were ready to "bear them." He illumined many sacred truths the moment Jesus poured out the gift of the Spirit upon the Church on the day of Pentecost (Acts 2; cf. Acts 1:8). As we will see, the Spirit continues to reveal glorious truths about Jesus and His eternal kingdom.

God dwells in unapproachable light (1 Tim. 6:16) and shrouds Himself in thick darkness (1 Kings 8:12). Similarly, He hides His secrets from the wise of this age, while revealing them to mere "babes" (Matt. 11:25; Luke 10:21), that is, the humble and those without worldly reputation, power, and position. He reveals "the hidden wisdom" of His gospel to those who earnestly seek Him and His mysteries (1 Cor. 2:7). The disposition of a person's heart, whether approaching Him with pride or humility, ultimately decides whether he or she stumbles over these mysteries or receives further insight. For this reason, it is insufficient to examine the cumulative evidence of everything that the Bible says about prophecy, while attempting to resolve the many apparent paradoxes and contradictions. Prophecy ultimately tests the heart, and it is designed to stumble the pride and self-confidence of man.

There are many reasons for studying Bible prophecy: First, Jesus expects His people to discern the times in which we live. He told the scribes and Pharisees, "When it is evening you say, 'It will be fair weather, for the sky is red'; and in the morning, 'It will be foul weather today, for the sky is red and threatening.' Hypocrites! You know how to discern the face of the sky, but you cannot discern the signs of the times" (Matt. 16:2-3; cf. Luke 12:54-56). This warning indicates that we should not be ignorant of the divinely appointed "times and seasons" in which we live or of the prophetic events which are falling into place around us. This can only be true if we, like the prophet Daniel, have sought wisdom and understanding of Bible prophecy.

Second, Christ has commanded us to pay attention to the prophecies of Scripture. To illustrate, He warned, "But take heed; see, I have told you all things beforehand" (Mark 13:23). As such, prophecies inform us of future events so that we do not fear and are not taken off guard when they take place. The messages of the holy prophets and apostles encourage, protect, equip, and warn Christians.

> And the Lord God of their fathers sent warnings to them by His messengers, rising up early and sending them, because He had compassion

on His people and on His dwelling place. But they mocked the messengers of God, despised His words, and scoffed at His prophets, until the wrath of the Lord arose against His people, till there was no remedy. (2 Chron. 36:15-16)

Third, prophecy is a powerful resource for engendering faith. For example, Jesus promised that the Holy Spirit would teach us "all things," and He told us about future events so that we would believe when those events were fulfilled (John 14:26, 29). Consequently, fulfilled prophecy finds a central place in the Christian gospels, as evidenced by the phrases "that it might be fulfilled," "thus it is written," "what was spoken by the prophet," and the like. As the angel told the apostle John, "The testimony of Jesus is the spirit of prophecy" (Rev. 19:10). This remarkable statement encapsulates the idea that the gospel, our testimony about the Person and energies of Christ, is the very essence of prophecy. This is why prophecy provides the basis for Christian evangelism and demonstrable reasons for compelling others to believe the gospel. Furthermore, Christ provided us with a solution for the common objection that prophecy is too difficult to understand, specifically, that the Spirit teaches us "all things"—everything we need to know.

Fourth, God reveals His divine actions to us as evidence of our friendship with Him. Jesus announced, "No longer do I call you servants, for a servant does not know what his master is doing; but I have called you friends, for all things that I heard from My Father I have made known to you" (John 15:15). This friendship is precisely why the Lord did not withhold from the patriarch Abraham the things which He was about to do (Gen. 18:17). What a delight to be friends with Jesus! What a privilege to be given an understanding of what the Master is about to do!

Fifth, Christians are stewards of the mysteries of God. The apostle Paul wrote, "Let a man so consider us, as servants of Christ and stewards of the mysteries of God. Moreover, it is required in stewards that one be found faithful" (1 Cor. 4:1-2). The Master has entrusted us, as servant-stewards, with the task of understanding and caring for His divine secrets. He will undoubtedly require us to give an account of what we did with them on the day of judgment.

Sixth, we will receive special blessings if we read, understand, and obey the prophecies of Scripture. The book of Revelation conveys this specific promise: "Blessed is he who reads and those who hear the words of this prophecy, and keep those things which are written in it" (Rev. 1:3; cf. Rev. 22:7). Those who trust in the words of the Lord's prophets and apostles will receive godly prosperity (2 Chron. 20:20).

Seventh, prophecy is so important and precious that the ancient prophets, and even the angels in heaven, have longed to understand it.

> Of this salvation the prophets have inquired and searched carefully, who prophesied of the grace that would come to you, searching what, or what manner of time, the Spirit of Christ who was in them was indicating when He testified beforehand the sufferings of Christ and the glories that would follow. To them it was revealed that, not to themselves, but to us they were ministering the things which now have been reported to you through those who have preached the gospel to you by the Holy Spirit sent from heaven—things which angels desire to look into. (1 Pet. 1:10-12)

How great is the value of prophecy! The prophets did not fully understand their own prophecies at times, yet they "inquired and searched carefully" to understand their content and the timing of their fulfillment (1 Pet. 1:11). The Spirit who was in them designated that the gospel of Christ, about which they prophesied, would be revealed at a future time and for the benefit of a future people. This people is the holy and apostolic Church, those who follow Christ and His commandments. God has given this grace and salvation to people!

Like the ancient prophets, we should wrestle with Bible prophecy, searching and studying to understand it. We, like the ancients, should search the prophecies carefully and inquire from God to properly understand their content and the timing of these prophetic events. We should do this because "it is the glory of God to conceal a matter, but the glory of kings is to search out a matter" (Prov. 25:2). This pursuit is an angelic and royal enterprise!

The prophecies that we will explore throughout this book pertain to the events surrounding the glorious return of Jesus Christ. The theological study of end-time events is called eschatology.[2] The Hebrew prophets and Christ's apostles spoke often about eschatological events. For example, the apostles Peter, James, and John were eyewitnesses of Christ's glory on the Mount of Transfiguration (Matt. 17:1-9; Mark 9:2-13; Luke 9:28-36; 2 Pet. 1:17-18), and Peter regarded this event as a prophetic message about "the power and coming of our Lord Jesus Christ." In other words, the vision which they saw of Jesus on the mountain was a prophetic foreshadowing that He will return in glory:

> For we did not follow cunningly devised fables when we made known to you the power and coming of our Lord Jesus Christ, but were eyewitnesses of His majesty . . . And so we have the prophetic word confirmed, which you do well to heed as a light that shines in a dark place, until the day dawns and the morning star rises in your hearts. (2 Pet. 1:16, 19)

As we eagerly await the Second Coming of Christ, I invite you to diligently study the prophecies of Scripture and to pray for understanding by the Holy Spirit. In so doing, we will heed the instruction of our resurrected Lord that "He who has an ear, let him hear what the Spirit says to the churches" (Rev. 2:7, 11, 17, 29; 3:6, 13, 22). As you "take and eat" the words of prophecy, you may discover that reading about God's judgments "makes your stomach bitter," but rest assured, His redemptive purposes will be "as sweet as honey" (Rev. 10:9). I invite you to come and see!

---

2   The study of the last days or last things.

2

THE PROPHETIC PUZZLE

IN THIS CHAPTER, we will examine several prophecies of the book of Daniel. We will discover that these prophecies are intended to be read together, as a beautiful puzzle, where each prophecy adds additional pieces to the overall panorama. I will demonstrate that each of the five primary visions of the book, Daniel 2, 7, 8, 9, and 10-12, portray a series of events which will terminate at the time of the end, when Jesus Christ will return in glory. Predictably, these prophecies describe many of the same events, with each prophecy providing different angles and unique details of the larger eschatological drama.

The first vision is King Nebuchadnezzar's prophetic dream, which the prophet Daniel interpreted. The prophet told the king that the vision was how God was making known to him "what will be in the latter days" (Dan. 2:28). The earlier prophets had described Israel's "latter days" as the time when God would set up His kingdom upon the earth, restore His glorious presence to Jerusalem, and bring the Jews back to the land which had been promised to the patriarchs and their offspring. Commentators generally agree that the end of Nebuchadnezzar's dream refers to this same period of latter days. As we evaluate the details of the dream, it will become clear that the dream is not limited to this period of latter days, but the final portion of the dream specifically focuses on this period; this pattern is consistent with the other prophecies of the book.

Daniel provided the details of the king's dream:

> You, O king, were watching; and behold, a great image! This great image, whose splendor was excellent, stood before you; and its form was awesome. This image's head was of fine gold, its chest and arms of silver, its belly and thighs of bronze, its legs of iron, its feet partly of iron and partly of clay. You watched while a stone was cut out without hands, which struck the image on its feet of iron and clay, and broke them in pieces. Then the iron, the clay, the bronze, the

silver, and the gold were crushed together, and became like chaff from the summer threshing floors; the wind carried them away so that no trace of them was found. And the stone that struck the image became a great mountain and filled the whole earth. (Dan. 2:31-35)

The king saw an enormous statue or image of a man, comprised of four metals, corresponding to four successive kingdoms of man (Dan. 2:26ff). The inspired interpretation given to Daniel shows that the image's golden head represents King Nebuchadnezzar, the first king of the Neo-Babylonian Empire ("you are this head of gold" Dan. 2:38). The chest and arms of silver pointed to the Media-Persian or Achaemenid Kingdom ("another kingdom inferior to yours" Dan. 2:39)[1], and the bronze belly and thighs represent the Macedonian or Greek Kingdom ("then another, a third kingdom . . . which shall rule over all the earth" Dan. 2:39). The fourth kingdom, symbolized by the statue's iron legs, is commonly understood to represent the Roman Empire, which chronologically followed the Macedonian Kingdom ("the fourth kingdom . . . will break in pieces and crush all the others" in Dan. 2:40). As the two arms of the second kingdom likely represent the Medes and Persians (cf. Dan. 8:3), the two legs of the fourth kingdom may hint that the Roman Empire was later divided into a western half, administered from Rome, and an eastern half, with its capital at Byzantium (later renamed Constantinople).

This fourth and final kingdom would become a divided kingdom (Dan. 2:33-35, 41-43) but this means more than an East-West division. The "feet and toes" of the image were a composite of strong iron and potter's clay (Dan. 2:33, 41). The iron within the feet and toes indicates that they represent, in part, a continuation of the fourth kingdom (cf. Dan. 7:3, 17, 23) and its strength, as opposed to representing an altogether separate, fifth kingdom. However, the addition of ceramic clay implies a fundamental change in the latter period of this fourth

---

[1]   Cf. "Your kingdom has been divided, and given to the Medes and Persians" (Dan. 5:28).

kingdom. Some commentators have speculated that the addition of clay could point to the parsing up of the Roman Empire into individual nation-states and/or the incursions into the Empire by Islamic invaders, but the text reveals only that the kingdom would be divided so that it is "partly strong and partly fragile" (Dan. 2:41-42).[2]

A LIKENESS OF NEBUCHADNEZZAR'S STATUE IN THE PLAIN OF DURA

GOLD "This image's head was of fine **gold**,

SILVER its chest and arms of **silver**,

BRONZE its belly and thighs of **bronze**,

IRON its legs of iron,

IRON AND CLAY its **feet partly of iron and partly of clay**." (Daniel 2:32–33, NKJV)

Regardless of how we identity the feet and toes, the prophet explained that all four kingdoms will end abruptly because of the sudden arrival of God's kingdom:

> Then the iron, the clay, the bronze, the silver, and the gold were crushed together, and became like chaff from the summer threshing floors; the wind carried them away so that no trace of them was found. And the stone that struck the image became a great mountain and filled the whole earth . . . And in the days of these kings the God of heaven will set up a kingdom which shall never be destroyed; and the kingdom shall not be left to other people; it shall break in pieces and consume all these kingdoms, and it shall stand forever. (Dan. 2:35, 44)

---

2   Verse 43 explains the composite of iron and clay to mean that "they will mingle with the seed of men; but they will not adhere to one another."

Daniel saw a stone "cut out of the mountain without hands," which struck the image's brittle feet, crushing the entire image (Dan. 2:45; cf. Ps. 2:9).[3] The idea is that the world's great kingdoms will be completely destroyed at the same moment of time ("crushed together" Dan. 2:35) and blown away like chaff in the wind ("no trace of them was found"! Dan. 2:35; cf. Ps. 1:4). The prophet explained that the God of heaven will "set up a kingdom which shall never be destroyed" (Dan. 2:44); this divine action contrasts sharply with the emergence of the world's kingdoms, which human hands built and defended (cf. 2 Cor. 5:1; Heb. 9:24). Then God's kingdom will become a "great mountain," filling the entire earth (Dan. 2:35). The book of Revelation describes this end-time event as occurring at the return of Christ: "The kingdoms of this world have become the kingdoms of our Lord and of His Christ, and He shall reign forever and ever!" (Rev. 11:15).

Consistent with the four kingdoms of Daniel 2, the prophet saw four beasts in his vision in Daniel 7:

> I saw in my vision by night, and behold, the four winds of heaven were stirring up the Great Sea. And four great beasts came up from the sea, each different from the other. The first was like a lion, and had eagle's wings. I watched till its wings were plucked off; and it was lifted up from the earth and made to stand on two feet like a man, and a man's heart was given to it. And suddenly another beast, a second, like a bear. It was raised up on one side, and had three ribs in its mouth between its teeth. And they said thus to it: "Arise, devour much flesh!" After this I looked, and there was another, like a leopard, which had on its back four wings of a bird. The beast also had four heads, and dominion was given to it. After this I saw in the night

---

3   Similarly, Jesus, in the parable of the wicked vinedressers, warned, "And whoever falls on this stone will be broken; but on whomever it falls, it will grind him to powder" (Matt. 21:44). This is a deliberate play on words using the same vocalization of the Hebrew words eben ("stone") and ben ("Son").

visions, and behold, a fourth beast, dreadful and terrible, exceedingly strong. It had huge iron teeth; it was devouring, breaking in pieces, and trampling the residue with its feet. It was different from all the beasts that were before it, and it had ten horns. (Dan. 7:2-7)

Daniel saw four great beasts emerging from the turbulent waters of the Mediterranean Sea. He explained that these four beasts represent four kings, and more particularly, four kingdoms (Dan. 7:17, 23; cf. Zech. 1:18-20). The first beast was a lion with eagle's wings whose wings were plucked off so that it stood upon its two feet and received "a man's heart" (Dan. 7:4). This verse is an allusion to the removal of Nebuchadnezzar's reign during his period of insanity ("let his heart be changed from that of a man, let him be given the heart of a beast" Dan. 4:16) and his subsequent restoration to the throne (Dan. 4:34). This lion represents the Neo-Babylonian Empire, the same kingdom which was symbolized by the head of gold in Daniel 2.

The second beast was a bear which "raised up on one side" and had three ribs between its teeth so that it could "devour much flesh" (Dan. 7:5). The identity of this kingdom becomes clear by comparing it with

Daniel's vision in the subsequent chapter. There, in the vision of the ram and the goat, the prophet relayed, "Then I lifted my eyes and saw, and there, standing beside the river, was a ram which had two horns, and the two horns were high; but one was higher than the other, and the higher one came up last. I saw the ram pushing westward, northward, and southward" (Dan. 8:3-4). As the bear of chapter 7 was elevated on one side, one of this ram's two horns was elevated higher than the other. The prophet was told that these two horns represent "the kings of Media and Persia" (Dan. 8:20), in other words, the unified Achaemenid Kingdom of the Medes and Persians. Also, as the bear's mouth had three ribs, the ram pushed in three directions, westward, northward, and southward, to solidify its territorial withholdings. The bear, like the ram in the subsequent chapter, represents the Achaemenid Kingdom.

The third beast was a leopard with four heads and four wings (Dan. 7:6). Once again, significant parallels exist between these symbols and those found in the vision of the ram and goat. In the latter vision, the goat used its prominent horn to break off the ram's two horns. Then this horn was itself broken off and replaced by four prominent horns, which were divided "toward the four winds of heaven" (Dan. 8:8; cf. Dan.

8:22; 11:4). The four heads and four wings of the leopard beast correspond to the goat's four horns which pointed toward the four winds. In Daniel 8, the prophet identified the ram as Persia, the goat as Greece, and the goat's conspicuous horn as the first king of the Greek kingdom (Dan. 8:2, 21; cf. Dan. 11:2-3). This preeminent king of Greece was Alexander the Great, who experienced premature death. The four horns represent four primary ("notable") kingdoms which emerged from the Macedonian kingdom (Dan. 8:22; cf. Dan. 11:2-4); these horns were ruled over by Alexander's successors, the Diadochi. The biblical parallels between the leopard of chapter 7 and the goat of chapter 8 strongly suggest that the third beast is the Macedonian kingdom.

Daniel did not describe the fourth beast as a particular animal, but he described it as dreadful, terrible, and exceedingly strong (Dan. 7:7, 19). The fourth kingdom in Nebuchadnezzar's dream was strong like iron so that it crushed, broke in pieces, and shattered everything, including what remained of the three previous kingdoms (Dan. 2:40-41). Similarly, the prophet described the fourth beast as a fourth kingdom which was exceedingly strong and had iron teeth with which it devoured, broke in pieces, and trampled the entire earth "with its feet"

(Dan. 7:7, 19, 23). We may infer, based on the parallels with Daniel 2, that the ten toes of the fourth kingdom should be equated with the ten horns upon the head of the fourth beast (Dan. 2:33, 41 with Dan. 7:7, 20). Once again, using the interpretive method of Scripture interpreting Scripture, the fourth beast with iron features in Daniel 7 should be equated with the fourth kingdom of iron in Daniel 2. Nearly all commentators have identified this fourth beast kingdom as the Roman Empire, a claim which we will evaluate momentarily.

The vision of the four beasts in Daniel 7 strongly emphasizes the unique characteristics of the fourth beast. For example, the beast's head sported ten horns, symbolizing ten kings who will arise from the fourth kingdom (Dan. 7:24). The prophet observed an additional "little" horn, which will arise among the previous ten horns (Dan. 7:8). He identified this horn as a king who will arise "after" and "among" the ten kings to become "greater than his fellows" (Dan. 7:8, 20, 24). Daniel saw that this horn will pluck three of the ten horns out "by the roots," indicating that this emerging king will forcefully and overwhelmingly subdue three of the ten kingdoms (Dan. 7:8, 24).

The prophecy of Daniel 7 provides several clues for identifying the great king ("the little horn") and the ten kings. For example, Daniel saw the little horn will have the eyes "of a man" and a mouth speaking pompous words against God (Dan. 7:8, 20, 25). This self-exalting king will speak blasphemies, persecute and kill God's saints, and attempt to change the times and laws during a mysterious period of "a time and times and half a time" (Dan. 7:21, 25). These blasphemies will end when the beast itself is slain and its body given over to the fiery flame (Dan. 7:11), in other words, once the fourth kingdom has been completely destroyed in Christ's glorious presence.[4] The dominion of this wicked king will end precisely when the heavenly court is seated, and God gives His everlasting kingdom to His saints:

> I was watching; and the same horn was making war against the saints, and prevailing against them, until the Ancient of Days came, and a judgment was made in favor of the saints of the Most High, and the time came for the saints to possess the kingdom . . . But the court shall be seated, and they shall take away his [the self-exalting king's] dominion, to consume and destroy it forever. Then the kingdom and dominion, and the greatness of the kingdoms under the whole heaven, shall be given to the people, the saints of the Most High. His kingdom is an everlasting kingdom, and all dominions shall serve and obey Him. (Dan. 7:21-22, 26-27; cf. Dan. 7:9-10; 18)

This passage provides the biggest clue for identifying this self-exalting king. He will be the final ruler who will be destroyed when the kingdoms "under the whole heaven" are given to the saints, when God's everlasting kingdom will arrive. Clearly, no king or sovereign of the ancient world fulfilled the details of this prophecy. To drive home

---

4   Daniel saw that the first three beasts would each lose their dominion, but their lives would be prolonged "for a season and a time" (Dan. 7:12; cf. Rev. 17:10; 20:3, 5, 7), that is, until the time of unprecedented tribulation when they will rise up together as part of the composite Beast (Rev. 13:1-2).

this point, the prophet also connected the arrival of God's kingdom with the glorious arrival of the Son of Man:

> I was watching in the night visions, and behold, One like the Son of Man, coming with the clouds of heaven! He came to the Ancient of Days, and they brought Him near before Him. Then to Him was given dominion and glory and a kingdom that all peoples, nations, and languages should serve Him. His dominion is an everlasting dominion, which shall not pass away, and His kingdom the one which shall not be destroyed." (Dan. 7:13-14; cf. Matt. 28:18-20)

Christ identified Himself as the Son of Man who will arrive with the clouds of heaven. For instance, He prophesied, "All the tribes of the earth will mourn, and they will see the Son of Man coming on the clouds of heaven with power and great glory" (Matt. 24:30; cf. Zech. 12:10-12; Mark 13:26; Luke 21:27; Rev. 1:7; 14:14). The context of this and similar statements show that Jesus and His apostles regarded His coming in the clouds as a future event, even at the time when John wrote the book of Revelation. This means that Christ's "coming with the clouds of heaven" (Dan. 7:13) cannot be equated with His ascension into heaven (i.e., His coming "*to* the Ancient of Days" Dan. 7:13, emphasis added), but must refer to His glorious return.

The fourth beast of Daniel 7 and the composite Beast of Revelation 13 share numerous similarities. These similarities demonstrate beyond reasonable doubt that they describe the same final kingdom of the world that will reign at the time of the end. The Revelation prophecy reads as follows:

> Then I stood on the sand of the sea. And I saw a beast rising up out of the sea, having seven heads and ten horns, and on his horns ten crowns, and on his heads a blasphemous name. Now the beast which I saw was like a leopard, his feet were like the feet of a bear, and his mouth like the mouth of a lion. The dragon gave him his power, his

throne, and great authority. . . They worshiped the beast, saying, "Who is like the beast? Who is able to make war with him?" And he was given a mouth speaking great things and blasphemies, and he was given authority to continue for forty-two months. Then he opened his mouth in blasphemy against God, to blaspheme His name, His tabernacle, and those who dwell in heaven. It was granted to him to make war with the saints and to overcome them. (Rev. 13:1-2, 4-7)

The Beast in this passage shares striking similarities with the fourth beast of Daniel 7: First, both beasts emerge from the sea (Dan. 7:2 and Rev. 13:1). Second, both beasts have ten horns, that is, ten kings (or crowns) (Dan. 7:7, 20, 24 and Rev. 13:1). Third, both beasts "make war" with the saints and overcome them (Dan. 7:21, 25 and Rev. 13:4, 7). Fourth, the little horn of Daniel's fourth beast and the Beast of the Apocalypse both have a mouth speaking pompous words and blasphemies against God and the saints (Dan. 7:8, 20, 25 and Rev. 13:5-6). Fifth, both beasts maintain their authority for "a time, times, and half a time" or its equivalent of forty-two months (Dan. 7:21, 25 and Rev. 11:2-3; 13:5). As we will see in subsequent chapters, these beasts exhibit many other similarities. To the faithful interpreter, these parallels lead to the conclusion that the fourth beast of Daniel 7 should be equated with John's Beast, the Antichrist's kingdom.

This evidence begs an important question: Do these prophecies incorrectly place the return of Jesus Christ in the period of the ancient Roman Empire? Undoubtedly, the decline and fall of the Roman Empire has pushed many commentators to seek alternative interpretations. Preterist interpreters,[5] for example, contend that the Beast was the ancient Roman Empire, while many futurists argue that the Roman Empire will be revived. At least one recent interpretation has sought to skip the Roman Empire entirely, arguing that the Beast will be an

---

5   Preterists believe that many eschatological events, such as the coming of the Son of Man, were fulfilled in the past. For a thorough critique of preterism, see my book *Debunking Preterism: How Over-Realized Eschatology Misses the Not Yet of Bible Prophecy*.

exclusively Islamic Antichrist. These interpretive options contain weaknesses, as we will see in subsequent chapters.

To answer this question, we can correctly identify the Beast by first recognizing that it will have a composite nature. In other words, the apostle's description of the Beast incorporates the primary characteristics of all four of the beast kingdoms of Daniel 7. For example, John described the Beast as "like a leopard," but also having the feet of "a bear" and a mouth "like a lion" (Rev. 13:2), meaning that the primary features of the first three kingdoms will remain with the Beast. Furthermore, the Beast will also have "ten horns and seven heads" (Rev. 13:1), a description which combines all four of Daniel's beasts: the lion's head (Babylon), the bear's head (Media-Persia), the four leopard heads (the Greek Diadochi), and one head with ten horns (Rome with its final end-time kings). It is likely that Daniel, unlike John, did not see the full composite nature of the Beast. Yet John's vision indicates that the Beast will combine the fullness of the previous three beasts into its fourth and final form, but only during the final forty-two months before the Lord's return (Rev. 13:3-8). We will revisit this idea later in the book.

Admittedly, even the book of Daniel provides clues which suggest that the fourth kingdom will be *composite* in nature. For example, the fourth beast of Daniel 7 will have iron teeth, reminiscent of the fourth kingdom of Nebuchadnezzar's statue, and bronze claws, alluding to the third kingdom (Dan. 7:19). Finally, as we saw previously, the vision of Nebuchadnezzar's statue depicts all four kingdoms crashing down together, at one moment, at the time of the consummation of God's everlasting kingdom. This cannot occur as depicted in the vision unless, in a real sense, the kingdoms of Babylon, Media-Persia, and Greece will be carried forward into the kingdom of the fourth beast—the composite Beast (cf. Dan. 7:12).

The Beast does not refer exclusively to the Roman Empire for other reasons. An angel revealed the following mystery to the apostle John:

Here is the mind which has wisdom: The seven heads are seven mountains on which the woman sits. There are also seven kings. Five have
fallen, one is, and the other has not yet come. And when he comes, he
must continue a short time. The beast that was, and is not, is himself
also the eighth, and is of the seven, and is going to perdition. The ten
horns which you saw are ten kings who have received no kingdom as
yet, but they receive authority for one hour as kings with the beast.
These are of one mind, and they will give their power and authority
to the beast. These will make war with the Lamb, and the Lamb will
overcome them, for He is Lord of lords and King of kings; and those
who are with Him are called, chosen, and faithful. (Rev. 17:9-14)

The prophetic interpretation of the seven heads is that they represent
seven mountains and seven kings (Rev. 17:9-10). In Daniel's vision of
the four beasts, the heads symbolize kingdoms, and as we have seen,
"kings" sometimes also refers to kingdoms (Dan. 7:6, 17). Likewise,
"mountains" in apocalyptic literature often symbolizes kingdoms (Jer.
51:25; Dan. 2:35, 45; Zech. 4:7). The angel revealed to John that "Five
have fallen, one is, and the other has not yet come. And when he comes,
he must continue a short time" (Rev. 17:10). In other words, the apostle
was told that five of the seven kingdoms were already in the past ("five
have fallen"), whereas the sixth kingdom was present when John wrote
down the vision ("one is"), and the seventh kingdom was yet future
("the other has not yet come"). This has led many commentators to
interpret the seven heads as the great kingdoms which have oppressed
God's people: Egypt, Assyria, Babylon, Media-Persia, Greece, Rome,
and the future Antichrist kingdom.[6] Based on this evidence, it is reasonable to conclude that the Beast will include, but is not limited to,
the region and authority of the Roman Empire. It is preferable to see
the kingdom of Rome as having morphed into a divided, fragmented
kingdom ("iron and clay") until it finds its final, composite form under

[6] We will discuss the eighth head in a subsequent chapter of this book.

the Antichrist (cf. "a short time . . . an hour" Rev. 17:10, 12) at the time of the end (Dan. 2:33-35, 41-43).

The angel also revealed to John that the ten horns represent ten kings, who were future at the time of John's writing ("who have received no kingdom as yet" Rev. 17:12), who will be coregents with the Antichrist ("they receive authority for one hour as kings with the beast" Rev. 17:12). No kings in antiquity can answer the prophetic expectations of these ten kings. For example, the line of the Roman Caesars does not fit the requirements because many of these kings had already died by the time John wrote and because they reigned consecutively, not as co-reigning rulers. In addition, John saw that the ten kings will burn up the harlot city at the time of the end (Rev. 17:16; cf. Rev. 18), hardly a feat worthy of dead kings in history. The apostle was also told that the ten kings "will make war with the Lamb, and the Lamb will overcome them" (Rev. 17:14); this final war against the Lamb is described later in the book, and it will occur at the Second Coming of Jesus Christ (Rev. 19:19). In all these details, the actions of the ten kings are decidedly future events.

3

THE ABOMINATION OF DESOLATION

BEFORE CHRIST WENT TO THE CROSS, He lamented, "O Jerusalem, Jerusalem, the one who kills the prophets and stones those who are sent to her! How often I wanted to gather your children together, as a hen gathers her chicks under her wings, but you were not willing! See! Your house is left to you desolate" (Matt. 23:37-38; cf. Luke 13:34-35). In this passage, we see the heart of Jesus for His people. He mourned over the very city responsible for murdering the prophets, even with the knowledge that they would soon crucify Him. He also prophesied that their house—the holy temple—would become a desolation (Matt. 23:38; Luke 19:41-44). Furthermore, the people of the Holy City would not see Him again until they proclaimed, "Blessed is He who comes in the name of the Lord" (Matt. 23:39). This was a well-rehearsed verse from one of the Hallel psalms, Psalm 118, which extols Yahweh (יְהֹוָה) (i.e., the Lord) for His eternal faithfulness to the Jewish nation. Jesus' statement demonstrates that the nation will welcome Him as Lord when He returns in glory!

As Jesus left the temple, His disciples pointed out the magnificent architectural beauty of its buildings. In response, He prophesied the destruction of these buildings: "Assuredly, I say to you, not one stone shall be left here upon another, that shall not be thrown down" (Matt. 24:2; Mark 13:2; Luke 21:6). Previously, He had predicted details of the same event: "Your enemies will build an embankment around you, surround you and close you in on every side, and level you, and your children within you, to the ground" (Luke 19:43; cf. Dan. 9:26; Luke 23:27-31). It is a matter of historical record that the Roman legions commanded by General Titus completely dismantled the temple within forty years, in AD 70, exactly as Christ had prophesied.

Later, Jesus sat with His apostles on the Mount of Olives, according to their custom.[1] They asked, "*When* will these things [the events of the temple's destruction] be, and *what* will be the sign of Your coming and of the end of the age?" (Matt. 24:3, emphasis added).[2] Their twofold question betrays that they connected the Jerusalem temple's destruction with His glorious coming at the end of the age. Why did they connect this destruction with His return? To correctly answer this question, we must remember that the disciples had spent more than three years learning at their Master's feet. More importantly for our purposes, they had become the primary teachers of the gospel or good news about God's kingdom, in other words, the message that Jesus was fulfilling the expectations of the Prophets. As we will see, because the prophet Daniel had connected the destruction of the holy sanctuary with the Messiah's glorious arrival, the apostles had correctly connected these prophetic events.

Although the apostles correctly understood the content and sequence of these prophetic events, they were initially ignorant of the timing of their fulfillment. To illustrate, they incorrectly assumed that God's kingdom

---

1   The historical backdrop includes King David and his followers having previously ascended the Mount of Olives to weep with their heads covered while barefoot (2 Sam. 15:30; cf. Zech. 14:1-4).

2   Luke paraphrased the questions: "Teacher, but when will these things be? And what sign will there be when these things are about to take place?" (Luke 21:7; cf. Mark 13:4).

would arrive immediately (Luke 19:11), and after Christ's resurrection from the dead, they asked Him, "Lord, will you at this time restore the kingdom to Israel?" (Acts 1:6). In both instances, the apostles betrayed that they were perplexed about the timing of eschatological events.

The reason for the apostles' confusion about timing is that they did not yet understand that the Lord would "go away" to the Father (John 16:16-19) and that He would remain at God's right hand for an extended inter-advent period of nearly two thousand years. Prior to the day of Pentecost, Christ's session at the Father's right hand remained a concealed mystery (cf. Acts 2:30-36). However, the apostolic Church soon understood the concept of a delay, especially once the apostle Paul taught the mystery of the Gentiles, specifically, that non-Jews would trust in the Messiah during the period of widespread Jewish resistance to the gospel.

Because of historical retrospect, modern Christians know about many events related to the Jewish nation which the earliest disciples did not. For example, we know that the destruction of the Second Temple in AD 70 did not usher in the return of Jesus Christ.[3] In addition, it is certain that the apostles did not foresee the long dispersion of Jews throughout the nations. Neither did they realize that the land of Israel would lie desolate for two thousand years nor that the Jews would return to establish the modern State of Israel in 1947-48, much less that the Israeli Defense Forces would recapture Jerusalem in 1967. Against all odds, the Jews have maintained their unique ethnic and national identity, miraculously surviving the Crusades, pogroms, assimilation, the Holocaust, and several Middle Eastern wars which Israel won despite overwhelming Arab forces.

As a result of this ignorance, the apostles incorrectly assumed that Christ's glorious arrival would be connected with the destruction of the Second Temple and did not conceive of a Third Temple. Yet in the twenty-first century, the Orthodox Jews of the Temple Institute

---

3   The holy Church grappled with this dilemma—"the delay of the Parousia"—the perceived postponement of His return.

have finished preparing the temple furniture, Levitical vestments, and sacred vessels in preparation for building the Third Temple. Jewish priests and Levites have annually prepared mock sacrifices for Passover and have performed water-drawing rituals for the feast of Tabernacles. Most recently, in 2022, five red heifers arrived in Israel in preparation for obtaining the ashes of a red heifer, a necessary requirement to purify the priests according to Jewish law (Heb. 9:13). Furthermore, the Jewish Sanhedrin has reconvened in Israel and has rendered judicial decisions. I argue that the apostles' ignorance of a Third Temple is one of the reasons that Jesus answered their questions in the manner that He did in the Olivet Prophecy.

At this point it is imperative that we clarify a common misunderstanding about a rebuilt temple in Jerusalem. The holy Church has always taught that Jesus Christ is the final, perfect sacrifice for all sins and transgressions. Christ has offered Himself up as the ransom for sin (Mark 10:45), and He has provided redemption and forgiveness of sins by His blood (Eph. 1:7; Heb. 7:27; 9:12-15, 25-26; 10:4, 11; cf. Rom. 3:25). The writer of Hebrews reminded us that "it is not possible that the blood of bulls and goats could take away sins" (Heb. 10:4). As such, it is inappropriate for anyone, even the Jews, to return to the sacrificial system of the Old Testament, especially after the destruction of the Second Temple in AD 70. Nevertheless, we will soon see that the Holy Scriptures predict exactly this scenario, namely, the Jewish nation returning to the "shadows" of these Mosaic sacrifices and offerings. They will once again insist on keeping the law of Moses as a means of "establishing their own righteousness," instead of submitting to God's righteousness (Rom. 10:3), but it will spell disaster for the nation.

At any rate, Christ began to answer the apostles' questions by warning against large-scale deception (Matt. 24:4). He predicted the emergence of false Christs (literally "anointings") and false prophets, wars and rumors of wars, and famines, pestilences, and earthquakes in unexpected places (Matt. 24:5-7, 11). Then He explained that Christians would be delivered over to legal trials and that many of them would be betrayed, hated, and martyred for the faith (Matt. 24:9-10). Also, lawlessness would run rampant, and love would "grow cold," yet despite this, the gospel would be preached to all nations before "the end of the age" (Matt. 24:12-14). As we will see in subsequent chapters, all these prophetic events, like labor pains, will increase in intensity as the end draws near.

As a central feature of the Olivet Prophecy, Jesus explained that the event known as "the abomination of desolation" will be the primary harbinger which will signal a period of great and unprecedented tribulation.

> Therefore when you see the "abomination of desolation," spoken of by Daniel the prophet, standing in the holy place (whoever reads, let him understand), then let those who are in Judea flee to the mountains. Let him who is on the housetop not go down to take anything out of his house.[4] And let him who is in the field not go back to get his clothes. But woe to those who are pregnant and to those who are nursing babies in those days! And pray that your flight may not be in winter or on the Sabbath. For then there will be great tribulation, such as has not been since the beginning of the world until this time, no, nor ever shall be. And unless those days were shortened, no flesh would be saved; but for the elect's sake those days will be shortened. (Matt. 24:15-22; cf. Mark 13:14-20)

This passage reveals many details about the abomination of desolation. First, the abomination will be a visible and identifiable sign ("when you *see* the abomination of desolation" Matt. 24:15, emphasis added). The "you" here is not restricted to the Lord's first-century disciples, although the grammar does not prohibit this interpretation. Rather, as the remainder of the Synoptic Gospels reveals, the early disciples ("you") serve as representatives for Christ's disciples more generally, that is, the apostolic Church.[5]

---

4   Houses with flat roofs and patios are common in ancient and modern Israel.

5   This is evident based on a comprehensive word study of the second person plural "you" in the Synoptic Gospels, especially the five primary didactic sections in the book of Matthew.

Second, Jesus specifically instructed His disciples to search the prophecies of Daniel to understand the abomination of desolation; He explained that this is the very event which was "spoken of by Daniel the prophet" (Matt. 24:15). The phrase "whoever reads, let him understand" is the key to unlocking the meaning of this abomination (Matt. 24:15); it does not mean that Matthew was instructing his readers to "read" and "understand" the words of Jesus but that Jesus Himself was telling His disciples to read and understand the prophecies of Daniel. This is evident because this same statement appears in Mark's parallel account.

Third, the abomination will stand in the holy place (Matt. 24:15). In other words, the abomination will be an idol which will be erected inside the holy place (i.e., the inner courtyard), and most likely, within the most holy place (i.e., the inner precinct) of the Jerusalem temple. As we will see, the prophecies of Daniel confirm that the abomination refers to an idol that will be set up inside the temple sanctuary.

Fourth, the abomination will start the period of great and unprecedented tribulation ("*when* you see . . . *then* there will be great tribulation" Matt. 24:15, 21, emphasis added). This tribulation will be particularly intense ("great") and unrepeatable ("such as has not been since the beginning of the world until this time, no, nor ever shall be" Matt. 24:21). Jesus quoted Daniel 12:1 almost verbatim, demonstrating that He had in mind the unprecedented tribulation that Daniel also prophesied (Dan. 12:1-4; cf. "spoken of by Daniel the prophet" Matt. 24:15). These words of Jesus show that the great tribulation could never be duplicated; the language prohibits, in the truest sense, any double fulfillment, that is, a prophecy fulfilled completely on two occasions.

Fifth, the Jews in Judea must flee Jerusalem and go into the mountains when they see the abomination (Matt. 24:16; Mark 13:14). To refuse immediate flight ("not go down" and "not go back" Matt. 24:17; Mark 13:15-16) will place them in the epicenter of the great tribulation. The necessity of immediate evacuation is evidenced by the fact that pregnancy, winter weather conditions, and Sabbath travel restrictions could result in delay and death (Matt. 24:19-20; Mark 13:17-18).

As Jesus commanded, we will now read about the abomination of desolation in the prophecies of Daniel so that we can understand it. The abomination appears four times in the book of Daniel (Dan. 8:11-13, 9:27, 11:31, and 12:11; see Table 1), and it always describes a self-exalting ruler who uses military force to desecrate the temple sanctuary with two simultaneous actions: First, he will remove the daily offering of the temple; three of the four references clearly identify this offering as the tamid (Daniel 8:11-13, 11:31, and 12:11), the burnt offering of lambs, which the Levites were commanded to offer every evening and morning on the bronze altar of the Jerusalem temple. Second, at this same time, the ruler will erect the abomination of desolation, an idol, in the temple sanctuary. The idea is that the abomination will replace the tamid offering. These four passages read as follows:

He [the little horn] even exalted himself as high as the Prince of the host; and by him the daily sacrifices were taken away, and the place of His sanctuary was cast down. Because of transgression, an army was given over to the horn to oppose the daily sacrifices; and he cast truth down to the ground. He did all this and prospered . . . "How long will the vision be, concerning the daily sacrifices and the transgression of desolation, the giving of both the sanctuary and the host to be trampled underfoot?" (Dan. 8:11-12, 13)

The people of the prince who is to come shall destroy the city and the sanctuary. . . Then he shall confirm a covenant with many for one week; but in the middle of the week, he shall bring an end to sacrifice and offering. And on the wing of abominations shall be one who makes desolate, even until the consummation, which is determined, is poured out on the desolate. (Dan. 9:26, 27)

And forces shall be mustered by him [the king of the north], and they shall defile the sanctuary fortress; then they shall take away the daily sacrifices, and place there the abomination of desolation. (Dan. 11:31)

And from the time that the daily sacrifice is taken away and the abomination of desolation is set up there shall be one thousand two hundred and ninety days. (Dan. 12:11)

Regarding the prophecy of Daniel 9:26-27 (above), many commentators have argued that the ruler who will "bring an end to sacrifice and offering" (Dan. 9:27) is the Messiah who would be "cut off, but not for Himself" (Dan. 9:26). While it is correct to identify the slain Messiah (Dan. 9:26) as Jesus Christ, who died for the sins of the world, it is untenable to identify Him with the prince who will end "sacrifice and offering" (Dan. 9:27). Based on the Hebrew grammar, the nearest antecedent for the one who will end the sacrifice and offering (Dan. 9:27) is the coming prince whose people would destroy the temple and its sanctuary (Dan. 9:26). This identification becomes certain once a comparison is made between this passage (Dan. 9:26-27) and the other related prophecies in the book which clearly communicate that *the self-exalting ruler* will forcefully remove the tamid and set up the abomination of desolation (Dan. 8:11-13; 11:31; 12:11).

This coming prince will abruptly stop sacrifices and offerings in the middle of the final "week" of years (Dan. 9:27),[6] that is, three and a half years before the terminus of the prophecy. It should not escape our notice that this period roughly corresponds to the 1,290 days of Daniel 12:11, the period which will begin with these same events ("from the time that the daily sacrifice is taken away and the abomination of desolation is set up there shall be one thousand two hundred and ninety days" Dan. 12:11) and terminate at the end ("But you, go your way till the end; for you shall rest, and will arise to your inheritance at

---

6   Each heptad of seven years was called a Shemittah (i.e., Sabbatical year).

the end of the days" Dan. 12:13). Consequently, the final grouping of seven years will end with the final consummation, which is the answer to Daniel's prayer recorded at the beginning of the chapter, a prayer that the Lord will redeem the Jewish nation and restore Jerusalem and its holy sanctuary (Dan. 9:1-19). This period will "bring in everlasting righteousness" for the prophet's people and his Holy City (Dan. 9:24).

The other prophecies about the abomination of desolation also contain specific time indicators which demonstrate that they pertain to the time of the end. For example, in the prophecy of Daniel 8, Daniel was told that "the vision refers to the time of the end" (Dan. 8:17) and "the latter time of the indignation . . . at the appointed time, the end" (Dan. 8:19; cf. Dan. 11:27). In addition, four times in the vision of Daniel 10-12, we are told that the vision would not be completely understood until the time of the end (Dan. 11:40; 12:4, 9, 13). As such, the exhaustive fulfillment of these prophecies did not occur in history, such as during the period of the Maccabees, with the actions of Antiochus IV Epiphanes, as many commentators argue.

In the Olivet Discourse, Christ mentioned only one abomination of desolation. Then He identified it as the particular abomination of which Daniel wrote. Jesus did not say that the abomination would be like the one spoken of by Daniel, nor did He indicate that it would be an event only foreshadowed by the abomination of Daniel's prophecies. Rather, as we have seen, several verses confirm that Jesus had in mind *the same* abomination of which Daniel wrote. Consistent with this idea, Jesus borrowed His phrase "the abomination of desolation" (Matt. 24:15) from Daniel 11:31 and 12:11 (LXX). This phrase is only similar to the abomination statement in Daniel 9:27, although there is no doubt that Jesus also had this verse in mind as part of a larger constellation of verses about the same event.

As in the Olivet Discourse, the great and unprecedented tribulation appears in the book of Daniel:

At that time Michael shall stand up, the great prince who stands watch over the sons of your people; and there shall be a time of trouble, such as never was since there was a nation, even to that time. And at that time your people shall be delivered, everyone who is found written in the book. And many of those who sleep in the dust of the earth shall awake, some to everlasting life, some to shame and everlasting contempt. Those who are wise shall shine like the brightness of the firmament, and those who turn many to righteousness like the stars forever and ever. (Dan. 12:1-3)

This prophecy demonstrates that the great tribulation will occur when the abomination of desolation is set up. The phrase "at that time" appears twice in one verse (Dan. 12:1), the first of which serves to connect the standing up of Michael the archangel (Dan. 12:1; cf. Rev. 12:7) and the period of the Jewish nation's unprecedented tribulation (Dan. 12:1) with the events discussed in the immediately preceding verses (Dan. 11:31-45). In other words, the great tribulation will occur when ("at that time") the latter events of the previous chapter take place, including the northern king setting up the abomination of desolation in the Jerusalem sanctuary (Dan. 11:31-35), exalting himself above all gods (11:36-39), and being killed in the Holy Land (11:40-45). We will examine these verses in detail in subsequent chapters of this book.

Daniel was told that the great tribulation will end when God resurrects the dead. The second appearance of the phrase "at that time" (Dan. 12:1) connects the time of the deliverance of the prophet's people and the resurrection with the unprecedented tribulation mentioned previously in the same verse. Read as a unit, this prophecy demonstrates that the unprecedented tribulation will occur when the self-exalting king sets up the abomination and that this period will end with the deliverance of the Jewish people and the resurrection of the dead. As an aside, scholars have long noted that the Olivet Discourse is largely Christ's exposition of this portion of Daniel's prophecy, which explains why He reiterated the same themes to His apostles (Matt. 24:15-22).

The reader should note that the prophecy of Daniel 12:1-4 is the most unambiguous prediction about the resurrection of the dead in the Old Testament, and in one sense, it forms the bedrock for the New Testament doctrine of the resurrection. Christ and the apostle Paul cited the passage in defense of the resurrection (John 5:28-29; Acts 24:14-15). Consequently, those who claim that the resurrection in Daniel should be understood figuratively, and not actually and bodily, compromise a central tenet of Christianity. Therefore, the tribulation cannot be detached from the return of Christ and the bodily resurrection of the dead.

Daniel 12 establishes the length of the great tribulation. A few verses after Daniel's prophecy about the unprecedented tribulation, "the man clothed in linen"[7] answers the angel's question "How long shall the fulfillment of these wonders be?" with "it shall be for a time, times, and half a time; and when the power of the holy people has been completely shattered, all these things shall be finished" (Dan. 12:6, 7). As we discovered previously, this phrase "a time, times, and half a time" also appears in Daniel 7:25 with reference to the period when the "little horn" will speak blasphemies and wage war against the saints before his death at the Son of Man's cloud-coming. The exact length of this period is confirmed by the apostle John, who equated the "time, times, and half a time" with 1,260 days (Rev. 12:6, 14); this is the second half of Daniel's final "week" of years (Dan. 9:27; 12:11). Likewise, Daniel received explicit time indicators for the unprecedented tribulation:

And he said, "Go your way, Daniel, for the words are closed up and sealed till the *time of the end*. Many shall be purified, made white, and refined, but the wicked shall do wickedly; and none of the wicked shall understand, but the wise shall understand. And from the time that the daily sacrifice is taken away, and the abomination of desolation is set up, there shall be one thousand two hundred and ninety days . . . but you, go your way till *the end*; for you shall rest, and will arise to your inheritance at *the end of the days*." (Dan. 12:9-11, 13, emphasis added)

---

7   The identity of this "man" is likely the Angel of the Lord, the pre-incarnate Christophany of the second Person of the Holy Trinity—Jesus Christ (cf. Rev. 1:13-15).

The angel did not introduce a new abomination of desolation in verse 11 but merely alluded to the same one he had previously spoken about in detail earlier in the same vision (Dan. 11:31). Once again, we see that the tamid offering will be removed when the abomination is erected, and this twofold event will begin a specific period of 1,290 days (Dan. 12:11), only one month longer than the 1,260 days of great tribulation, as revealed to the apostle John. These prophetic events will occur when the righteous are "made purified, white, and refined" (Dan. 12:10), the same events as foretold earlier in the vision (Dan. 11:35; cf. Rev. 3:5; 7:14).

This portion of Daniel's vision contains three separate time statements which reveal that it will be fulfilled at the time of the end ("the time of the end" 12:4; "the end" 12:9; "the end of the days" 12:13). Furthermore, the prophecy reveals that "the man clothed in linen" came to bring understanding to the prophet about "what will happen to your people in the latter days, for the vision refers to many days yet to come" (Dan. 10:14). Continuing the resurrection theme of Daniel 12:1-4, the prophet was told that he would rest (a euphemism for his death) and would be resurrected to receive his inheritance (implicitly, in the Promised Land) at "the end of the days" (Dan. 12:13).

Like the Lord Jesus Christ, the apostle Paul reiterated these Danielic themes regarding the abomination of desolation:

> Now, brethren, concerning the coming of our Lord Jesus Christ and our gathering together to Him, we ask you, not to be soon shaken in mind or troubled, either by spirit or by word or by letter, as if from us, as though the day of Christ had come. Let no one deceive you by any means; for that Day will not come unless the falling away comes first, and the man of sin is revealed, the son of perdition, who opposes and exalts himself above all that is called God or that is worshiped, so that he sits as God in the temple of God, showing himself that he is God. (2 Thess. 2:1-4)

The apostle taught that the day of Christ's return to "gather together" His Church into His presence (2 Thess. 2:1, 3; cf. Matt. 24:30-31; 1 Thess. 4:15-18) will not take place until after the unprecedented tribulation. Two events must first occur ("comes first"): The Man of Sin must be revealed, the man who will exalt himself and sit in God's temple (2 Thess. 2:3-4). Also, the apostasy ("the falling away" 2 Thess. 2:3), a massive departure from the truth, must occur (cf. 2 Thess. 2:9-12). This prophecy is consistent with Christ's teaching that He will return in glory only after massive deception (Matt. 24:4-13, 23-26) and after the great tribulation ("immediately after the tribulation of those days" Matt. 24:29), which tribulation will take place once the abomination of desolation is placed (Matt. 24:15ff). Based on such verses, we clearly see Christ's *post*-tribulation return.

The apostle Paul, like Daniel and Christ, expected a future fulfillment for the abomination of desolation. He quoted Daniel 11:36 (LXX) when he wrote that this Man of Sin will "exalt himself above all that is called God or that is worshipped" (2 Thess. 2:4). By quoting this verse from Daniel, Paul equated the Man of Sin with the self-exalting king (Dan. 11:36) who will remove the tamid and set up his abomination in the Jerusalem temple sanctuary (Dan. 11:31). Like Daniel, Paul taught the Thessalonians that this lawless man will take his seat "as God in the temple" in order to set himself up to be worshipped as God Himself (2 Thess. 2:4). Paul, like Daniel, also predicted that Christ will return in glory to kill this wicked man ("whom the Lord will consume with the breath of His mouth and destroy with the brightness of His coming" 2 Thess. 2:8; cf. Isa. 11:4 LXX; Dan. 7:11, 13, 21-22; Rev. 19:20-21).

In addition to these three primary witnesses (i.e., Daniel, Jesus Christ, and Paul), the apostle John also repeated these themes about the abomination of desolation. He saw a vision in which the Gentiles will trample the outer court of God's temple and tread upon the Holy City for forty-two months, which he equates with 1,260 days.

Then I was given a reed like a measuring rod. And the angel stood, saying, "Rise and measure the temple of God, the altar, and those who worship there. But leave out the court which is outside the temple, and do not measure it, for it has been given to the Gentiles. And they will tread the holy city underfoot for forty-two months . . . one thousand two hundred and sixty days" (Rev. 11:1-2, 3)

In the next chapter, John saw a heavenly woman fleeing from the presence of Satan (Rev. 12:1-6, 13-17), reminiscent of the flight of the people of Judea in the Olivet Discourse (Matt. 24:15-22). In this vision, he learned that the flight will continue for 1,260 days (Rev. 12:6), which he equated with "a time, times, and half a time" (Rev. 12:14; cf. Dan. 7:25; 12:7). If his readers still had any doubt that this refers to the unprecedented tribulation mentioned in Daniel 12, the apostle alluded to the ancient prophecy again, writing that Michael will cast Satan out of heaven to begin these forty-two months of intense tribulation (Rev. 12:7-17 with Dan. 12:1).

In addition, in the next chapter of the Apocalypse, the apostle alluded to the "little horn" prophecy of Daniel 7, relaying that the final Beast will have "a mouth speaking great things and blasphemies" and that this will "continue for forty-two months" (Rev. 13:5; cf. Dan. 7:8, 11, 20, 25; 11:36). This tightly corresponds with the length of the little horn's reign of terror for "a time, times, and half a time" (Dan. 7:25; cf. Dan. 12:7; Rev. 12:14). John also explained that the entire world will worship the image (or idol) of the Beast during this forty-two-month period (Rev. 13:5-8, 14-15). This passage identifies the abomination of desolation as an image or icon of the self-exalting king himself!

We have seen that the book of Revelation equates the "time, times, and half a time," the forty-two months, and the 1,260 days. In addition, a grammatical comparison of the Beast described by the apostle John with the Man of Sin (2 Thess. 2:3-12) demonstrates beyond reasonable doubt that both apostles prophesied about the same man—the Antichrist. I have provided a comparative table at the end of this book

(Table 2). These facts argue strongly in favor of a future unprecedented tribulation, under the reign of the Antichrist, which will last for three and a half years. This literal interpretation which foresees a concise, definite period of great tribulation is all the more evident when we recognize that Daniel wrote about overlapping periods of 1,290 days and 1,335 days (Dan. 12:11-12), figures which do not lend themselves well to a figurative interpretation.

The eschatological prophecies given by Daniel, Paul, and John present Christ's arrival from heaven to violently kill this wicked villain and to give the heavenly kingdom to His saints (Dan. 7:11, 26; 11:45; 2 Thess. 2:8; Rev. 19:20; cf. Isa. 11:4 LXX; Dan. 9:27). This demonstrates that the same wicked man who will remove the daily offering and erect his abomination in the Jerusalem temple will be killed by the returning Christ. This fact alone sufficiently prohibits *any* interpretation that attempts to regard the abomination of desolation as being set up outside the years that will immediately precede the Lord's return![8] The importance of this temporal connection, and its implications for eschatology, cannot be overemphasized.

The Bible tells us that every word must be established by the testimony of two or three witnesses. These four prophetic witnesses, Daniel, Paul, John, and Jesus Himself, provided us with the same basic prophetic elements. This "prophetic puzzle," when put together by the help of the Holy Spirit, constructs a clear sequence of eschatological events. The Antichrist's abomination of desolation will start the three and a half years of unprecedented tribulation, which will continue until the Son of Man arrives with the clouds to destroy him. Consequently, any attempt to divide these prophetic events or to disrupt this essential timeline can only be explained by sheer ignorance or a strong desire to protect another theological commitment. As our Lord declared, "Therefore, what God has put together, let not man separate!" (Matt. 19:6; Mark 10:9).

---

[8]   This dismantles preterist and historicist interpretations which envision an extended, two-thousand-year great tribulation.

4

THE WAR BEGINS

WE SAW THAT THE ABOMINATION OF DESOLATION will involve the Antichrist's military invasion of Jerusalem, which will initiate forty-two months of unparalleled tribulation. Consistent with this theme, the prophets depicted a large, multi-national invasion of the land of Israel at the time of the end. For example, in his prophecy of the Gog and Magog War, Ezekiel outlined the invasion of Israel by a figure called Gog, the chief prince from the north (Ezek. 38-39). The Lord instructed the prophet to prophecy against this man:

> Son of man, set your face against Gog, of the land of Magog, the prince of Rosh, Meshech, and Tubal, and prophesy against him, and say, "Thus says the Lord God: 'Behold, I am against you, O Gog, the prince of Rosh, Meshech, and Tubal. I will turn you around, put hooks into your jaws, and lead you out, with all your army, horses, and horsemen, all splendidly clothed, a great company with bucklers and shields, all of

them handling swords. Persia, Ethiopia, and Libya are with them, all of them with shield and helmet; Gomer and all its troops; the house of Togarmah from the far north and all its troops—many people are with you. Prepare yourself and be ready, you and all your companies that are gathered about you; and be a guard for them. After many days you will be visited. In the latter years you will come into the land of those brought back from the sword and gathered from many people on the mountains of Israel, which had long been desolate; they were brought out of the nations, and now all of them dwell safely. You will ascend, coming like a storm, covering the land like a cloud, you and all your troops and many peoples with you . . . Then you will come from your place out of the far north, you and many peoples with you, all of them riding on horses, a great company and a mighty army. You will come up against My people Israel like a cloud, to cover the land. It will be in the latter days that I will bring you against My land, so that the nations may know Me, when I am hallowed in you, O Gog, before their eyes . . . Are you he of whom I have spoken in former days by My servants the prophets of Israel, who prophesied for years in those days that I would bring you against them?'." (Ezek. 38:2-9, 15-16, 17)

This mysterious prince called Gog will arise from the land of Magog (Ezek. 38:2; cf. "Gog" Num. 24:7 LXX), and this prophecy calls him the "chief prince" of Meshech and Tubal (Ezek. 38:2-3; cf. Ezek. 39:1). These regions are most often associated with modern Turkey, and possibly also Cappadocia. The prophecy explains that the coalition under Gog's command will include several Middle Eastern nations, including Persia (modern Iran), Ethiopia, Libya, Gomer (modern Turkey), and Togarmah "from the far north" (modern Turkey or possibly further north, Ezek. 38:5-6, 15). His vast hordes of armies will ascend like a storm and will cover the land of Israel like a massive cloud (Ezek. 38:9, 16).

This prophecy specifies that its visions will be fulfilled "after many days" (Ezek. 38:8), "in the latter years" (Ezek. 38:8), and "in the latter days" (Ezek. 38:16). Ezekiel wrote, "In the latter years you [Gog] will come into the land of those brought back from the sword and gathered from many people on the mountains of Israel, which had long been desolate; they were brought out of the nations, and now all of them dwell safely" (Ezek. 38:8). This verse implies that the Jewish people will have only *recently* been gathered back to their land after a *long* period of desolation. Similarly, Isaiah prophesied, "Your holy people have possessed it but a little while; our adversaries have trodden down Your sanctuary" (Isa. 63:18). The conditions described by Isaiah and Ezekiel have never existed in history and must refer to the modern State of Israel. The conditions which existed in the years immediately prior to the Roman destruction of Jerusalem and its temple in AD 70 contrasted sharply with those described in the prophecies. That destruction took place after the Jews had possessed the land for several centuries.

Other features of Ezekiel's prophecy help us to conclude that it refers to the time of the end. For example, the prophet predicted that the Lord will destroy Gog's multinational military with an earthquake, fire, and hailstones (Ezek. 38:18-23; 39:4-6). From that day forward, Israel and all the other nations will come to know the Lord (Ezek. 38:23; 39:6-7, 22), Israel will never again profane God's holy name (Ezek. 39:7), and God will no longer hide His face from the nation but will pour His Spirit upon them (Ezek. 39:29). In other words, the war will continue until the final deliverance of the Jewish nation (Dan. 9:26 with 12:1). Clearly then, this prophecy was not fulfilled any time in history. Coupling this evidence with what we learned in previous chapters, we can conclude that the war of Gog and Magog will continue for forty-two months, from the initial invasion at the time of the abomination until Christ returns in glory. We will explore these events in more detail in subsequent chapters.

Some teachers insist that Ezekiel's mention of ancient weapons cannot depict modern warfare. Admittedly, it is challenging to interpret the presence of "horses, and horsemen, all splendidly clothed, a great company with bucklers and shields, all of them handling swords" (Ezek. 38:4; cf. Ezek. 39:9) as describing current military weaponry.

However, we should understand that the prophet was utilizing accommodation, which is, employing the language and concepts familiar to his immediate audience to convey a message about the distant future. The Lord inspired the writing of Scripture but He did not override the human authorship by providing futuristic terminology that would not be understood for thousands of years, such as providing words such as tanks, jets, artillery, missiles, rifles, and so forth. Instead, the ancient prophets utilized the linguistic conventions and concepts which were already found in their contemporary context.

In the prophecy, God asks this northern prince a startling and rhetorical question regarding his identity: "Are you he of whom I have spoken in former days by My servants the prophets of Israel, who prophesied for years in those days that I would bring you against them?" (Ezek. 38:17). This man will not be a mere prince but the Antichrist, the cruel ruler whom all the prophets predicted will invade the land of Israel. While the Lord opposes the Antichrist ("I am against you," Ezek. 38:3) and has ordained him for condemnation, He also decreed that this man will make a U-turn when He sovereignly puts hooks into his "jaws" so to speak and "leads him out" like a beast to invade the land of Israel (Ezek. 38:4; cf. Job 41:1-2; Isa. 37:29).

Throughout the vast majority of Israel's history, the Arab neighbors which appear in the coalition of nations under the command of Gog (the Antichrist) have been a military threat to the nation. The psalmist Asaph sang about some of these nations:

> They have taken crafty counsel against Your people and consulted together against Your sheltered ones. They have said, "Come, and let us cut them off from being a nation, that the name of Israel may be remembered no more." For they have consulted together with one consent; they form a confederacy against You: The tents of Edom and the Ishmaelites; Moab and the Hagrites; Gebal, Ammon, and Amalek; Philistia with the inhabitants of Tyre; Assyria also has joined with them; they have helped the children of Lot. Selah (Ps. 83:3-8)

It is quite possible that the confederacy of ten nations described in this psalm will comprise the ten horns and kings, that is, the military arm of the Beast. These ten nations are typically identified with the following modern nations and peoples:

1. Edom—Jordan

2. Ishmaelites—Saudi Arabia

3. Moab (Lot's children)—Jordan

4. Hagrites—Egypt

5. Gebal - Lebanon

6. Ammon (Lot's children)—Jordan

7. Amalek—Egypt (Sinai region)

8. Philistia—Palestinians (Gaza strip)

9. Tyre—Lebanon

10. Assyria—Iraq and Syria

When the prophet Zechariah spoke about this international siege of Jerusalem, he pronounced that the invaders will be Israel's neighbors: "Behold, I will make Jerusalem a cup of drunkenness to all the surrounding peoples, when they lay siege against Judah and Jerusalem" (Zech. 12:2). Just two chapters later, God warned, "And your spoil will be divided in your midst. For I will gather all the nations to battle against Jerusalem; the city shall be taken, the houses rifled and the women ravished. Half of the city shall go into captivity, but the remnant of the people shall not be cut off from the city" (Zech. 14:1-2). The coalition of "all nations" which will attack Jerusalem does not refer to every nation on the planet but echoes the reference to "all the surrounding" nations in the former passage. Zechariah foresaw that the Holy City will be invaded with spoils taken, houses plundered, and women raped (Zech. 14:2; cf. Isa. 13:16).

Zechariah's prophecies clearly refer to the future invasion of Jerusalem at the time of the end. He prophesied that God will ultimately destroy the military invaders and deliver Judah and Jerusalem (Zech. 12:4, 6-9; 14:3, 5, 12-15). Once again, these prophetic expectations did not happen any time in history. To illustrate, the opposite scenario played out during the First Jewish-Roman War of AD 66-70; the Roman legions were entirely victorious over Judea and Jerusalem, and they decimated the Jewish nation without any miraculous deliverance. The prophecy continues with the following prediction:

> It shall be in that day that I will seek to destroy all the nations that come against Jerusalem. And I will pour on the house of David and on the inhabitants of Jerusalem the Spirit of grace and supplication; then they will look on Me whom they pierced. Yes, they will mourn for Him as one mourns for his only son and grieve for Him as one grieves for a firstborn. In that day there shall be a great mourning in Jerusalem, like the mourning at Hadad Rimmon in the plain of Megiddo. And the land shall mourn, every family by itself. (Zech. 12:9-12)

On at least two occasions, Jesus quoted and applied verse 10 to the Second Coming, specifically, when everyone will look upon Him—the pierced Lord—and will mourn because of Him (Matt. 24:30; Rev. 1:7). Also, the theme of God pouring out His Spirit upon the Jewish people found here also appears in several other prophecies which describe the nation receiving the final redemption under the new covenant (Isa. 32:15; 44:3; Jer. 31:33; Ezek. 11:19; 36:26-27; 39:29; Joel 2:28-29). Throughout the Prophets, the phrase "the Spirit of grace and supplication"[1] is used with reference to the complete regathering of the surviving remnant of Jews to their ancestral land (Jer. 31:9; Dan. 9:17-18, 23; cf. Jer. 50:4-5). Such passages indicate national repentance, including newfound submission to the Jewish Messiah. By connecting these redemptive themes to the battle over Jerusalem in particular, the prophet clearly foresaw the end-time war over Jerusalem. Much stronger arguments can demonstrate the futurity of the battle in Zechariah 14, as we will see in a subsequent chapter of this book.

One astonishing feature of this Zechariah 14 prophecy is that half of the city of Jerusalem will be taken captive and many of its inhabitants taken captive, while the remainder of its inhabitants will experience neither death nor captivity, presumably because of divine protection (Zech. 14:2; cf. Isa. 1:7-9). Despite the Holocaust in the last century and the frequently used Jewish reaction "Never again!", this prophecy clearly predicts a *future* captivity of the city (cf. Isa. 6:12). Christ made a similar prediction in Luke's version of the Olivet Discourse:

> But when you see Jerusalem surrounded by armies, then know that its desolation is near. Then let those who are in Judea flee to the mountains, let those who are in the midst of her depart, and let not those who are in the country enter her. For these are the days of vengeance, that all things which are written may be fulfilled. But woe to those who are pregnant and to those who are nursing babies in those days! For there will be great distress in the land and wrath upon this people. And they will fall by the edge of the sword, and be led away captive into all nations. And Jerusalem will be trampled by Gentiles until the times of the Gentiles are fulfilled. (Luke 21:20-24)

Saint Luke replaced the statement found in Matthew and Mark ("when you see the abomination of desolation") with "when you see Jerusalem surrounded by armies . . . its desolation is near" (Luke 21:20).

---

[1]   Alternatively translated "the Spirit of grace *and pleas of mercy*" (emphasis added).

Likely, Luke designed this transposition for his largely Gentile audience. Both phrases are consistent with Daniel's prophecies, which reveal that the Antichrist will forcefully remove the temple sacrifices and set up his abomination by sending his armies to desolate the Holy City. Also, Christ's statements about "the days of vengeance" (Luke 21:22) and "wrath" against the Jewish people ("great distress in the land and wrath upon this people" Luke 21:23) reflect the overall end-time predictions conveyed by the Old Testament prophets (Deut. 32:43; Isa. 1:24; 10:6; 61:2; 63:4; Hosea 8:1). These prophetic events must happen in order "that all things which are written [in the Prophets] may be fulfilled" (Luke 21:22).

As Zechariah's prophecy indicates the end-time captivity of Jerusalem ("half of the city shall go into captivity" Zech. 14:2), Luke's rendition of the Discourse reveals that many of the Jews who survive the initial invasion will be "led away captive into all nations" (Luke 21:24; cf. Ezek. 39:28). This does not refer primarily to the First Jewish-Roman War in AD 66-70 but to the Antichrist's final assault against Jerusalem. Admittedly, Luke's version of the prophecy appears to allow for a mysterious versatility of fulfillment or application that includes the destruction of Judea and Jerusalem during and after AD 70.

During the final battle over Jerusalem, the Jewish people will be "drunk" with the "wine" of God's wrath so to speak, which is consistent with Luke's statements, and many corpses will be strewn about because of famine and war (Isa. 51:17-20; cf. Zeph. 1:10-11). The prophet Isaiah also explained that many people will be robbed of their goods, and the survivors will be trapped in holes and incarcerated in prisons (Isa. 42:22; 49:9; cf. Zech. 14:2). Some of the surviving inhabitants of Judah and Jerusalem will be sold as prisoners to the region which now includes modern Turkey[2] (Joel 3:6); this is consistent with Luke's statement of Jesus about their captivity into all nations (Luke 21:24).

Christ's declaration that Jerusalem will be "trampled by Gentiles"

---

2   This ancient region also included modern Greece.

during the period called "the times of the Gentiles" (Luke 21:24) is echoed by the apostle John's statement that the Gentiles will "tread the holy city underfoot for forty-two months" (Rev. 11:2; cf. Isa. 63:18). Although Gentiles have been treading upon Jerusalem during the long period of the Jewish Diaspora, from the destruction of the Second Temple in AD 70 until the establishment of the modern State of Israel, we cannot easily dismiss the thematic and linguistic parallels between Christ's statement and John's statement. In addition, the parallel passages in Matthew and Mark conclusively demonstrate that Jesus was speaking about the final end-time assault on Jerusalem. This position is further buttressed by the prophet Ezekiel's reference to "the time of the Gentiles," in which the singular "time" denotes the day of the Lord (Ezek. 30:3-4).

In the Olivet Discourse, Jesus told His disciples that the Judean Jews must flee to the mountains once they see the abomination of desolation (Matt. 24:16; Mark 13:14) or the simultaneous event of the Antichrist's armies surrounding the Holy City (Luke 21:21). Drawing from this prophecy, the apostle John saw the heavenly woman fleeing from the presence of the serpent-dragon to a place of protection in the desert:

> Now a great sign appeared in heaven: a woman clothed with the sun, with the moon under her feet, and on her head a garland of twelve stars. Then being with child, she cried out in labor and in pain to give birth. . . And the dragon stood before the woman who was ready to give birth, to devour her Child as soon as it was born. She bore a male Child who was to rule all nations with a rod of iron. And her Child was caught up to God and His throne. Then the woman fled into the wilderness, where she has a place prepared by God, that they should feed her there one thousand two hundred and sixty days. (Rev. 12:1-2, 4-6)

The apostle depicted the heavenly women, the mother Church at the time of Christ's birth, the Jewish nation consisting of twelve tribes, symbolized by twelve stars (cf. Gen. 37:9), as experiencing the "labor pains" of tribulation before giving birth to Christ, the male Child destined to reign over all the nations (Rev. 12:5, 13; cf. Matt. 24:8, 15). This Child was then "caught up to God and His throne" (Rev. 12:5), a vivid image of Christ's ascension to God's right hand, which John saw as occurring prior to the final "travail" of great tribulation (Rev. 12:5-6, 13; cf. Isa. 66:7).[3] The end-time Jerusalem Church, and almost certainly, those Jews who will become Christians after the flight, will flee into the desert to receive divine nourishment and protection away from the serpent during this tribulation, which tribulation will continue for 1,260 days and "a time and times and half a time" (Rev. 12:6, 14).[4]

The prophet Isaiah provided an additional prophetic backdrop for John's vision of the heavenly mother with Child in his prophecy that the holy nation will miraculously "give birth" to her children at once, on a single day (Isa. 66:7-13). This is a powerful symbol for the glorious resurrection at the end of the unprecedented tribulation (Isa. 26:17-19; cf. Dan. 12:1-4).

Continuing this theme of the perpetual enmity between the serpent's seed and the woman's Seed (cf. Gen. 3:15), the apostle John described this cosmic struggle:

> Now when the dragon saw that he had been cast to the earth, he persecuted the woman who gave birth to the male Child. But the woman was given two wings of a great eagle, that she might fly into the wilderness to her place, where she is nourished for a time and times and half a time, from the presence of the serpent. So the serpent spewed water out of his mouth like a flood after the woman, that he might cause her to be carried away by the flood. But the earth helped

---

[3] As Daniel described the death of the Messiah immediately before describing the events of the final tribulation (Dan. 9:26-27), the apostle John depicted the ascension of the male Child, Jesus Christ, to God's throne immediately prior to depicting the events of the unprecedented tribulation (Rev. 12:5ff).

[4] The holy Virgin mother of Christ, the Theotokos, and her flight into Egypt to save the holy Child from King Herod's slaughter of the innocents (Matt. 2:13-18) prophetically foreshadow the flight of the holy Jerusalem church and her children from the presence of the Antichrist.

the woman, and the earth opened its mouth and swallowed up the flood which the dragon had spewed out of his mouth. And the dragon was enraged with the woman, and he went to make war with the rest of her offspring, who keep the commandments of God and have the testimony of Jesus Christ. (Rev. 12:13-17)

The holy refugees of Jews will flee to the desert with "two wings of a great eagle" (Rev. 12:14). The prophetic backdrop for this exodus imagery is God bearing the children of Israel "on eagles' wings" to bring them through the desert on their way to the Promised Land (Exod. 19:4). John's depiction of the earth helping the woman by swallowing up the flood (Rev. 12:15-16) is a reference to the Antichrist's armies, elsewhere symbolized as a flood (Isa. 59:19; Dan. 9:26; 11:22), being prevented from killing the fleeing Jews of Judea and Jerusalem. After Satan recognizes that he is unable to continue his persecution of the Jews who have fled, he will ferociously attack the Christians throughout the remainder of the world ("makes war with the rest of her offspring, who keep the commandments of God and have the testimony of Jesus Christ" Rev. 12:17; cf. Gen. 3:15).

Although some commentators have suggested that the desert is only a metaphor, we should notice that the prophets also spoke about the surviving Jews receiving divine comfort and blessing in the desert. For example, Jeremiah taught that many who survive the sword will find grace in the desert (Jer. 31:2). The Lord promised, "Therefore, behold, I will allure her, will bring her into the wilderness, and speak comfort to her" (Hosea 2:14). The prophet Ezekiel drew from the desert wanderings of the exodus to describe how the Lord will ultimately bring many of the people of Israel into the desert and into relationship with Him:

And I will bring you into the wilderness of the peoples, and there I will plead My case with you face to face. Just as I pleaded My case with your fathers in the wilderness of the land of Egypt, so I will plead My case with you . . . I will make you pass under the rod, and

I will bring you into the bond of the covenant; I will purge the rebels from among you, and those who transgress against Me; I will bring them out of the country where they dwell, but they shall not enter the land of Israel. Then you will know that I am the Lord. (Ezek. 20:35-36, 37-38)

In this passage, the Lord promised to bring many of the Jews into "the desert of the nations" to plead His legal case with them (Ezek. 20:35). As sheep pass under a shepherd's rod so that one in every ten becomes a holy tithe before Him (cf. Lev. 27:32; Isa. 6:13), the Good Shepherd will divide the Jewish people and purge the disobedient ones ("rebels") in order to prepare a holy people for Himself ("I will make you pass under the rod" Ezek. 20:37; cf. Ezek. 20:36-38; Amos 9:9-10). It is not altogether clear how He will plead His case with them but it will necessarily require the gospel ("the bond of the covenant . . . then you will know that I am the Lord" Ezek. 20:37).

It is unlikely that the desert is used metaphorically in these passages. To the contrary, the evidence supports a literal interpretation where many Jews will find protection in the desert region of Bozrah (meaning sheepfold) and Kedar, specifically, the vast system of rocky enclaves known as Sela or Petra (often translated "rock") in modern Jordan (Isa. 16:1-5; 42:11-13; Mic. 2:12; cf. Isa. 26:20). This correlates well with the statement of the prophet Daniel that the nation of Jordan will be delivered from the final assault of the Antichrist ("but these shall escape from his hand: Edom, Moab, and the prominent people of Ammon" Dan. 11:41). Clearly, this desert wandering will be a crucial part of a second and greater exodus!

5

THE MYSTERY OF THE GAP

THE PROPHECY OF THE SEVENTY WEEKS serves a critical purpose for the study of eschatology. The angel Gabriel gave it to Daniel in response to his penitential prayer in which he petitioned the Lord to bring the Jews back to their homeland after their exile of seventy years in Babylon (Dan. 9:1-19; cf. 1 Kings 8:46-53; 2 Chron. 6:36-40). The prophet prayed for God to turn His wrath away from His Holy City, Jerusalem, and to show favor to the desolate sanctuary of His holy temple (vv. 16-17). The prophecy continues as follows:

> Seventy weeks are determined for your people and for your holy city, to finish the transgression, to make an end of sins, to make reconciliation for iniquity, to bring in everlasting righteousness, to seal up vision and prophecy, and to anoint the Most Holy. Know therefore and understand, that from the going forth of the command to restore and build Jerusalem until Messiah the Prince, there shall be seven weeks

and sixty-two weeks; the street shall be built again, and the wall, even in troublesome times. And after the sixty-two weeks Messiah shall be cut off, but not for Himself; and the people of the prince who is to come shall destroy the city and the sanctuary. The end of it shall be with a flood, and till the end of the war desolations are determined. Then he shall confirm a covenant with many for one week; but in the middle of the week he shall bring an end to sacrifice and offering. And on the wing of abominations shall be one who makes desolate, even until the consummation, which is determined, is poured out on the desolate. (Dan. 9:24-27)

Commentators generally agree regarding several features of this prophecy. First, it is an expansion of Jeremiah's prophecy which predicts the return of the Jews to the land of Israel after seventy years of Babylonian reign (2 Chron. 36:21; Jer. 25:11-12; 29:10; cf. Dan. 9:2; Zech. 1:12), enumerating the events that would occur during a period of seventy "weeks"; the Hebrew is translated literally "sevens" or "heptads." These seventy "weeks" are almost universally understood to mean seventy groupings of seven years (70 x 7 years = 490 years[1]; cf. Gen. 29:27-28). Second, the prophecy pertains to the prophet's people, the Jews, and the Holy City Jerusalem (Dan. 9:24). Third, the 490-year period consummates the following divine purposes: "to finish the transgression, to make an end of sins, to make reconciliation for iniquity, to bring in everlasting righteousness, to seal up vision and prophecy, and to anoint the Most Holy" (Dan. 9:24). Some scholars have attempted, with limited degrees of success, to connect all six redemptive actions to the First Advent of Jesus Christ. Fourth, most conservative Christian interpreters understand "an anointed one" who would be "cut off" and "have nothing" after the first sixty-nine weeks (483 years) to refer to Christ and His death on the cross (Dan. 9:26; cf. Isa. 53:8).

Scholars, however, vehemently disagree regarding the timing and

---

[1] This is ten Jubilee cycles.

events of the Seventieth Week, the final seven years of the prophecy. For example, preterists usually identify "the prince who is to come" (Dan. 9:26) as Emperor Vespasian or General Titus, whereas many futurists see this figure to be the future Antichrist. Most interpreters see the destruction of the city (Dan. 9:26) as a reference to the Roman invasion of Jerusalem in AD 70, although most futurists interpret it as referring to the city's future destruction by the Antichrist or as a double entendre.

As a reminder, some commentators interpret the one who will "confirm a covenant with many for one week; but in the middle of the week, he shall bring an end to sacrifice and offering" (Dan. 9:27) as a reference to the ministry and death of Christ (cf. Matt. 26:28). Others interpret the verse as describing the Antichrist, who will deceptively enter into the holy covenant with Israel and with "many" other nations (Dan. 8:25; 11:21-24, 27-28; cf. Isa. 28:14-16, 18; Ezek. 38:8, 11, 14; 1 Thess. 5:3). He will then violate the covenant by setting up the abomination of desolation at the midpoint of the final seven years: "for half of the week he shall put an end to sacrifice and offering. . . . On the wing of abominations shall come one who makes desolate" (Dan. 9:27; cf. Isa. 10:22-23).

As we saw previously, this event will include the forced cessation of the daily sacrifice in the Third Temple (Dan. 9:27; 11:31; 12:11; Matt. 24:15; 2 Thess. 2:4). Consistent with this motif, our futurist interpretation of Daniel 9:26-27 applies all these actions to the Antichrist as seen in the table below.

TABLE 3: PRETERIST AND FUTURIST INTERPRETATIONS OF DANIEL 9:26-27

Daniel 9:26-27	Preterist Interpretation	Futurist Interpretation
And the people of the prince who is to come shall destroy the city and the sanctuary	Vespasian or Titus	The Antichrist
And he shall make a strong covenant with many for one week,	Christ	The Antichrist
and for half of the week he shall put an end to sacrifice and offering.	Christ	The Antichrist
And on the wing of abominations shall come one who makes desolate,	Titus	The Antichrist
until the decreed end is poured out on the desolator.	Titus	The Antichrist

Most futurists interpret Daniel's Seventieth Week as referring to the final seven years prior to the return of Jesus. This requires a gap of nearly two thousand years between the sixty-ninth and seventieth weeks. While the prophecy does not specify a gap, the grammatical construction of the passage divides the 490 years into distinct periods of "seven weeks and sixty-two weeks" (49 years + 434 years = 483 years), and "one week" (7 years). This allows for the possibility of at least one gap, especially since the angel specified that certain prophetic events would signal the start and completion of each period.

All eschatological systems of interpretation must leave room for a gap before Daniel's final "week" of years. Many preterists, following Saint Clement of Alexandria, allow for a forty-year gap between the "cutting off" of the Messiah after the sixty-ninth week and the destruction of Jerusalem during the seventieth week. Nevertheless, other preterist interpretations reject a gap altogether and place the "cutting off" of the Messiah in the midpoint of the seventieth week, instead of immediately after the sixty-ninth week. They claim that the termination of the Seventieth Week occurred three and a half years after Christ's crucifixion, when the evangelistic focus of the apostles shifted from the Jews to the Gentiles.

This preterist interpretation is incorrect. The prophet Daniel had prayed for the Lord to show mercy to the Jewish nation by turning them from their iniquities and putting an end to the desolations that had come upon Jerusalem (Dan. 9:1-19). But their interpretation strongly implies that the divine answer to these prayers was to send the Roman armies to bring ultimate desolation upon Jerusalem. In addition, the preterist interpretation necessarily separates the abomination of desolation from the removal of the daily sacrifice because they teach that Jesus removed the daily sacrifices and that General Titus set up the abomination nearly four decades later, after the Seventieth Week (cf. Dan. 9:26-27). On the other hand, the futurist position is that the fulfillment of the prophecy must include the final redemption of Jerusalem and the glorious return of Jesus to usher in "everlasting righteousness" for the Jewish nation.

The traditional futurist interpretation teaches that the Lord will fulfill His promise to redeem Daniel's nation, city, and temple, albeit after a mysterious delay. This delay does not mean that God was "slack concerning His promise" but that He is patiently waiting for His people to repent (2 Peter 3:9). Ironically, the preterist position denies God's faithfulness because it places the terminus ad quem (i.e., end point) of Daniel's prophecy in the first century AD, without the Lord having answered his prayers and supplications for His desolate nation, city, and sanctuary (Dan. 9:1-19). While the angel predicted specific prophetic events related to the final redemption of the nation (Dan. 9:24; cf. Dan. 12:7; Zech. 12:10; Rom. 11:25-27), the preterist interpretation teaches the exact opposite, that is, that the fulfillment of this prophecy was the destruction of the Jewish kingdom in AD 70 and the ultimate and permanent rejection of Daniel's people!

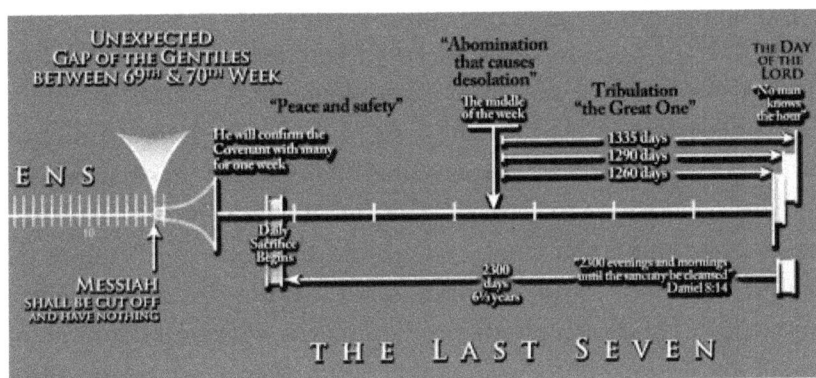

The presence of this mysterious gap in Daniel 9:27 is not a modern contrivance. To the contrary, the holy Church fathers taught that the Seventieth Week, and more particularly the final three and a half years, has been reserved for fulfillment in their future. They held a firm conviction that the Antichrist will erect the abomination of desolation in the Jerusalem temple and that the returning Christ will destroy him three and a half years later. For example, Justin Martyr (c. AD 160) wrote that Jesus will gloriously return from heaven once this "man of apostasy" has spoken blasphemies "against the Most High" and has persecuted Christians.[2] Similarly, Saint Irenaeus of Lyons (c. AD 180) believed that the Antichrist should be equated with the "lawless one" and "the son of perdition" who will seek "to be worshipped as God" (cf. 2 Thess. 2:3-4). According to Irenaeus, this man will be "endowed with all of the power of the devil" and will arise from a ten-kingdom confederacy to "reign over the earth for three years and six months" and will "sit in the temple at Jerusalem" until the Lord returns from heaven in clouds.[3] Irenaeus saw at least the final half of the Seventieth Week of Daniel 9:27

---

2   Justin Martyr 1.253, 254 in Bercot, David W. *A Dictionary of Early Christian Beliefs: A Reference Guide to More Than 700 Topics Discussed by the Early Church Fathers.* Peabody, MA: Hendrickson Publishers, Inc., 1998.

3   Irenaeus 1.553, 1.554, 1.560 in Bercot 1998.

as speaking about the final years prior to the return of Christ.

Saint Hippolytus of Rome (c. AD 200) taught that the entire final week of Daniel 9:27 refers to "the last week that is to be at the end of the whole world."[4] He identified the Beast as the future Antichrist who will seek to be worshipped as God.[5] Hippolytus believed that the Antichrist will reign for "a time, times, and a half," which he explained means three and a half years, and rebuild Jerusalem and "restore the [temple] sanctuary" while "exalting himself above all kings and above every god."[6] He also taught that the Antichrist will reveal the abomination of desolation and remove "sacrifice and oblation" in the middle of the last week (Dan. 9:27):

> For when the sixty-two weeks are fulfilled, and Christ has come, and the gospel is preached in every place, the times will then be accomplished. Then, there will remain only one week (the last) . . . And in the middle of it [the Seventieth Week], the abomination of desolation will be manifested. This is the Antichrist, announcing desolation to the world. And when he comes, the sacrifice and oblation will be removed.[7]

Tertullian (c. AD 210) taught that the resurrection of the dead will occur immediately after "the destruction of the Antichrist."[8] Origen (c. AD 248) referenced Daniel 11:31 to teach that the Antichrist will establish the abomination of desolation "on the temple" so that he "sits in the temple of God, showing himself that he is God" (2 Thess. 2:4).[9] Saints Cyprian, Victorinus, and Lactantius each wrote (c. AD 250-280) that the

---

4   Hippolytus 5.213 in Bercot 1998.

5   Hippolytus 5.214, 5.215 in Bercot 1998.

6   Hippolytus 5.190, 5.184 in Bercot 1998.

7   Hippolytus 5.182 in Bercot 1998.

8   Tertullian 3.565 in Bercot 1998.

9   Origen 4.593-94 in Bercot 1998.

future Antichrist will persecute God's saints.[10] Victorinus believed that number 666 referred to the name of the Antichrist.[11] Lactantius taught that Jesus will return to destroy the Antichrist, who will be the wicked man who requires worship of himself, calls himself God, and performs demonic signs and wonders. He explained that the Antichrist will also attempt to destroy the temple of God and persecute the righteous during the forty-two months of "distress and tribulation, such as there never has been from the beginning of the world" (Matt. 24:21).[12]

The fathers of the Church recorded many of the above statements only a few decades after the destruction of the Second Temple. The fact that they expected a future fulfillment of these events at that time demonstrates that these events did not occur in AD 70. They certainly did not believe that these prophecies of Christ and the holy apostles were fulfilled in the first century! But they expected that these events were yet future, and as such, they are also in our future.

The mysterious gap in the prophecy of the Seventy Weeks fits well with the mystery of the Gentiles taught by the apostle Paul (Rom. 11:25-26; 16:25-26; Eph. 3:3-6; Col. 1:26-27). This mystery, namely, that believing Jews and Gentiles are "fellow heirs" of Israel's promises, was concealed during the Old Testament period but was revealed to the Lord's apostles (Rom. 16:25; Eph. 3:5, 9; Col. 1:26). This inclusion of the Gentiles is concurrent with Christ's inter-advent period.

The mystery of the gap is not unique to the prophecy of the Seventy Weeks. In point of fact, such a gap appears in *every* eschatological prophecy in the book of Daniel. For example, Nebuchadnezzar's dream about the statue of the four kingdoms requires a gap because the entire statue, representing the four great kingdoms of man (i.e., Babylon, Media-Persia, Greece, and Rome), will be simultaneously demolished

---

10   Cyprian 5.346, 349, 556; Victorinus in Bercot 1998.

11   Victorinus 7.456 in Bercot 1998.

12   Lactantius 4.593-95; 5.204-19; 7.215 in Bercot 1998.

(without a trace found!) when Christ consummates His kingdom (Dan. 2:35, 45). The same is true with Daniel's vision of the four beasts because the final beast will be destroyed and burned at the Son of Man's cloud-coming (Dan. 7:11). Regardless of whether we identify the final kingdom as the Roman Empire or not, the terminus ad quem of these prophecies is definitely in our future, which requires a significant gap of time beyond the world of antiquity. Likewise, the latter events of Daniel 11-12, including the setting up of the abomination of desolation, the destruction of the self-exalting king, the unprecedented tribulation, and the resurrection of the dead, are decidedly future, thus requiring a gap of several centuries.

Similarly, many other eschatological passages in the Old Testament Prophets necessitate a chronological "gap"; this is a literary device that modern biblical scholars call the prophetic perspective, and it is characterized by juxtaposing future and far future prophetic events without any mention of a chronological delay. The New Testament reveals the mystery of Christ's two advents, and this significantly assists the reader to identify the portions of the Old Testament prophecies that have been fulfilled and those that will be fulfilled at the end of the age.

One classic example of this phenomena is recorded in the Gospel of Luke. The passage explains that Jesus opened the scroll of Isaiah (Isa. 61:1-2) and read the following passage: "The Spirit of the Lord is upon Me because He has anointed Me to preach the gospel to the poor; He has sent Me to heal the brokenhearted, to proclaim liberty to the captives and recovery of sight to the blind, to set at liberty those who are oppressed; to proclaim the acceptable year of the Lord" (Luke 4:18-19). Then He proclaimed, "Today this Scripture is fulfilled in your hearing" (Luke 4:21). Notably, He quoted the portion of this prophecy that He was presently fulfilling, but midsentence, He refrained from declaring the following portion: "and the day of vengeance of our God; to comfort all who mourn, to console those who mourn in Zion, to give them beauty for ashes, the oil of joy for mourning, the garment of praise for the spirit of heaviness; that they may be called trees of righteousness, the planting of the Lord, that He may be glorified" (Isa. 61:2-3). Christ did not recite this latter portion of the prophecy, which is concerned with "the day of vengeance of our God" (Isa. 61:2; cf. Luke 21:22), also known as the day of the Lord (cf. Isa. 34:8), because it awaited fulfillment at His Second Advent. These prophetic events do not match any first-century events but describe a prophetic fulfillment in our future.

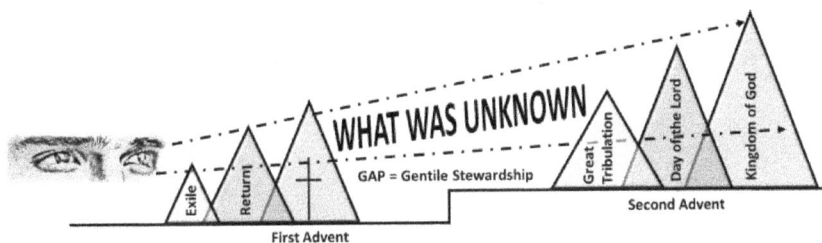

6

ORIGIN OF THE ANTICHRIST

THE MYSTERIOUS GAP which we saw in Daniel's Seventieth Week also appears in the prophetic vision of the little horn in Daniel 8. As mentioned previously in this book, the four notable horns of the goat (Dan. 8:8, 22), like the four heads of the leopard beast (Dan. 7:6), represent the four primary Diadochi (successors to Alexander the Great) which emerged from the Macedonian kingdom (Dan. 11:4). Yet the vision itself indicates on four occasions that its contents pertain to the time of the end.

> The vision refers to the time of the end. . . I am making known to you what shall happen in the latter time of the indignation; for at the appointed time the end shall be. . . Therefore, seal up the vision, for it refers to many days in the future. (Dan. 8:17, 19, 26)

Consequently, we might expect that the end of the vision depicts many of the same end-time events as the other visions in the book of

Daniel. The larger passage reads as follows:

> Therefore the male goat grew very great; but when he became strong, the large horn was broken, and in place of it four notable ones came up toward the four winds of heaven. And out of one of them came a little horn which grew exceedingly great toward the south, toward the east, and toward the Glorious Land. And it grew up to the host of heaven; and it cast down some of the host and some of the stars to the ground, and trampled them. He even exalted himself as high as the Prince of the host; and by him the daily sacrifices were taken away, and the place of His sanctuary was cast down. Because of transgression, an army was given over to the horn to oppose the daily sacrifices; and he cast truth down to the ground. He did all this and prospered. (Dan. 8:8-12)

The "little horn" in this prophecy is the Antichrist. Only two chapters in Scripture, the adjacent chapters of Daniel 7 and 8, mention the little horn, and both prophecies specify that its contents pertain to the time of the end. Unfortunately, while most conservative scholars correctly identify the little horn of Daniel 7 as referring to the Antichrist, they usually maintain that the little horn in the subsequent chapter is an entirely different figure—Antiochus IV Epiphanes. This view is not primarily based on exegetical considerations or solid hermeneutical principles but on a vested interest in protecting the Antiochus interpretation. However, when the inspired text clearly specifies that the vision pertains to end-time events, we should not interpret the vision as having been fulfilled in the ancient world! Admittedly, the little horn in Daniel 7 arises from the fourth beast of Rome, while in Daniel 8 it will arise in "the latter time" out of one of the four divisions of the kingdom of Greece (Dan. 8:23), but we should remember that the final expression of the Beast is composite in nature.

Daniel 8 also provides a primary clue about the origin of the "little horn" king. Grammatically, the little horn would arise from one of the four horns ("out of one of them" Dan. 8:9), or less likely from one of "the four winds of heaven" (Dan. 8:8). Both interpretations lead to the same conclusion, namely, that this king will arise from the fourfold division of Alexander the Great's kingdom, from one of the divisions of Alexander's kingdom, in other words, from the kingdoms of Seleucus, Ptolemy, Cassander, or Lysimachus. In other words, the Antichrist will begin his reign in the geographical region of one of these four primary (notable) kingdoms.

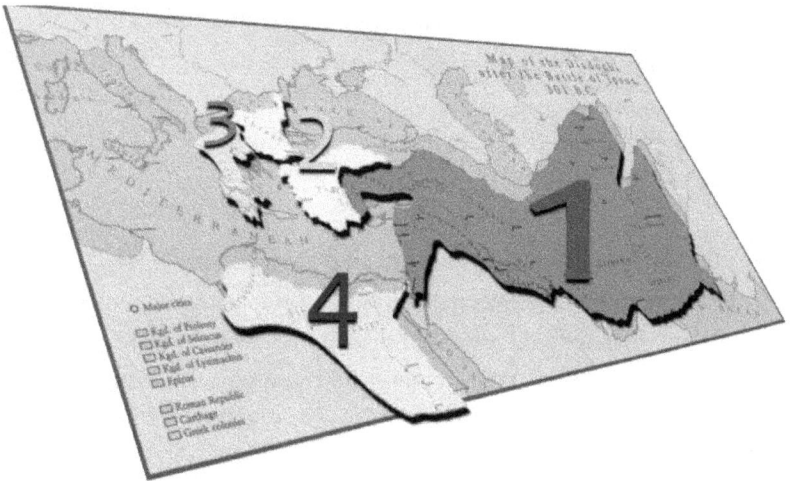

Since most of the Ptolemaic kingdom was south of Israel and Cassandri was to the west, it is nearly certain that the Antichrist will arise from either the region of the Seleucid kingdom or the Lysimachi kingdom to Israel's north. This means that he will emerge as a king in one of the northern nations of the Middle East. According to Daniel's prophecy, his kingdom will expand toward the south, the east, and the land of Israel (Dan. 8:9), and he will cast down some of the heavenly army and trample some of the stars, powerful symbols depicting the persecution of the saints (Dan. 8:10, 24; cf. Dan. 12:3; Rev. 12:4). This king will exalt himself as high as the Prince of the host (Dan. 8:11; cf. Dan. 8:25; 11:36-37), who is later called "the Prince of princes" (Dan. 8:25; cf. Rev. 17:14; 19:16); this Prince is the Commander of the heavenly host—Jesus Christ (cf. Jos. 5:14; Dan. 9:25). Finally, as we saw previously, this prophecy also reveals that the Antichrist's soldiers will trample the temple sanctuary, set up the abomination of desolation ("transgression of desolation" Dan. 8:13), and remove the tamid offering (Dan. 8:11-12).

> And in the latter time of their kingdom, when the transgressors have reached their fullness, a king shall arise, having fierce features, who understands sinister schemes. His power shall be mighty, but not by his own power; He shall destroy fearfully and shall prosper and thrive; he shall destroy the mighty, and also the holy people. Through his cunning he shall cause deceit to prosper under his rule; and he shall exalt himself in his heart. He shall destroy many in their prosperity. He shall even rise against the Prince of princes; but he shall be broken without human means. And the vision of the evenings and mornings which was told is true; therefore, seal up the vision, for it refers to many days in the future. (Dan. 8:23-26)

This angelic interpretation of the little horn vision describes the Antichrist. He will arise "not by his own power" (Dan. 8:24) because Satan will give him "his power, his throne, and great authority" (Rev. 13:2). However, the Antichrist will oppose the Prince of princes but will be "broken without human means" (Dan. 8:25). In other words, Christ will personally kill him when He returns from heaven (Rev. 19:19-20; cf. Dan. 7:26; 11:45). The prophet Daniel was instructed to "seal up" this vision because it pertained to the distant future, a reference to the time of the end (Dan. 8:26; cf. Dan. 12:4, 9). The prophet witnessed the "holy ones" discussing the duration of the end-time fulfillment of this prophecy:

Then I heard a holy one speaking; and another holy one said to that certain one who was speaking, "How long will the vision be, concerning the daily sacrifices and the transgression of desolation, the giving of both the sanctuary and the host to be trampled underfoot?" And he said to me, "For two thousand three hundred days; then the sanctuary shall be cleansed." (Dan. 8:13-14)

The duration of the fulfillment of the end-time portion of this vision will be 2,300 days, a period of less than six years and four months (Dan. 8:14, 26). The word translated "days" here is literally rendered "evenings and mornings," a phrase which points to the tamid sacrifice, which was to be offered twice daily by the priests as a continual burnt offering (Exod. 29:38-42; Num. 28:1-8; cf. Gen. 1:5). The calculation of 2,300 days will begin with the restoration of the tamid offering upon the Temple Mount, a sacrifice that the Antichrist will remove at the midpoint of the final seven years, and the period will terminate with the purification of the temple sanctuary 2,300 days later ("then the sanctuary shall be cleansed" Dan. 8:14; cf. Dan. 9:24).[1] In chapter 18, we will revisit the mysterious concept of the temple's dedication and its cleansing.

Most scholars correctly understand the contents of Daniel 8 and Daniel 11 as ending with the same series of events. Many conservative futurist commentators categorize the various sections of the final vision of Daniel as follows: The transition from Medo-Persian rule to Macedonian rule under Alexander the Great (Dan. 11:2-3), the Seleucid and Ptolemaic dynasties, with a special emphasis on Antiochus IV Epiphanes (11:4-35), and the reign of the Antichrist (11:36-45). On the other hand, many preterists see the self-exalting king described in Daniel 11:36ff as one of several first-century rulers. Still other commentators attempt to find Antiochus IV Epiphanes in the details of

---

[1] The eight months between the beginning of the final seven years and the final 2,300 days (six years and four months) may be because it will take time to obtain the ashes of the red heifer before sacrifices can begin.

this section of the prophecy. However, as I demonstrated in previous chapters of this book, the abomination of desolation (11:31-45; 12:11-12), the unprecedented tribulation (12:1), and the resurrection of the dead (12:1-3, 13) are temporally inseparable from the time of the end.

Several pieces of evidence demonstrate that the time of the end is in view as early as Daniel 11:21. First, the vision of Daniel 10-12 is a solitary vision, and the "man clothed in linen" provided the prophetic interpretation of the vision in chapter 12. Because the angel explained that the events of chapter 12, including the unprecedented tribulation and resurrection of the dead, refer to the time of the end, the larger explanation of these same events found in chapter 11 must refer to this same period. For example, the mention of the removal of the tamid and setting up of the abomination of desolation (Dan. 12:11) alludes to the same events which were detailed earlier in the vision (Dan. 11:31-45). Similarly, the refinement, purification, and making white of the wise and understanding people (Dan. 12:10) point back to these same events in the previous chapter (Dan. 11:33-35).

Second, Daniel's statement about the invasion of ships from Cyprus or "the western coastlands" (Dan. 11:30) is an allusion to Balaam's prophecy, in which he foretold that "ships shall come from the coasts of Cyprus" (Num. 24:24; cf. v. 23), wherein the prophet predicted that this same event would occur "in the latter days" (Num. 24:14). Furthermore, this time indicator is a technical phrase in the Old Testament, and it always refers to the period leading up to the eschaton (the end of the age), a period which does not fit with Antiochus IV Epiphanes' reign in the second century BC. Nevertheless, it fits well with the reign of the Antichrist during the great tribulation, as outlined in Daniel 12.

Third, the reference to the self-exalting king ("the king" Dan. 11:36) does not appear abruptly and unannounced at this point in Daniel's prophecy, as some conservative commentators suppose; rather, its ante-cedent is "the vile person" introduced as early as verse 21. This contempt-ible king is described using the third person singular pronouns ("he/him") throughout this section of the prophecy (Dan. 11:21-35), without any indication of a change in the subject. Furthermore, verse 36 mentions "the king" without any indication of a subject change. The absence of any subject change throughout verses 21-45 contrasts sharply with the multiple subject changes prior to verse 21. This strongly suggests that the self-exalting king is the primary subject of the actions in verses 21-45.

Fourth, the self-exalting king will "exalt himself and magnify himself above every god" (Dan. 11:36). The apostle Paul alluded to this passage with reference to the Man of Sin, the Antichrist, who will enter the temple of God (2 Thess. 2:3-4; cf. Rev. 13:5-6). From the standpoint of the Thessalonian letters, this event was to take place in the future, and the apostle connected it with the glorious return of Jesus Christ from heaven (2 Thess. 2:1, 8). The totality of this evidence demonstrates beyond reasonable doubt that the Antichrist is the subject of Daniel 11:21-45 in its entirety. The textual evidence can be seen in more detail in Table 4.

Furthermore, Antiochus IV Epiphanes (175-164 BC) was *never* a "little horn" (cf. Dan. 8:9), not in the sense that the book of Daniel uses the term. To the contrary, Antiochus ruled over the most expansive of the four "notable" horns of Alexander the Great's kingdom—the expansive Seleucid Empire! Nevertheless, this ancient king served as a prophetic foreshadowing of the Antichrist because his actions appeared to fulfill many of the prophetic details of the northern king of Daniel 11:21-35. The Antiochus' interpretation is well established, with much in its defense, so I will not reiterate it here. However, the futurist position that the final Antichrist will completely fulfill these verses is highly defensible, and this interpretation is based on several incontrovertible pieces of evidence.

Therefore, in one sense, the historical actions of Antiochus Epiphanes function as a historical distractor that divinely conceals the true identity of the self-exalting king—the Antichrist. This identity will become evident when the prophetic vision is unsealed and fulfilled at the time of the end. At any rate, as demonstrated in previous chapters of this book, Jesus alluded to Daniel's abomination of desolation in His Olivet Prophecy (Matt. 24:15-16; Mark 13:14; cf. Dan. 9:27; 11:31,

45; 12:11), and He spoke of it as awaiting a future fulfillment at the end of the age. Everything points to the conclusion that the abomination of desolation did not find an exhaustive fulfillment in Antiochus' desecration of the Jerusalem temple in 168 BC.

A LIKENESS OF ANTIOCHUS IV EPIPHANES

Some commentators have argued that Daniel 11:21-35 is an example of double fulfillment, but this does not work, as evidenced by the temporal relationship of the northern king's actions with the abomination of desolation, the unprecedented tribulation, and the resurrection of the dead (Dan. 11:30-45; 12:1-3, 11). Consequently, the ultimate, plenary fulfillment of Daniel 8:9ff and 11:21ff must include the Antichrist setting up the abomination in the Jerusalem temple. It is preferable to consider Antiochus IV to be the partial fulfillment of these prophecies and the Antichrist as the complete fulfillment, illustrative of the "near and far" pattern characteristic of many biblical prophecies. This wicked king, Antiochus Epiphanes, brought covenant discipline upon the Jews by outlawing the observance of God's commandments, desecrating the holy temple, demanding idol worship, and subjugating and attempting to destroy the nation. As such, he functions as a shadow for the type of the Antichrist.

The larger prophecy of Daniel 11, beginning with verse 21, reads as follows:

> And in his place shall arise a vile person, to whom they will not give the honor of royalty; but he shall come in peaceably, and seize the kingdom by intrigue. With the force of a flood they shall be swept away from before him and be broken, and also the prince of the covenant. And after the league is made with him, he shall act deceitfully, for he shall come up and become strong with a small number of people. He shall enter peaceably, even into the richest places of the province; and he shall do what his fathers have not done, nor his forefathers: he shall disperse among them the plunder, spoil, and riches; and he shall devise his plans against the strongholds, but only for a time. (Dan. 11:21-24)

The Antichrist is the vile person who will arise in the "place" of antiquity's "king of the north," specifically, in the place of Seleucus IV Philopator (187-76 BC) (Dan. 11:21). The northern king at that time, Seleucus IV, commissioned Heliodorus the tax collector ("one who imposes taxes on the glorious kingdom" Dan. 11:20). This is a strong indicator that the Antichrist will not arise from the region of the Lysimachi but from the region of the former Seleucid Empire, as did Antiochus IV Epiphanes. As we should expect, most of this region of the Seleucids was later occupied by the Roman Empire, the fourth beast of Daniel 7. This interpretation understands that the mysterious gap exists between Daniel 11:20 and 11:21, just as we saw a chronological division between Daniel 8:8 and 8:9 and between Daniel 9:26 and 9:27.

Antiochus IV Epiphanes did not fulfill many of the other details of Daniel 11. First, the prophecy teaches that this northern ruler will not be given "the honor or royalty" (Dan. 11:21); however, the Roman Republic installed Antiochus as the Seleucid king, and he reigned as a legitimate heir to the Seleucid throne (cf. Dan. 11:21), albeit in the place of his murdered older brother.

Second, he did not begin as the ruler of a small political power or nation, yet the prophecy shows that the northern king will "come up and become strong with a small people"[2] *after* a league is made with him (Dan. 11:23). The text more accurately is translated "a small people," not "a small number of people" (NKJV). Many translations include the words "number of" in a failed attempt to provide clarity because the translators assume the correctness of the Antiochus' interpretation. The Antichrist, the true little horn, will deceitfully become strong with a small nation or people group (Dan. 11:23). Therefore, he will not begin as the leader of a notable or mighty nation ("great" or "notable" horn), such as Russia, Turkey, or Iran. This small people could refer to an ethnic or cultural group, such as the Palestinians, or to a new, fledgling nation that attempts to gain independence. Regardless, the Antichrist will use this opportunity to seize his kingdom using deceit and military stealth (Dan. 11:21-24).

Third, this king would "peaceably" ascend the throne "in a time of tranquility" (Dan. 11:21, 24; cf. "all of them dwell securely" Ezek. 38:8; "in their prosperity" Dan. 8:25). However, Antiochus violently seized the throne while he left his nephew and brother's true heir, Demetrius, stranded in Rome. These events occurred during a civil war and against the backdrop of massive violent uprisings, not during a period of tranquility.

Fourth, the Antichrist, the self-exalting king, will "magnify himself above every god" and will not regard the gods of his fathers (Dan. 11:36-37; cf. 2 Thess. 2:4). To the contrary, Antiochus IV worshipped Zeus and set up an idol of him in the Jerusalem temple (2 Macc. 6:2); by definition, this was the gods of his fathers!

Daniel's prophecy details the Antichrist's self-exaltation:

Then the king shall do according to his own will: he shall exalt and magnify himself above every god, shall speak blasphemies against the God of gods, and shall prosper till the wrath has been accomplished;

---

2   This translation was added by the author.

for what has been determined shall be done. He shall regard neither the god of his fathers nor the desire of women, nor regard any god; for he shall exalt himself above them all. But in their place, he shall honor a god of fortresses; and a god which his fathers did not know he shall honor with gold and silver, with precious stones and pleasant things. Thus he shall act against the strongest fortresses with a foreign god, which he shall acknowledge, and advance its glory; and he shall cause them to rule over many, and divide the land for gain. (Dan. 11:36-39)

Critical scholars readily admit that Antiochus did not fulfill many of the latter details of this prophecy (Dan. 11:36-45). Due to the non-fulfillment by Antiochus, they invented the notion that the prophet Daniel was a second-century BC pseudo-Daniel who passed off "history as prophecy," having incorrectly predicted the details about Antiochus' military exploits! Even the Jewish rabbis did not dare to interpret these prophecies of Daniel as describing Antiochus; most of them taught that they were fulfilled by various individuals during the First Jewish-Roman War.

The Antichrist's undivided commitment to self-exaltation and self-deification is reiterated multiple times in the Scriptures. For example, the book of Daniel reveals that he will not regard "the desire of women" (Dan. 11:37). Some commentators have speculated that this could be a reference to the worship of the goddess Artemis or to homosexuality; however, this phrase probably refers to his disinterest in the typical desires of men, such as marriage and the sexual pursuit of women. At any rate, he will declare himself to be God ("above every god" Dan. 11:36), dismissing all other deities ("nor regard any god" Dan. 11:37), which undoubtedly includes those of Hinduism, Buddhism, Judaism, Christianity, and Islam (since he will derive from a predominantly Islamic region, Allah will likely be the "god of his fathers" Dan. 11:37). This verse does not contradict the expressions in the next two verses that this king will honor a foreign god with riches, "a god which his fathers did not know" and "a god of fortresses," so as to destroy military strongholds (Dan. 11:38-39; cf. 2 Cor. 10:4). Rather, as we will see in the next chapter of this book, this foreign god is himself the Antichrist.

As we should expect, the end-time portion of Daniel 11 shares over-lapping themes with the prophet's Seventieth Week (Dan. 9:26-27). In both passages, the northern king's armies are depicted as a destroying flood which sweeps away his enemies (Dan. 9:26; 11:22; cf. Isa. 28:2, 15, 18). But more importantly, both passages refer to "the covenant" (Dan. 9:27; 11:22). The latter passage reveals that the northern king will kill "the prince of the covenant" through his military exploits (Dan. 11:22). Because this covenant is proximate to the "league" or "alliance" in the next verse, the interpreter should expect that they are themati-cally and/or chronologically related. This covenant is identified as "the holy covenant" in three of its four appearances in the same prophecy (Dan. 11:28, 30a, 30b, not v. 32). Therefore, it is preferable to see the alliance or league in verse 23 as the Antichrist's political confirmation of the holy covenant of verse 22 (cf. Dan. 9:27).

The holy covenant of Daniel 11 is the covenant which God made with the patriarchs and their offspring (Gen. 12:1-3; 15:18-21; 17:2-8; cf. Luke 1:72). Foremost, the larger context of the chapter links the northern king's violation of this covenant with the military invasion of the land of Israel (Dan. 11:28-32), the land which God promised to the patriarchs and their seed as an eternal inheritance. The northern king will not intend to keep the terms of this holy covenant; even while he confirms it, he will act deceptively against it, with every intention of violating it at an opportune time (Dan. 11:23)! The next verse describes him as entering the province in a perceptively peaceful manner, yet he will destroy military strongholds and disperse "plunder, spoil, and riches" (Dan. 11:24; cf. Ezek. 38:12-13). Apparently, the league will provide an immediate political advantage for the northern king.

According to Daniel, the Antichrist will not create a new covenant but will strengthen or confirm an existing covenant: "Then he shall confirm a covenant with many for one week; but in the middle of the week, he shall bring an end to sacrifice and offering. And on the wing of abominations shall be one who makes desolate" (Dan. 9:27). The fact that this king will remove the sacrifices and offerings at the midpoint of the final seven years implies that his strengthening of the holy covenant will make provision for the Jews to restart their sacrifices in the Jerusalem temple, or at least, that they will exploit this as an opportunity to do so. Furthermore, the Jews do not need a fully rebuilt temple to begin offering the tamid, as evidenced by the fact that the Jews who returned from the Babylonian exile offered this sacrifice before they even laid the foundation of the Second Temple (Ezra. 3:1-6); this appears to be the most likely scenario for the Third Temple because the sacrifices will be restarted late in the first year after the alliance is made (cf. Dan. 8:14).

Also, Daniel's prophecy does not demonstrate that the covenant will be designed to last only seven years. The most likely scenario is that the nations will intend for the alliance or league to continue indefinitely, but Christ will put an end to the Antichrist after the final seven years.

The Israeli government will not knowingly enter into covenant with the Antichrist. He will join the international peace agreement ("the league" Dan. 11:23) while still a little horn, and likely, as only one leader among many international players ("with many" Dan. 9:27). The Jews will imagine that the peace pact will bring prosperity and security to their nation and to the larger region of Middle Eastern nations. It is almost certain that some of the world's superpowers, such as the United States and Russia, and possibly China, will back this pact of "peace and security" in the region; otherwise, it is unthinkable that the many other nations, most particularly Israel, would consider this arrangement to be valuable and enduring.

In addition, history has demonstrated that most of the Arab world will not agree to a major peace treaty with Israel, guaranteeing Jewish rights to the land, and possibly, to Jerusalem and the Temple Mount, unless the region has recently experienced war or the imminent threat of war. Consequently, we should anticipate this event to be the next major event to take place on the prophetic timetable.[3] Something must

---

3   As of 2022, the conflict between Russia and Ukraine and the restless threats of China, North Korea, Iran, Hezbollah, and others could easily precipitate an imminent threat, even the threat of global conflict or nuclear war.

break the deadlock on the Temple Mount between the Jews and their Arab antagonists.

Daniel was not the first prophet to speak about this end-time agreement. The prophet Isaiah spoke about the leadership of Jerusalem making "a covenant with death . . . and Sheol [hades or hell]," (cf. Rev. 6:8), which will result in the destruction of the Jewish nation:

> Therefore hear the word of the Lord you scornful men who rule this people who are in Jerusalem, because you have said, "We have made a covenant with death, and with Sheol we are in agreement. When the overflowing scourge passes through, it will not come to us for we have made lies our refuge, and under falsehood we have hidden ourselves." . . . Your covenant with death will be annulled, and your agreement with Sheol will not stand; when the overflowing scourge passes through, then you will be trampled down by it. As often as it goes out it will take you; for morning by morning it will pass over, and by day and by night; it will be a terror just to understand the report. For the bed is too short to stretch out on, and the covering so narrow that one cannot wrap himself in it. For the Lord will rise up as at Mount Perazim, He will be angry as in the Valley of Gibeon—that He may do His work, His awesome work, and bring to pass His act, His unusual act. Now therefore, do not be mockers, lest your bonds be made strong; for I have heard from the Lord God of hosts, a destruction determined even upon the whole earth. (Isa. 28: 14-15, 18-22)

The covenant will unwittingly involve an agreement with death and hell because it is based upon a deceptive, misplaced trust in mere mortal man. This agreement was prefigured by King Hezekiah's frail alliance with Egypt, which provided a false confidence of protection from "the Assyrian" (cf. Isa. 30:1-7; 36:6-9). As in the days of Hezekiah, the scornful rulers of Jerusalem ("scornful men" Isa. 28:14; "the mockers" Isa. 28:22; cf. 2 Pet. 3:3) will neglect the true righteousness and trust in Christ, favoring a humanistic trust in the international league ("lies our refuge . . . under falsehood" Isa. 28:15). Nevertheless, the northern king will nullify the peace treaty by bringing the terror of military destruction ("the overflowing scourge" Isa. 28:15; cf. Isa. 59:19; Dan. 9:26; 11:22; Rev. 12:15-16), which will pass through the land (cf. Jer. 4:10). This divinely decreed destruction that begins in Jerusalem will overcome "the whole earth" (Isa. 28:22; cf. 2 Pet. 3:3-7).

Nevertheless, the prophet continued by conveying that the Lord Himself will eventually destroy the enemy invaders, as King David destroyed the Philistines in the vicinity of Jerusalem ("as at Mount Perazim. He will be angry as in the Valley of Gibeon" Isa. 28:21; cf. 1 Chron. 14:11-16). This intervention will be God's "awesome work" and "unusual act" (Isa. 28:21; cf. Isa. 29:20; Hab. 1:5). During his apostolic ministry, the apostle Paul taught that this divine intervention was yet future (Acts 13:41).

The prophecy of Daniel 11 continues by outlining the Antichrist's military maneuvers:

> He shall stir up his power and his courage against the king of the South with a great army. And the king of the South shall be stirred up to battle with a very great and mighty army; but he shall not stand, for they shall devise plans against him. Yes, those who eat of the portion of his delicacies shall destroy him; his army shall be swept away, and many shall fall down slain. Both these kings' hearts shall be bent on evil, and they shall speak lies at the same table; but it shall not prosper, for the end will still be at the appointed time. While returning to his land with great riches, his heart shall be moved against the holy covenant; so, he shall do damage and return to his own land. (Dan. 11:25-28)

This passage describes the Antichrist's first incursion into the region to the south of the land of Israel. Although his forces will initially be outnumbered by those of the southern kingdom, he will defeat these forces because the southern king's closest advisors will betray him from within (Dan. 11:25-26). Then the Antichrist ("the king of the north") and the southern king will lie to each other at the negotiation table and will be unable to agree to terms at that time (Dan. 11:27). However, after the Antichrist has returned to his own country, he will take action against the holy covenant (Dan. 11:28), although the text does not specify the nature of his actions. While the Ptolemaic Kingdom of Egypt foreshadowed this southern kingdom, we should not assume that the end-time fulfillment will be modern Egypt. It is quite possible that the Kingdom of Saudi Arabia is in view, and Daniel 11 may differentiate between Egypt and the southern kingdom.

The prophet Ezekiel described the Lord's response to Gog (i.e., the Antichrist) regarding his invasion of the land of Israel:

> On that day it shall come to pass that thoughts will arise in your mind, and you will make an evil plan: You will say, "I will go up against a land of unwalled villages; I will go to a peaceful people, who dwell safely, all of them dwelling without walls, and having neither bars nor gates"—to take plunder and to take booty, to stretch out your hand against the waste places that are again inhabited, and against a people gathered from the nations, who have acquired livestock and goods, who dwell in the midst of the land. Sheba, Dedan, the merchants of Tarshish, and all their young lions will say to you, "Have you come to take plunder? Have you gathered your army to take booty, to carry away silver and gold, to take away livestock and goods, to take great plunder?" Therefore, son of man, prophesy and say to Gog . . . "On that day when My people Israel dwell safely, will you not know it?" (Ezek. 38:10-14)

This prophecy contains many of the same themes as Daniel 11. For example, both prophecies describe the Antichrist as the king from the north (Ezek. 38:6, 15; 39:2; Dan. 11:25, 29, 40). In addition, both passages describe a period of peace immediately preceding the king assaulting the land of Israel; Ezekiel described the Jewish nation as "a land of unwalled villages . . . a peaceful people, who dwell safely, all of them dwelling without walls, having neither bars nor gates" (Ezek. 38:11; cf. Jer. 49:31), whereas Daniel wrote that the king will deceptively enter the region "in a time of tranquility" before plundering it (Dan. 11:21, 24). These peaceful conditions ("peace and safety" 1 Thess. 5:3) will have only been recently achieved by the international alliance formed at the beginning of the final seven years (Dan. 9:27). The implication is that the Jewish nation will be caught completely off guard by the Antichrist's invasion. Even Israel's southern neighbors, including Sheba, Dedan, and Tarshish, will also be startled by the northern king's arrival (Ezek. 38:13); these are the modern Gulf States which, as of the writing of this book, recently have become allies of the State of Israel. Finally, Ezekiel predicted that the Antichrist will take plunder, silver, gold, livestock, and goods (Ezek. 38:12-13), and Daniel prophesied that he will take plunder, spoils, and riches (Dan. 11:24, 28).

At the time of the Antichrist's invasion ("in the latter years" Ezek. 38:8), the Jews will have previously been regathered from the nations to inhabit the continual "waste places" of the Promised Land. Ezekiel wrote that the Antichrist will invade Israel, ascending upon "the land of those brought back from the sword and gathered from many people on the mountains of Israel, which had long been desolate; they were brought out of the nations, and now all of them dwell safely" (Ezek. 38:8, 12). This nation will have only recently been regathered to the land after it had experienced "the desolations of many generations" (Isa. 61:4; "long been desolate" Ezek. 38:8), conditions which have existed only since the creation of the State of Israel in 1947-48.

During the first half of the final "week" of years, the Antichrist will invade the kingdom of the south to solidify his reign in the Middle East. This invasion will be an intensification of the "birth pains" which must precede the arrival of Jesus Christ. Christ taught, "And you will hear of wars and rumors of wars. See that you are not troubled; for all these things must come to pass, but the end is not yet. For nation will rise against nation, and kingdom against kingdom. And there will be famines, pestilences, and earthquakes in various places. All these are the beginning of sorrows" (Matt. 24:6-8; cf. Jer. 6:24).

Christ's expression "kingdom against kingdom" is a direct quote from a prophecy about Egypt's future civil war and its ultimate fall to the Antichrist's forces (Isa. 19:2). Jesus' words indicate that this war will be representative of the toppling of other governments throughout the world at this time. The larger context of Isaiah's prophecy reads as follows: "I will set Egyptians against Egyptians; everyone will fight against his brother and everyone against his neighbor, city against city, kingdom against kingdom. . . And the Egyptians I will give into the hand of a cruel master, and a fierce king will rule over them" (Isa. 19:2, 4). The Antichrist's victory over Egypt will be utterly devastating for the region, and he ("a cruel master . . . a fierce king" Isa. 19:4; cf. Jer. 30:15) will forcefully subjugate the region of North Africa.

Whereas the Antichrist's first invasion of the southern kingdom will take place during the first half of Daniel's final "week" of years, his second invasion will occur just before the abomination of desolation, at the midpoint of the final seven years. The prophet continued recounting the vision by describing the second invasion:

> At the appointed time he shall return and go toward the south; but it shall not be like the former or the latter. For ships from Cyprus shall come against him; therefore, he shall be grieved, and return in rage against the holy covenant, and do damage. So, he shall return and show regard for those who forsake the holy covenant. And forces shall be mustered by him, and they shall defile the sanctuary fortress; then they shall take away the daily sacrifices, and place there the abomination of desolation. Those who do wickedly against the covenant he shall corrupt with flattery. (Dan. 11:29-32)

When the Antichrist threatens the security of the region, naval ships from Cyprus (alternatively "the western coastlands") will attack his troops or maneuver to threaten them (Dan. 11:30). It is probable that this will be the West's response to him threatening the international peace terms. In response, he will retreat from his southern advance in Africa and turn his rage against the holy covenant by recruiting other nations to forsake the Jewish nation (Dan. 11:30; cf. Isa. 37:7, 29). Then his multinational military will suddenly invade Israel and desecrate the Jerusalem temple by forcefully removing the tamid offering and setting up the abomination of desolation (Dan. 11:31).

As mentioned previously, the oracle of Balaam forecasts the arrival of the ships from Cyprus in the latter days (Num. 24:14, 23-24). The prophet stated, "Alas! Who shall live when God does this? But ships shall come from the coasts of Cyprus, and they shall afflict Asshur and afflict Eber, and so shall Amalek, until he perishes" (Num. 24:23-24). The ships will afflict Asshur, a likely reference to a city in ancient Assyria, a feature which may identify this general area as the region of the Antichrist's origin. Eber may be a reference to the people on "the other side" of the Euphrates River, which also highlights the region of Assyria.

The southern king will attack the Antichrist a third time at the end of the unprecedented tribulation ("At the time of the end" Dan. 11:40).

> At the time of the end the king of the South shall attack him; and the king of the North shall come against him like a whirlwind, with chariots, horsemen, and with many ships; and he shall enter the countries, overwhelm them, and pass through. He shall also enter the Glorious Land, and many countries shall be overthrown; but these shall escape from his hand: Edom, Moab, and the prominent people of Ammon. He shall stretch out his hand against the countries, and the land of Egypt shall not escape. He shall have power over the treasures of gold and silver, and over all the precious things of Egypt; also, the Libyans and Ethiopians shall follow at his heels. (Dan. 11:40-43)

At the beginning of this invasion, the Antichrist will demonstrate overwhelming air, sea, and land superiority ("like a whirlwind, with chariots, horsemen, and with many ships; and he shall enter the countries, overwhelm them, and pass through" Dan. 11:40). However, this passage depicts the final unraveling of the Antichrist's kingdom. Yet no enemy rival, including the southern kingdom, including Egypt, Libya, and Ethiopia, will be any match for the Antichrist's overwhelming forces ("Egypt shall not escape . . . also, the Libyans and Ethiopians shall follow at his heels" 11:42, 43).

7

THE MYSTERY OF INIQUITY

IN THE OLIVET DISCOURSE, Jesus emphasized the antichrist deception which will characterize the period leading up to His glorious return: "Take heed that no one deceives you. For many will come in My name, saying, 'I am the Christ,' and will deceive many" (Matt. 24:4-5). Christ taught that pretenders will arise: "I have come in My Father's name, and you do not receive Me; if another comes in his own name, him you will receive" (John 5:43).

The league of far-reaching peace in the first half of the final seven years will create the illusion of a "golden age" of peace and security, and messianic pretenders will capitalize on this during this short-lived era of change. Many Jews will undoubtedly believe that the messianic era has dawned, and they will likely follow at least one so-called Messiah.[1] As

---

[1] Many leading Orthodox rabbis have recently claimed that their Messiah is alive and will soon appear and that they have met him and witnessed his miracles.

in the days of Jeremiah, when the Jews trusted in the lying words of the false prophets who told them to place their confidence in the Jerusalem temple (Jer. 7:4), they will do the same during the final years before the return of Christ. Yet Jeremiah revealed that the nation will eventually understand "in the latter days" that these pretenders are not the Lord's prophets (Jer. 23:20-23; cf. Jer. 30:24). The false prophets in antiquity seduced the Jews by claiming, "'Peace!' when there is no peace" (Ezek. 13:10), which is the very situation that will be recapitulated during the first half of the final "week" of years.

Even after the Antichrist sets up the abomination of desolation (Matt. 24:15ff), many people will be deceived by false messianic figures ("christs," literally "false anointings") and false prophets:

> Then if anyone says to you, "Look, here is the Christ!" or "There!" do not believe it. For false christs and false prophets will rise and show great signs and wonders to deceive, if possible, even the elect. See, I have told you beforehand. Therefore if they say to you, "Look, He is in the desert!" do not go out; or "Look, He is in the inner rooms!" do not believe it. For as the lightning comes from the east and flashes to the west, so also will the coming of the Son of Man be. For wherever the carcass is, there the eagles will be gathered together. (Matt. 24:23-28; cf. Mark 13:21-23; Luke 17:23-24, 37)

These imposters will pose as legitimate messianic claimants and other prophetic figures. They will command cult followings (Matt. 24:26) and claim that "the time has drawn near!" (Luke 21:8) but Jesus warned us that no one should follow them, especially by following them into remote places such as deserts (Matt. 24:26). By contrast, no one will need to search for the Person of Christ because His glorious return will be an instantaneous and observable event, such as when lightning flashing across the sky (Matt. 24:26-27; Luke 17:23-24). No one can miss His return; it is certain like the arrival of vultures when a carcass is in the vicinity (Matt. 24:28; Luke 17:37).

Jesus warned us beforehand that these messianic deceivers will perform "great signs and wonders" (Matt. 24:24-25). The intensity of this end-time deception will even threaten to deceive God's elect, His chosen people (Matt. 24:24). Christ included the phrase "if possible" to teach that the elect, those divinely ordained to inherit salvation, will not be ultimately and completely deceived by these satanic imposters. However, it is likely that some Orthodox Christians will become partially and temporarily deceived, and many who profess Christ's name will be completely deceived, as many have throughout history. Consequently, the saints need to be prepared for satanic deception by walking in the Holy Spirit and acquiring an awareness of the devil's schemes (2 Cor. 2:11).

The apostle Paul warned, "Let no one deceive you by any means" (2 Thess. 2:3), a phrase which expresses his concern that some Christians had incorrectly concluded that the return of Jesus Christ will occur before the Antichrist's arrival. But as we saw previously, Paul warned that the widespread apostasy and the revealing of the Antichrist must occur *before* that day (2 Thess. 2:1-4). Regarding this apostasy, he prophesied, "Now the Spirit expressly says that in latter times some will depart from the faith, giving heed to deceiving spirits and doctrines of demons, speaking lies in hypocrisy, having their own conscience seared with a hot iron" (1 Tim. 4:1-2). Christ asked whether His gospel ("the faith") will be on the earth by the time He returns ("will He really find [the] faith on the earth?" Luke 18:8),[2] which is a hyperbolic expression emphasizing the fact that the apostolic faith will become scarce after this apostasy has taken place.

Saint Paul received his sequence of prophetic events from Daniel's prophecies and Christ's Olivet Prophecy, and he had previously taught these doctrines to the Thessalonian saints ("when I was still with you, I told you these things" 2 Thess. 2:5). Consequently, he had taught them that this lawless man, known as the Man of Sin and the son of perdition, will exalt himself above God and all other deities, taking his

---

[2] Brackets added to reflect the presence of the definite article in the Greek manuscripts.

seat in the holy temple for the purpose of "showing himself that he is God" (2 Thess. 2:4; cf. Dan. 11:36). The apostle continued his teaching regarding the Antichrist:

> Do you not remember that when I was still with you, I told you these things? And now you know what is restraining, that he may be revealed in his own time. For the mystery of lawlessness is already at work; only He who now restrains will do so until He is taken out of the way. And then the lawless one will be revealed, whom the Lord will consume with the breath of His mouth and destroy with the brightness of His coming. The coming of the lawless one is according to the working of Satan, with all power, signs, and lying wonders, and with all unrighteous deception among those who perish, because they did not receive the love of the truth, that they might be saved. And for this reason God will send them strong delusion, that they should believe the lie, that they all may be condemned who did not believe the truth but had pleasure in unrighteousness. (2 Thess. 2:5-12)

Commentators have spilled much ink in defense of their particular identification of "the restrainer" (2 Thess. 2:6-7). The prophecy specifies that at the divinely ordained time, this restrainer will be removed ("taken out of the way") so that the end-time revelation of the Antichrist can take place (2 Thess. 2:6-8). The text identifies the restrainer as a person ("he who now restrains") and a force or condition ("you know what is restraining"), which has led many commentators to contend that one of the Roman emperors ("he") and the empire itself ("what") are in view. Nevertheless, other commentators, somewhat convincingly, have argued that Michael the Archangel is the one who has been restraining the revelation of the Antichrist.

Others have contended that Satan is the restrainer in verses 6-8. They point out that the devil will no longer prevent the revelation of the Antichrist once the archangel Michael forcefully removes him from heaven (Rev. 12:7-12). This interpretation is evidenced by the fact that

Paul's prophecy connects the revelation of the Antichrist with him taking his seat in God's temple (2 Thess. 2:4; cf. "the abomination of desolation" Matt. 24:15), an event which I demonstrated will occur at the midpoint of the final seven years. As we have seen, this event will chronologically correspond with Satan's forced removal from heaven, thus beginning his "short time" of wrath upon the earth and sea, namely, during the unprecedented tribulation (Rev. 12:12; cf. Rev. 20:3). This tribulation will continue for "a time and times and half a time" (Rev. 12:14), which is variously equated with 1,260 days (Rev. 12:6) and forty-two months (Rev. 13:5), a period which will be terminated by the return of Jesus Christ. Therefore, Satan temporarily prevents the great tribulation by restraining the revelation of the Antichrist, and as a result, he attempts to prevent the Lord's return. This motif of angelic restraint finds precedent in Daniel's vision of the demonic "prince" of Persia temporarily restraining ("withstanding") the arrival of God's Angel (Dan. 10:13).

The apostle Paul explains that "the mystery of lawlessness" will find its climax when the Antichrist is revealed (2 Thess. 2:6-7). Paul reminded the saints in Thessalonica that this mystery was "already at work" (2 Thess. 2:7; cf. 1 John 2:18); in other words, the various forms of lawlessness were already operational, although lawlessness will reach a climax in an incarnational form in the man known as the Antichrist. He will be the last dictator on earth, and unlike previous antichrists, he will be accompanied with the *full* power of Satan, with "*all* power, signs, and lying wonders" and "*all* unrighteous deception" (2 Thess. 2:9-10, emphasis added). The Antichrist's mighty power and authority will not be the result of human strength ("not by his own power" Dan. 8:24) but by Satan himself ("the dragon gave him his power" Rev. 13:2). The Antichrist and his work will be the "strong delusion" and "the lie" which God will use to condemn a wicked world which has rejected the gospel (2 Thess. 2:10-12). When God Himself sends strong delusion, how great is that delusion! The apostle reminds us that the Lord Jesus will return in brilliant glory to kill the Antichrist with His powerful word ("the breath of His mouth" 2 Thess. 2:8; cf. Isa. 11:4; Rev. 19:15, 20-21).

To recap what we have learned this far, the abomination of desolation will begin the forty-two months of unprecedented tribulation (Dan. 9:27; 12:1-3, 11; Rev. 11:1-3), the period during which the Antichrist will be revealed with a *fullness* of satanic deception, power, and miracles (cf. Rev. 12:6, 12, 14; 13:3-8). At this time, at the midpoint of the final seven years, Michael the archangel will successfully defeat Satan in heavenly battle and will cast him down to the earth:

> And war broke out in heaven: Michael and his angels fought with the dragon; and the dragon and his angels fought, but they did not prevail, nor was a place found for them in heaven any longer. So the great dragon was cast out, that serpent of old, called the Devil and Satan, who deceives the whole world; he was cast to the earth, and his angels were cast out with him. . . "Woe to the inhabitants of the earth and the sea! For the devil has come down to you, having great wrath, because he knows that he has a short time." (Rev. 12:7-9, 12)

Three events—Satan's ousting from heaven, the abomination of desolation, and the revelation of the Antichrist with all satanic power and wonders—will begin at the midpoint of the final seven years. The temporal alignment of these prophetic events strongly suggests that the devil will come down to inhabit the human person of the Antichrist (cf. John 13:27). As such, the very hypostasis or person of Satan will incarnate this wicked man. Consequently, Paul's "mystery of lawlessness," as revealed in the Antichrist (2 Thess. 2:7), will be the antithesis of what he later terms "the mystery of godliness," as revealed in Christ ("God was manifested in the flesh" 1 Tim. 3:16). As such, this son of perdition, the individual seed of the serpent, will be the demonic counterfeit of the promised Seed of the woman—the incarnate Son of God (cf. Gen. 3:15).

Michael casting out Satan from heaven at the midpoint of the final seven years presents some interpretive difficulties. This can be seen in

Jesus' statement that He saw Satan "fall like lightning from heaven," which he pronounced after the ministry of the seventy whom He had sent to preach the gospel (Luke 10:18). However, this statement may function anticipatorily; in other words, Christ prophetically saw Satan's future ousting from heaven in the then present because His kingdom authority was already being revealed in the ministry of these seventy evangelists. Similarly, Jesus spoke about the casting out of Satan in the context of His imminent death on the cross: "Now is the judgment of this world; now the ruler of this world will be cast out" (John 12:31). If this interpretation is correct, such passages serve as examples of inaugurated eschatology, the "already and not yet" principle of God's kingdom (see chapter 20). The idea is that the cross of Christ is the ground and basis for Satan losing his heavenly authority (cf. Col. 2:14-15); notwithstanding, the full manifestation and final outworking of His victory over Satan will take place at the time of the kingdom's consummation, at the end.[3]

Christ's statements about Satan's fall contain allusions to Old Testament prophecies about Lucifer, the king of Babylon (Isa. 14:12-14) and the prince/king of Tyre (Ezek. 28:2-5, 12-19). Isaiah's prophecy reads as follows:

> "How you are fallen from heaven, O Lucifer, son of the morning! How you are cut down to the ground, you who weakened the nations! For you have said in your heart: 'I will ascend into heaven, I will exalt my throne above the stars of God; I will also sit on the mount of the congregation on the farthest sides of the north; I will ascend above the heights of the clouds, I will be like the Most High.' " (Isa. 14:12-14)

The passage specifies that Lucifer (literally "shining one" or "morning star") is the king of Babylon (Isa. 14:4) who exalted himself

---

[3] Alternatively, Satan may be cast out of heaven twice, once after Christ's crucifixion, so that he now inhabits the Abyss, and a second time, after he is defeated by Michael the archangel, following his release from the Abyss.

"above the stars of God" (Isa. 14:13; cf. Job 38:7; Jer. 49:16; Obad. 4; Hab. 2:9). This self-exalting king ultimately refers to the Antichrist for several reasons: First, Jesus alluded to this passage when he spoke about Satan's fall from heaven (Luke 10:18; cf. Rev. 12:7-13).

Second, the prophet Daniel alluded to this prophecy when he wrote about the self-exaltation of the Antichrist's throne above the stars: "And it [the little horn] grew up to the host of heaven; and it cast down some of the host and some of the stars to the ground, and trampled them. He even exalted himself as high as the Prince of the host . . . and the place of His sanctuary was cast down" (Dan. 8:10-11; cf. Rev. 12:4).

Third, the king of Babylon was described as attempting to "sit on the mount of the congregation on the farthest sides of the north" (Isa. 14:13), which refers to Satan's desire to exalt himself within God's temple. This phrase occurs only once more in Scripture, where it pertains to Jerusalem, the Holy City: "Beautiful in elevation . . . is Mount Zion on the sides of the north" (Ps. 48:2). The location likely refers to Jerusalem's Temple Mount, which is directly to the north of Mount Zion.

Fourth, the king's statement that he would become "like the Most High" (Isa. 14:14) alludes to the Genesis narrative of the serpent tempting the woman to transgress so that she could "be like God, knowing good and evil" (Gen. 3:5). To further demonstrate this connection, the Antichrist will exalt himself above all gods, taking his seat in God's temple for the purpose of "showing himself that he is God" (2 Thess. 2:4; cf. Dan. 11:36).

Ezekiel's prophecy regarding the prince of Tyre shares many of the same features as Isaiah's prophecy:

"Son of man, say to the prince of Tyre, 'Thus says the Lord God: "Because your heart is lifted up, and you say, 'I am a god, I sit in the seat of gods, in the midst of the seas,' yet you are a man, and not a god, though you set your heart as the heart of a god (Behold, you are wiser than Daniel! There is no secret that can be hidden from you! With your wisdom and your understanding you have gained riches for yourself and gathered gold and silver into your treasuries; by your great wisdom in trade you have increased your riches, and your heart is lifted up because of your riches)." ' " (Ezek. 28:2-5)

As with Isaiah's prophecy about the king of Babylon, this passage also speaks beyond its immediate referent of a contemporary prince of Tyre to the self-exalting Antichrist. Once again, we see that the prince lifts himself up to declare, "I am a god, I sit in the seat of gods," reminiscent of the verse about the Man of Sin ("who opposes and exalts himself above all that is called God or that is worshiped, so that he sits as God in the temple of God, showing himself that he is God" 2 Thess. 2:4). This king's royal throne "in the midst of the seas" (Ezek. 28:2) may parallel the phrase "between the seas," the location of the holy mountain Jerusalem, where the Antichrist will erect his palatial tents (Dan. 11:45). Ezekiel included a parenthetical reference to the wisdom and understanding of his contemporary, the young prophet Daniel (Ezek. 28:3), to highlight the Antichrist's "wisdom" and "understanding" (Ezek. 28:4; cf. Dan. 8:23). Furthermore, the book of Daniel alludes to Ezekiel's prophecy when referring to the Antichrist's southward invasion; just as Ezekiel wrote that the prince gained riches, including gold and silver, for his treasuries (Ezek. 28:4), Daniel specified that the Antichrist would have "power over the treasuries of gold and silver" (Dan. 11:43).

Ezekiel continued the prophecy by addressing the king of Tyre, who is presumed to be the father of the prince of Tyre (or a reference to the prince who later becomes king) mentioned in the initial verses of the same chapter (cf. Ezek. 28:1-10):

"Son of man, take up a lamentation for the king of Tyre, and say to him, 'Thus says the Lord God: "You were the seal of perfection, full of wisdom and perfect in beauty. You were in Eden, the garden of God; every precious stone was your covering: The sardius, topaz, and diamond, beryl, onyx, and jasper, sapphire, turquoise, and emerald with gold. The workmanship of your timbrels and pipes was prepared for you on the day you were created. You were the anointed cherub who covers; I established you; you were on the holy mountain of God; you walked back and forth in the midst of fiery stones. You were perfect in your ways from the day you were created, till iniquity was found in you. By the abundance of your trading you became filled with violence within and you sinned; therefore, I cast you as a profane thing out of the mountain of God; and I destroyed you, O covering cherub, from the midst of the fiery stones. Your heart was lifted up because of your beauty; you corrupted your wisdom for the sake of your splendor; I cast you to the ground, I laid you before kings that they might gaze at you. You defiled your sanctuaries by the multitude of your iniquities, by the iniquity of your trading; therefore, I brought fire from your midst; it devoured you, and I turned you to ashes upon the earth in the sight of all who saw you. All who knew you among the peoples are astonished at you; you have become a horror and shall be no more forever." ' " (Ezek. 28:12-19)

The prophet depicted the king of Tyre as Satan. He described the king as "the seal of perfection, full of wisdom and perfect in beauty" when he was in the garden of Eden (Ezek. 28:13; cf. Gen. 3:1-2). The Lord created the king with a beautiful covering of precious stones, reminiscent of a priestly breastplate, and He gave him musical instruments (Ezek. 28:13, 17). He is called the "anointed cherub who covers," a cryptic reference to Satan (cf. 2 Cor. 4:3-4; 11:14), and he is described as walking back and forth among flaming stones upon God's holy mountain (Ezek. 28:14-16). However, he committed sin and became violent, so God cast him out of His heavenly mountain to the earth (Ezek. 28:15-17; cf. Gen. 3:14). Consistent with the prophecies regarding the Antichrist, the king of Tyre defiled sanctuaries, and the Lord slayed him, burned him with fire, and sent him to eternal destruction (Ezek. 28:17-19). Yet because the prince of Tyre will set his heart "as the heart of a god," God promised to bring foreigners from among the nations to assault his beauty, wisdom, and splendor, and to kill him in battle (Ezek. 28:6-8).

The cumulative biblical evidence reveals that Satan performs the same actions as the Antichrist (Lucifer and the prince/king of Tyre). Another connection between the two is the apostle John's description of Michael casting Satan out of heaven (Rev. 12:5-12; cf. Ezek. 28:15-17), which is immediately followed by a description of the serpent pursuing the woman who gave birth to the man Child (Rev. 12:13-17). Part of the literary background of these verses is the protoevangelium, the first biblical prophecy about the Messiah, and for that matter, about the Antichrist (Gen. 3:15).

In the narrative leading up to this prophecy, the serpent, who is a cunning beast, tempted the woman, who had been created in God's image, telling her that she would become "like God" if she disobeyed God (Gen. 1:26-27; 3:1-5). After her transgression, God decreed that she would experience intensified labor pains when bringing forth children (Gen. 3:16; cf. Isa. 66:7), which, as we have seen, will find its greatest fulfilment in the birth pains of the great tribulation (Rev. 12:2). In addition, the Lord prophesied that the wounded "Seed" of the woman would bruise the head of the "seed" of the serpent (Gen. 3:15; cf. Isa. 66:7). The first part of this prophecy was fulfilled when the individual Seed of the woman, the male Child (i.e., Jesus Christ), was pierced for sins and transgressions ("you shall bruise His heel" Gen. 3:15), dying on the cross in order to reconcile "the image of God" (i.e., mankind) back to Himself so that we can reenter Paradise. In addition, Christ will eventually crush the serpent's head ("He shall bruise your head" Gen. 3:15; cf. Isa. 27:1; Rom. 16:20; Rev. 13:3).

The Old Testament description of Leviathan, the legendary serpent-dragon of the sea, shares many similarities with the Antichrist. For example, Job described Leviathan as the king "over all the children of pride" and one with whom no one can make a covenant, pierce with a hook, or defeat in war (Job 41:1-2, 4, 8-9, 34; cf. Num. 21:6, 8-9; Judg. 5:26). Also, the psalmist told God that He had crushed the multiple heads of Leviathan (Ps. 74:14; cf. Job 26:13). Finally, the Leviathan motif appears again in the apostle John's depiction of Satan as a fiery red dragon with seven crowned heads (i.e., seven kingdoms) and ten horns (i.e., ten kings) and its reflection in the Antichrist's composite kingdom with seven heads and ten crowned horns (Rev. 12:3 with 13:1; 17:3, 7, 12, 16; cf. Dan. 7:7, 20, 24). Then John saw that the sea Beast will receive the deadly head wound of the protoevangelium, the head wound of Genesis 3:15.

> And I saw one of his heads as if it had been mortally wounded, and his deadly wound was healed. And all the world marveled and followed the beast. So they worshiped the dragon who gave authority to the beast; and they worshiped the beast, saying, "Who is like the beast? Who is able to make war with him?" And he was given a mouth speaking great things and blasphemies, and he was given authority to continue for forty-two months. (Rev. 13:3-5)

As the seventh head of the Beast, the Antichrist will reign for only a brief period before he will be violently killed ("he must continue a short time" Rev. 17:10). Then he will be resurrected ("his deadly wound was healed" Rev. 13:3), a demonic parody of Christ's own resurrection from the dead. In this manner, the Antichrist will become an eighth head, which will be a resurrection of the seventh head, of the seven-headed Beast ("the beast that was, and is not, is himself also the eighth, and is of the seven" Rev. 17:11). Nevertheless, after his resurrection, he will not be just one head at the end of a series of seven other heads; rather, he will become a composite fullness of *all* the previous kingdoms ("of the seven" Rev. 17:11), the fullness of satanic power and authority which the previous kingdoms only received in part (cf. Rev. 13:1-2). The Antichrist will not receive a resurrection unto eternal life but a resurrection of eternal death because through this divine miracle (performed by God, not Satan) he will become the incarnation of Satan, presumably having been emptied through his depravity and death of any remaining vestige of God's likeness.

The Antichrist's resurrection will initiate the final forty-two months of unprecedented tribulation (Rev. 13:5), which will coincide with

Satan's fall from heaven, thus revealing the mystery of iniquity, the incarnation of Satan in the individual seed of the serpent (Gen. 3:15). After his resurrection, the entire world will "marvel" at the Beast and will worship him. From this point on, they will recognize that the world's military forces cannot defeat him.

> Then he opened his mouth in blasphemy against God, to blaspheme His name, His tabernacle, and those who dwell in heaven. It was granted to him to make war with the saints and to overcome them. And authority was given him over every tribe, tongue, and nation. All who dwell on the earth will worship him, whose names have not been written in the Book of Life of the Lamb slain from the foundation of the world. If anyone has an ear, let him hear. He who leads into captivity shall go into captivity; he who kills with the sword must be killed with the sword. Here is the patience and the faith of the saints. (Rev. 13:6-10; cf. Rev. 17:8)

As an aside, the devil recognizes that he will be permitted to give people great authority throughout the kingdoms of this world in return for worshipping him. He offered to give the world's kingdoms ("all the kingdoms of the world and their glory") to Christ in exchange for worshipping him (Matt. 4:8-9; Luke 4:5-7), a temptation which would have been empty if God had not determined to legitimately give this authority to Satan. Consistent with this theme, the apostle John wrote that the entire world was already under the influence of the devil (1 John 5:19).

During the final forty-two months of unprecedented tribulation, the Antichrist will be given authority over the nations of the world ("over every tribe, tongue, and nation" Rev. 13:7; "all who dwell on the earth" Rev. 13:8). People whose names have been written in the Lamb's Book of Life will refuse to worship the Beast, which will result in the mass martyrdom of Christians (Rev. 13:8-10; 20:4). However, the Lord will return in brilliant glory to kill the Antichrist with His sharp sword, identified as the word proceeding from His mouth (Rev. 19:15, 20-21;

"the breath of His mouth" 2 Thess. 2:8; cf. Isa. 11:4 LXX). When Christ pierces the Man of Sin, lawlessness in all its forms will be replaced by the consummated kingdom of God.

In addition to the sea Beast, the apostle saw another beast arising from the earth at the beginning of the unprecedented tribulation.

> Then I saw another beast coming up out of the earth, and he had two horns like a lamb and spoke like a dragon. And he exercises all the authority of the first beast in his presence, and causes the earth and those who dwell in it to worship the first beast, whose deadly wound was healed. He performs great signs, so that he even makes fire come down from heaven on the earth in the sight of men. And he deceives those who dwell on the earth by those signs which he was granted to do in the sight of the beast, telling those who dwell on the earth to make an image to the beast who was wounded by the sword and lived. He was granted power to give breath to the image of the beast, that the image of the beast should both speak and cause as many as would not worship the image of the beast to be killed. He causes all, both small and great, rich and poor, free and slave, to receive a mark on their right hand or on their foreheads, and that no one may buy or sell except one who has the mark or the name of the beast, or the number of his name. Here is wisdom. Let him who has understanding calculate the number of the beast, for it is the number of a man: His number is 666. (Rev. 13:11-18)

Elsewhere, the apostle identified the land beast simply as "the false prophet" (Rev. 16:13; 19:20; 20:10). The literary backdrop for this beast is Behemoth, the mammoth creature depicted by Job (Job 40:15-24), which is set alongside his description of Leviathan (Job 41:1-34). John explained that the false prophet will present himself as a man of peace ("two horns like a lamb" Rev. 13:11) yet he will speak with the words of Satan himself (Rev. 13:11).[4] As a deceiver who promotes a false peace, he may be a religious figure, such as a Roman pontiff or a powerful Imam. Some have suggested that the two horns may represent the powers of "church and state," such as an ecumenical merger between the nation-states and the Roman papacy or a satanic merger of apostate Christianity with Islam (i.e., "Chrislam").

The false prophet will deceive the inhabitants of the earth by performing demonic signs as part of his demonic strategy to compel people to worship the Antichrist. His miraculous powers will include summoning fire down from the sky (Rev. 13:13), reminiscent of Elijah's divine miracles (1 Kings 18:23-38; 2 Kings 1:10-14), to "prepare the way" (cf. Exod. 23:20; Isa. 40:3; Mal. 3:1, 3) for the Antichrist. Because he will perform demonic miracles, the intensity of which the world has never seen, those who dwell upon the earth will worship the Antichrist. Seemingly overnight, the world's inhabitants will forsake their religious traditions, even the secular humanism of the West, in order to worship this resurrected man (Rev. 13:12, 14).

The false prophet will kill those who refuse to make images to the Antichrist and to worship them (Rev. 13:14-15). We may speculate whether people will create individual images, as in the ancient world, participate in a computerized singularity with a centralized system connecting them directly to the Antichrist, engage in transhumanism, or interact with some other demonically inspired technology or artificial intelligence. Regardless, the primary image will be the desecrating sacrilege, the abomination of desolation, which is the Antichrist's own image that he will set up in the Jerusalem sanctuary. The power of Satan within the false prophet will animate this idol with the energies of the resurrected Antichrist, such as speech (Rev. 13:14-15).

The worship of the Beast's image finds a close parallel in the narrative of King Nebuchadnezzar's statue. According to the narrative, the

---

4   It is uncertain whether the false prophet should be identified as the "worthless shepherd" (Zech. 11:17).

king commanded the peoples of every nation and language within his dominion to "fall down and worship the gold image" of himself which he erected in the plain of Dura. Those who refused to worship his image were thrown into a fiery furnace (Dan. 3:4-6, 12-15). The Angel of the Lord, undoubtedly a Christophany (a preincarnate revelation of Christ), was seen in the fiery furnace with the three righteous men, Shadrach, Meshach, and Abednego, who had refused to worship the image, and He miraculously delivered them from being burned (Dan. 3:25, 28). Then the king exclaimed: "They have frustrated the king's word, and yielded their bodies, that they should not serve nor worship any god except their own God!" (Dan. 3:28). This passage of Scripture provides assurance that Jesus will also be with those of us who refuse to worship the Beast and his image.

The false prophet will also force all peoples to receive "the mark" of the Antichrist, an identifying mark placed upon the right hand or forehead, without which no one will be able to engage in commerce or any financial transaction (Rev. 13:16-17). Consequently, those who refuse to receive this mark will experience starvation, eviction from their homes, prison sentences, and other unspeakable forms of persecution (Rev. 20:4). The apostle John's audience would be able to recognize his description of the mark as a parody of the Jewish practice of donning phylacteries, two leather boxes that religious Jewish men strap to their forehead and non-dominant arm and hand when engaged in prayer; it symbolized their covenant with God (Exod. 13:16; Deut. 6:8; 11:18; Matt. 23:5). In the literary context of the Apocalypse, the mark is a parody of the seal of the living God (Rev. 7:2-3; 9:4; 14:1). The mark of the Beast will be much more than a newly developed technology, such as an electronic tattoo or RFID microchip implant, required for economic exchange. Whatever technology is used, no one will receive it without understanding its purpose as a sign of voluntary allegiance and worship of the Antichrist.

The apostle reveals that the number "six hundred sixty-six" (not 6-6-6) is the number of the Antichrist ("the number of the beast . . . of a man" Rev. 13:18). John's audience would have understood this calculation as referring to the common practice of Greek isopsephy, where one adds all the numeric values of letters in a person's name in order to obtain a sum. The number six-hundred sixty-six is associated with the names of a limited number of potential men, one of whom will be the name of the Antichrist. Whether the Antichrist will be identifiable by Greek isopsephy or by a modern and more obvious method of calculation, we do not yet know.

The significance of the number six in Hebrew thought is primarily due to it being one less than seven, the number associated with completeness or perfection. This number appears in several biblical passages which contain themes related to the Antichrist. For example, Goliath of Gath, the giant whom King David slayed by crushing his head with a stone, stood at a height of six cubits and a span (1 Sam. 17:4). Likewise, the image which King Nebuchadnezzar required the people of Babylon to worship had a height of sixty cubits and width of six cubits (Dan. 3:1). More directly, King Solomon received an annual amount of gold which weighed six hundred and sixty-six talents (1 Kings 10:14; 2 Chron. 9:13). This illustrates the pattern of prophetic foreshadowing which can be seen throughout sacred Scripture.

The apostle John penned the following admonitions to equip Christians to escape the deception of the Antichrist:

> Little children, it is the last hour; and as you have heard that the Antichrist is coming, even now many antichrists have come, by which we know that it is the last hour . . . But you have an anointing from the Holy One, and you know all things . . . Who is a liar but he who denies that Jesus is the Christ? He is antichrist who denies the Father and the Son. Whoever denies the Son does not have the Father either; he who acknowledges the Son has the Father also. (1 John 2:18, 20, 22-23)

> Beloved, do not believe every spirit, but test the spirits, whether they are of God; because many false prophets have gone out into the world. By this you know the Spirit of God: Every spirit that confesses that

Jesus Christ has come in the flesh is of God, and every spirit that does not confess that Jesus Christ has come in the flesh is not of God. And this is the spirit of the Antichrist, which you have heard was coming, and is now already in the world. You are of God, little children, and have overcome them, because He who is in you is greater than he who is in the world. They are of the world. Therefore, they speak as of the world, and the world hears them. (1 John 4:1-5; cf. 1 John 2:18)

John defined an antichrist as a person who denies that Jesus Christ is the Son of God, thereby denying the Father (1 John 2:22-23). He wrote that those who do not adhere to the Orthodox teachings regarding Christology, such as those who deny that the divine Person of Christ has become incarnate, belong to the spirit of the Antichrist and should not be received into Christian fellowship (1 John 4:3-4; 2 John 1:7). In the lifetime of the apostles, many deceivers had already been involved in the local parishes but later abandoned them, revealing that they did not belong to the apostolic faith (1 John 2:19, 26). Even false apostles posed as true ones (Rev. 2:2), and the apostle Paul described them as deceivers who functioned like Satan, who "transforms himself into an angel of light" (2 Cor. 11:13-15). Elsewhere, he warned them about false teachers: "For the time will come when they will not endure sound doctrine, but according to their own desires, because they have itching ears, they will heap up for themselves teachers; and they will turn their ears away from the truth, and be turned aside to fables" (2 Tim. 4:3-4).

Although the saints whom John addressed in his epistles understood the concepts relating to the final Antichrist, he reminded them that many antichrists had arrived already (1 John 2:18; 2 John 1:7). Consistent with Paul's doctrine of the mystery of lawlessness which was "already at work" during the apostles' ministry (2 Thess. 2:7), John asserted that the *spirit* of the Antichrist (not the Antichrist himself!) was "already in the world" (1 John 4:3). In addition, many false prophets had already arrived (1 John 4:1). The arrival of such deceivers before the time of the end demonstrates the "already and not yet" principle, in other words, "the last hour" of the present evil age has already broken into history before the eschaton (see chapter 20).

The apostle John reminded us that the gift of the Holy Spirit equips the holy Church to test teachers and prophets to see if they accord with apostolic truth or heresy. This divine anointing teaches us "all things," including how to discern the spirits and test them to determine whether they are from God or the world (1 John 2:20, 27; cf. Rev. 2:2). The Lord Himself taught us that we can distinguish between true and false prophets by evaluating "their fruits," in other words, by observing their deeds and assessing the veracity of their prophecies (Matt. 7:15-20). This is one of the sacred tasks of Christians in these last days.

8

YOU WILL BE MY WITNESSES

SATAN'S EVICTION FROM HEAVEN will result in victory for the children of God. The heavenly voice declared to the apostle John that God's kingdom will arrive with salvation, strength, and power when this happens:

> Then I heard a loud voice saying in heaven, "Now salvation, and strength, and the kingdom of our God, and the power of His Christ have come, for the accuser of our brethren, who accused them before our God day and night, has been cast down. And they overcame him by the blood of the Lamb and by the word of their testimony, and they did not love their lives to the death. Therefore rejoice, O heavens, and you who dwell in them!" (Rev. 12:10-12)

By the midpoint of the final seven years, Satan will no longer be able to maintain a heavenly domain. The archangel Michael and his angels will prevail over Satan in heaven and cast him to the earth, which will trigger the period of unprecedented tribulation. As a result of this final persecution, the saints of God will boldly proclaim the gospel of Christ ("the word of their testimony" v. 11) and embody His martyr-witness testimony ("they did not love their lives to the death" v. 11).

Satan's fall means that he will no longer be able to accuse Christians of transgressions before God's throne ("for the accuser of our brethren . . . has been cast down" v. 10; cf. Zech. 3:1-2). Consequently, the consciences of Christians will be free from his direct assaults. As a result, the kingdom of God will arrive at that time ("Now salvation, and strength, and the kingdom of our God, and the power of His Christ have come" Rev. 12:10). Some interpret this verse to be an anticipatory statement conveying the idea that Christ will arrive to consummate His kingdom forty-two months later; however, it is preferable to regard it as indicating that the holy Church will experience a Pentecost-like endowment of power at the midpoint of the final seven years.

The Antichrist will persecute and murder the saints during the tribulation, necessitating this special grace and power. Certainly Christians will be targeted in this persecution, as the apostle John prophesied just verses later: "And the dragon was enraged with the woman, and he went to make war with the rest of her offspring, who keep the commandments of God and have the testimony of Jesus Christ" (Rev. 12:17).

But it was Moses who had prophesied about the end-time relationship between the nations and the Jewish nation. The Song of Moses includes this statement: "They [the children of Israel] have provoked Me to jealousy by what is not God; they have moved Me to anger by their foolish idols. But I will provoke them to jealousy by those who are not a nation; I will move them to anger by a foolish nation" (Deut. 32:21). This verse does not speak about the foreign invaders, "a nation whose language you will not understand . . . a nation of fierce countenance," who will be the instruments of covenantal judgment upon the land of Israel (Deut. 28:49-50; cf. Dan. 8:23). Rather, it refers to the "foolish nation," the predominantly Gentile Church, proclaiming and living out the gospel so as to "provoke them [the Jews] to jealousy" for their Messiah (Rom. 10:19; 11:11).

The prophet Isaiah prophesied that the Gentiles would preach the gospel to the Jews during the period leading up to the day of the Lord:

> For with stammering lips and another tongue He will speak to this people to whom He said, "This is the rest with which you may cause the weary to rest," and, "This is the refreshing"; yet they would not hear. But the word of the Lord was to them, "Precept upon precept, precept upon precept, line upon line, line upon line, here a little, there a little," that they might go and fall backward, and be broken and snared and caught . . . Therefore thus says the Lord God: "Behold, I lay in Zion a stone for a foundation, a tried stone, a precious cornerstone, a sure foundation; whoever believes will not act hastily." (Isa. 28:11-13, 16)

God promised to use a people "with stammering lips and another tongue" (i.e., the Gentiles; cf. 1 Cor. 14:21-22) to proclaim the gospel ("the rest" and "the refreshing") to the Jews, despite the nation's reluctance to receive it ("yet they would not hear"; cf. Isa. 6:9-10). As Isaiah elsewhere lamented, "In returning and rest you shall be saved; in quietness and confidence shall be your strength. But you would not" (Isa. 30:15). This message of rest and trust refers to trusting in the Lord, as Jesus Himself taught, "Come to Me, all you who labor and are heavy laden, and I will give you rest" (Matt. 11:28). The apostles identified Zion's stone of the corner in Isaiah 28:16 as Christ (Rom. 9:33; 1 Pet. 2:6; cf. Eph. 2:20), and they called their hearers to believe in Him ("Whoever believes on Him will not be put to shame" Rom. 10:11).

The Lord, however, promised to reveal the gospel to the humble among the people so that they could teach others. Because the priests and prophets were no longer able to teach Israel the message, Isaiah warned, "Whom will he teach knowledge? And whom will he make to understand the message? Those just weaned from milk? Those just drawn from the breasts? For precept must be upon precept, precept upon precept, line upon line, line upon line, here a little, there a little" (Isa. 28:9-10; cf. Isa. 53:1; 1 Cor. 14:20). Jesus, alluding to this passage, explained that the Father has hidden the message from the proud ("the wise and prudent") and has revealed it to the humble (mere "babes" in Matt. 11:25; cf. Isa. 8:16).

The result of ignoring this message while continuing to trust in the arm of flesh is that the Jewish nation would stumble over this Stone (i.e., Christ) and "go and fall backward, and be broken and snared and caught" (Isa. 28:13; cf. Ps. 118:22-23; Isa. 8:14-15; Matt. 21:44; John 16:1). Echoes of this passage are found in Daniel's prophecy about the unprecedented tribulation:

> Those who do wickedly against the covenant he [the northern king] shall corrupt with flattery; but the people who know their God shall be strong and carry out great exploits. And those of the people who understand shall instruct many; yet for many days they shall fall by sword and flame, by captivity and plundering. Now when they fall, they shall be aided with a little help; but many shall join with them by intrigue. And some of those of understanding shall fall, to refine them, purify them, and make them white, until the time of the end; because it is still for the appointed time. (Dan. 11:32-35)

The Antichrist will deceive with flattery those who seek to undermine the holy covenant, yet Christians ("the people who know their God" Dan. 11:32) will show strength and perform miracles ("carry out great exploits" Dan. 11:32). The believing saints will "instruct many," leading them to a proper understanding of the gospel, yet many will become martyrs ("they shall fall by sword and flame, by captivity and plundering" Dan. 11:33). The Man clothed in linen instructed the prophet, "But you, Daniel, shut up the words, and seal the book until the time of the end" (Dan. 12:4), and he also stated that the hidden meaning of the prophecy will be revealed to them by these gospel witnesses ("many shall run to and fro, and knowledge shall increase" Dan. 12:4; cf. Amos 8:12).

Among these end-time witnesses of the gospel, two witnesses will play a particularly significant role:

> And I will give power to my two witnesses, and they will prophesy one thousand two hundred and sixty days, clothed in sackcloth. These are the two olive trees and the two lampstands standing before the God of the earth. And if anyone wants to harm them, fire proceeds from their mouth and devours their enemies. And if anyone wants to harm them, he must be killed in this manner. These have power to shut heaven, so that no rain falls in the days of their prophecy; and they have power over waters to turn them to blood, and to strike the earth with all plagues, as often as they desire. (Rev. 11:3-6)

The prophetic backdrop for the two witnesses includes the Old Testament prophets Moses and Elijah the Tishbite. The literary connection between the witnesses and Elijah is well established: First, Elijah also commanded ("except at my word") that no rain would fall throughout the land of Israel (1 Kings 17:1). According to Jesus and his brother James, the drought in Elijah's day continued in the land for three years and six months (Luke 4:25; James 5:17-18). As such, this prophet's ministry prefigured the ministry of the two witnesses, who will prophesy for the same duration ("one thousand two hundred and sixty days" Rev. 11:3). Second, the two witnesses will also speak words of fire that "devours their enemies" (Rev. 11:5), reminiscent of Elijah calling fire from heaven to devour King Ahab's emissaries (2 Kings 1:10-14; cf. 1 Kings 18:23-38).

Third, the Scriptures predict that Elijah will return to "prepare the way" for the Messiah before the day of the Lord. The Lord spoke through the prophet Malachi that He would send "My messenger"[1] who would "prepare the way before Me" (Mal. 3:1). He identified the messenger as Elijah in the next chapter: "Behold, I will send you Elijah

---

[1] "My messenger" is a word play; the name Malachi means "my messenger."

the prophet before the coming of the great and dreadful day of the Lord. And he will turn the hearts of the fathers to the children, and the hearts of the children to their fathers, lest I come and strike the earth with a curse" (Mal. 4:5-6). Notice that Elijah will bring repentance to the nation before the day of the Lord so that He would not "strike the earth with a curse." John picked up this language in his description of the two prophets' power "to strike the earth with all plagues" (Rev. 11:6). Jews have expected Elijah's return since his ascension (Matt. 27:47, 49; Mark 15:35-36), and to this day, religious Jews leave an empty chair for the prophet at each Passover Seder, and they open their door and summon him to return to them.

Notably, the New Testament identifies John the Baptizer as the Elijah who was expected to come (Matt. 11:10; 14-15; 17:11-13; Mark 1:2; 9:11-13). John distinguished himself by dressing in garb similar to that of Elijah (Matt. 3:4; Mark 1:6). In addition, the angel who spoke to John's father prophesied, "And he [John] will turn many of the children of Israel to the Lord their God. He will also go before Him in the spirit and power of Elijah, 'to turn the hearts of the fathers to the children,' and the disobedient to the wisdom of the just, to make ready a people prepared for the Lord" (Luke 1:16-17). Also, Jesus identified John as the messenger of Malachi's prophecy (Mal. 3:1; cf. Matt. 11:10; Mark 1:2), and when the disciples questioned Him about Elijah's arrival, He declared, "Indeed, Elijah is coming first and will restore all things. But I say to you that Elijah has come already" (Matt. 17:11-12; cf. Matt. 11:14-15; Mark 9:12-13). As Jesus came to suffer and die, and later to come again in glory, John the Baptizer came before Jesus to fulfill the first of Elijah's two comings ("is coming . . . has already come"). The Baptizer proclaimed a message of repentance in "the spirit and power of Elijah," which resulted in his own rejection and death, and Elijah will come again to "restore all things" prior to the day of the Lord.

The two witnesses were also prefigured by Moses. To demonstrate, John wrote that the witnesses will powerfully turn waters into blood and "strike the earth will all plagues," as Moses did against Egypt (Exod. 7-11 esp. 7:14-25 with Rev. 11:6). Such miraculous power explains how the witnesses will be divinely protected from the Antichrist and his forces until the completion of their prophetic ministry.

The Scriptures provide other examples of two prophets working in tandem, such as Eldad and Medad, who prophesied "in the camp" of the children of Israel (Num. 11:26-27); Moses and Aaron during the exodus; and Elijah and Elisha during the period of the kings of Israel. However, the New Testament highlights that Moses and Elijah appeared to Jesus before Peter, James, and John on the Mount of Transfiguration (Matt. 16:28-7:9; Mark 9:2-10; Luke 9:27-36; cf. Zech. 4:14; 2 Pet. 1:16-18). This strengthens the likelihood that the two witnesses will be prophets who will minister in "the spirit and power" of these two forerunners—Moses and Elijah.

It is less likely, although far from impossible, that the two witnesses will be Moses and Elijah. The evidence in favor of this view is that Elijah appears to have bypassed natural death when the Lord raptured him to heaven in a chariot of heavenly glory (2 Kings 2:11-13) and Moses' death led to speculation about his body (Deut. 34:5-6; Jude 1:9), which may hint that he would be resuscitated at some point. This view would require Moses to be "resurrected" only to die a second time (Rev. 11:7). The apostolic teaching that "it is appointed for men to die once" (Heb. 9:27) may be why some of the Church fathers[2] taught that the two witnesses would be Elijah and Enoch, another man whom God miraculously took to heaven without having tasted death (Gen. 5:24; Heb. 11:5). Others have argued that such views represent an over-literalization of the intended typology.

The apostle John also identified the two witnesses as "the two olive trees and the two lampstands standing before the God of the earth" (Rev. 11:4), echoing a prophecy of Zechariah:

---

2   E.g. Tertullian, Irenaeus, and Hippolytus of Rome

> Then I answered and said to him, "What are these two olive trees—at the right of the lampstand and at its left?" And I further answered and said to him, "What are these two olive branches that drip into the receptacles of the two gold pipes from which the golden oil drains?" Then he answered me and said, "Do you not know what these are?" And I said, "No, my lord." So he said, "These are the two anointed ones, who stand beside the Lord of the whole earth." (Zech. 4:11-14)

In Zechariah's prophecy, the two olive trees ("two sons of the oil") symbolized Joshua, the high priest, and Zerubbabel, the royal governor of Judah, at the time of the restoration of the Jews from Babylonian captivity. The Lord had ordained and consecrated these two men to construct and complete the Jerusalem temple by the power of the Holy Spirit ("but by My Spirit" Zech. 4:6). These men also stood as powerful symbols for the two roles of the coming Messiah—Jesus Christ—the ultimate High Priest and King of Jerusalem (cf. Heb. 6:19-7:17).[3] The book of Revelation borrows the imagery of these two men to prefigure the two final heralds of the final return from exile—the two witnesses of Jerusalem (Rev. 11:3-14).

During the great tribulation, the two witnesses will mourn over the wickedness of man (hence "clothed in sackcloth" Rev. 11:3), prophesy of coming judgments, perform confirmatory signs and wonders, and proclaim the gospel of Christ to the Jewish nation and the world as preparation for the return of our Lord. Until they complete their 1,260 days of testimony, God will divinely protect them from premature death by the Antichrist, as He protected Moses and Aaron from Pharaoh. Once these two prophets complete their testimony, the resurrected Antichrist will receive divine authority to martyr them:

> When they finish their testimony, the beast that ascends out of the bottomless pit will make war against them, overcome them, and kill

---

3   See *Moshiach Now* by Tzemach David (pen name for this author).

them. And their dead bodies will lie in the street of the great city which spiritually is called Sodom and Egypt, where also our Lord was crucified. Then those from the peoples, tribes, tongues, and nations will see their dead bodies three-and-a-half days, and not allow their dead bodies to be put into graves. And those who dwell on the earth will rejoice over them, make merry, and send gifts to one another, because these two prophets tormented those who dwell on the earth. Now after the three-and-a-half days the breath of life from God entered them, and they stood on their feet, and great fear fell on those who saw them. And they heard a loud voice from heaven saying to them, "Come up here." And they ascended to heaven in a cloud, and their enemies saw them. In the same hour there was a great earthquake, and a tenth of the city fell. In the earthquake seven thousand people were killed, and the rest were afraid and gave glory to the God of heaven. The second woe is past. Behold, the third woe is coming quickly. (Rev. 11:7-14)

Commentators differ widely about the identity of the two witnesses. The interpretation that they symbolize the holy Church at large (or the Jews and the predominantly Gentile Church) should be summarily dismissed based on the literal view of the 1,260 days, which we have established, coupled with the fact that the Beast will not be given authority to kill the witnesses until after the days of their prophecy (Rev. 11:4-8), in other words, until after the great tribulation. In contradistinction, many Christians will not be afforded this protection from physical death but will become martyrs during the tribulation. In addition, the two witnesses will be raptured after the sixth trumpet, that is, at the time of the second woe (Rev. 11:12-14), whereas the Church will not be raptured until the last trumpet, at the third woe, most specifically, at the glorious return of our Lord.

Some interpreters have posited that the two witnesses will prophecy during the first half of the final seven years, instead of during the second half, and they argue that the Antichrist will kill them as soon as he ascends from the bottomless pit, specifically, at the midpoint of the final week. But this is a faulty premise, the text requiring only that the Beast kills them sometime after his ascension (Rev. 11:7). Furthermore, placing the testimony of the two prophets in the first half of the final week creates an additional obstacle because, as stated above, the completion of their prophecy will occur at the end of the great tribulation, after the sixth trumpet, at the time of the second woe, which occurs just before the last trumpet (Rev. 11:12-15).

Other interpreters view the two witnesses as symbols for the Law and the Prophets, or variously, for the Law and the gospel (or the Old and New Testaments), but such interpretations crumble on similar grounds. For although the Antichrist will "intend to change times and law" and will wage a seemingly successful war against Christians during the final forty-two months (Dan. 7:25), the Scriptures do not indicate that he will destroy all the Bibles in the world, much less, that he will eliminate the Church's prophetic testimony about Christ. Besides, the Beast's attempt to destroy this witness will almost certainly take place long before the completion of the great tribulation, when the two witnesses will be martyred.

The corpses of the two witnesses will not be given the decency of burial but will remain exposed in one of Jerusalem's streets for three and a half days (Rev. 11:9-10). John's readers were familiar with the Hebrew Bible and would have easily identified Jerusalem as the great city "where also our Lord was crucified" (Rev. 11:8; cf. Matt. 27:35; Mark 15:24-32; Luke 23:33), which was spiritually (i.e., symbolically) called "Sodom and Egypt" (Rev. 11:8). The prophet Isaiah called the elders of Jerusalem "the rulers of Sodom" (Isa. 1:9-10), and Moses prophesied that the destruction of the nation of Israel would be like the destruction of Sodom (Deut. 29:23; 32:32; Isa. 3:9). And as the righteous fled the wicked cities immediately before God brought devastation upon Sodom (Gen. 19:12-25) and Egypt (Exod. 7-12), our Lord Jesus warned the inhabitants of Jerusalem that they must flee before His fiery judgments fall upon the city (Matt. 24:17; Mark 13:15; Luke 17:31), and He likened this flight to Lot's escape from Sodom (Luke 17:29).

The world's inhabitants ("peoples, tribes, tongues, and nations") will be aware of the death of the two prophets, and they will gloat over them, even celebrating with gifts, because their prophecies and plagues will be odious to them (Rev. 11:9-10). Nevertheless, three and a half days after their death, the Lord will resurrect and subsequently rapture these men into heaven in the presence of their onlookers (Rev. 11:11-12). This will coincide with a massive earthquake, resulting in the collapse of a tenth of Jerusalem and the deaths of seven thousand people (Rev. 11:13). It is uncertain if this earthquake is the one that will occur on the day of the Lord or if it is simply a foreshock. At any rate, the people who remain alive after the earthquake in Jerusalem will give glory to God at that time (Rev. 11:13), a rare occasion of apparent repentance in the book of Revelation.

These two prophets will be two martyrs at the end of a long history of Christian martyrs. Jesus had warned His disciples about the intensity of the coming persecution, even to the degree that "brother will betray brother to death, and a father his child; and children will rise up against parents and cause them to be put to death" (Mark 13:12; cf. Matt. 10:21). This statement encapsulates the persecution during the long sweep of Christian history, most particularly against those engaged in evangelism, but it is not limited to the period of great tribulation (Matt. 10:21ff. The Lord also warned the disciples that they would be beaten after being dragged before synagogue courts and would appear before kings as a testimony of gospel witness (Mark 13:9; John 16:2; cf. Isa. 66:5; Luke 21:12). This persecution began during the lifetime of the apostles, as the book of Acts communicates, and it functions as a template for how we should endure persecution for the cause of Christ.

Jesus encouraged an undaunted proclamation of the gospel and a fearless wisdom which recognizes that many will become martyr witnesses. He reminds us that we should fear God alone and not fear the persecution and death which may result from our testimony (Matt. 10:22, 27). Christ did not come to bring peace to the earth but a sword

(Matt. 10:34)! He taught, "Yes, the time is coming that whoever kills you will think that he offers God service. And these things they will do to you because they have not known the Father nor Me. But these things I have told you, that when the time comes, you may remember that I told you of them" (John 16:2-4). Yet the absolute sovereignty of the Father does not allow even the tiniest insult to our bodies or souls, unless He has decreed it within the parameters of His providential love (Matt. 10:29-31).

> Then they will deliver you up to tribulation and kill you, and you will be hated by all nations for My name's sake. And then many will be offended, will betray one another, and will hate one another. Then many false prophets will rise up and deceive many. And because lawlessness will abound, the love of many will grow cold. But he who endures to the end shall be saved. And this gospel of the kingdom will be preached in all the world as a witness to all the nations, and then the end will come. (Matt. 24:9-14)

In one sense, this passage depicts the general sweep of tribulation which Christians have experienced from the era of the apostles until the unprecedented tribulation (Acts 14:22; Rev. 1:9; 2:10, 13; cf. 1 Pet. 5:9). Nevertheless, the book of Revelation in particular, coupled with other eschatological prophecies, reveal that tribulation will reach a crescendo during the period of the great tribulation (cf. Matt. 24:15ff). As Jesus indicated, the "labor pains" of tribulation will increase in intensity just prior to God's final deliverance of His people at the day of His return (Matt. 24:8; cf. 1 Thess. 5:3).

During that period of unprecedented tribulation, the holy Church will complete the task of the Great Commission, which Christ commanded us, saying, "Go into all the world and preach the gospel to every creature" (Mark 16:15). Because the harvest fields are always white and plentiful for the purposes of evangelism, even some of the towns of Israel will not have received gospel witnesses before He returns in glory

(Matt. 10:23)! However, once the gospel has been proclaimed to all the nations, the end of the age will arrive (Matt. 24:14). The apostle John saw one aspect of the end-time completion of the Great Commission in a prophecy which anticipates the final push of the gospel witness just before the day of Jesus Christ:

> Then I saw another angel flying in the midst of heaven, having the everlasting gospel to preach to those who dwell on the earth—to every nation, tribe, tongue, and people—saying with a loud voice, "Fear God and give glory to Him, for the hour of His judgment has come; and worship Him who made heaven and earth, the sea and springs of water." (Rev. 14:6-7)

During our earthly abode, the apostle Paul taught us to "glory in tribulations" because they produce perseverance, character, and an eager expectation of eternal verities (Rom. 5:3-5). Christians can also experience the peace of God in the midst of tribulation, recognizing that Jesus has "overcome the world" (John 16:33). In addition, the apostles encouraged us to be patient and joyful in tribulation (Rom. 12:12; 2 Cor. 7:4; 2 Thess. 1:4-5; 1 Pet. 4:12; Rev. 1:9) and to take pleasure in persecutions and distresses (2 Cor. 12:9-10). Also, we should certainly not despair in the midst of persecution because "our light affliction, which is but for a moment, is working for us a far more exceeding and eternal weight of glory, while we do not look at the things which are seen, but at the things which are not seen" (2 Cor. 4:17-18). And if we become martyrs, we should recognize that it is God who leads us in the triumphal procession of death in Christ (2 Cor. 2:14; cf. 2 Cor. 4:7-11; Phil. 1:29).

We should trust God through tribulations while comforting others with the same comfort that He affords us (2 Cor. 1:4, 9). This is because as we become weak from persecution, Christ's power and life effectively work in our bodies so that we are walking billboards of the crucified Christ (2 Cor. 4:7-11); he wrote, "For when I am weak, then I am strong" (2 Cor. 12:10). The risen Lord explained that He provides grace during such times so that His own strength operates in us and is "made perfect in [our] weakness" (2 Cor. 12:9).

Satan often asks God permission to sift people as wheat during times of weakness, but rest assured, the risen Lord intercedes for us before the Father so that our faith does not fail (Luke 22:31-32; cf. Rom. 8:27; Heb. 7:25). The apostle Peter taught that Christians should vigilantly resist the devil because he "walks about like a roaring lion, seeking whom he may devour" (1 Pet. 5:8-9). The hope of the elect lies in the promise that all the persecution that the enemy throws our way cannot separate us from the Father's eternal love:

> Who shall separate us from the love of Christ? Shall tribulation, or distress, or persecution, or famine, or nakedness, or peril, or sword? As it is written: "For Your sake we are killed all day long; we are accounted as sheep for the slaughter." Yet in all these things we are more than conquerors through Him who loved us. For I am persuaded that neither death nor life, nor angels nor principalities nor powers, nor things present nor things to come, nor height nor depth, nor any other created thing, shall be able to separate us from the love of God which is in Christ Jesus our Lord. (Rom. 8:35-39)

The certainty remains that those who live godly in Christ Jesus will experience temptations, betrayal, persecution, suffering, and for some, martyrdom (Matt. 13:21; 24:3-14; 2 Tim. 3:12). Tribulation is necessary so that we may be considered worthy of God's kingdom (2 Thess. 1:4-5; 1 Pet. 4:12-13; Rev. 2:10). The apostle Peter reminded, "Beloved, do not think it strange concerning the fiery trial which is to try you, as though some strange thing happened to you; but rejoice to the extent that you partake of Christ's sufferings, that when His glory is revealed, you may also be glad with exceeding joy" (1 Pet. 4:12-13).

Our Father in heaven will greatly reward those who are persecuted for the sake of His name (Matt. 5:10-12; 20:21-23; 1 Pet. 4:13). Jesus promised that He Himself will confess us before the Father if we confess

Him before men (Matt. 10:32) and that He will save those who "endure to the end" (Matt. 24:13); He taught, "He who loses his life for My sake will find it" (Matt. 10:39; cf. Rev. 2:13). We should ask ourselves whether we able to drink the cup of the Lord's suffering and to be baptized with the baptism of His death (Matt. 20:21-23). Our prayer should be that we, by the grace given to us by the Spirit of truth, will stand up as bold witnesses who endure hardships and the persecution which the Father has prepared for us.

When the apostle John opened the fifth seal he

> saw under the altar the souls of those who had been slain for the word of God and for the testimony which they held. And they cried with a loud voice, saying, "How long, O Lord, holy and true, until You judge and avenge our blood on those who dwell on the earth?" Then a white robe was given to each of them; and it was said to them that they should rest a little while longer, until both the number of their fellow servants and their brethren, who would be killed as they were, was completed. (Rev. 6:9-11)

The unified cry of the martyrs in their question "How long?" expresses the inward groaning of all God's people who long for Christ Jesus to take vengeance against those who persecute us and to reward His faithful disciples. The apostle heard the souls of the martyrs being told to rest "a little while" longer for the time of the great tribulation, when countless Christians will become martyrs. Then in the next chapter, John saw

> a great multitude which no one could number, of all nations, tribes, peoples, and tongues, standing before the throne and before the Lamb, clothed with white robes, with palm branches in their hands, and crying out with a loud voice, saying, "Salvation belongs to our God who sits on the throne, and to the Lamb!" All the angels stood around the throne and the elders and the four living creatures, and fell

on their faces before the throne and worshiped God, saying: "Amen! Blessing and glory and wisdom, thanksgiving and honor and power and might, be to our God forever and ever. Amen." (Rev. 7:9-12)

The apostle did not initially know the identity of these heavenly worshippers; however, one of the heavenly presbyters explained:

"These are the ones who come out of the great tribulation, and washed their robes and made them white in the blood of the Lamb. Therefore they are before the throne of God, and serve Him day and night in His temple. And He who sits on the throne will dwell among them. They shall neither hunger anymore nor thirst anymore; the sun shall not strike them, nor any heat; for the Lamb who is in the midst of the throne will shepherd them and lead them to living fountains of waters. And God will wipe away every tear from their eyes." (Rev. 7:14-17)

Clearly then, this great multitude does not represent those who, according to some, will have been raptured before experiencing the great tribulation. Rather, they will worship the Lamb in the presence of the Father because they are faithful unto death; these men and women will have "washed their robes and made them white in the blood of the Lamb" (Rev. 7:14), indicating that they will be killed for following Christ. The imagery of washing their robes in Christ's blood emphasizes that they will not give up their own lives so much as they will participate, by the grace given to them, in His death.

John depicted a harlot riding upon a scarlet beast with seven heads and ten horns, a symbol for the Antichrist's kingdom. This woman was garbed in royal attire and holding a golden chalice of divine wrath from which she became intoxicated with the blood of the Christian saints and martyrs (cf. Rev. 14:8):

Come, I will show you the judgment of the great harlot who sits on many waters, with whom the kings of the earth committed fornication, and the inhabitants of the earth were made drunk with the wine of her fornication." So he carried me away in the Spirit into the wilderness. And I saw a woman sitting on a scarlet beast which was full of names of blasphemy, having seven heads and ten horns. The woman was arrayed in purple and scarlet, and adorned with gold and precious stones and pearls, having in her hand a golden cup full of abominations and the filthiness of her fornication. And on her forehead a name was written: MYSTERY, BABYLON THE GREAT, THE MOTHER OF HARLOTS AND OF THE ABOMINATIONS OF THE EARTH. I saw the woman, drunk with the blood of the saints and with the blood of the martyrs of Jesus. And when I saw her, I marveled with great amazement . . . The waters which you saw, where the harlot sits, are peoples, multitudes, nations, and tongues. And the ten horns which you saw on the beast, these will hate the harlot, make her desolate and naked, eat her flesh and burn her with fire. For God has put it into their hearts to fulfill His purpose, to be of one mind, and to give their kingdom to the beast, until the words of God are fulfilled. And the woman whom you saw is that great city which reigns over the kings of the earth. (Rev. 17:1-6, 15-18)

The ancient, pagan city of Babylon served as the capital of the Neo-Babylonian Empire, also called Babylon. The prophet Jeremiah described this ancient capital as "a golden cup in the Lord's hand that made all the earth drunk" and the nations deranged (Jer. 51:7; cf. Isa. 51:21-23; Rev. 14:8) and as sitting "by many waters" (Jer. 51:13; cf. Rev. 17:1). The apostle John enigmatically drew upon these features to characterize "the great harlot," and by extension, the larger kingdom of the Antichrist, which he called Babylon (or Mystery Babylon).

Ascertaining the identity of this harlot constitutes one of the most difficult tasks for the interpreter of the Apocalypse. The primary candidates presented in commentaries are pagan Rome, ancient Jerusalem, Vatican City, and the ubiquitous "city of man." Less commonly, commentators consider modern Jerusalem, New York City, Mecca, or another city in Saudi Arabia to be among the prospects. One's interpretation of the harlot is often predicated upon how he or she identifies the Beast and the healing of its mortal head wound (Rev. 13:1-8; 17:3, 7-9).

The interpretation that apostate Jerusalem is the harlot has much to commend it.[4] For example, the prophets depicted Jerusalem as a harlot (Isa. 1:21), and they depicted Israel and Judah in the same manner (Num. 15:39; 25:1-2; Deut. 31:16; Isa. 1:21; Hosea 1:2; 2:4-5). Furthermore, Christ hyperbolically portrayed Jerusalem as the place where all the prophets had been martyred ("it cannot be that a prophet should perish outside of Jerusalem" Luke 13:33; cf. Acts 7:51-52), and as such, as filling up the cup of divine wrath (Matt. 23:31-35; 1 Thess. 2:15-16; cf. Rev. 14:8). Furthermore, Jerusalem maintained an unholy alliance with the Roman Empire (cf. "sitting on a scarlet beast" Rev. 17:3), as evidenced by their mutual condemnation of Christ and the chief priests' declaration that they served "no king but Caesar!" (John 19:15). This interpretation sees the harlot as the apostate people of Jerusalem, carefully distinguishing it from the geographical city in the strictest sense.

Although the Old Testament portrays Israel's idolatry as "harlotry," the prophets described other nations as committing harlotry with their gods (Exod. 34:14-16; Lev. 17:7). Admittedly, this is not reason enough to reject the identification of Jerusalem as the harlot of the Apocalypse. If the interpretation is correct, the apostate city will receive eternal, fiery destruction at the day of Christ (Rev. 14:8, 10-11; 18), a complete forty-two months after the Beast and his ten-nation confederacy first burn the city ("these will hate the harlot, make her desolate and naked, eat her flesh and burn her with fire" Rev. 17:16; cf. Lev. 21:9).

Those who identify the harlot as Rome, the capital of the ancient Roman Empire, typically do so for three primary reasons: First, the apostle John identified the harlot city as sitting on seven mountains or hills (Rev. 17:9), which many commentaries argue is a symbol for Rome,

---

4   The apostle Paul contrasted two cities, the heavenly Jerusalem, corresponding to the new covenant, with the earthly Jerusalem, corresponding to the Mosaic law (Gal. 4:22-26; cf. Rev. 12:1; 17:1).

known widely as the city of seven hills. Second, the apostle Peter greeted the church "in Babylon" (1 Pet. 5:13), an almost certain euphemism for Rome. Third, Rome served as the primary capital for the Roman Empire, which the prophet Daniel identified as the fourth and final beast kingdom (see chapter 2). Fourth, the Apocalypse records that the woman "sits on many waters" (Rev. 17:1), reflecting the fact that this city "reigns over the kings of the earth" and over "peoples, multitudes, nations, and tongues" (Rev. 17:15, 18; v. 2). Many later commentators identified the harlot as the Roman papal Church, which ruled over the Western Roman Empire, a view which is largely an interpretation of necessity for those who recognize that the Empire no longer exists but want to maintain that Rome is the harlot.[5]

Others argue that the harlot sitting upon "seven heads" may reflect her ubiquitous presence upon many "mountains" (i.e., kingdoms), wherein the number seven is typically seen as representing the totality of all the beast kingdoms. In this view, the harlot signifies the transhistorical capital of the Beast, wherever its kingdoms have existed throughout history. As such, she reigned from many imperial capitals, such as Ramesses, Nineveh, Babylon, Susa, Athens, Rome (when the apostle wrote), and so forth. This view maintains that the harlot signifies the spiritual capital of the Beast, seeing her as the originator ("the mother of harlots") of all idolatries committed upon the earth (Rev. 17:5).

---

[5] This interpretation creates a further difficulty because it implicates the patriarchate of Rome, and presumably, all the Western churches under its jurisdiction, even prior to the Great Schism of AD 1054, of complicity with the fourth beast kingdom. The Protestant Reformers identified the papacy as the harlot, but it is difficult to see how this view does not also implicate the entirety of Christendom, along with its ecumenical councils.

9

SEALS, TRUMPETS, AND BOWLS

THE FOUR HORSEMEN OF THE APOCALYPSE (Rev. 6:1-8) find their primary prophetic backdrop in the four groups of horses in the vision of Zechariah the prophet (Zech. 6:1-8; cf. Zech. 1:8-15). The four colors of the horses in both passages are nearly identical, specified as white, red, black, and pale color ("dappled" in Zechariah). Zechariah's four groups of horses were identified as heavenly "spirits" sent out to patrol the earth and to punish the oppressors of the Jewish people. Similarly, the four horses and their riders in the book of Revelation will be commissioned by Christ to punish those who oppress the holy Church of God.

The emergence of the four horses with their riders, as seen by the apostle John, will occur when Jesus, the Lamb of God, breaks the first four seals of the heavenly inheritance. The cultural background for this passage is that first-century Roman inheritance scrolls (i.e., wills) were sealed with seven seals. The key feature of the larger context is that only the slain and resurrected Lamb is worthy to break the seals and to sovereignly allow the prophetic events contained within the scroll (Rev. 5:2-9). As John saw, the breaking of the first seal will result in the release of the first horse and its rider:

> Now I saw when the Lamb opened one of the seals; and I heard one of the four living creatures saying with a voice like thunder, "Come and see." And I looked, and behold, a white horse. He who sat on it had a bow; and a crown was given to him, and he went out conquering and to conquer. (Rev. 6:1-2)

We should not confuse this white horse rider with the returning King of kings who John saw mounted upon a white horse in Revelation 19:11-21. The similarities between the two white horses and their riders exist to highlight their royal power and the fact that they both usher in a period of "peace and security." The former rider was seen wearing a royal crown and holding a bow without any mention of arrows (Rev. 6:2); this rider and its horse likely symbolize the arrival of temporary, humanistic peace, as evidenced by the contrast with the subsequent horse, the red horse of war (Rev. 6:3-4). By stark contrast, Christ will return to usher in everlasting peace to the nations. Consequently, the white horse rider of the first seal likely symbolizes the false peace which will exist during the first half of the final seven years before Christ returns. As I demonstrated previously, many false prophets and false christs ("anointings"), including the Antichrist himself, will arise during this short-lived peace. A second opinion, which many commentators embrace, is that the white horse and its rider symbolize the advancement of the gospel of Christ.

> When He opened the second seal, I heard the second living creature saying, "Come and see." Another horse, fiery red, went out. And it was granted to the one who sat on it to take peace from the earth, and that people should kill one another; and there was given to him a great sword. When He opened the third seal, I heard the third living creature say, "Come and see." So I looked, and behold, a black horse, and he who sat on it had a pair of scales in his hand. And I heard a voice in the midst of the four living creatures saying, "A quart of wheat for a denarius, and three quarts of barley for a denarius; and do not harm the oil and the wine." (Rev. 6:3-6)

The apostle saw that the red horse of war, whose rider will remove peace from the earth, wields "a great sword." As we can infer from our previous timeline, a regional war will break out just prior to the midpoint of the final "week" of years when the Antichrist invades the kingdom of the South (Dan. 11:29-30). However, when he invades Jerusalem and sets up his abomination of desolation in the Jerusalem temple, the red horse's rider will quickly "take peace from the earth"

(Rev. 6:4). The false peace agreement will be seen for what it truly is, an illusion of the world's humanistic aspirations.

This world war will almost certainly result in a precipitous decline of the global economy, which will teeter on the brink of collapse. Severe agricultural scarcity and inflated prices for cereal grains will ensue, as symbolized by the black horse rider holding a pair of scales and by the heavenly statement "a quart of wheat for a denarius, and three quarts of barley for a denarius" (Rev. 6:5-6; cf. 2 Kings 7:1; Ezek. 4:10, 16). Other food items, such as olive oil and wine—products of olive trees and viticulture respectively—will be preserved ("do not harm the oil and the wine" Rev. 6:6); this may indicate that the downturn of the global economy will stop short of total collapse. This will undoubtedly prepare the way for the mark of the Antichrist.

> When He opened the fourth seal, I heard the voice of the fourth living creature saying, "Come and see." So I looked, and behold, a pale horse. And the name of him who sat on it was Death, and Hades followed with him. And power was given to them over a fourth of the earth, to kill with sword, with hunger, with death, and by the beasts of the earth. (Rev. 6:7-8)

The fourth rider, with its pale (lit. "pale green") horse, symbolizes widespread death, which will be accompanied by its personified counterpart, hades or hell (cf. Ezek. 14:21). The text indicates that a fourth of the earth will die from the war, pestilence, and starvation (cf. Lev. 26:18-28; Deut. 32:24-26). It is uncertain whether a quarter of the world's population ("a fourth of the earth" Rev. 6:8) will die or whether those who live within a specific geographical region, that is, within a fourth part of the planet's surface area, will die. This verse likely speaks about the total number of casualties within the entire forty-two-month war of the Antichrist, otherwise known as the war of Gog and Magog.

In addition to the seven seals, the apostle John heard seven trumpet blasts, resulting in specific judgments upon the earth and sea, and he saw seven bowls, which will be poured out in divine judgment, completing the plagues of the unprecedented tribulation. However, God will not permit His angels to bring about the trumpet judgments until His servants have been sealed on their foreheads with the divine seal of protection (Rev. 7:1-3; 9:4). Therefore, John saw 144,000 people being sealed, 12,000 from each of the twelve tribes of Israel (Rev. 7:4-8). This indicates the preciseness of Christ's divine protection; not one person whom He chooses will be missing. Whether the 144,000 righteous individuals become martyrs at the hands of the Beast or live until Christ's return, every one of them will "follow the Lamb wherever He goes" and be redeemed from the Earth to stand with Christ upon Mount Zion[1] (Rev. 14:1-5). How comforting to trust in the Lord's mercies and unswerving commitment to preserve and protect His elect!

The majority of commentators regard the 144,000 as signifying the *spiritual* descendants of Jacob, all living Jews and Gentiles who trust in Christ, who will be spiritually protected during the trumpet judgments. This traditional interpretation is supported by several pieces of evidence: First, John's list of the twelve tribes is unique among biblical census. For example, "the tribe of Joseph" replaced the tribe of Ephraim (Rev. 7:8), and no other biblical list or census does this. In addition, John's census uniquely lists Levi as a tribe, indicating that the Levites will receive a kingdom inheritance in the Promised Land (Rev. 7:7). Finally, the tribe of Dan is uniquely omitted from John's list of the tribes (cf. Gen. 49:17), whereas Ezekiel prophesied that this tribe would be included in the eternal land allotments in the messianic era (Ezek. 48:1-2), the latter verses demonstrating that this tribe will not cease to exist.

Second, scholars have correctly argued that John's prophecy contains features of the military census lists of the Old Testament, and consistent with this motif, the prophecy identifies the 144,000 as young men (Rev. 14:4). More particularly, they are described as male virgins (Rev. 14:4). However, there is no clear textual reason why the Lord will

---

[1]   A metonym for Jerusalem.

not seal women and married men with the same divine protection. This evidence strongly favors seeing the 144,000 men as symbolic.

Third, elsewhere in the book of Revelation, the apostle received visions in which he described hearing a heavenly proclamation and seeing a vision which revealed its underlying meaning, and in these other occurrences, the content of what he saw more fully explained what he had heard. For example, the apostle heard a voice instructing him to see the Lion of the tribe of Judah (Rev. 5:5), but when he looked, he saw "a Lamb as though it had been slain" (Rev. 5:6); in this case, both the statement and the vision revealed different aspects of the same object, namely, the Person of Jesus Christ. In the passage concerning the 144,000, the apostle heard the precise numbers of those sealed, and he immediately saw a great heavenly multitude coming out of the great tribulation, which consisted of people from every nation, ethnic group, and language (Rev. 7:9-17). If this interpretation is correct, it means that the 144,000 Israelites is a symbol for this great multitude from among all nations.

On the other hand, a minority of commentators have contended that the 144,000 sealed men will be literal descendants of Jacob whom God will physically protect during the great tribulation so that they receive salvation. According to this interpretation, the sealed virgins will eventually become a faithful remnant of Jews within the holy Church. The primary strength of this position is that the majority of occurrences in the New Testament of the twelve tribes of Israel refer to ethnic descendants of Jacob, and the holy Church is not identified as the twelve tribes, with the possible exception of James 1:1 (cf. 1 Pet. 1:1-2). This interpretation lends itself to the idea that the 144,000 will be a specified number of Jewish male virgins, who will be converted to the Christian faith early in the tribulation. If this is correct, they will undoubtedly be some of the "wise ones" who will bring many Jews to follow Jesus Christ (Dan. 12:3).

At any rate, the book of Revelation communicates the concept that God protects and preserves His people, whether Jews or Gentiles, from temporal, divine judgments and from eternal condemnation. One example is Christ's promise to "keep" the church in Philadelphia from the great tribulation: "Because you have kept My command to persevere, I also will keep you from the hour of trial which shall come upon the whole world, to test those who dwell on the earth" (Rev. 3:10). The implication is that even if the church had continued until the great tribulation ("the hour of trial which shall come upon the whole world"), Christ would give them the grace to patiently endure it in such a manner that they would not lose their eternal reward. This verse does not indicate a pre-tribulation rapture of the Church![2] To the contrary, the same Greek verb translated "keep" is found in the Lord's High Priestly Prayer for His elect: "I do not pray that You should take them out of the world, but that You should keep them from the evil one" (John 17:15; cf. John 17:11). The idea, made explicit in the latter passage, is that the Lord will not remove His people from the world to protect them but would give them the grace to faithfully endure *in the midst of* tribulation and temptation.

The divine judgments during the great tribulation will be terrifying and will have a largescale impact throughout the world. Jesus warned, "And there will be signs in the sun, in the moon, and in the stars; and on the earth distress of nations, with perplexity, the sea and the waves roaring; men's hearts failing them from fear and the expectation of those things which are coming on the earth, for the powers of the heavens will be shaken" (Luke 21:25-26; cf. v. 11). These prophetic events herald the nearness of the Son of Man's return from heaven, although this will only be perceived by those with eyes to see. These divine judgments will enable the inhabitants of the earth to learn about God's righteousness (Isa. 26:9).

The seven trumpets in the Apocalypse provide examples of these divine judgments. The first four trumpet judgments may occur when the Lamb opens the second seal, during the time that the red horse of

---

2   Some modern Protestants teach that Christ will take all Christians to heaven before the great tribulation so that Christians will not be on earth during it.

war rides forth to "take peace from the earth" (Rev. 6:4). Consider the results of the angelic blowing of the first four trumpets:

1. Hail and fire followed, mingled with blood, and they were thrown to the earth. And a third of the trees were burned up, and all green grass was burned up. (Rev. 8:7)

2. Something like a great mountain burning with fire was thrown into the sea, and a third of the sea became blood. And a third of the living creatures in the sea died, and a third of the ships were destroyed. (Rev. 8:8-9)

3. A great star fell from heaven, burning like a torch, and it fell on a third of the rivers and on the springs of water. The name of the star is Wormwood. A third of the waters became wormwood, and many men died from the water, because it was made bitter. (Rev. 8:10-11)

4. A third of the sun was struck, a third of the moon, and a third of the stars, so that a third of them were darkened. A third of the day did not shine, and likewise the night. (Rev. 8:12)

Many of the plagues and judgments depicted in the book of Revelation share similarities with the ten plagues that came upon Egypt during the days of Moses (Exod. 7-10; Deut. 4:30, 28:27, 60-61). For example, the first trumpet will result in a mixture of hail, fire, and blood, reminiscent of the seventh plague upon Egypt (Rev. 8:7 with Exod. 9:13-35). Similarly, the second trumpet will result in the waters being transformed into blood, answering to the first plague of Egypt (Rev. 8:8-9 with Exod. 7:14-25). Likewise, the third trumpet will bring the bitterness of wormwood to the waters, likely hearkening back to the bitterness of the waters of Marah (Exod. 15:23; cf. Deut. 29:17-18; Jer. 9:15; 23:15), and the fourth trumpet alludes to the thick darkness which fell upon Egypt (Exod. 10:22; cf. Amos 8:9). A further observation is that the Pharaoh in the book of Exodus serves as a prototype for the Antichrist in the Apocalypse, and Yahweh arriving at Mount Sinai at the time of the exodus (Exod. 19:16-18) foreshadows the Son of Man's arrival with clouds to deliver His saints at the final exodus.

Although the first four trumpet judgments could result from "natural" phenomena, it is certainly possible that at least some of them describe modern warfare. To illustrate, the first trumpet will result in hailstones, pellets of ice which are formed through strong, upward motions of air, which typically form during a thunderstorm. The fact that the stones will be mixed with fire and blood has led some to see this as describing volcanic activity or meteorites; however, others have argued that this verse could just as easily describe the results of a nuclear detonation. Theoretically, any of these events could result in the conditions described in the verse (Rev. 8:7). Similarly, while the second trumpet appears to depict a meteorite ("something like a great mountain burning with fire" Rev. 8:8), some have envisioned a nuclear bomb used to destroy military ships. As they point out, this trumpet will result in the destruction of a third of the ships in the sea, and we might expect the Antichrist to retaliate against the naval ships in the Mediterranean Sea after they have maneuvered against him during his southern advance (Dan. 11:30; cf. Num. 24:24).

While it may sound somewhat sensational, we may speculate that the fourth trumpet judgment (Rev. 8:12) presents a scenario consistent with modern space warfare. Those critical of biblical cosmology have used such verses to contend that they present a pre-modern view of the universe which has been "disproven" by modern science. They argue that the rotational force of the Earth on its axis prohibits the Sun, Moon, and stars from being darkened for "a third" of the day and night because atmospheric debris, necessary to obstruct cosmic light, would rotate with a similar velocity as the Earth. But to the contrary, the cosmology presented in this verse likely indicates the presence of debris outside of Earth's atmosphere. This would mean that the debris will appear to remain stationary while Earth continues to rotate normally. If this assessment is correct, the fourth trumpet judgment may envision a scenario in which satellite communication systems have been destroyed, perhaps by missiles launched in space, resulting in stellar darkness for a third of the day and a third of the night, from the visual perspective of many people on Earth.

The text is unclear whether the extent of the first four trumpet judgments will be localized or global. The absence of contextual clues mitigates against the interpretation that they describe local judgments, which will be limited to a certain region, such as the Middle East (cf. Ezek. 5:2, 12; Zech. 13:8-9). However, if they describe the results of an extensive nuclear exchange, the global interpretation may be unlikely, although not altogether impossible. The evidence appears inconclusive, and it is unclear whether the judgments will be "natural" or manmade. Therefore, it is prudent to emphasize that the risen Lamb of God has sovereign control over all these judgments and that we should remain cautiously open to the possibility that these verses could describe natural disasters, nuclear exchanges with fallout, or other potential scenarios.

The final three trumpet judgments are identified as the three imprecatory "woes" (Rev. 9:12), presumably because of the over-whelming terror that these judgments will bring. The apostle John heard an angel pronouncing, "Woe, woe, woe to the inhabitants of the earth, because of the remaining blasts of the trumpet of the three angels who are about to sound!" (Rev. 8:13). The first of these three woes is the fifth trumpet judgment:

Then the fifth angel sounded: And I saw a star fallen from heaven to the earth. To him was given the key to the bottomless pit. And he opened the bottomless pit, and smoke arose out of the pit like the smoke of a great furnace. So the sun and the air were darkened because of the smoke of the pit. Then out of the smoke locusts came upon the earth. And to them was given power, as the scorpions of the earth have power. They were commanded not to harm the grass of the earth, or any green thing, or any tree, but only those men who do not have the seal of God on their foreheads. And they were not given authority to kill them, but to torment them for five months. Their torment was like the torment of a scorpion when it strikes a man. In those days men will seek death and will not find it; they will desire to die, and death will flee from them. The shape of the locusts was like horses prepared for battle. On their heads were crowns of something like gold, and their faces were like the faces of men. They had hair like women's hair, and their teeth were like lions' teeth. And they had breastplates like breastplates of iron, and the sound of their wings was like the sound of chariots with many horses running into battle. They had tails like scorpions, and there were stings in their tails. Their power was to hurt men five months. And they had as king over them the angel of the bottomless pit, whose name in Hebrew is Abaddon, but in Greek he has the name Apollyon. One woe is past. Behold, still two more woes are coming after these things. (Rev. 9:1-12)

The fallen star will be given the key to the Abyss, the realm of the departed spirits (Rev. 9:1-2). This likely indicates that the "star" is an angelic being (cf. Job 38:7; Isa. 14:12), and he may be the demon ("the angel of the bottomless pit" Rev. 9:11) known as the destroyer (Exod. 12:23; 1 Cor. 10:10; Rev. 9:11; cf. Jer. 4:7). It is quite likely that the locusts who ascend from the Abyss are also demons, especially since regarding actual insects, one Proverb specifies that "locusts have no king" (Prov. 30:27), whereas these locusts have a chief demon as their king (Rev. 9:11). The fact that they will not be actual insects is also seen by the fact that they will be prohibited from consuming vegetation but will be commissioned to torment the wicked with intense pain for five months (Rev. 9:4-5). This time indicator of "five months" provides the clue that this judgment cannot occur less than five months before Christ's return. These demons will ascend from the bottomless pit, the Abyss, to bring divine chastisements against the wicked ("only those men who do not have the seal of God on their foreheads" Rev. 9:4).

While this plague is reminiscent of the locust plague that God brought against Egypt just prior to the exodus (Exod. 10:1-6, 12-20; Deut. 28:38-39, 42; Ps. 105:33-35), the primary backdrop for John's prophecy is the locust visions in the book of Joel (Joel 1:4ff; 2:2-11, 25; cf. Jer. 51:27). The evidence for this is that the apostle frequently alluded to Joel's locust prophecies, and both men described the sounding of the trumpet alongside their description of the locust invasion (Joel 2:1, 15; Rev. 9:1). In addition, John portrayed his locusts as having fang-like teeth "like lions" (Rev. 9:8), similar to Joel's initial description (Joel 1:6). The careful reader, however, should not equate the locust judgments in the book of Joel with the locust judgment of the fifth trumpet of the Apocalypse. They must be separate locust invasions because the locusts in Joel ate all the vegetation (Joel 1:4-5, 7, 9-13, 16-18; 2:24-26), whereas the demonic locusts in the book of Revelation will be prohibited from touching any vegetation (Rev. 9:4).

Similar to the locust judgment in the Apocalypse, Joel's locust visions serve as a harbinger of the day of the Lord. In his initial description of the locusts, the prophet declared, "Alas for the day! For the day of the Lord is at hand; it shall come as destruction from the Almighty" (Joel 1:15; cf. Joel 2:1). Although the Hebrew grammar allows for the possibility that this judgment will occur on the day of the Lord, it is preferable to regard this verse as signaling that the locust invasion is a harbinger that the day will take place very soon ("at hand"). Simply put, Joel was uninterested in parsing out a detailed chronology of the judgments of the great tribulation but chose instead to refer to the day of the Lord as including the events leading up to it.

Joel, unlike the apostle John, described the locust horde as a nation that would come against the land of Israel (Joel 1:6). He calls the locusts "a people, great and strong" (Joel 2:2), and the Lord called them His "great army" (Joel 2:25; cf. Joel 2:11). The prophet also described this people as great, "the like of whom has never been; nor will there be any such after them," a phrase which is similar to statements describing the unprecedented tribulation (Jer. 30:7[3]; Dan. 12:1; Matt. 24:21; Mark 13:19). While these descriptions envision a military force, some commentators think that the prophet may be envisioning actual insects as an army.

Nevertheless, by the end of Joel's prophecy, he clearly employed the imagery of a locust horde to symbolize the northern army's invasion of the land of Israel. For example, he wrote that the land in front of the locusts will be like the garden of Eden but their fire will make the land like a desert after they pass (Joel 2:3; cf. Ezek. 38:12-13). While many translations render this phrase as "the northern army" (Joel 2:20), the Hebrew text is better rendered "the northern one," a likely reference to the Antichrist, the leader of the great locust army which the Lord will send as His instrument of indignation. Consistent with the message of the other prophets, Joel assured the reader that this northern one would be destroyed in the land of Israel, followed by the messianic blessings upon the land (Joel 2:20ff).

Some popular prophecy teachers have suggested that the locusts in the book of Revelation depict modern military technology, such as helicopters, fighter jets, or attack drones. One strength of this view is that the apostle described the locusts as having breastplates similar to iron and producing a terrifying sound with their wings, like horses rushing into battle (Rev. 9:9; cf. v. 17). But admittedly, such descriptions do not alleviate the fact that actual locust invasions produce similar sounds, and the locusts in Joel's prophecy also made a similar clamor (Joel 2:4-5). But more to the point, the locusts in Revelation will not be given authority to kill men but only to cause excruciating pain for five months with their scorpion-like stingers, and to selectively harm only those people without God's seal upon their foreheads (Rev. 9:4-6). It is unimaginable that this passage envisions a military invasion that will not result in any deaths.

After the fifth trumpet judgment, the apostle John warned, "One

---

3   This passage, like the prophecy of Joel, referred to the days of unprecedented tribulation leading up to the day of the LORD.

woe is past. Behold, still two more woes are coming after these things"
(Rev. 9:12). The second of the three woes is the sixth trumpet. The
sixth trumpet judgment and many, if not all, the bowl judgments
contain the events of the final battle of the Antichrist's war. We should
not confuse the final battle, known as the battle of Armageddon, with
this larger three and a half year war (i.e., the war of Gog and Magog).
Rather, as we will see shortly, this location of Armageddon, in the Valley
of Megiddo, will be the epicenter of the climactic battle that will take
place at the end of the war.

> Then the sixth angel sounded . . . "Release the four angels who are
> bound at the great river Euphrates." So the four angels, who had been
> prepared for the hour and day and month and year, were released to
> kill a third of mankind. Now the number of the army of the horsemen
> was two hundred million; I heard the number of them. And thus I
> saw the horses in the vision: those who sat on them had breastplates
> of fiery red, hyacinth blue, and sulfur yellow; and the heads of the
> horses were like the heads of lions; and out of their mouths came fire,
> smoke, and brimstone. By these three plagues a third of mankind was
> killed—by the fire and the smoke and the brimstone which came out
> of their mouths. For their power is in their mouth and in their tails;
> for their tails are like serpents, having heads; and with them they do
> harm. (Rev. 9:13, 14-19)

The sixth trumpet blast will result in four demons being released
from the Euphrates River who will then embolden two hundred million soldiers to arrive there (Rev. 9:14, 16). Many have noted that the
current numbers of Chinese military are sufficient to fit this description,
and it is likely that the Oriental kings depicted in the sixth bowl judgment will commission these very troops from beyond the Euphrates
(Rev. 16:12-16). This military force will arrive at the exact moment
("for the hour and day and month and year" Rev. 9:15) that God has
sovereignly ordained for them to appear (Rev. 9:15). They will slay

one-third of the world's inhabitants during the final portion of the war (Rev. 9:15, 18), and they will unleash the powers of hell—fire, smoke, and brimstone from serpent-like heads upon their tails (Rev. 9:17-18). Despite God's mercy that many people will remain alive on the earth after these plagues, the apostle adamantly declared that these people will not repent of their sins (Rev. 9:20-21).

The third woe should be equated with the seventh trumpet (Rev. 8:13), which is also evidenced by its mention one verse before the seventh angel sounds ("The second woe is past. Behold, the third woe is coming quickly" Rev. 11:14). This trumpet blast will result in the kingdom of the world giving way to the arrival of the glorious, eternal kingdom of Christ Jesus (Rev. 11:15). As we will later see, this is also the day of the Lord, the day when God will suddenly and completely destroy the great city Babylon, the ubiquitous city of man, which is the world with all its wickedness (Rev. 16:8-11; 18:1ff). The Son of Man will return in glory and will personally judge the wicked, resulting in the angels throwing the wicked into the fiery, eternal destruction in hell (Rev. 11:18; 20:9-10, 14-15). This will be the most terrifying woe of all!

The seven trumpet judgments will fulfill the typology inherent in the ancient destruction of the city of Jericho (Jos. 6:1-21). In the biblical narrative, the prophet Joshua instructed his soldiers to march around the city once during each of the first six days and seven times on the seventh day. Also, seven priests blew seven trumpets made of rams' horns (i.e., shofars) during each of the seven days. Then, on the seventh day, the congregation of Israel collectively shouted, and the walls of Jericho fell to the ground. This account closely parallels the prophecy in the Apocalypse wherein seven angels blow seven consecutive trumpets, followed by the fall of the great city Babylon. Also corresponding to this narrative, the apostle Paul taught that Jesus will descend from heaven with a commanding shout when the final trumpet sounds (1 Thess. 4:13-18; cf. 1 Cor. 15:50-54).

The apostle presented us with "the seven last plagues," which will complete God's righteous wrath upon the Earth (Rev. 15:1; 16:1, 5-6).

As each of seven angels consecutively pours his bowl of judgment upon the planet, plagues will result. The first five bowl judgments will result in the following plagues:

1. Earth: "A foul and loathsome sore came upon the men who had the mark of the beast and those who worshiped his image." (Rev. 16:2; cf. Exod. 9:9-11)

2. Sea: "It became blood as of a dead man; and every living creature in the sea died." (Rev. 16:3)

3. Rivers and Springs of Water: "They became blood. . . For they have shed the blood of saints and prophets, and You have given them blood to drink." (Rev. 16:4, 6)

4. Sun: It will "scorch men with fire. And men were scorched with great heat, and they blasphemed the name of God who has power over these plagues." (Rev. 16:8-9)

5. The kingdom of the Beast (i.e., Antichrist): It "became full of darkness; and they gnawed their tongues because of the pain. They blasphemed the God of heaven because of their pains and their sores, and did not repent of their deeds." (Rev. 16:10-11)

At this point we should remind ourselves that the bowls and trumpets are not designed to inflict wrath upon Christians (cf. Rom. 5:9; 1 Thess. 5:9-10). John pointed out that the bowl judgments will specifically target those who have received the mark of the Antichrist and have worshipped him (Rev. 16:2), those who have "shed the blood of saints and prophets" (Rev. 16:6), and the kingdom of the Antichrist (Rev. 16:10). Similarly, the Lord is able to protect His people in the midst of such judgments, as He protected His people in the land of Goshen from the plagues against Egypt (Exod. 8:22-24;

9:4-7, 26; 10:21-23; cf. Rev. 3:10). This sovereign protection is one of the primary purposes of the seal of the living God (Rev. 9:4), and it is also evident in the prophecy of God preparing a place in the desert for the heavenly woman to flee for safety during the 1,260 days of the Antichrist's persecution (Rev. 12:6).

God has designed these specific judgments to vindicate His persecuted Church. The Lord Jesus reminded His disciples, "Shall God not avenge His own elect who cry out day and night to Him, though He bears long with them? I tell you that He will avenge them speedily" (Luke 18:7-8). Consistent with this theme, the apostle John saw that an angel offered incense, which was mixed "with the prayers of all the saints," upon the altar in heaven (Rev. 8:3-4). Then immediately, the angel filled a censer with fire from the altar and threw it upon the earth, resulting in cosmic disturbances and the seven angels preparing to sound their trumpets (Rev. 8:3-6). Some, if not all, of God's judgments upon the earth are "measure for measure" (lex talionis), according to the manner in which the earth's inhabitants have persecuted His saints and prophets (Rev. 16:6; cf. Ps. 79:3, 10, 12).

The sixth bowl judgment will result in the final gathering of the nations for the battle of Armageddon:

> Then the sixth angel poured out his bowl on the great river Euphrates, and its water was dried up, so that the way of the kings from the east might be prepared. And I saw three unclean spirits like frogs coming out of the mouth of the dragon, out of the mouth of the beast, and out of the mouth of the false prophet. For they are spirits of demons, performing signs, which go out to the kings of the earth and of the whole world, to gather them to the battle of that great day of God Almighty. "Behold, I am coming as a thief. Blessed is he who watches, and keeps his garments, lest he walk naked and they see his shame." And they gathered them together to the place called in Hebrew, Armageddon. (Rev. 16:12-16)

The partial drying up of the Euphrates River is no small feat, and it could be the result of a dam, nuclear detonation, or less likely, extreme drought (cf. Exod. 14:21-22). The prophet Isaiah prophesied that the Egyptian Sea and "the River" (the Euphrates or the River of Egypt) will be divided into seven small streams, which will eventually enable the surviving Jews to return to their ancestral homeland (Isa. 11:15; cf. Isa. 44:27; 50:2; 51:10). Numerous seas and rivers will become dry, resulting in decaying fish carcasses (Isa. 50:2; Nah. 1:4). For instance, the Nile River basin will be dried up and its river and tributaries will be polluted ("turn foul") and its reeds will wither, possibly as a result of vaporization from the use of nuclear weapons or other tactical weapons against Cairo (Isa. 19:5-6; cf. Zech. 10:11).

As mentioned previously, the phrase "the kings from the east" in Revelation 16 likely refers to the national leaders of the Far East, such as China and North Korea, and possibly India, Pakistan, Japan, and others. The demonic spirits sent by the unholy trinity—Satan, the Antichrist, and the false prophet—will be "like frogs," reminiscent of the plague of frogs which God sent against Egypt during the exodus (cf. Exod. 8:2-13). These demons will perform "signs" designed to inspire these Oriental kings and the leaders of the other nations on Earth ("the kings of the earth and of the whole world" Rev. 16:14) to send their militaries into the land of Israel. Their purpose will not be to destroy Jerusalem, which the Antichrist will have largely already accomplished (see chapters 3 and 4), but more probably to depose and destroy the Antichrist, although their attempt will be unsuccessful. By the end of the war, the Antichrist will have crushed and oppressed the world and its leaders to the point that they rebel against him, desperately attempting to remove his oppressive yoke. The arrival of this Oriental horde will likely fulfill Daniel's prophecy: "But news from the east and the north shall trouble him [the Antichrist]; therefore, he shall go out with great fury to destroy and annihilate many" (Dan. 11:44).

This international endeavor will be futile, even presumptuous, for at least two reasons: First, no military on earth will be able to overpower the Antichrist's forces because the full power of Satan will be at work in him. Second, Christ has already decreed that He alone will destroy the Antichrist and only after this wicked man has reigned for forty-two months. We need not speculate the reason why Satan and his chief minions will inspire this great battle against their own kind, but it may simply be that this "house divided against itself" (Luke 11:17) will intend to annihilate ("to steal, and to kill, and to destroy" John 10:10) as many people as possible, sending them into eternal damnation.

The purpose of this gathering of the world's military leaders at Armageddon will be to engage in "the battle of that great day of God Almighty" (Rev. 16:14), the final battle to accomplish "the war to end all wars" (cf. Rev. 19:19; 20:8). We should equate "that great day of God Almighty" (Rev. 16:14) with the day of the Lord, also known as the day of Jesus Christ or one of its derivatives. To demonstrate, a search of the phrase "the day of God" reveals that it appears in one other verse, specifically 2 Peter 3:12 (cf. Joel 2:11, 31; Zeph. 1:14). In the larger context of the apostle Peter's prophecy, he clearly equated the day of God with the day of the Lord, which he taught will arrive "as a thief in the night, in which the heavens will pass away with a great noise, and the elements will melt with fervent heat" (2 Pet. 3:10; cf. Matt. 24:35, 42-44). The ungodly will receive their judgment on this day (2 Pet. 3:7; cf. Matt. 25:31-46). This will be no ordinary day of reckoning; this is judgment day!

Consistent with this motif, the risen Lord interjected a parenthetical statement into the middle of John's prophecy about the battle of Armageddon: "Behold, I am coming as a thief. Blessed is he who watches, and keeps his garments, lest he walk naked and they see his shame" (Rev. 16:15; cf. Matt. 24:43; Luke 12:39; Rev. 3:3, 11). The awkward placement of this warning in the middle of a verse about the final battle is intended to emphasize the point that Christ will return to preemptively interrupt this battle, to prevent humanity from destroying itself (cf. Matt. 24:22; Rev. 11:18; 19:19-21). The tragic irony is that even at this final stage in the eschatological drama, the wicked will remain oblivious to the fact that Jesus will soon return to consummate His kingdom. Yet the apostles frequently warned that the Son of Man will come like a thief in the night to an unprepared and undiscerning world continuing in wickedness (1 Thess. 5:1-10; cf. "like a snare" Luke 21:35).

The epicenter for the final gathering of the world's military forces will be at Armageddon (Rev. 16:16). Years ago, my wife and I traveled throughout the Middle East, and we visited Armageddon (Har-Megiddo), which is now an archaeological site, a large hill situated in a very large, fertile plain known as the Jezreel Valley. The sprawling valley is majestic to behold, and it stretches from the northwest to the southeast across the vastness of the land of Israel. Historically, because of its key location, many foreign armies invaded the valley to gain access to the interior of the land and to conquer it. Megiddo's rich military history can be seen by the fact that it has been conquered and rebuilt at least twenty times. This location will serve as a strategic epicenter for the largescale, international conflagration designed to destroy humanity.

The Old Testament details several battles which were fought in the Valley of Jezreel. As we might expect, they each serve as a prophetic foreshadowing for the battle of Armageddon. For example, the Canaanite kings led a battle against Sisera and his armies by the waters of Megiddo; this battle is depicted as a war fought in heaven amongst the stars, reflecting the ancient Near East cosmology of the heavenly court of angelic beings presiding over the affairs of mankind (Judg. 5:19-21; cf. Rev. 12:1ff). Furthermore, the Spirit of the Lord came upon Israel's judge Gideon so that he led a successful battle against the soldiers of the East who had "gathered together" as a vast "multitude" in the Valley of Jezreel (Judg. 6:33-34).

> Now the Midianites and Amalekites, all the people of the East, were lying in the valley as numerous as locusts . . . "When I [Gideon] blow the trumpet, I and all who are with me, then you also blow the trumpets on every side of the whole camp, and say, 'The sword of the Lord and of Gideon!' ". . . and they blew the trumpets and broke the pitchers that were in their hands . . . and every man stood in his

place all around the camp; and the whole army ran and cried out and fled. When the three hundred blew the trumpets, the Lord set every man's sword against his companion throughout the whole camp; and the army fled. (Judg. 7:12, 18-22)

God has sovereignly decreed that the people of the East will once again gather "as numerous as locusts" to make war in the Valley of Jezreel, this time for the battle of Armageddon. They will gather to oppose the Antichrist in clear defiance of the prophetic words of the holy prophets and apostles, which is paramount to opposing the returning Son of God (Rev. 19:19). As typified in Gideon's battle, the Lord Jesus Christ will complete the final battle with the trumpet blast (1 Cor. 15:51-54; 1 Thess. 4:16; Rev. 10:7; 11:15, 18), a shout of command (1 Thess. 4:16), and the sword of the Lord (Rev. 19:15; cf. Isa. 11:4; Rev. 1:16), and the Lord's enemies will attack each other in a chaotic frenzy of fear and confusion (Ezek. 38:21; Hag. 2:22; Zech. 14:13). At Christ's glorious return, He will resurrect His saints, revealing His glory in our earthen vessels (2 Cor. 4:7, 17-18; cf. Gen. 2:7), like Gideon revealed his army along with the fire within the broken jars of clay.

Finally, the Lord prophesied through the prophet Hosea that "in a little while" the nation of Israel would be utterly defeated in the Valley of Jezreel: "It shall come to pass in that day[4] that I will break the bow of Israel in the Valley of Jezreel" (Hosea 1:5; cf. 2 Kings 10:11; Hosea 1:4). The battle of Armageddon will be the final battle of the forty-two month war, during which time the power of the Jewish people will be completely shattered (Deut. 32:36; Dan. 12:7). However, the final gathering of the surviving remnant of Israel will occur at the day of God ("For great will be the day of Jezreel!" Hosea 1:11), and they will receive their final salvation from Christ in the very place where the nation had been destroyed ("in the place . . . it shall be said to them,

---

[4] The prophets frequently employed the phrase "in that day" (variously "at/on that day") as a shorthand designation for the day of the Lord.

'You are sons of the living God' " Hosea 1:10).

The prophet Joel wrote about a mysterious place called the Valley of Jehoshaphat, also known as the Valley of Judgment and the Valley of Decision. The Lord warned, "I will also gather all nations and bring them down to the Valley of Jehoshaphat; and I will enter into judgment with them there on account of My people, My heritage Israel, whom they have scattered among the nations; they have also divided up My land. They have cast lots for My people" (Joel 3:2-3). The Valley of Jehoshaphat may be a synonym for the Valley of Jezreel, although the former has frequently been associated with the Kidron Valley, located between the Old City and the Mount of Olives. This suggestion is appealing because Jerusalem is the target for this multinational invasion of Israel (Zech. 14:1ff; Rev. 14:20). The purpose for this battle is for the Lord to gather the nations for judgment because they will have exiled the Jews and divided the Promised Land ("Whom they have scattered among the nations; they have also divided up My land" Joel 3:2; cf. Zech. 14:2; Luke 21:24).

The prophet continued his prediction about the multitudes of nations being assembled in the Valley of Jehoshaphat:

> "Prepare for war! Wake up the mighty men, let all the men of war draw near, let them come up. Beat your plowshares into swords and your pruning hooks into spears; Let the weak say, 'I am strong.' Assemble and come, all you nations, and gather together all around. Cause Your mighty ones to go down there, O Lord. Let the nations be wakened and come up to the Valley of Jehoshaphat; for there I will sit to judge all the surrounding nations. Put in the sickle, for the harvest is ripe. Come, go down; for the winepress is full, the vats overflow—for their wickedness is great." Multitudes, multitudes in the valley of decision! For the day of the Lord is near in the valley of decision. (Joel 3:9-14)

This prophecy shares many features with the apostle John's description of the Son of Man's coming with a cloud at the end-time harvest

(Rev. 14:14-20; cf. Matt. 13:36-43). First, the apostle saw the Son of Man, accompanied by angels, arriving to harvest the earth, which is reflected in Joel's statement that the Lord will descend upon the armies with His "mighty ones" (Joel 3:11, 13; cf. Isa. 13:3). Second, the angel's statement to Christ to "thrust in Your sickle and reap . . . for the harvest of the earth is ripe" (Rev. 14:14-15) echoes the prophet's command to "put in the sickle, for the harvest is ripe" (Joel 3:13). Third, the apostle picked up Joel's imagery of a winepress overflowing with the blood of grapes as divine judgment for the wickedness of the nations (Joel 3:13 with Rev. 14:18-20).

Furthermore, in the Olivet Discourse Jesus alluded to the prophet Joel's statement about God sitting to judge the nations and gathering them together ("all you nations, and gather together all around . . . for there I will sit to judge all the surrounding nations" Joel 3:11, 12). Christ taught, "When the Son of Man comes in His glory, and all the holy angels with Him, then He will sit on the throne of His glory. All the nations will be gathered before Him" (Matt. 25:31-32; cf. Joel 3:12). Clearly then, the Son of Man will return to judge the world at the time of this final conflagration of the nations in the Valley of Decision.

The apostle John's vision of the Son of Man's harvest further depicts His divine wrath and judgment against the nations:

> Then I looked, and behold, a white cloud, and on the cloud sat One like the Son of Man, having on His head a golden crown, and in His hand a sharp sickle. And another angel came out of the temple, crying with a loud voice to Him who sat on the cloud, "Thrust in Your sickle and reap, for the time has come for You to reap, for the harvest of the earth is ripe." So He who sat on the cloud thrust in His sickle on the earth, and the earth was reaped . . . "Thrust in your sharp sickle and gather the clusters of the vine of the earth, for her grapes are fully ripe." So the angel thrust his sickle into the earth and gathered the vine of the earth, and threw it into the great winepress of the wrath of God. And the winepress was trampled outside the city, and blood

came out of the winepress, up to the horses' bridles, for one thousand six hundred furlongs. (Rev. 14:14-16, 18-20)

The final battle will create extensive carnage and destruction, the likes of which the world has never seen. The reference to "the city" in verse 20 is almost certainly Jerusalem,[5] and the winepress overflowing with wine evokes a vivid image of how blood will freely flow from the wounded and dead soldiers. These "rivers" of blood will rise to four feet in depth and will continue flowing for two hundred miles ("up to the horse's bridles, for one thousand six hundred furlongs" Rev. 14:20)! Clearly then, the battle of these innumerable soldiers will not be limited to the vicinity of Jerusalem.

Jerusalem is the Holy City where God has promised to establish His name forever (2 Chron. 6:6; 12:13; 33:4, 7; cf. Deut. 12:5-7; Zech. 2:12).

Why do the nations rage, and the people plot a vain thing? The kings of the earth set themselves, and the rulers take counsel together, against the Lord and against His Anointed, saying, "Let us break Their bonds in pieces and cast away Their cords from us." He who sits in the heavens shall laugh; the Lord shall hold them in derision. Then He shall speak to them in His wrath, and distress them in His deep displeasure: "Yet I have set My King on My holy hill of Zion." (Ps. 2:1-6)

In their perpetual rage, the nations and their rulers strategize against His plan for His Son to eternally reign from this place (Ps. 2:1-8; Rev. 19:19). To be sure, this is humanity's general approach to cast off moral restraint ("break Their bonds . . . cast away Their cords" Ps. 2:3), to destroy the yoke of Christ. According to Luke, this same rage against God's covenant provoked the kings of the earth to crucify our Lord (Acts 4:25-28).

---

5   The Jerusalem Temple Mount was built on an ancient threshing floor (2 Sam. 24:18-25; 1 Chron. 21:18-25; cf. "Thrust in Your sickle and reap" Rev. 14:15).

How great is the enemy's strategy to usurp Jerusalem for himself! Yet how much greater is the Father's power to redeem it in righteousness and to consummate His eternal kingdom! Consequently, God mocks the insolence of the nations, and He will reveal His purposes to the entire world by establishing King Jesus upon that small hill in the Middle East—the Holy Mount Zion (Ps. 2:6-8). This is His everlasting decree ("I have set my King"), and He who is faithful will do it! Because Christ's rod-iron rule will bring divine wrath against the nations and their kings (Ps. 2:5; cf. Rev. 2:27), the psalmist warned them to avoid this wrath by honoring ("kiss the Son") and submitting to the Son of God (Ps. 2:9-12).

At this point, I will digress in order to discuss how we should understand the order of the seven heptads of judgment—the seven seals, seven trumpets, and seven bowls—in the book of Revelation. Admittedly, the apostle John saw the seven seals before seeing the seven trumpet judgments and the seven bowl judgments. However, the interpreter should not assume that the prophetic events will take place in the exact sequence as they were seen by the apostle in his visions. While each heptad contains seven judgments that will be fulfilled chronologically (e.g., the first seal will occur before second seal, and so forth), the judgments contained in the three heptads will not take place sequentially in relationship to those of the other two heptads. To illustrate, the seven trumpet judgments will overlap with the timing of some of the seal and bowl judgments. Most scholars admit a high degree of recapitulation with these judgments and throughout the book of Revelation more generally. This literary feature allows subsequent visions to take the readers behind the scenes to understand the deeper meaning of events and the narrative flow of the book.

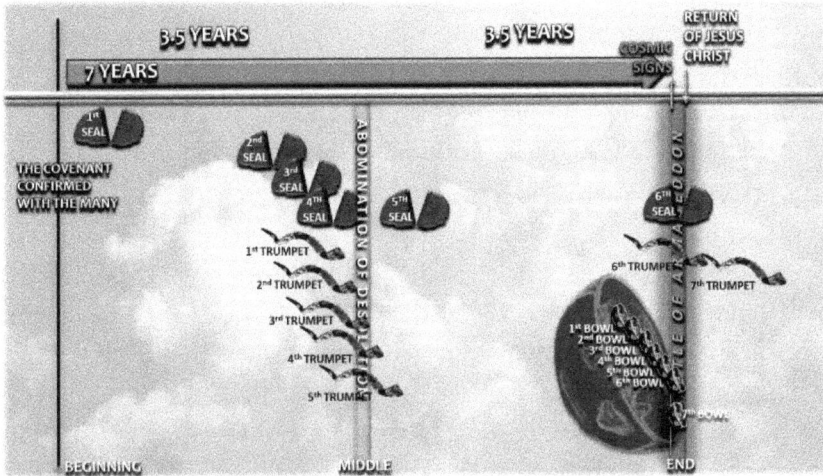

The evidence for this method of interpretation, as it pertains to the heptads, is twofold: First, the language of the seals and trumpets demonstrate that they describe many of the same prophetic events, although seen from different angles and vantage points. Second, all three heptads, the seals, the trumpets, and the bowls, share the same terminus—the day of Jesus Christ.

One example of such overlapping events is that the earthquake of unprecedented magnitude will occur after the sixth seal (Rev. 6:12), at the seventh trumpet (Rev. 11:19), and at the seventh bowl (Rev. 16:18-21). The linguistic similarities shared by these three passages strongly suggest that the same great earthquake is in view.

Sixth Seal: "Behold, there was a great earthquake . . . and every mountain and island was moved out of its place." (Rev. 6:12)

Seventh Trumpet: "And there were lightnings, noises, thunderings, an earthquake, and great hail." (Rev. 11:19)

Seventh Bowl: "And there were noises and thunderings and lightnings; and there was a great earthquake, such a mighty and great earthquake as has not occurred since men were on the earth . . . and the cities of the nations fell. . . Then every island fled away, and the mountains were not found. And great hail from heaven fell upon men." (Rev. 16:18, 19, 20-21)

Notice that the description of the seventh bowl judgment combines the language of the sixth seal and the seventh trumpet. The likelihood that the Apocalypse presents different earthquakes of this magnitude, using much of the same language, is highly suspect.

More decisive, the apostle explained that the seals, the trumpets, and the bowls all terminate at the day of Jesus Christ. To demonstrate, the sixth seal concludes with the statement "for the great day of His wrath has come, and who is able to stand?" (Rev. 6:17). Similarly, the seventh trumpet will be blown when "the mystery of God would be finished" (Rev. 10:7) and "the kingdoms of this world [will] have become the kingdoms of our Lord and of His Christ, and He shall reign forever and ever!" (Rev. 11:15). This will also be "the time of the dead, that they should be judged, and that [God] should reward [His] servants the prophets and the saints" (Rev. 11:18). Other Scriptures demonstrate that the consummation of God's kingdom, the resurrection of the dead, and the judgment seat of Christ will take place on the day of Christ. Finally, the seventh bowl takes place on "the great day of God Almighty" (Rev. 16:14), and it is immediately followed by the destruction of Babylon (Rev. 18) and the glorious arrival of the Son of Man (Rev. 19:11-21). We must conclude that all three series of judgments—the seals, trumpets, and bowls—will end in the same place: the day of the Lord.

10

THE DAY OF JESUS CHRIST

THE BIBLICAL AUTHORS gave various names for the day of the Lord
(יום יהוה).[1] For example, the prophets variously called it the day of the
Lord of hosts (Isa. 2:12), the day of the Lord God of hosts (Jer. 46:10),
the great and awesome day of the Lord (Joel 2:31; Acts 2:20), and the
great and dreadful day of the Lord (Mal. 4:5). In characteristic fashion,
the apostle Paul substituted the name Jesus for Yahweh, restyling the
day of the Lord as the day of our Lord Jesus Christ (1 Cor. 1:8), the day
of the Lord Jesus (1 Cor. 5:5; 2 Cor. 1:14), the day of Jesus Christ (Phil.
1:6), and the day of Christ (Phil. 1:10; 2:16; 2 Thess. 2:2). The New
Testament writers also termed it the day of God (2 Pet. 3:12), that great
day of God Almighty (Rev. 16:14), the great day (Jude 1:6), the great
day of His wrath (Rev. 6:17; cf. Isa. 34:8), and in characteristic short-

---

[1]   Isa. 13:6, 9; Ezek. 13:5; 30:3; Joel 1:15; 2:1, 11; 3:14; Amos 5:16, 18, 20; Obad. 1:15; Zeph. 1:7,
      14; Zech. 14:1; 1 Thess. 5:2; 2 Pet. 3:10.

hand, the day[2] and that day.[3] Jesus simply rendered it the day of judgment (Matt. 10:15; 11:22-24; 12:36; Mark 6:11; Acts 17:31; 2 Pet. 2:9; 3:7; 1 John 4:17; cf. "His day" Luke 17:24) and the last day (John 6:39-40, 44, 54; 11:24; 12:48). The apostles also used descriptive terms, such as Paul's "the day of wrath and revelation of the righteous judgment of God" (Rom. 2:5), "the day when God will judge the secrets of men by Jesus Christ" (Rom. 2:16), "the day of redemption" (Eph. 4:30), and Peter's "the day of visitation" (1 Pet. 2:12).

The versatility of language employed for the day of the Lord does not give license to imagine that the various expressions indicate multiple days of the Lord. As we have seen, the apostle Peter equated "the day of the Lord" with "the day of God" (2 Pet. 3:10, 12; cf. Rev. 16:14). He also considered this to be judgment day ("the day of judgment and perdition of ungodly men" 2 Pet. 3:7) and the day when the Lord Jesus Christ will fulfill His promise to return in glory (2 Pet. 3:4-5). An exhaustive study of the linguistic variations for the day of the Lord serve to demonstrate that any attempt to divide this solitary day into multiple days or to extend it over a period of months or years is forced and contrived.

Most of the Old Testament prophecies concerning the day of the Lord, in one sense, point to localized judgments which took place in antiquity. Based on this fact, many commentators assume that the Prophets contain many "days of the Lord" which occurred in history and that those days only foreshadowed the final day of the Lord. However, based on abundant biblical evidence, it is preferable to understand these historical judgments as revealing aspects of the day of the Lord, the solitary day which is penultimate and in our future.

The primary reason for this is that the many prophecies about the day of the Lord form a single patchwork of overlapping events, wherein each prophecy provides details about the day, while leaving out other

---

[2]   Joel 1:15; Matt. 25:13; Luke 17:30; Rom. 13:12-13; 1 Cor. 3:13; 1 Thess. 5:5, 8; 2 Thess. 2:3; Heb. 10:25; 2 Pet. 1:19.

[3]   Matt. 7:22; 24:36; Luke 6:23; 10:12; 21:34; John 14:20; 16:23, 26; 2 Thess. 1:10; 2:3; 2 Tim. 1:18; 4:8.

details. Consequently, the careful reader can observe the same recurring themes in these various passages; this collective weight of evidence strongly argues in favor of the interpretation that they all refer to the same day of the Lord. When comparing the Old Testament prophecies regarding the day of the Lord with the New Testament passages about the day of Jesus Christ, we can deduce that the apostles equated the day of the Lord with the day of Christ, the day upon which Jesus will return from heaven to save His people, judge His enemies, and consummate His kingdom.

The day of Jesus Christ will not take place until a specific constellation of signs takes place. The prophet Joel prophesied that these signs will arrive before the day of the Lord: "And I [the Lord] will show wonders in the heavens and in the earth: Blood and fire and pillars of smoke. The sun shall be turned into darkness and the moon into blood before the coming of the great and awesome day of the Lord" (Joel 2:30-31). In addition, Christ taught that these cosmic signs and His glorious return will not take place until "immediately after" the unprecedented tribulation: "Immediately after the tribulation of those days the sun will be darkened, and the moon will not give its light; the stars will fall from heaven, and the powers of the heavens will be shaken. Then the sign of the Son of Man will appear in heaven" (Matt. 24:29-30; cf. Mark 13:24-25; Luke 21:26-27).

Based on such texts, we can establish the exact order of eschatological occurrences. Consequently, the great tribulation will end with the great stellar signs in the heavens and the return of Christ (Matt. 24:29-30), but the day of the Lord cannot begin until these signs occur first (Joel 2:30-31). In short, the cosmic darkness will take place after the tribulation but before the day of the Lord. Furthermore, as I will soon demonstrate, the other prophets prophesied that these cosmic signs will occur on, not simply before, the day of the Lord. The way to reconcile this with Joel's statement about this chronology is simply to see the cosmic signs as occurring at the very beginning of the day of the Lord. Finally, I have already established that the battle of Armageddon will take place on that day (Rev. 16:14-16).

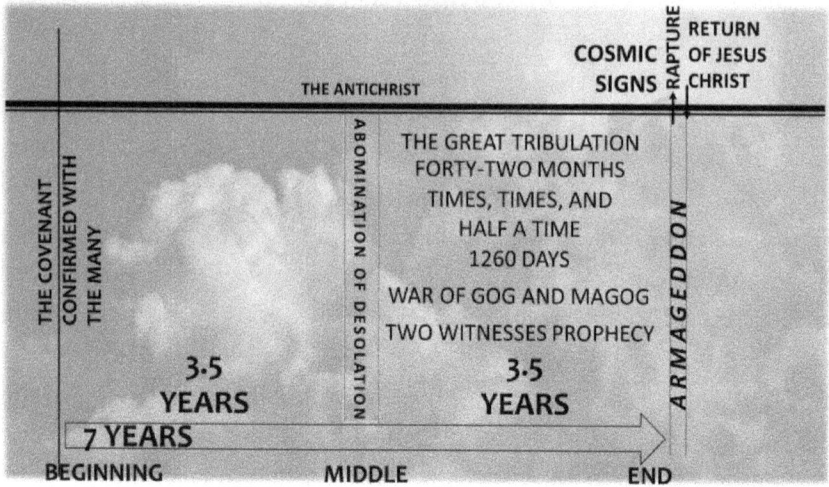

In the previous chapter, we evaluated the Scriptural evidence for the battle of Armageddon. We will now examine the other events that will take place on the day of the Lord, and I will demonstrate that they include the events listed in the following table:

Events of the Day of the Lord
The Battle of Armageddon
A Great Earthquake and Heaven Shaking
Cosmic Darkness—Clouds and Pillars of Smoke
People Taking Shelter
A Massive Hailstorm
A Fiery Inferno
The Return of Jesus Christ

One of the other primary signs of the day of the Lord will be an earthquake of unprecedented magnitude (Rev. 6:12, 14; 16:18-20). The prophet John described it in this manner: "There was a great earthquake, such a mighty and great earthquake as had not occurred since men were on the earth" (Rev. 16:18). This quake will cause all the inhabitants of the land of Israel to tremble (Joel 2:1; cf. Nah. 1:5). Ezekiel described it in the following prophecy:

> For in My jealousy and in the fire of My wrath I have spoken: "Surely in that day there shall be a great earthquake in the land of Israel, so that the fish of the sea, the birds of the heavens, the beasts of the field, all creeping things that creep on the earth, and all men who are on the face of the earth shall shake at My presence. The mountains shall be thrown down, the steep places shall fall, and every wall shall fall to the ground." (Ezek. 38:19-20)

The prophets taught that Earth will shake mightily (Isa. 2:12, 19, 21; Nah. 1:5-6) and will "move out of her place" (Isa. 13:13). The mountains and hills will teeter back and forth (Jer. 4:24; Nah. 1:5) and will be removed from their place (Isa. 54:10; Rev. 6:14; 16:20). Consequently, every island will be submerged underneath the oceans (Rev. 16:20; cf. Rev. 6:14). The prophet Isaiah wrote, "Every valley shall be exalted and every mountain and hill brought low; the crooked places shall be made straight and the rough places smooth" (Isa. 40:4; cf. Isa. 42:16). The world's cities will also be demolished in the earthquake (Jer. 4:26; Rev. 16:19). Isaiah called this "the day of the great slaughter, when the towers fall" (Isa. 30:25). King David wrote to the Lord: "You have made the earth tremble; You have broken it; heal its breaches, for it is shaking. You have shown Your people hard things; You have made us drink the wine of confusion" (Ps. 60:2-3).

Isaiah borrowed imagery from the flood narrative in the book of Genesis to describe this earthquake:

The windows from on high are open, and the foundations of the earth are shaken. The earth is violently broken, the earth is split open, the earth is shaken exceedingly. The earth shall reel to and fro like a drunkard, and shall totter like a hut; its transgression shall be heavy upon it, and it will fall, and not rise again. (Isa. 24:18-20)

The prophet also predicted that this great earthquake will cause people to take shelter in the caverns of the earth:

Enter into the rock and hide in the dust from the terror of the Lord and the glory of His majesty. The lofty looks of man shall be humbled, the haughtiness of men shall be bowed down, and the Lord alone shall be exalted in that day. For the day of the Lord of hosts shall come upon everything proud and lofty, upon everything lifted up—and it shall be brought low . . . They shall go into the holes of the rocks and into the caves of the earth from the terror of the Lord and the glory of His majesty, when He arises to shake the earth mightily. In that day a man will cast away his idols . . . to go into the clefts of the rocks, and into the crags of the rugged rocks, from the terror of the Lord and the glory of His majesty, when He arises to shake the earth mightily. (Isa. 2:10-21)

The primary purpose of the earthquake will be to humble or bring down the pride of humanity so that "the Lord alone shall be exalted on that day" (Isa. 2:11, 17; cf. Isa. 13:12). The prophecy continues with a lengthy description of the great earthquake which will demolish everything that exudes pride—the largest trees, the tallest mountains, the highest towers, the fortified walls, and massive seafaring vessels (Isa. 2:13-16). People will no longer value their foreign deities but will fearfully cast their idols aside in order to enter into the chambers of the earth to find protection from the earthquake (Isa. 2:18-21).

The most prominent feature of the day of the Lord, prior to the glorious return of Christ, will be stellar darkness. The Sun, Moon, and stars will be darkened at that time (Isa. 13:10; Joel 2:10, 30-31; 3:15;

Matt. 24:29; Mark 13:25; Luke 21:26; cf. Isa. 24:23). The prophets often described this day as "a day of darkness and gloominess, a day of clouds and thick darkness" (Joel 2:2; cf. Isa. 13:10; Jer. 4:23, 28; Ezek. 30:3; Amos 5:18, 20; Zeph. 1:15; Nah. 1:3). Consequently, deep darkness will shroud the Earth and its inhabitants (Isa. 60:2; cf. Isa. 9:2) so that people will walk like blind men (Zeph. 1:17). The prophet Zechariah wrote, "It shall come to pass in that day that there will be no light; the lights will diminish. It shall be one day which is known to the Lord—neither day nor night" (Zech. 14:6-7; cf. Matt. 24:36); as an aside, this verse indicates that the day of the Lord will be a twenty-four-hour day. In addition, John used personification to depict the Sun as wearing black sackcloth, a mourner's garb, and the Moon as acquiring a blood-like appearance, an appropriate symbol that will reflect the concurrent carnage on Earth (Rev. 6:12; cf. Isa. 50:3). This likely speaks of the crimson hue that the Moon will appear to exude once small particulates have entered the Earth's atmosphere.

Consistent with this atmospheric change, the prophets predicted that fire and smoke will accompany the stellar darkness. The Lord warned, "And I will show wonders in the heavens and in the earth: Blood and fire and pillars of smoke. The sun shall be turned into darkness and the moon into blood, before the coming of the great and awesome day of the Lord" (Joel 2:30-31; cf. Acts 2:19-20). The blood in verse 30 is elucidated by the subsequent verse as referring to the scarlet color of the Moon. The "pillars of smoke" denotes visible columns of smoke vapors, and possibly, mushroom clouds from nuclear detonations. This is consistent with the prophets' insistence that the day of the Lord will be "a day of clouds," a likely reference to these clouds of smoke. While other prophecies envision the cosmic darkness on the day of the Lord, Joel mentioned that the cosmic darkness will occur before the day. As mentioned previously, this discrepancy is easily reconciled by seeing the darkness as heralding the beginning of the day.

Christ also prophesied that the stellar darkness will be attended by stars falling from the sky (Matt. 24:29; cf. Mark 13:24; Luke 21:26).

Similarly, the apostle John saw stars descending to Earth "as a fig tree drops its late figs when it is shaken by a mighty wind" (Rev. 6:13; cf. Isa. 34:4). In first-century Greek literature, the word translated "stars" carries a broad semantic range; in other words, the word is often not limited to stars, as narrowly defined within the discipline of modern astronomy, but it could refer to any flaming body in the heavens, such as meteors, asteroids, and comets. It is evident that Jesus and John were not claiming that multiple suns from other galaxies will fall to the Earth. Rather, much smaller objects of burning debris will plummet from the atmosphere and strike the planet.

Another feature of the day of the Lord will be a giant hailstorm (Ezek. 38:22; Rev. 16:21; cf. Isa. 28:17). The Lord asked, "Have you seen the treasury of hail, which I have reserved for the time of trouble, for the day of battle and war?" (Job 38:22-23). God will send a flurry of giant hailstones, rain, fire, and brimstone to descend upon the Antichrist's unsuspecting armies and upon those who live securely in the coastlands of the earth (Ezek. 38:22; 39:6; cf. Zeph. 1:18). The soldiers will be astonished because they will initially see that each other's faces will appear to have been set ablaze (Isa. 13:8). The apostle John described the size of the hailstones: "And great hail from heaven fell upon men, each hailstone about the weight of a talent. Men blasphemed God because of the plague of the hail, since that plague was exceedingly great" (Rev. 16:21).

Malachi prophesied about this fiery conflagration: "Behold, the day is coming, burning like an oven, and all the proud, yes, all who do wickedly will be stubble. And the day which is coming shall burn them up . . . [it] will leave them neither root nor branch' " (Mal. 4:1; cf. Zeph. 2:2). This devouring fire will be an expression of the Lord's fury against sinners and His jealousy on behalf of His people Israel (Nah. 1:6; Zeph. 1:18; 2:2). Isaiah relayed the extent of this burning: "Therefore the curse has devoured the earth, and those who dwell in it are desolate. Therefore the inhabitants of the earth are burned, and few men are left" (Isa. 24:6; cf. Isa. 24:3; Jer. 4:25, 27; Zeph. 1:18)! Elsewhere, the Lord declared, "I will make a mortal more rare than fine gold, a man more than the golden wedge of Ophir" (Isa. 13:12). Similarly, He spoke through the prophet Zephaniah: "I will utterly consume everything from the face of the land. . . I will consume man and beast; I will consume the birds of the heavens, the fish of the sea . . . I will cut off man from the face of the land" (Zeph. 1:2-3).

On the day of Christ, He will arrive with flaming fire to consume His enemies (Ps. 50:3; 97:3; Mal. 3:2). Malachi asked, "But who can endure the day of His coming? And who can stand when He appears? For He is like a refiner's fire and like launderers' soap" (Mal. 3:2). As we have seen, His return will be accompanied by lightning, earthquakes, and clouds of smoke (Ps. 97:2-6; 144:5-6). The intense heat will create valleys and transform mountains into molten lava (Ps. 97:5; Mic. 1:4). The seas will roar and the created things itself will be in a state of tumult, cheering and clapping for the Lord's return so to speak (Ps. 98:7-9; cf. Rom. 8:19-22).

The prophets warned that God will also shake the heavens on the day of the Lord (Joel 2:10; 3:16; Isa. 13:13; Hag. 2:6, 21; Heb. 12:26-27). For example, the Lord spoke through the prophet Haggai, saying, "Once more (it is a little while) I will shake heaven and earth, the sea and dry land" (Hag. 2:6; cf. v. 21; Heb. 12:26-27). The Lord Jesus taught that "the powers of the heavens will be shaken" (Matt. 24:29; cf. Mark 13:24; Luke 21:26), and the apostle John saw that the sky will be rolled up "as a scroll" (Rev. 6:14). This is an allusion to the prophecy of Isaiah, who wrote, "All the host of heaven shall be dissolved, and the heavens shall be rolled up like a scroll; all their host shall fall down as the leaf falls from the vine, and as fruit falling from a fig tree" (Isa. 34:4; cf. Rev. 6:13).

In Revelation 6, the apostle John coalesced all the events of the day of the Lord together into one prophecy:

I looked when He opened the sixth seal, and behold, there was a great earthquake; and the sun became black as sackcloth of hair, and the moon became like blood. And the stars of heaven fell to the earth, as a fig tree drops its late figs when it is shaken by a mighty wind. Then the sky receded as a scroll when it is rolled up, and every mountain and island was moved out of its place. And the kings of the earth, the great men, the rich men, the commanders, the mighty men, every slave and every free man, hid themselves in the caves and in the rocks of the mountains, and said to the mountains and rocks, "Fall on us and hide us from the face of Him who sits on the throne and from the wrath of the Lamb! For the great day of His wrath has come, and who is able to stand?" (Rev. 6:12-17)

Here we see the following features: (1) the unprecedented earthquake, (2) cosmic darkness, (3) stars falling to the earth, (4) the sky receding as a scroll, (5) people taking shelter, and (6) the earth dwellers recognizing that the day of the Lamb's wrath has arrived. The question "Who is able to stand?" (Rev. 6:17) echoes a prophecy of Malachi ("But who can endure the day of His coming? And who can stand when He appears" Mal. 3:2; cf. Joel 2:11; Nah. 1:6) and a statement that Christ made in His Olivet Discourse regarding His glorious appearance ("that you may be counted worthy to escape all these things . . . and to stand before the Son of Man" Luke 21:36).

All the aforementioned events will be accompanied by the fiery destruction of the Earth on the day of the Lord. For example, the apostle Peter wrote about this destruction of the cosmos:

For this they [the scoffers] willfully forget: that by the word of God the heavens were of old, and the earth standing out of water and in the water, by which the world that then existed perished, being flooded with water. But the heavens and the earth which are now preserved by the same word, are reserved for fire until the day of judgment and perdition of ungodly men . . . But the day of the Lord will come as a thief in the night, in which the heavens will pass away with a great noise, and the elements will melt with fervent heat; both the earth and the works that are in it will be burned up. Therefore, since all these things will be dissolved, what manner of persons ought you to be in holy conduct and godliness, looking for and hastening the coming of the day of God, because of which the heavens will be dissolved, being on fire, and the elements will melt with fervent heat? (2 Pet. 3:5-7; 10-12; cf. 1 Pet. 1:8, 13)

The apostle did not mince words when he prophesied that the day will include the fiery destruction of the planet ("the heavens and the earth" 2 Pet. 3:5, 7-8, 10; cf. Gen. 1:1-2; 2:1, 4). The atmosphere will "pass away with a great noise," while the elements will melt "with fervent heat" (2 Pet. 3:7, 10-12). Saint Peter certainly did not envision a cataclysm after which life will carry on as usual. To the contrary, the Earth will experience fundamental changes, which will render it largely uninhabitable and useless, much like it was during the Flood of Noah's day (2 Pet. 3:6; cf. Gen. 7:1-8:19; Isa. 24:1, 4; 54:9-10). The Lord Jesus summarized, "Heaven and earth will pass away, but My words will by no means pass away" (Matt. 24:35; Mark 13:31; Luke 21:33; cf. 1 John 2:17), reminiscent of Isaiah's statement about the day of the Lord: "The grass withers, the flower fades, but the word of our God stands forever" (Isa. 40:8; cf. Isa. 54:9-10). Peter also called this the day of judgment when God will bring perdition to the ungodly people of this age (2 Pet. 3:7).

Because the present world will be dissolved by fire, the apostle Peter warned Christians to conduct their lives in godliness, while anticipating and "hastening the coming of the day of God" (2 Pet. 3:11-12). The day of Jesus Christ cannot arrive before its divinely appointed time, yet because of our ignorance of the timing of its arrival, we hasten its arrival through our prayers and obedience. Similarly, the prophet Zephaniah counseled his contrite hearers to humbly seek the Lord and His righteousness, and held out the possibility that some people may be "hidden in the day of the Lord's anger" (Zeph. 2:3). Likewise, the apostle John encouraged the saints to do the will of God because the world and its desires are "passing away" (1 John 2:17). The writer to the Hebrews argues that the shaking of the heaven and the Earth will remove the realities of this fallen world:

But now He has promised, saying, "Yet once more I shake not only the earth, but also heaven." Now this, "Yet once more," indicates the removal of those things that are being shaken, as of things that are made, that the things which cannot be shaken may remain. Therefore, since we are receiving a kingdom which cannot be shaken, let us have grace, by which we may serve God acceptably with reverence and godly fear. For our God is a consuming fire. (Heb. 12:26-29)

This cosmic disturbance is much more than the wobbling of the Earth upon its axis and the trembling of the atmosphere. To elucidate this concept, the writer to the Hebrews expressed that the purpose of the shaking of our created universe will be to remove temporary realities in order to reveal the eternal verities—the kingdom of God (Heb. 12:27). Consistent with the theme of fiery cataclysm on the day of the Lord, the author included the phrase "for our God is a consuming fire" (Heb. 12:29; cf. Exod. 24:17; Deut. 4:24; 9:3; 32:21-22). As with Peter's prophecy, this passage also connects the destruction of the cosmos with the glorious revelation of the heavenly Jerusalem (Heb. 12:22, 27-28 and 2 Pet. 3:13); we will revisit this concept in chapter 18.

The apostle John explained that the unbelieving world, symbolized by the mysterious city Babylon, will be completely burned up at this time (Rev. 18:8-9, 18; cf. Rev. 14:8). These plagues will come upon the city "in one day" and "in one hour" (Rev. 18:8, 10, 19). John also connected the unprecedented earthquake with Babylon's desolation (Rev. 16:18-19). Isaiah too prophesied this city's everlasting destruction: "Its streams shall be turned into pitch and its dust into brimstone; its land shall become burning pitch. It shall not be quenched night or day; its smoke shall ascend forever. From generation to generation it shall lie waste; no one shall pass through it forever and ever" (Isa. 34:9-10; cf. Isa. 34:11ff; Rev. 14:8-11; 18).

The prophets attributed the impending judgments of the day of the Lord to the Almighty (Isa. 13:6; Joel 1:15), and these judgments will express His wrath and divine recompense for the evil deeds performed of mankind (Isa. 13:9, 11, 13; 34:8; Ezek. 38:19; Obad. 1:15; Nah. 1:6; Zeph. 1:15, 17-18; 2:2-3; Rev. 16:19). The Lord warned, "I will punish the world for its evil and the wicked for their iniquity; I will halt the arrogance of the proud, and will lay low the haughtiness of the terrible" (Isa. 13:11). Elsewhere, Isaiah wrote that the Earth will be destroyed "because they have transgressed the laws, changed the ordinance, broken the everlasting covenant" (Isa. 24:5; cf. Isa. 26:21). This divine vengeance is not arbitrary but is because the inhabitants of the Earth have violated the everlasting covenant, a likely reference to the promise given to the patriarchs and their seed regarding the land of Israel (Gen. 17:7-8; 1 Chron. 16:15-22; Ps. 105:8-15). As a result of these judgments, people will cry out and experience intense fear on that day (Isa. 13:6-8; Jer. 30:5; Ezek. 30:2; Joel 2:1; Zeph. 1:14, 17), and they will be gripped with pain like the labor pains of a pregnant woman (Isa. 13:7-8; Jer. 30:6; Mic. 5:3; 1 Thess. 5:2-3; cf. Matt. 24:8). The sounds of trumpet blasts and emergency alarms will be heard (Joel 2:1; Zeph. 1:14, 16).

Some Christians have proposed that the constellation of divine judgments on the day of the Lord could be the result of nuclear warfare instead of "natural disasters." I will avoid engaging in speculative theology at this point, except to briefly mention some merits of this interpretation. First, as we have seen, world war appears in the immediate context for the day of God, and the final cluster of judgments on this day will begin only once the armies of the world have assembled themselves for the battle of Armageddon. Second, the conditions of nuclear fallout are consistent with the prophetic depictions of fiery debris descending, "pillars of smoke" darkening the atmosphere, and the like. Third, Jesus taught that He will return to cut short the great tribulation, in order to prevent humanity from being completely destroyed ("no flesh would be saved" Matt. 24:22; Mark 13:20; cf. Rom. 9:28-29), and the Apocalypse promises that God will "destroy those who destroy the earth" (Rev. 11:18). While these verses are inconclusive regarding this consideration, they provide a plausible framework for the world's militaries nearing the precipice of eliminating life on the planet through the detonation of nuclear warheads, or by using a comparable military technology, at the very moment that Christ returns to save His creation.

At any rate, the judgments on the day of Jesus Christ will give way to God's eternal salvation of His people. The psalm of the sons of Korah highlights His deliverance on that day:

> God is our refuge and strength, a very present help in trouble. Therefore we will not fear, even though the earth be removed, and though the mountains be carried into the midst of the sea; though its waters roar and be troubled, though the mountains shake with its swelling. Selah . . . God shall help her [the city of God], just at the break of dawn. The nations raged, the kingdoms were moved; He uttered His voice, the earth melted . . . Come, behold the works of the Lord, who has made desolations in the earth. (Ps. 46:1-3, 5-6, 8; cf. 1 Kings 19:11-12; Ps. 18:9-10)

The psalm reveals that God will publicly display His wrath against the nations while faithfully delivering His saints. Because Christ is with us, even during unimaginable tribulation ("our refuge and strength, a very present help in trouble" Ps. 46:1) and in the day of His wrath, Christians should never fear ("Therefore we will not fear" Ps. 46:2). Because of this eternal verity, the psalmist summons us to "Come, behold the works of our Lord!" (Ps. 46:8).

11

DESTRUCTION OF THE ANTICHRIST

ON THE DAY OF JESUS CHRIST, the Lord will consummate His kingdom and put an abrupt end to war and conflicts throughout the world. The sons of Korah sang, "He makes wars cease to the end of the earth; He breaks the bow and cuts the spear in two; He burns the chariot in the fire" (Ps. 46:9; cf. Hosea 2:18). God promised to destroy chariots, horses, and battle bows (i.e., military transports and weaponry) in Jerusalem and throughout the nation of Israel when He establishes His reign of peace "from sea to sea, and from the River to the ends of the earth" (Zech. 9:10; cf. Ps. 72:8; Mic. 5:4).

The God of Israel promised to plunder the nations which plunder the Promised Land because those who molest the Jewish nation touch "the apple of His eye" (Zech. 2:1-9; cf. Deut. 32:10), the very nation that will join other nations to follow the Lord in that day (Zech. 2:10-13). This destruction will demonstrate His fiery wrath against these invaders and His jealousy for the nation (Ezek. 38:18-19; cf. Zeph.

3:8). God's anger will continue until the time of the end, when He will have "performed the intents of His heart" (Jer. 30:24), and He will stop bringing judgments against the Jewish nation when He casts out their final enemy (Zeph. 3:14-15).

As we have seen, the Antichrist will bring his multinational forces to invade the land of Israel at the time of the end (Ezek. 38:16, 18). However, God is opposed to this chief prince[1] over the nations, and ultimately He plans to bring him from the region of the far north to fall upon the "mountains of Israel"[2] so that He can violently disarm him there ("knock the bow out . . . and cause the arrows to fall out") and kill him and his troops on the open field (Ezek. 39:1-3, 5; cf. Isa. 14:25). The book of Daniel reveals that the Antichrist will "plant the tents of his palace between the seas and the glorious holy mountain; yet he shall come to his end, and no one will help him" (Dan. 11:45). The Lord will slay the Antichrist in order that that the nations will come to learn that He is the Holy One of Israel and so the people of Israel will know Him and never again profane His holy name (Ezek. 38:16, 23; 39:6-7). This will be no ordinary day but it will be the day frequently highlighted in the Holy Scriptures—the day of Jesus Christ ("This is the day of which I have spoken" Ezek. 39:8).

The Lord of armies will punish the invaders of Jerusalem with "thunder and earthquake and great noise, with storm and tempest and the flame of devouring fire" (Isa. 29:6). He will bring "flooding rain, great hailstones, fire, and brimstone" down upon the Antichrist's military (Ezek. 38:22; 39:6) at the time that the unprecedented earthquake shakes the land of Israel and crumbles the mountains and cities (Ezek. 38:19-20). As a result of the earthquake, the Antichrist's forces will experience confusion, resulting in large-scale friendly fire ("every man's sword will be against his brother" Ezek. 38:21; cf. Zeph. 2:22; Zech. 14:13). The prophet Zechariah provided more details about this event:

---

1   The prophet Daniel, a contemporary of Ezekiel, often used the title "prince" to refer to angels and demons (Dan. 10:13, 20-22; 12:1; cf. Dan. 8:11, 25; 9:25, 26).

2   A synecdoche for the larger nation.

"And it shall happen in that day that I will make Jerusalem a very heavy stone for all peoples; all who would heave it away will surely be cut in pieces, though all nations of the earth are gathered against it. In that day," says the Lord, "I will strike every horse with confusion, and its rider with madness; I will open My eyes on the house of Judah, and will strike every horse of the peoples with blindness." (Zech. 12:3-4)

As discussed previously in this book, it is unlikely that such passages indicate that the Middle East will return to horse warfare. Rather, the prophet Zechariah, like Ezekiel, employed the language of accommodation to express modern ideas. In other words, they presented truths by adopting the conventions of their particular culture and setting so that their immediate audience could understand. The meaning of Zechariah's prophecy is that the multinational invaders of Jerusalem will become greatly confused, and their weapons, which they had intended to use to annihilate the Jews, will malfunction. Isaiah explained that these oppressors will assemble for war but will ultimately fall and be condemned in judgment for the sake of Israel because "no weapon formed against you shall prosper, and every tongue which rises against you in judgment you shall condemn" (Isa. 54:15, 17; cf. Isa. 59:19).

As the Israelites fled from Pharaoh's armies by crossing through the Red Sea (Exod. 14), the surviving Jews in Jerusalem will flee from the Antichrist's forces by passing through the newly created mountain valley, which will have been formed by a mighty earthquake (Zech. 14:4-5). The earthquake in this verse may not be the unprecedented earthquake at the day of the Lord but may refer to the earthquake which will precede it at the second woe, in other words, at the sixth trumpet and after the rapture of the two prophets, which will cause a tenth of Jerusalem to collapse (Rev. 11:13). This final remnant of escaping Jews will flee through this valley and remain sovereignly protected until the glorious return of Jesus Christ:

> And the Mount of Olives shall be split in two, from east to west, making a very large valley; half of the mountain shall move toward the north and half of it toward the south. Then you shall flee through My mountain valley, for the mountain valley shall reach to Azal. Yes, you shall flee as you fled from the earthquake in the days of Uzziah king of Judah. Thus the Lord my God will come, and all the saints with You. (Zech. 14:4-5)

A few chapters later, Zechariah explained that the Lord Himself will "go forth and fight against those nations, as He fights in the day of battle" (Zech. 14:3; cf. Zech. 12:7-8). To terminate this final battle, Christ will return with His fiery, heavenly chariots to judge "all flesh" and to slaughter His enemies with the sword (Isa. 66:6, 15-16). The result will be that the multitude of nations which fights against Mount Zion will suddenly and instantly pass away like chaff (Isa. 29:5-8; cf. Ps. 1:4; Dan. 2:35). Consequently, they will wake up to the realization that their innermost cravings will not have been satisfied, despite their dreams that consuming Jerusalem would satiate their souls (Isa. 29:6-8). The Lord of hosts will be like a lion roaring over its prey when He "come[s] down to fight for Mount Zion and for its hill" (Isa. 31:4). When He defends Jerusalem, He will create a new Passover by "passing over" the remnant of Israel to deliver it from its enemies (Isa. 31:5). He will rescue the city "just at the break of dawn" (Ps. 46:4-5).

The prophets portrayed the Lord as a mighty warrior who will go forth with a shout to prevail against His enemies (Isa. 42:13; 1 Thess. 4:16). Isaiah depicted Him as garbed in a breastplate of righteousness, a helmet of salvation, garments of vengeance, and a cloak of zeal, and as returning to Jerusalem to bring justice to the earth and recompense to His enemies (Isa. 59:15-18; cf. Isa. 66:6; Eph. 6:10-17). Consistent with this theme, the Song of Moses reveals that God will take vengeance upon those who hate Him by killing them with His "glittering sword"; His intentions will be to avenge the blood of His servants, the martyrs (Deut. 32:40-43; cf. Ps. 45:3). Christ illustrated this in the parable of the wedding feast: "But when the king heard about it, he was furious. And he sent out his armies, destroyed those murderers, and burned up their city" (Matt. 22:7).

In the Apocalypse, the prophecy about the Lamb's wedding supper begins with the return of the divine Word of God:

> Now I saw heaven opened, and behold, a white horse. And He who sat on him was called Faithful and True, and in righteousness He judges and makes war. His eyes were like a flame of fire, and on His head were many crowns. He had a name written that no one knew except Himself. He was clothed with a robe dipped in blood, and His name is called The Word of God. And the armies in heaven, clothed in fine linen, white and clean, followed Him on white horses. Now out of His mouth goes a sharp sword, that with it He should strike the nations. And He Himself will rule them with a rod of iron. He Himself treads the winepress of the fierceness and wrath of Almighty God. And He has on His robe and on His thigh a name written: KING OF KINGS AND LORD OF LORDS. (Rev. 19:11-16)

Jesus Christ is portrayed here in His role as the victorious Warrior-King. Some people interpret this passage in an overly literal manner, arguing that He will sport an actual thigh tattoo while galloping out of heaven on a white horse. However, the symbolic imagery in the Apocalypse typically conveys a layer of meaning which transcends its imagery. Despite this interpretive difficulty, we clearly see the glorious return of Jesus, the faithful and true Logos, who will descend from heaven to judge men and to war against the Antichrist and his armies. The apostle emphasized Christ's resplendent glory ("eyes were like a flame of fire" Rev. 19:12; cf. Dan. 10:6; Rev. 1:14) and royal majesty ("many crowns" Rev. 19:12; cf. v. 16). The King of kings and Lord of lords (Rev. 19:16; cf. Dan. 2:37) is coming to take back what is rightfully His—the Earth.

Part of the prophetic background for this passage derives from the patriarch Jacob's blessing upon the tribe of Judah (Gen. 49:8-12). In the blessing, which is about "the latter days," he prophesied that Judah would act as a lion which had been roused from consuming prey (Gen. 49:1, 9). This motif provides the backdrop for Christ's title "the Lion of the tribe of Judah" (Rev. 5:5). In addition, Jacob's prophecy predicts that Judah, the royal tribe from which Jesus emerged, would wash "his garments in wine, and his clothes in the blood of grapes" (Gen. 49:11). He also revealed that the royal dynasty ("the scepter") would not depart from this tribe until the Messiah arrived as King (Gen. 49:10).

The apostle John also saw that Christ's robe will be dipped in blood (Rev. 19:13, 16), specifically, the blood of the wicked (Isa. 63:2-4; Rev. 19:17-21; cf. Rev. 14:20).[3] John also saw the heavenly armies comprised of holy angels,[4] and very probably the glorified saints (1 Thess. 3:13; 4:14 cf. Rev. 19:7-8) clothed in white linen, characteristic of priestly vestments, and following Him on white horses (Rev. 19:14). As we will see, these heavenly hosts will participate in the destruction of the wicked. Jesus will tread the winepress of God's fierce wrath so to speak, resulting in the blood of His enemies being pressed out under His feet like grapes in a winepress (Rev. 19:15; cf. Isa. 63:2-3; Rev. 14:20). In the Song of Moses, the Lord poetically declared, "I will make My arrows drunk with blood, and My sword shall devour flesh, with the blood of the slain" (Deut. 32:42).

Christ will strike the nations with His sharp, two-edged sword, which proceeds from His mouth, and He will rule these nations with an iron rod (Rev. 19:15; cf. Rev. 1:16). This verse is an allusion to two prophecies, one which shows that the Messiah will inherit the peoples of the world after breaking the nations into pieces like a rod of iron shatters pottery (Ps. 2:8-9; cf. Dan. 2:35, 44-45), and the other revealing that Christ will "strike the earth with the rod of His mouth" and slay the wicked one with "the breath of His lips" (Isa. 11:4 LXX; cf. Isa. 49:2).

---

3   The blood may be a double entendre also meant to remind us that Christ's own blood has purified His people (cf. Rev. 19:14).

4   Matt. 13:40-42; 16:27; 24:30-31; 25:31-32; Mark 8:38; Luke 9:26; 2 Thess. 1:7; Jude 14-15.

The wicked one here is the Man of Sin, whom Jesus will "consume with the breath of His mouth and destroy with the brightness of His coming" (2 Thess. 2:8). In other words, the Lord's powerful voice and blazing glory will instantaneously kill the Antichrist and his companions!

At this point, I will digress to provide some literary background. The motif of the Davidic Messiah slaying the Antichrist with the breath or rod of His mouth derives from the Assyrian prophecies of Isaiah (Isa. 7-14; cf. Mic. 5:5-6). As briefly mentioned in chapter 6, the Assyrian in those passages does not chiefly point to a historical king, such as Sennacherib, but ultimately to the final oppressor from this region: the Antichrist. The prophecies themselves envision Christ as killing this wicked king, thereby removing his dictatorial authority over Israel in order to usher in His own eternal kingdom (Isa. 11:4).

The Antichrist ("the Assyrian"), "the rod of My [God's] anger" (Isa. 10:5) will inflict wrath upon those living in Jerusalem ("He shall strike you with a rod and lift up his staff against you" Isa. 10:24), like Pharaoh did to the Israelites ("in the manner of Egypt" Isa. 10:24). However, after the great tribulation ("for yet a very little while" Isa. 10:25; cf. Rev. 6:11; 20:3), the Antichrist will cease his harsh treatment of the Jews because God will lift up His rod in the manner that His servant Moses lifted it up over the Red Sea (Isa. 10:26). At that time, the Messiah will slay the Antichrist: "He shall strike the earth with the rod of His mouth, and with the breath of His lips He shall slay the wicked [one][5]" (Isa. 11:4; cf. 2 Thess. 2:8; Rev. 2:16; 19:15, 21).

Continuing the motif of the Assyrian, the prophets predicted that God will forcefully remove the Antichrist's burdensome "yoke" from Israel's neck (Isa. 10:26-27; Jer. 30:8-9). For example, Isaiah wrote, "It shall come to pass in that day that his burden will be taken away from your shoulder and his yoke from your neck" (Isa. 10:27). One chapter

---

5   The Septuagint (LXX) and *Targum Jonathan* translate this as "the wicked one" and not as "the wicked" in a general sense. The Targum further identifies this wicked person as Gog—the Antichrist.

earlier, the prophet explained that God will establish Christ's everlasting kingdom ("the government will be upon His shoulder"; Isa. 9:1-3, 6-7) by breaking the Antichrist's yoke of burden and "the staff of his shoulder, the rod of his oppressor, as in the day of Midian" (Isa. 9:4; cf. Isa. 14:25).[6] In addition, Isaiah predicted that the Antichrist will be broken on the mountains of Israel (Isa. 14:25), a theme later picked up by Ezekiel (Ezek. 38:8; 39:2, 4, 17). The prophet borrowed these earlier themes to communicate that God will break the wicked king's yoke so that the Jewish people can serve their risen Messiah (Jer. 30:8-9).

As we return to John's wedding supper prophecy, we see that he continued by depicting the banquet guests and menu items:

> Then I saw an angel standing in the sun; and he cried with a loud voice, saying to all the birds that fly in the midst of heaven, "Come and gather together for the supper of the great God, that you may eat the flesh of kings, the flesh of captains, the flesh of mighty men, the flesh of horses and of those who sit on them, and the flesh of all people, free and slave, both small and great". . . And the rest were killed with the sword which proceeded from the mouth of Him who sat on the horse. And all the birds were filled with their flesh. (Rev. 19:17-18, 21)

The irony of this passage should not be overlooked. Whereas the wedding supper of the Lord will include a lavish feast of aged wines and choice meats with marrow for His people (Isa. 25:6), this prophecy portrays scavenger raptors as invited guests and the world leaders and their militaries as the menu items. Ezekiel's Gog and Magog prophecy provides some of the backdrop for this banquet imagery. In the prophecy, the Lord made this pronouncement to the Antichrist: "I will give you to birds of prey of every sort and to the beasts of the field to be devoured"

---

6   Gideon's slaughter of the two Midianite princes, Oreb and Zeeb (Judg. 7:25; 8:21), prophetically foreshadows Christ violently killing the Antichrist and his false prophet (cf. Ps. 83:11; Isa. 9:4; 10:26).

(Ezek. 39:4). At that time, the predatory beasts and birds will assemble together to fill themselves with the fat and blood of the corpses, like ancient worshippers partaking of the sacrificial offerings of livestock:

> "Speak to every sort of bird and to every beast of the field: 'Assemble yourselves and come; gather together from all sides to My sacrificial meal which I am sacrificing for you, a great sacrificial meal on the mountains of Israel, that you may eat flesh and drink blood. You shall eat the flesh of the mighty, drink the blood of the princes of the earth, of rams and lambs, of goats and bulls, all of them fatlings of Bashan. You shall eat fat till you are full, and drink blood till you are drunk at My sacrificial meal which I am sacrificing for you. You shall be filled at My table with horses and riders, with mighty men and with all the men of war,' " says the Lord God. (Ezek. 39:17-20)

Other prophets also framed the day of the Lord within a sacrificial context. Zephaniah marked, "The day of the Lord is at hand, for the Lord has prepared a sacrifice; He has invited His guests," and he added that this sacrifice will include the punishment of princes and violent men (Zeph. 1:7-9). Similarly, Isaiah prophesied that the Lord's sword will fall upon Edom, modern day Jordan, and the prophet likened the mangled bodies of those slaughtered to the blood and fat of sacrificial livestock (Isa. 34:5-7; cf. Zech. 9:15). In His wrath, God will hand the multinational forces over to slaughter (Isa. 34:2); the prophet expounded, "Their slain shall be thrown out; their stench shall rise from their corpses, and the mountains shall be melted with their blood. . . The sword of the Lord is filled with blood" (Isa. 34:3, 6). Those who will have oppressed Israel will consume their own flesh and become intoxicated by drinking their own blood so to speak, and everyone on earth will know that the Lord is the Savior and Redeemer of Israel and "the Mighty One of Jacob" (Isa. 49:25-26). The prophet later depicted the Second Coming by employing the metaphor of the nations becoming drunk by ingesting their own blood:

Who is this who comes from Edom, with dyed garments from Bozrah, this One who is glorious in His apparel, traveling in the greatness of His strength?—"I who speak in righteousness, mighty to save." Why is Your apparel red, and Your garments like one who treads in the winepress? "I have trodden the winepress alone, and from the peoples no one was with Me. For I have trodden them in My anger and trampled them in My fury; their blood is sprinkled upon My garments, and I have stained all My robes. For the day of vengeance is in My heart, and the year of My redeemed has come. I looked, but there was no one to help, and I wondered that there was no one to uphold; therefore, My own arm brought salvation for Me; and My own fury, it sustained Me. I have trodden down the peoples in My anger, made them drunk in My fury, and brought down their strength to the earth." (Isa. 63:1-6; cf. Isa. 59:15-18)

The imagery here portrays the returning Christ as wearing blood-splattered robes from the carnage of His enemies ("their blood is sprinkled upon My garments, and I have stained all My robes" Isa. 63:3; cf. Rev. 19:13, 16). Consequently, He will appear as a man wearing crimson-dyed garments from Bozrah, a city in Jordan, and the blood on His feet will have the characteristic appearance of one who has trampled the red grapes of a winepress. The prophet explained that the nations will not deliver Israel, so the Lord Himself will come down to save and redeem His nation ("I have trodden the winepress alone" Isa. 63:3; cf. Rev. 19:15). He alone suffered and spilled His blood at the cross for the forgiveness of sins, and He alone will deliver His people at His Second Advent ("no one was with Me" Isa. 63:3). While Jesus may be covered with His enemies' blood at His return, it may be unnecessary to press the details of this passage in such a literal fashion. Others have argued that this depiction is a mere metaphor for the fact that He will kill His enemies when He returns (cf. Matt. 22:2, 7-14).

At any rate, Isaiah calls the time of Christ's return "the day of vengeance . . . the year of My redeemed" (Isa. 63:4). This echoes his previous statements regarding "the day of the Lord's vengeance, the year of recompense for the cause of Zion," which he later terms "the day of vengeance of our God" upon which He will "console those who mourn in Zion" (Isa. 34:8; 61:2, 3; cf. Jer. 51:6). The Lord will return to Jerusalem to save Israel and to punish those who have injured His people (Isa. 35:4; cf. Isa. 63:3, 6). In Luke's version of the Olivet Discourse, Jesus called the great tribulation, which will culminate in the day of His wrath, "the days of vengeance," during which "all things which are written [in the Scriptures] may be fulfilled" (Luke 21:22).

Zechariah provided a terrifying description of the destruction of the multinational military which will fight against Jerusalem:

> And this shall be the plague with which the Lord will strike all the people who fought against Jerusalem: Their flesh shall dissolve while they stand on their feet, their eyes shall dissolve in their sockets, and their tongues shall dissolve in their mouths. It shall come to pass in that day that a great panic from the Lord will be among them. Everyone will seize the hand of his neighbor and raise his hand against his neighbor's hand . . . Such also shall be the plague on the horse and the mule, on the camel and the donkey, and on all the cattle that will be in those camps. So shall this plague be. (Zech. 14:12-13, 15)

The prophet and his contemporaries would have easily recognized that no contemporary, manmade weapon could cause such devastation. However, many prophecy teachers have noted that nuclear technology is more than capable of causing instantaneous vaporization, such as the conditions which Zechariah described ("Their flesh shall dissolve while they stand on their feet, their eyes shall dissolve in their sockets, and their tongues shall dissolve in their mouths" Zech. 14:12). Alternatively, Christ's own glory will result in their destruction (cf. 2 Thess. 1:6-10). As we saw previously, the utter destruction of Jerusalem's invaders will follow on the heels of the friendly fire amongst those who have assembled to destroy the city ("a great panic from the Lord will be among them. Everyone will seize the hand of his neighbor and raise his hand against his neighbor's hand" Zech. 14:13). This event will also destroy all the vehicles and mobilized units ("the horse and the mule, on the camel and the donkey, and on all the cattle" Zech. 14:15). These verses appear to support the view that this destruction will be the result of nuclear exchange between enemies. Regardless of the secondary cause of this plague, it will ultimately come "from the Lord" (Zech. 14:13).

By such means, God will completely destroy all the nations where the Jews have been scattered (Jer. 30:11; 46:28). To illustrate, the Lord will destroy the territory of Jordan so that it becomes "like Gomorrah— overrun with weeds and saltpits, and a perpetual desolation," and He will make the land of Iraq utterly desolate (Zeph. 2:9, 13-15). The prophet Balaam prophesied that the Star from Jacob, that is, Israel's Messiah, will destroy the wicked people of Moab, Edom, and Seir (i.e., modern Jordan) "in the latter days" (Num. 24:14, 17-19). In addition, many wicked Ethiopians will be slain by the sword of the Lord (Zeph. 2:12). Furthermore, God will send "saviors," a probable reference to the holy angels and glorified saints, to descend from Mount Zion in order to accomplish this destruction (Obad. 1:21).

Following the battle of Armageddon, the soiled uniforms of the soldiers will be utilized as combustible fuel (Isa. 9:5). Ezekiel expanded on this concept in his prophecy about the defeat of Gog and his armies: "Then those who dwell in the cities of Israel will go out and set on fire and burn the weapons, both the shields and bucklers, the bows and arrows, the javelins and spears; and they will make fires with them for seven years . . . They will make fires with the weapons" (Ezek. 39:9, 10). In other words, the primary energy source for the people living in Israel will come from their enemies, likely, their nuclear energy and the fossil fuels which they once manufactured for mechanized weaponry. This will sufficiently meet the energy demands of the nation for seven years beyond the day of Christ!

Reminiscent of how the Israelites plundered Egypt during the first exodus (Exod. 12:36), the surviving Jews will plunder the goods of those who had invaded their land during the final battle (Isa. 9:3; Ezek. 39:10). Some plunder will be taken from the residents of the Gaza Strip and Jordan, and their neighbors will once again submit to Israel (Isa. 11:14; cf. Zeph. 2:4-5, 9). Zechariah explained, "And the wealth of all the surrounding nations shall be gathered together: Gold, silver, and apparel in great abundance" (Zech. 14:14). In addition, Israel will take these people as prisoners of war (Jer. 30:16; Zeph. 3:8; Zech. 2:8), and the surviving invaders will become Israel's servants and maids (Isa. 14:2; Zeph. 2:9). Also, some of the enemies of the Jews will become incarcerated workers in Yemen (Joel 3:8).

During the Antichrist's systematic persecution of Jews and Christians, the enemy nations will incarcerate many of them, likely detaining them in prisons, work and refugee camps, and concentration camps. Nevertheless, as with the Christians, the Lord promised to deliver the surviving Jews from these places of internment "because of the blood of your covenant" (Zech. 9:11). In other words, He will spare those who will survive the tribulation so that they receive the benefits of Christ's sacrificial death on the cross. Consequently, He will release these prisoners when He appears in glory (Zech. 9:11-14) so that those sitting in darkness will see a great Light—the returning Christ (Isa. 9:2; 42:7; cf. Matt. 4:16)! He will then give these "prisoners of hope" twofold as many blessings compared to the difficulties they experienced through persecution (Zech. 9:12; cf. Job 42:10).

Several prophecies depict the surviving Jews waging a successful battle against their enemies on the day of the Lord. For example, the Lord announced through the prophet Malachi, "You shall trample the wicked, for they shall be ashes under the soles of your feet on the day that I do this" (Mal. 4:3). Another example is Isaiah's prophecy that the people of Jerusalem will trample upon their enemies, including those in the Gaza Strip and Jordan, as straw is trampled upon and thrown into a trash dump (Isa. 25:10; Zeph. 2:4-5), and they will "thresh" these people like sheaves upon a threshing floor (Mic. 4:13). Similarly, the survivors in Jerusalem and Israel will fight valiantly against their enemies, including against the wicked men from the region of modern Turkey (Zech. 9:13, 15; 10:3).

The returning Lord will defend and empower them so that they can defeat their enemies: "Then the Lord will be seen over them, and His arrow will go forth like lightning. The Lord God will blow the trumpet, and go with whirlwinds from the south. The Lord of hosts will defend them" (Zech. 9:14-15; cf. Zech. 10:3-5). As a result, these valiant soldiers will "tread down their enemies in the mire of the streets in the battle. They shall fight because the Lord is with them" (Zech. 10:5; cf. Zech. 14:14). Zechariah revealed that the captains of the forces of southern Israel will become like a fiery torch that ignites sheaves which will "devour all the surrounding peoples on the right hand and on the left" (Zech. 12:6). The prophet described how the soldiers will defeat their enemies:

> The Lord will save the tents of Judah first, so that the glory of the house of David and the glory of the inhabitants of Jerusalem shall not become greater than that of Judah. In that day the Lord will defend the inhabitants of Jerusalem; the one who is feeble among them in that day shall be like David, and the house of David shall be like God, like the Angel of the Lord before them. It shall be in that day that I will seek to destroy all the nations that come against Jerusalem. (Zech. 12:7-9)

The Lord will defend and save the remnant of the Jewish nation. The weakest of the soldiers will be transformed into a strong warrior, like King David, and the house of David, that is, Christ and His heavenly armies, will personally lead the charge ("like God, like the Angel of the Lord before them" Zech. 12:8). This verse may be echoed in Jesus' statement that in the resurrection, the righteous will be "like angels of God" (Matt. 22:30; cf. Mark 12:25; Luke 20:35). One interpretive difficulty is whether to interpret the victorious soldiers in all the above passages as the surviving remnant of Jews who will come to saving faith when they look upon the returning Christ (see chapter 14) or as the resurrected saints who will descend with Christ in glory (cf. 1 Thess. 3:13; 4:14; Rev. 19:7-8, 14), or both. In addition, it is uncertain whether Israel's defeated enemies, including the recently captured prisoners of war, refer to the wicked being captured so that they can be thrown into hellfire.

At any rate, the apostle John continued his prophecy by describing the eternal destruction of the Antichrist:

> And I saw the beast, the kings of the earth, and their armies, gathered together to make war against Him who sat on the horse and against His army. Then the beast was captured, and with him the false prophet who worked signs in his presence, by which he deceived those who received the mark of the beast and those who worshiped his image. These two were cast alive into the lake of fire burning with brimstone. (Rev. 19:19-20)

The idea here is not that the Antichrist will literally turn military weapons against the returning Christ and His heavenly army. Rather, the war against Jesus Christ is the Antichrist's subjugation of the nations and the international leaders' attempt to overthrow his yoke because God has ordained that Christ alone will defeat the Antichrist and his kings. Christ will slay the Antichrist and his ten kings (Rev. 19:15, 18-21), reminiscent of the execution of Haman and his ten sons (Esther 9:14). In addition to killing these ten kings, the Lord Jesus will likely slay other wicked rulers, as King David explained, "The Lord is at Your right hand; He shall execute kings in the day of His wrath. He shall judge among the nations, He shall fill the places with dead bodies, He shall execute the heads of many countries" (Ps. 110:5-6). Similarly, the prophet Haggai declared that God will topple "the thrones" of nations when He shakes heaven and Earth (Hag. 2:21-22).

When Christ descends from heaven, the unholy trinity—Satan, the Antichrist, and the false prophet—will be thrown "alive" into the lake of hellfire and brimstone (Rev. 19:20; 20:10; cf. Num. 16:33; Isa. 14:9-11,

15). This lake of fire (i.e., hell) will be set ablaze by a fiery stream of brimstone which will proceed from the Lord's mouth, that is, from His word of command (Isa. 30:33 with Dan. 7:9-11). Isaiah described the dead leaders of the nations and the other inhabitants of hell as greeting the Antichrist when he arrives there (Isa. 14:9). Those who see the Antichrist will marvel at his humiliated state: "Is this the man who made the earth tremble, who shook kingdoms, who made the world as a wilderness and destroyed its cities, who did not open the house of his prisoners?" (Isa. 14:16-17). The Antichrist and his false prophet will not be resurrected again but will be eternally punished and destroyed, and they will eventually be forgotten by God's people (Isa. 26:13-14).

The Antichrist's death will bring with it the destruction of his worldwide kingdom, which kingdom is symbolized by the sea Beast with seven heads and ten horns (cf. Rev. 13:1-8; 17:3, 7-14), known since ancient times by the name Leviathan. Isaiah remarked, "In that day the Lord with His severe sword, great and strong, will punish Leviathan the fleeing serpent, Leviathan that twisted serpent; and He will slay the reptile that is in the sea" (Isa. 27:1; cf. Isa. 51:9; Job. 26:13). To summarize, when Christ returns to destroy the serpent's individual seed, the Antichrist (cf. Gen. 3:15), He will effectively put an end to the serpent's worldwide kingdom (Rev. 19:15, 19-21).[7] This is consistent with the prophetic declaration that Israel's Messiah "shall be higher than Gog, and His kingdom shall be exalted" (Num. 24:7 LXX).[8] As such, the eschatological victory belongs to Jesus!

A few passages communicate that the Antichrist's corpse will experience corruption and decay. For example, Isaiah predicted that his corpse

---

[7] The death of the Philistine at the hands of King David also prefigured the Antichrist's death by Jesus, the Son of David. As David slung a stone from his slingshot which crushed Goliath's forehead, and he subsequently completely severed the giant's head with a sword (1 Sam. 17:49-51), Christ will do the same to the Antichrist.

[8] Whereas most English translations of this verse read Agag (cf. 1 Sam. 15:33), the Greek Septuagint renders it Gog, the title for the Antichrist picked up by Ezekiel in his prophecy of Gog and Magog (Ezek. 38:2-3; 14, 16, 18, 21; 39:1, 11, 15; cf. Rev. 20:8).

will be tossed out of his grave to be trodden underfoot (Isa. 14:19; cf. Ezek. 28:6-8), and he prophesied, "The maggot is spread under you [the king of Babylon], and worms cover you" (Isa. 14:11). Likewise, God promised Israel that He would "remove far from you the northern army and will drive him away into a barren and desolate land, with his face toward the eastern sea and his back toward the western sea; his stench will come up, and his foul odor will rise, because he has done monstrous things" (Joel 2:20). This verse could refer to the Antichrist's army ("the northern army"), which will be slaughtered in the land of Israel, but the Hebrew text more closely reads "the northern [one]," which may indicate that the Antichrist will also experience death and corruption. At any rate, Ezekiel unequivocally described the burial of the Antichrist and his international forces:

> "It will come to pass in that day that I will give Gog a burial place there in Israel, the valley of those who pass by east of the sea; and it will obstruct travelers, because there they will bury Gog and all his multitude. Therefore, they will call it the Valley of Hamon Gog. For seven months the house of Israel will be burying them, in order to cleanse the land. Indeed all the people of the land will be burying, and they will gain renown for it on the day that I am glorified," says the Lord God. "They will set apart men regularly employed, with the help of a search party, to pass through the land and bury those bodies remaining on the ground, in order to cleanse it. At the end of seven months, they will make a search. The search party will pass through the land; and when anyone sees a man's bone, he shall set up a marker by it, till the buriers have buried it in the Valley of Hamon Gog. The name of the city will also be Hamonah. Thus, they shall cleanse the land." (Ezek. 39:11-16)

This prophecy communicates that Gog (i.e., the Antichrist) and his forces will be buried in the valley near the Sea of Galilee ("in Israel, the valley of those who pass by east of the sea" Ezek. 39:11), more specifically, in a city called Hamonah, in the Valley of Hamon Gog, meaning "the tumultuous multitude of Gog" (Ezek. 39:11, 15-16). The nation of Israel will finish burying the large quantity of corpses only after seven months, and this burial process will obstruct travelers from passing through the region (Ezek. 39:11-12).[9] Afterward, the nation will appoint a special task force, likely a company of angels, to meticulously search the land for any remaining corpses (Ezek. 39:14). Any remaining bones will receive a specific marker to ensure that they receive burial in the designated valley; this is intended to safeguard the purity of the land of Israel (Ezek. 39:16).

Similar to Ezekiel's prophecy about the corpses of the wicked, a prophecy of Isaiah elucidates the fate of the unrighteous dead. In this prophecy, the corpses of those slain by the returning Lord refer to their resurrected bodies, which will experience eternal destruction in hell. Isaiah explained that the worshippers from the nations will "go forth and look upon the corpses of the men who have transgressed against Me. For their worm does not die, and their fire is not quenched. They shall be an abhorrence to all flesh" (Isa. 66:24; cf. Isa. 14:11). Christ confirmed this passage as a resurrection prophecy by quoting Isaiah's phrase ("their worm does not die, and their fire is not quenched") with reference to the wicked receiving the recompense of eternal hellfire (Mark 9:44, 46, 48).[10] It is uncertain how the wicked dead will experience eternal, conscious torment while their corpses undergo eternal corruption, but it may suffice to simply recognize that their resurrection will be categorically dissimilar from the glorious resurrection of the righteous.

---

9   We will see in chapter 17 that hell will be outside the walls of the new Jerusalem.

10   The Valley of Hinnom (Greek: *Gehenna*), and the more specific location Tophet, were locations outside of Jerusalem's walls which came to exemplify what became known as hell.

12

THE UNKNOWN DAY AND HOUR

A COMMON MANTRA in the Prophets is that the day of the Lord is coming "near," "quickly," and "at hand." The immediate context of these statements includes robust warnings about God's proximate judgments upon the wicked:

> For the day of the Lord is at hand! . . . Behold, the day of the Lord comes. (Isa. 13:6, 9)

> For the day is near, even the day of the Lord is near. (Ezek. 30:3)

> For the day of the Lord is at hand. (Joel 1:15)

> For the day of the Lord is coming, for it is at hand. (Joel 2:1)

> For the day of the Lord upon all the nations is near. (Obad. 1:15)

For the day of the Lord is at hand. (Zeph. 1:7)

The great day of the Lord is near; it is near and hastens quickly. (Zeph. 1:14)

Behold, the day of the Lord is coming. (Zech. 14:1)

For behold, the day is coming. (Mal. 4:1)

With each of these statements, the individual prophet presented the future day of the Lord as impinging or pressing into his contemporary setting. Yahweh threatened to arrive as Judge and to interject His judgments into those settings, often accompanied with cataclysms and terror. As mentioned in chapter 10, the first installment of His divine wrath took place in antiquity but this wrath will be recapitulated through exhaustive fulfillment at the day of Jesus Christ. Those who reject the message of the prophets will be unprepared because humanity, whether living in antiquity or the future, needs repentance, and judgment day will ultimately come upon all the unprepared wicked. While "it is appointed for men to die once, but after this the judgment" (Heb. 9:27), the unrepentant wicked will die in their sins, not knowing when their life on this earth will be completed (Luke 12:16-20; James 4:14).

Similarly, the holy apostles and their contemporaries conveyed the concept of the nearness of Christ's return from heaven at the day of Jesus Christ. For example, the apostle Paul reminded, "Let your gentleness be known to all men. The Lord is at hand" (Phil. 4:5). Likewise, James wrote, "Therefore be patient, brethren, until the coming of the Lord. . . You also be patient. Establish your hearts, for the coming of the Lord is at hand. . . Behold, the Judge is standing at the door!" (James 5:7-8, 9). On the basis of such passages, we can correctly conclude that any interpreter who separates the day of the Lord (in the Old Testament) from the day of Jesus Christ (in the New Testament) manifests a studied interest in abrogating the clear teaching of Scripture in order to maintain his strongly held presuppositions.

The book of Revelation relays a similar nearness for the day of Jesus Christ. Consider the seven time statements contained in the prologue and epilogue for the book:

The Revelation of Jesus Christ, which God gave Him to show His servants—things which must shortly take place . . . Blessed is he who reads and those who hear the words of this prophecy, and keep those things which are written in it; for the time is near. (Rev. 1:1, 3)

And the Lord God of the holy prophets sent His angel to show His servants the things which must shortly take place. "Behold, I am coming quickly! Blessed is he who keeps the words of the prophecy of this book." (Rev. 22:6-7)

"Do not seal the words of the prophecy of this book, for the time is at hand . . . and behold, I am coming quickly, and My reward is with Me, to give to every one according to his work." (Rev. 22:10, 12)

He who testifies to these things says, "Surely I am coming quickly." Amen. Even so, come, Lord Jesus! (Rev. 22:20)

The Greek word groups translated "shortly" and "quickly" typically convey the idea of temporal nearness, so the meaning of these verses are that the prophetic events depicted throughout the Apocalypse will take place in the near future. The words themselves do not mean that these events will occur in quick succession only once they have begun, although this concept can also be derived from the details of the book. While the concept of nearness in the New Testament has puzzled many interpreters, specifically because the Lord has not returned within the subsequent centuries since it was written, this concept is consistent with the overall pattern of how the Hebrew prophets spoke about the day of the Lord.

As we would expect, the context of such statements emphasizes the need for expectancy and preparation for the day of Jesus Christ. The apostle John reminded his Christian audience to spiritually prepare for it by reading, hearing, and obeying his prophecy ("Blessed is he who reads and those who hear the words of this prophecy, and keep those things which are written in it" Rev. 1:3; cf. Rev. 22:7), and the reason he gave for this is the proximity of the eschatological events depicted in the book, including Christ's return ("for the time is near" Rev. 1:3; cf. Hab. 2:2-3 with Heb. 10:37; Rev. 22:6-7). In the immediate context, the apostle warned that the person who refuses to repent in the present, risks remaining in his unjust and filthy condition when Jesus returns to reward every person according to his deeds ("He who is unjust, let him be unjust still; he who is filthy, let him be filthy still" Rev. 22:11-12). Nevertheless, the revelation of Jesus Christ, which He has revealed throughout the Apocalypse, helps prepare the holy Church for His return.

The resurrected Jesus reiterated these warnings in His statements to the churches of Asia Minor. To the church of Ephesus, He stated, "Repent and do the first works, or else I will come to you quickly and remove your lampstand from its place—unless you repent" (Rev. 2:5). Likewise, He warned the Christians at Pergamos, saying, "Repent or else I will come to you quickly and will fight against them with the sword of My mouth" (Rev. 2:16; cf. Rev. 19:15, 21). Finally, He encouraged the saints at Philadelphia with His pronouncement "Behold, I am coming quickly! Hold fast what you have, that no one may take your crown" (Rev. 3:11). As we have seen, such verses do not teach that Christ could arrive at any moment! Rather, they function as warnings to repent and live godly lives now and so avoid the catastrophic judgments at His return. He taught His disciples to watch and prepare for His return, regardless of when He arrives ("in the evening, at midnight, at the crowing of the rooster, or in the morning" Mark 13:35), "lest, coming suddenly, he find you sleeping" (Mark 13:36).

The Scriptures do not teach the doctrine of imminence, as taught within Protestant dispensationalism. This is the teaching that Christ can return at any moment and without preliminary signs. The apostles did not expect that He could return at any moment, as indicated by their expectations of specific, preceding events, such as the worldwide preaching of the gospel (Matt. 24:14), the end-time ministry of Elijah (Mal. 3:1; 4:5), the revelation of the Antichrist in the Jerusalem temple (Matt. 24:15ff; 2 Thess. 2:1-5), and the cosmic disturbances of the day of the Lord (see chapter 10), all which must precede Christ's return. Furthermore, the apostles Paul and Peter anticipated their own deaths (2 Tim. 4:6-8; 2 Pet. 1:13-14), and Jesus specified that Peter would die a martyr's death (John 21:18-19). Clearly then, the earliest Christians did not expect that the Lord could potentially return at any moment, as we are led to believe by dispensationalists. As we will see, Jesus and His apostles taught the unknowability of the precise timing of His return ("that day or hour" Matt. 24:36; Mark 13:32).

The Gospel of John anticipated that Christ would not return within the apostle John's lifetime, as evident in the following conversation: "Jesus said to him [the apostle Peter], 'If I will that he [the apostle John] remain till I come, what is that to you? You follow Me.' Then this saying went out among the brethren that this disciple [John] would not die. Yet Jesus did not say to him that he would not die, but, 'If I will that he remain till I come, what is that to you?' (John 21:22-23). Saint John, and the Holy Spirit who inspired him, found it necessary to include this conversation, presumably so that Christians would not expect the Lord to return within the lifetime of John, the last of the twelve apostles to die.

Jesus also discussed the timing of His return in a series of parables found in the Olivet Discourse (Matt. 24:32-25:13; Mark 13:28-37; Luke 21:29-33). The first is the parable of the budding fig tree (Matt. 24:32-35; Mark 13:28-31; Luke 21:29-33). Matthew's version of the parable reads as follows:

Now learn this parable from the fig tree: When its branch has already become tender and puts forth leaves, you know that summer is near. So you also, when you see all these things, know that it is near—at the doors! Assuredly, I say to you, this generation will by no means pass away till all these things take place. (Matt. 24:32-34; cf. Mark 13:28-30)

There is insufficient reason to conjecture that the budding of the fig tree symbolizes a specific prophetic event, such as the creation of the State of Israel. Furthermore, Luke included the phrase "and all the trees" ("Look at the fig tree, and all the trees" Luke 21:29), which further lends credence to the traditional interpretation, namely, that the parable should be understood in a straightforward manner, as a common agricultural metaphor illustrating a basic concept about the nearness of Christ's return.

The parable communicates that the arrival of specific prophetic events ("when you see all these things" Matt. 24:33; Mark 13:29; cf. Luke 21:31) will signal the imminent arrival of Jesus Christ (Matt. 24:30; Mark 13:26; cf. Luke 21:27), like the budding leaves of the fig trees signal the nearness of summer. Once we have seen all these prophetic events, specifically, the abomination of desolation at the Jerusalem temple and the subsequent unprecedented tribulation (Matt. 24:15-15-28; Mark 13:14-23; Luke 21:20-24), followed by the cosmic darkness and disturbances (Matt. 24:29; Mark 13:24; cf. Luke 21:25), we can know that Christ's return is chronologically imminent ("it [He] is near—at the doors!"[1] Matt. 24:33; Mark 13:29). Luke's substitution of the phrase "the kingdom of God is near" reveals that Christ will consummate His kingdom when He returns (Luke 21:31; cf. Matt. 16:28; 2 Tim. 4:1; Rev. 11:15).

Immediately prior to the parable, Luke included a statement that indicates that the beginning of these prophetic events will signify the nearness of Christ's return: "Now when these things begin to happen, look up and lift up your heads, because your redemption draws near" (Luke 21:28). The phrase "look up and lift up your heads" means that once Christians begin to witness these prophetic events, we should expect the Lord's return from heaven in the very near future. The

---

[1] The language here is similar to James' statement "Behold, the Judge is standing at the door!" (James 5:9). However, James employed the language in a slightly different manner. His phrase does not indicate a chronological but an *existential* nearness ("the coming of the Lord is at hand" James 5:8).

"redemption" here is the return of Jesus; He will give faithful Christians the heavenly possession which He purchased by His death on the cross (Eph. 1:14). In other words, He will glorify our bodies in His presence and provide us entrance into His kingdom, as the holy prophets foretold.

Much scholarly discussion has focused upon Christ's phrase in the Olivet Discourse that "this generation will by no means pass away till all these things take place" (Matt. 24:34; Mark 13:30; Luke 21:32; cf. Matt. 23:36). A study of the phrase "this generation"[2] in the Synoptic Gospels reveals that it includes the contemporaries of Jesus but is not restricted to them.[3] The phrase is a technical term which carries a qualitative meaning, and it refers to wicked offspring or children. It typically does not carry a temporal nuance, and as such, it does not refer to a group of people living within a specific timeframe, much less to a narrow period of time. The Lord's phrase means that the wicked will continue to exist and so persecute His disciples (cf. Matt. 24:4-13, 15-26) until His glorious return. Because of the tedious points of this discussion, I included an academic defense of this interpretation as an appendix to this book.

The Lord repeated the phrase "all these things" in the subsequent verse (Matt. 24:34; Mark 13:30), reminding His hearers that all the prophetic events of the preceding verses must take place before His return. Based on grammatical considerations, the phrase "all these things" could exclude His glorious return; however, this is a moot point since the phrase necessarily includes the events of the unprecedented tribulation (Matt. 24:15-24) *and* the cosmic darkness which will signal His immediate return (Matt. 24:29).

We can recognize the arrival of specific signs that will precede the day of Christ. Because these signs enable us to "see the day approaching" in a progressive fashion, the writer of Hebrews could remind Christians not to forsake "the assembling of ourselves together, as is the manner

---

2   ἡ γενεὰ αὕτη

3   Matt. 12:39; 17:17; Mark 8:38; Luke 9:41; 11:29; cf. Acts 2:40; Phil. 2:15.

of some, but exhorting one another, and so much the more as you see the day approaching" (Heb. 10:25). As frightening occurrences and devastations increase upon the Earth, many people will choose isolation. In addition, it will also be illegal for Christians to meet together during the reign of the Antichrist. However, this verse reminds us of the increasing importance of frequent Christian fellowship and mutual exhortation within the context of local parishes. At some point during the great tribulation, this may require meeting in underground house churches. Nevertheless, we must continue meeting with one another for the purposes of fellowship, apostolic teaching, the sacraments, and prayer (cf. Acts 2:42). We will need each other in the coming days!

Jesus also spoke about the need for spiritual preparation and continued prayer as the day approaches:

> But take heed to yourselves, lest your hearts be weighed down with carousing, drunkenness, and cares of this life, and that day come on you unexpectedly. For it will come as a snare on all those who dwell on the face of the whole earth. Watch therefore, and pray always that you may be counted worthy to escape all these things that will come to pass, and to stand before the Son of Man. (Luke 21:34-36)

When we see terrifying signs in heaven and earth, the natural default for people will be to resort to using mind-altering substances, especially alcohol ("drunkenness"; cf. "all tables are full of vomit and filth" Isa. 28:8), and to engage in other activities which temporarily dull fears and diminish emotional and physical discomfort. However, Jesus reminded us to pay close attention to the condition of our hearts so that we do not burden ourselves with such activities. Rather, we must intentionally prepare and eagerly await the day of His return; otherwise, it will become a trap and snare that brings judgment, as it will be to most people on the planet ("all those who dwell on the face of the whole earth" Luke 21:35). We must not only watch but also "pray always" (Luke 21:36; cf. Mark 13:33; "pray without ceasing" in 1 Thess. 5:17) so that we may be worthy to escape the coming desolations and to stand victoriously before Christ when He returns (Mal. 3:2; Luke 21:36; Eph. 6:13; Rev. 6:17). The apostle Paul summarized, "Therefore, take up the whole armor of God that you may be able to withstand in the evil day, and having done all, to stand" (Eph. 6:13).

In the Olivet Discourse, Christ taught that the exact timing of His return is unknowable to everyone. During the self-emptying of His earthly sojourn, He chose not to display His divine knowledge of many future events (while retaining His divine omniscience), including the timing of His return (Mark 13:32). This does not mean that He did not avail Himself of a general understanding of the eschatological timeline, only that He, like all men and angels, did not know the exactness of the timing:

> But of that day and hour no one knows, not even the angels of heaven, but My Father only. But as the days of Noah were, so also will the coming of the Son of Man be. For as in the days before the flood, they were eating and drinking, marrying and giving in marriage, until the day that Noah entered the ark, and did not know until the flood came and took them all away, so also will the coming of the Son of Man be. . . Watch therefore, for you do not know what hour your Lord is coming. But know this, that if the master of the house had known what hour the thief would come, he would have watched and not allowed his house to be broken into. Therefore you also be ready, for the Son of Man is coming at an hour you do not expect. (Matt. 24:36-39; 42-44; cf. Luke 12:39-40)

The context demonstrates that Jesus' statement about timing is intended to provoke preparedness ("you also be ready" Matt. 24:44). As the world of Noah's day was engaged in everyday activities ("eating and drinking, marrying and giving in marriage" Matt. 24:38; cf. Luke 17:27), unaware of the coming flood ("did not know" Matt. 24:39), even until the day that he entered the ark for safety, people at the time of the end will also continue with their daily routines, not expecting the coming judgment at His return (Matt. 24:38-39; Luke 17:26-30; cf. 2 Pet. 2:5, 9). This does not imply that the world will be living peacefully when the Lord returns or that there will be no signs or prophetic witnesses during the great tribulation. Instead, many people at that time will not heed the warnings of Christ until it is too late. For this reason, we should always eagerly await and watch for His return, as people who do not know when He will arrive but certainly know that He will come (Matt. 24:42).

In Luke's parallel account, Christ included a second illustration, specifically, the salvation of Lot and the fiery destruction of the city of Sodom: "They [the people of Sodom] ate, they drank, they bought, they sold, they planted, they built; but on the day that Lot went out of Sodom it rained fire and brimstone from heaven and destroyed them all" (Luke 17:28-29). As Lot's wife looked back with the intention of returning to her old life in Sodom, and died as a result, those living at the end of the age (like people at all times) must lay down their lives in order to lay hold of eternal life. Those who seek to preserve their lives, symbolized by Lot's wife hesitating to maintain her belongings, will receive death and destruction on the day of Jesus Christ (Luke 17:31-33; cf. 2 Pet. 2:5-9; Jude 1:6-7). It should be noted that in Matthew's version of the Olivet Discourse, Jesus used similar language but in a slightly different manner (Matt. 24:17-18).[4]

The Master taught that we do not know the timing of His coming but we should always be prepared for it. He provided the illustration of a homeowner who knew the exact hour that a thief or burglar would arrive at his house, so he was able to prevent him from entering (Matt. 24:43; Luke 12:39). Similarly, faithful disciples should always watch and patiently wait for His return so that regardless of when He comes, we always remain ready (Matt. 24:44).

Picking up this theme, the apostle Paul reminded the Thessalonians that they needed no further instruction about "the times and seasons" (1

---

[4]   The context of Matthew's verse describes the flight of the Jews from Jerusalem at the time the Antichrist sets up his abomination (Matt. 24:15-22).

Thess. 5:1; cf. Dan. 2:21; Matt. 24:36; Acts 1:7) because they perfectly knew that the day of the Lord will come "as a thief in the night" (1 Thess. 5:2; cf. Luke 21:34). The wicked world will not escape destruction on that day because it will overtake them with "sudden destruction . . . as labor pains upon a pregnant woman" (1 Thess. 5:3; cf. Isa. 13:6-9). On the other hand, Christians are not in a state of spiritual darkness that they should be overtaken "as a thief" (1 Thess. 5:4). The Lord has appointed us to receive salvation, not wrath, at the day of Jesus Christ (1 Thess. 5:9).

Therefore, Paul called Christians to awaken from any remaining spiritual slumber (Rom. 13:11; "let us not sleep, as others do, but let us watch and be sober" 1 Thess. 5:6; cf. Mark 13:36; Luke 12:45). The reason is because the day of the Lord is "at hand" and our salvation is much closer now than when we first became believers in Christ Jesus (Rom. 13:11-12). Therefore, we must put away the deeds typically done in the darkness of night, such as drunkenness, sexual immorality, arguments, and jealousy (Rom. 13:13; 1 Thess. 5:7). We should remove evil deeds like one removes sleepwear and put on Jesus Christ as one who dresses himself for daytime (Rom. 13:14; 1 Thess. 5:8); this reflects the truth that Christians are children of spiritual "light" whose manner of living is consistent with the day (1 Thess. 5:5).

Because the return of Jesus will come "as a thief" to those living in spiritual darkness, the risen Jesus warned the churches of Asia Minor, and by extension all Christian churches (Mark 13:37), to watchfully prepare for His return: "Therefore if you will not watch, I will come upon you as a thief, and you will not know what hour I will come upon you" (Rev. 3:3; cf. v. 11). He later reiterated, "Behold, I am coming as a thief. Blessed is he who watches, and keeps his garments, lest he walk naked and they see his shame" (Rev. 16:15). To restate this, we must "watch" for Christ's return and maintain our garments of righteousness so that we do not walk in the shame of nakedness that results from disobedience (cf. Gen. 3:7). This theme of preparedness while maintaining our garments derives from the parable of the faithful servant:

Let your waist be girded and your lamps burning; and you yourselves be like men who wait for their master, when he will return from the wedding, that when he comes and knocks they may open to him immediately. Blessed are those servants whom the master, when he comes, will find watching. Assuredly, I say to you that he will gird himself and have them sit down to eat, and will come and serve them. And if he should come in the second watch, or come in the third watch, and find them so, blessed are those servants. (Luke 12:35-38; cf. Matt. 24:42-51; Mark 13:34-37).

Here Jesus illustrated the manner in which we should await His return from heaven (cf. Mark 13:33-37). This parable refers to the ancient custom of servants awaiting and preparing for the return of their master after a wedding. The servants in the parable do not know at what hour the master will return (Luke 12:38; cf. Mark 13:33-35), but because they had girded their inner garments around their loins and had kept their lamps burning late into the evening, they were able to immediately open the door for him as soon as he returned and knocked on the door (Luke 12:35-36). Similarly, when Christ returns at an unknown day and hour, He will serve His faithful servants, those who will have prepared and watched for Him (Luke 12:38; cf. John 13:1-17). As Jesus later promised, "Behold, I stand at the door and knock. If anyone hears My voice and opens the door, I will come in to him and dine with him, and he with Me" (Rev. 3:20).

Christ continued this motif by contrasting the actions of the faithful, wise servant with the actions of the wicked servant. The faithful servant, whom the master appointed to be head servant over his household, provided food for the others "in due season" (Matt. 24:45). This servant could refer to the bishops and presbyters of the holy Church, although it is more probable that it signifies more generally Christians who serve spiritual nourishment to others. The point is that when the Master returns, He will reward His faithful servants and appoint them as rulers over everything ("all his goods" Matt. 24:47), as the Scripture elsewhere says, "All things are yours: whether . . . the world or life or death, or things present or things to come—all are yours" (1 Cor. 3:21, 22).

By contrast, the wicked servant lives as if the Master has indefinitely delayed His coming (Matt. 24:48; cf. 2 Pet. 3:3-4). Examples of such a lifestyle include abusing others and participating in drinking parties, actions which the Master would never allow to be done in His presence (Matt. 24:49). However, the Master will return to the wicked servant in an unexpected hour ("when he is not looking for him and at an hour that he is not aware of" Matt. 24:50) and will "cut him in two and appoint him his portion with the hypocrites. There shall be weeping and gnashing of teeth" (Matt. 24:51). The imagery is intended to evoke dread and disgust at the horrors of eternal damnation which await the wicked on judgment day.

Jesus followed this with the parable of the ten virgins, which also emphasizes the importance of preparing for His return:

Then the kingdom of heaven shall be likened to ten virgins who took their lamps and went out to meet the bridegroom. Now five of them were wise, and five were foolish. Those who were foolish took their lamps and took no oil with them, but the wise took oil in their vessels with their lamps. But while the bridegroom was delayed, they all slumbered and slept. And at midnight a cry was heard: "Behold, the bridegroom is coming; go out to meet him!" Then all those virgins arose and trimmed their lamps. And the foolish said to the wise, "Give us some of your oil, for our lamps are going out." But the wise answered, saying, "No, lest there should not be enough for us and you; but go rather to those who sell, and buy for yourselves." And while they went to buy, the bridegroom came, and those who were ready went in with him to the wedding; and the door was shut. Afterward the other virgins came also, saying, "Lord, Lord, open to us!" But he answered and said, "Assuredly, I say to you, I do not know you." Watch therefore, for you know neither the day nor the hour in which the Son of Man is coming. (Matt. 25:1-13)

The idea is that God's people must prepare now to meet the Bridegroom. Those who do not prepare by obediently following Christ in the present will not be ready when He returns, when the shout is given to "go out to meet him" (Matt. 25:6). Only five of the ten bridesmaids were wise, and hence, adequately prepared to leave at any moment to meet the groom. The main point of the parable is that it will be too late for further preparation when the cry of command is heard to go meet Christ Jesus (Matt. 25:6-10). Those unprepared to meet Him will be stuck outside the banquet hall, and the door of entrance to His wedding feast will be closed forever (Matt. 25:10). And although many of the wicked will continue to plead for entrance into God's kingdom, the Lord will reject their request, answering, "Assuredly, I say to you, I do not know you" (Matt. 25:12; cf. Matt. 7:23; Luke 13:27). Then Jesus summarized the parable: "Watch therefore, for you know neither the day nor the hour in which the Son of Man is coming" (Matt. 25:13). As an aside, some interpreters have wondered whether the statement that all ten virgins were sleeping (Matt. 25:5) implies that all the righteous will experience a certain level of spiritual lethargy and unwatchfulness before Christ returns, but this may be reading too much into the parable.

The apostle Peter reminded his readers to pay attention to the warnings of the holy prophets and apostles because scoffers will appear in the last days, saying, "Where is the promise of His coming? For since the fathers fell asleep, all things continue as they were from the beginning of creation" (2 Pet. 3:4; cf. Isa. 28:14; 29:20; Hab. 1:5; Acts 13:41; 2 Pet. 3:1-4; Jude 1:18). Peter argued against the uniformitarianism of the scoffers who claim that Christ will not fulfill His promise to return soon (2 Pet. 3:1-4; cf. Exod. 32:1-4). He wrote, "But, beloved, do not forget this one thing, that with the Lord one day is as a thousand years, and a thousand years as one day. The Lord is not slack concerning His promise, as some count slackness, but is longsuffering toward us, not willing that any should perish but that all should come to repentance" (2 Pet. 3:8-9; cf. Ps. 90:4). In other words, God's timetable of eschatological events is very different than mere human reckoning of them ("as some count slackness" 2 Pet. 3:9). This is because God, being omniscient, understands and considers the broad scope of eternity ("one day is as a thousand years, and a thousand years as one day" 2 Pet. 3:8). On the other hand, people are "like grass" which live on earth for a relatively brief moment before being "cut down" in death (Ps. 90:6; cf. Isa. 40:6-8). The apostle argued that Christ is not negligent in fulfilling His promise to return but is longsuffering because He desires all people to repent (2 Pet. 3:9). The Father, however, will not wait indefinitely to send His Son from heaven.

The apostle Peter alluded to Christ's thief-like coming, a concept taught previously in the Olivet Discourse: "But the day of the Lord will come as a thief in the night, in which the heavens will pass away with a great noise" (2 Pet. 3:10). The immediate context reveals that the fiery dissolution of the heavens and the Earth (2 Pet. 3:5-7, 10-12) and the Lord's return from heaven will occur at the day of the Lord (2 Pet. 3:4, 9, 10; "the day of God" v. 12). The Lord's promise includes the arrival of the new heavens and earth "in which righteousness dwells" (2 Pet. 3:13; cf. Isa. 65:17; 66:22; Rev. 21:1-22:5).

At the world's final moments, at the sixth bowl judgment which signals the battle of Armageddon (Rev. 16:12-16), the thief-like return of Christ will still be future ("Behold, I am coming as a thief" Rev. 16:15). As in the present, the world's inhabitants will generally remain unprepared and unaware of Christ's now imminent return. At this point in the prophetic drama, the nations will have observed all the prophetic harbingers, including the revelation of the Antichrist, but they will be stunned when the Lord returns "as a thief." Clearly then, very few people will escape once God Himself has sent the "strong delusion" (2 Thess. 2:11). This is why Jesus warned His disciples multiple times about this unprecedented deception (Matt. 24:4-5, 11, 23-26; 2 Thess. 2:2-3).

Some interpreters have wondered whether the timing of the Lord's return will always remain unknowable, since it will take place "immediately after" the great tribulation (Matt. 24:29), a calculable period of forty-two months. However, the cumulative evidence demonstrates that the unknowability of the timing of Christ's return will continue even into the final days of the tribulation. First, we have learned that the Antichrist will immediately martyr the two witnesses as soon as they have finished their testimony of 1,260 days (Rev. 11:3, 7), and these two prophets will be resurrected and raptured three and a half days later at the sixth trumpet (a.k.a. "the second woe") (Rev. 11:14). Second, Christ will return at the seventh trumpet (a.k.a. "the third woe"), which will occur quickly after the sixth trumpet (Rev. 11:11-15). Third, Christ's return will immediately end the Antichrist's persecution of Christians, a persecution which will begin with the abomination of desolation in Jerusalem and continue forty-two months (Rev. 13:5; cf. Rev. 11:2; 12:6). Based on these three facts, we can deduce that Christ will return within a period of approximately twenty-eight days, and more precisely, shortly after the resurrection of the two witnesses (which will occur on day 1,263.5) and before the Antichrist can begin a forty-third month of persecution. However, the Scriptures do not appear to give us any further information on which to base our calculation. It stands to reason, then, that while we will eventually be able to calculate the precise month of Christ's return, we will still be unable to predict the precise day or hour, even as we approach the final moments before the end.

Jesus drove home this point when He delivered his admonition not to heed the "false flags" of deceivers that He has already returned (Matt. 24:23-28), and this warning appears in a portion of the Olivet Prophecy which describes the events of the unprecedented tribulation (Matt. 24:15-29). Yet once again, while we do not know the *exact* timing ("the day nor the hour"), the prophetic harbingers which precede His return demonstrate that we will eventually know its chronological proximity (by the abomination of desolation, even to within one month!) and be able to "see the day approaching" (cf. Heb. 10:25). This line of reasoning also suggests that the unknowability of the precise timing will remain in force until that moment of His return.

While a few prophecies reveal that the day of the Lord should be understood in its normative sense of twenty-four hours (Zech. 14:6-7), some commentators argue that other prophecies present the day as longer than an actual calendar day. Admittedly, a few biblical prophecies include the preliminary events of Christ's return in their description of the day of the Lord (Jer. 30:6-7; Joel 1:15; 2:1ff; 1 Thess. 5:1ff). For example, the apostle Paul taught that the abrupt cessation of the humanistic "peace and security"[5] will signal the day of the Lord (1 Thess. 5:1ff). However, as we saw in chapter 4, the Antichrist will begin the unprecedented tribulation forty-two months before the day of Jesus Christ. Furthermore, the great tribulation must precede the cosmic darkness ("immediately after the tribulation" Matt. 24:29), which will signal the arrival of the day of the Lord (Joel 2:31; Matt. 24:29).

To reconcile these prophecies, the modern reader must recognize that we cannot demand the holy prophets and apostles to have written in an overly parsed manner which differentiates the day of the Lord from the events leading up to it. To illustrate, people often use the name of a holiday when speaking about the celebratory season of events leading up to the holiday itself, such as when modern Christians referring to Christmas Eve or to the events of the holiday season simply as "Christmas." Yet rational people do not object to this short-hand way of speaking, nor do they deny that the holiday of Christmas (read Christmas Day), strictly speaking, is exactly twenty-four hours. Similarly, while the inspired writers of Scripture understood the day of Christ to be an actual twenty-four-hour day, they, on rare occasions, wrote about it while including a description of the preliminary events which will precede that day. To put it simply, the events of the great tribulation will precede and terminate with the day of the Lord proper.

---

5   These conditions will be established during the first half of the final seven years, as part of the international security pact with the Antichrist (Dan. 9:27; 11:22, 28-31, 44).

13

THE RETURN OF JESUS CHRIST

BEFORE JESUS CHRIST WAS BETRAYED AND CRUCIFIED, He told His disciples, "I am going away and coming back to you" (John 14:28; cf. vv. 3, 18). This prophecy will be exhaustively fulfilled when He returns from heaven to gather the holy Church into His kingdom (Matt. 24:31; John 14:3; 1 Thess. 4:15-17). Because He is coming back, the risen Christ identified Himself as the Lord "who is and who was and who is to come" (Rev. 1:4, 8). The writer of Hebrews wrote, "For yet a little while, and He who is coming will come and will not tarry" (Heb. 10:37; cf. Hab. 2:3). During this "little while" of Christ's delay, we should be "looking for the blessed hope and glorious appearing of our great God and Savior Jesus Christ" (Titus 2:13).

Christ's Church has always proclaimed His personal return to the earth. In point of fact, it is a central tenet of the historic Christian faith. The holy Creed reads as follows: "From thence [the Father's right hand] He [Jesus Christ] shall come again, with glory, to judge the living and the dead; whose kingdom shall have no end." The Orthodox Church, the Roman Catholic Church, and most Protestant churches accept the Creed as true and authoritative. As we will see, the Holy Scriptures also teach that Jesus will return to judge the living and the dead and to consummate His everlasting kingdom.

The apostle Peter preached a message showing that the Lord's return from heaven will result in refreshment and restoration:

> Repent therefore and be converted, that your sins may be blotted out, so that times of refreshing may come from the presence of the Lord, and that He may send Jesus Christ, who was preached to you before, whom heaven must receive until the times of restoration of all things, which God has spoken by the mouth of all His holy prophets since the world began. (Acts 3:19-21)

The phrase "restoration of all things" (Acts 3:21) refers to God restoring the Edenic bliss and personal fellowship with Christ that people experienced prior to the introduction of sin and death. According to the testimony of all God's prophets ("the mouth of all His holy prophets since the world began" Acts 3:21), the arrival of the messianic kingdom will produce peace, abundance, and life. The Lord will give these eternal blessings to all His people, whether Jew or Gentile, yet the complete repentance of the Jewish nation must coincide with the glorious return of Jesus Christ (see chapter 14). Consistent with this eschatological expectation, Peter appealed to the Jews to be converted ("Repent therefore and be converted" Acts 3:19) and so be forgiven ("that your sins may be blotted out" Acts 3:19) in order that they may receive refreshment and the restoration of everything that has been lost because of the fall (Acts 3:21).

The Scriptures emphasize that Christ will descend from heaven. For instance, the apostle Paul taught, "For the Lord Himself will descend from heaven" (1 Thess. 4:16). Likewise, King David prayed, "Bow down Your heavens, O Lord, and come down" (Ps. 144:5), and the prophet Isaiah echoed this theme, longingly praying, "Oh, that You would rend the heavens! That You would come down! That the mountains might shake at Your presence" (Isa. 64:1). Similarly, Micah prophesied, "Behold, the Lord is coming out of His place [heaven]; He will come down and tread on the high places of the earth" (Mic. 1:3; cf. Isa. 26:21; Hosea 5:15).

The apostle Paul encouraged us to eagerly wait for this revelation of Christ (1 Cor. 1:7; cf. 1 Pet. 1:13). Likewise, the prophets expected the Lord's glorious presence to be revealed to the world. For example, using the prophetic perfect tense, King David proclaimed that "all the peoples see His glory" (Ps. 97:6; cf. Isa. 35:2; Ezek. 39:21) and "all the ends of the earth have seen the salvation of our God" (Ps. 98:3). Also, Isaiah predicted, "The glory of the Lord shall be revealed, and all flesh shall see it together; for the mouth of the Lord has spoken" (Isa. 40:5; cf. Isa. 35:2). Isaiah elsewhere declared, "The Lord has made bare His holy arm in the eyes of all the nations; and all the ends of the earth shall see the salvation of our God" (Isa. 52:10; cf. Isa. 53:1). He also taught that many kings will become silent when Christ is publicly revealed because "what had not been told them they shall see, and what they had not heard they shall consider" (Isa. 52:15; cf. Isa. 53:1). In other words, they will look upon the crucified and risen Savior.

The Scriptures also emphasize that Christ will return in clouds (Ps. 97:2).[1] King David exhorted his readers to rejoice and "extol Him who rides on the clouds, by His name Yah" (Ps. 68:4). In addition, Luke meticulously recorded the account of the risen Lord's ascent from the Mount of Olives to heaven and the angelic promise for Him to return "in like manner":

---

[1] This was prefigured by the Angel of the Lord, the pre-incarnate Son of God, who descended in a thick cloud upon Mount Sinai: "Now all the people witnessed the thunderings, the lightning flashes, the sound of the trumpet, and the mountain smoking; and when the people saw it, they trembled and stood afar off" (Exod. 20:18).

Now when He had spoken these things, while they watched, He was taken up, and a cloud received Him out of their sight. And while they looked steadfastly toward heaven as He went up, behold, two men stood by them in white apparel, who also said, "Men of Galilee, why do you stand gazing up into heaven? This same Jesus, who was taken up from you into heaven, will so come in like manner as you saw Him go into heaven." (Acts 1:9-11)

This passage strongly emphasizes that the disciples watched Jesus ascend into a cloud. Five phrases in the narrative highlight the optical nature of this event: "they watched," "their sight," "while they looked steadfastly," "gazing up," and "as you saw Him go." In addition, Luke recorded that Jesus ascended into a cloud of heaven (Acts 1:9-10). In addition, the angels thrice repeated the fact that He went "into heaven" (Acts 1:11).

Since Jesus will return "in like manner" as the disciples saw Him ascend into heaven (Acts 1:11), it is evident that He will visibly return from heaven. This is consistent with several other prophecies that His descent will be unmistakably visible and accompanied with the clouds of heaven (Dan. 7:13; Matt. 24:30; 26:64; Mark 13:26; 14:62; Luke 21:27; Rev. 1:7; 14:14). As the prophet Zechariah announced, the Lord will return to stand upon the very place from which He ascended—the Mount of Olives ("in that day His feet will stand on the Mount of Olives. . . the Lord my God will come" Zech. 14:4, 5)!

The Scriptures attest that Christ will return in a publicly visible manner. For example, the apostle John declared, "Behold, He is coming with clouds, and every eye will see Him, even they who pierced Him" (Rev. 1:7; cf. Matt. 24:30).[2] This echoes Jesus' declaration before the Sanhedrin, the judges of the great assembly who were responsible for formally condemning Him, to whom He prophesied, "I say to you, hereafter you will see the Son of Man sitting at the right hand of the Power, and coming on the clouds of heaven" (Matt. 26:64). In partial

---

2   Revelation 1:7 is the theme verse for the book of Revelation.

fulfillment of this prophecy, these leaders witnessed the emergence of the apostolic Church, the expression of Christ's kingdom authority ("hereafter you will see the Son of Man sitting at the right hand of the Power" Matt. 26:64). These same leaders will see the glorified Jesus when He returns "on the clouds of heaven" (Matt. 26:64; cf. Dan. 7:13; Rev. 1:7). The idea is that all people, the living and the dead, will see Christ's glorious return.

The Lord's glorious presence will "shine forth" when He comes out of the heavenly Zion (Ps. 50:2-3). Isaiah celebrated, "Arise, shine; for your light has come! And the glory of the Lord is risen upon you. For behold, the darkness shall cover the earth, and deep darkness the people; but the Lord will arise over you, and His glory will be seen upon you" (Isa. 60:1-2). The darkness on the day of the Lord will give way to the brightness of Christ's presence. Consequently, those who have walked in cosmic (and by extension, spiritual) darkness will see "a great light" (Isa. 9:1-2). Presumably, the brilliant glory of Christ will penetrate through the Earth so that everyone, whether living or dead, will simultaneously see Him.

In the Olivet Discourse, Jesus provided us with a succinct sequence of prophetic events which will accompany His return:

> Immediately after the tribulation of those days the sun will be darkened, and the moon will not give its light; the stars will fall from heaven, and the powers of the heavens will be shaken. Then the sign of the Son of Man will appear in heaven, and then all the tribes of the earth will mourn, and they will see the Son of Man coming on the clouds of heaven with power and great glory. And He will send His angels with a great sound of a trumpet, and they will gather together His elect from the four winds, from one end of heaven to the other. (Matt. 24:29-31; cf. Mark 13:24-27; Luke 21:25-27)

According to this prophecy, the order of eschatological events will be as follows:

1. The unprecedented tribulation

2. The cosmic disturbances which will signal the day of the Lord

3. The sign of Christ appearing in heaven

4. The tribes of the earth weeping when they see Him returning on the clouds of heaven

To summarize the sequence of prophetic events, stellar darkness and several other cataclysmic signs will "immediately" follow forty-two months of great tribulation (see chapter 10). The Son of Man will return in glory on the same day—the day of Jesus Christ ("*Then* the sign" Matt. 24:30, emphasis added). Then Christ will be visibly seen by the world of men and angels at that time. It is probable that the phrase "the sign of the Son of Man" (Matt. 24:30) should be translated epexegetically, meaning "the sign, namely, the Son of Man."[3] All the peoples of the Earth will see Christ in heaven, and many of them will mourn when they see Him descend with the clouds with the "power and great glory" of God (cf. Dan. 7:13-14; Zech. 12:10-14).

Christ will return to gather "His elect" (Matt. 24:31), which, as we will see, refers to the resurrection and the rapture of His Church. Matthew wrote that the angels will gather the saints "from one end of heaven to the other" (Matt. 24:31; cf. Matt. 13:43), while Mark expanded this phrase to read "from the farthest part of earth to the farthest part of heaven" (Mark 13:27). Consequently, this gathering of Christians will include those who remain alive upon the earth and those who have already been with Christ in heaven, the latter group having died before this gathering takes place. In addition, this gathering will be signaled by "a great sound of a trumpet" (Matt. 24:31; cf. Isa. 27:13).

---

3   In koine Greek, this is also known as an explicative genitive or a genitive of apposition. If this interpretation is correct, "the sign" in this verse is the Son of Man's coming.

Many scholars correctly recognize that the apostle Paul patterned the eschatology of his Thessalonian letters after the Olivet Discourse. In his first letter, he detailed the gathering of God's chosen ones, which will take place at the sounding of the heavenly trumpet:

> But I do not want you to be ignorant, brethren, concerning those who have fallen asleep, lest you sorrow as others who have no hope. For if we believe that Jesus died and rose again, even so God will bring with Him those who sleep in Jesus. For this we say to you by the word of the Lord, that we who are alive and remain until the coming of the Lord will by no means precede those who are asleep. For the Lord Himself will descend from heaven with a shout, with the voice of an archangel, and with the trumpet of God. And the dead in Christ will rise first. Then we who are alive and remain shall be caught up together with them in the clouds to meet the Lord in the air. And thus we shall always be with the Lord. Therefore comfort one another with these words. (1 Thess. 4:13-18)

The apostle instructed Christians to comfort one other about those who have died in the Christian faith because the Lord will resurrect them after the likeness of His own resurrection (1 Thess. 4:13-14, 18). Then at His return, Christ will escort them to remain with Him forever (1 Thess. 4:14; cf. Zech. 14:5; Matt. 24:31; 1 Thess. 2:19; 3:13). Immediately after the righteous are resurrected and brought into Christ's glorious presence, the Christians who remain alive will also be glorified and raptured ("caught up together" 1 Thess. 4:17) into the clouds to meet Him and the resurrected saints. The implication is that the glorified bodies of all the saints, whether raptured or resurrected, will be the same ontologically. In addition, Christians will never again be apart from the glorified Jesus (1 Thess. 4:17).

The phrase "the word of the Lord" (1 Thess. 4:15) refers to a logion, that is, an authentic teaching of Christ during His earthly ministry (1 Cor. 7:10-11, 25; 9:14; 11:23-25), not to a revelatory message given by the Holy Spirit to the apostle Paul (cf. 1 Cor. 2:12-16; 7:40; 2 Cor. 13:3; 1 Thess. 2:13).[4] As such, this "word" here refers to the Olivet Discourse which Jesus delivered to His disciples, and more specifically, his teaching about His glorious return and the gathering of His elect (Matt. 24:30-31; Mark 13:26-27). The table below provides the parallels between the two passages, demonstrating that they refer to the same events, namely, to the descent of Jesus Christ from heaven and His gathering of the saints, the living and the dead.

TABLE 5: PARALLELS BETWEEN THE OLIVET DISCOURSE AND 1 THESSALONIANS 4-5:[5]

Matthew 24	1 Thessalonians 4:16-5:9
24:30 "[T]hey will see the Son of Man coming on the clouds of heaven."	4:16, 17 "For the Lord Himself will descend from heaven . . . in the clouds."
24:31 "His angels with a great sound of a trumpet, and they will gather together His elect from the four winds, from one end of heaven to the other" (cf. Mark 13:27 "from the farthest part of the earth to the farthest part of heaven").	4:16-17 "[W]ith the voice of an archangel, and with the trumpet of God. And the dead in Christ will rise first. Then we who are alive and remain shall be caught up together with them in the clouds to meet the Lord in the air."
24:36 "But of that day and hour no one knows."	5:1-2 "But concerning the times and the seasons, brethren, you have no need that I should write to you."

4   Except when the apostle quoted the Old Testament, he always referred to Jesus when he used the title "the Lord."

5   The linguistic signature of the Olivet Discourse finds duplication in this prophecy of Paul. The careful reader should notice the thematic parallels, the similar sequence of events, and the appearance of "now concerning" (περι δε) at the same point within each sequence.

24:39 "And did not know until the flood came and took them all away, so also will the coming of the Son of Man be" (cf. Luke 21:34, 36 "unexpectedly . . . pray always that you may be counted worth to escape").	5:3 "For when they say, "Peace and safety! Then sudden destruction comes upon them . . . and they shall not escape."
24:8 "sorrows"	5:3 "labor pains"
24:42-44 "Watch therefore, for you do not know what hour your Lord is coming. But know this, that if the master of the house had known what hour the thief would come, he would have watched and not allowed his house to be broken into. Therefore, you also be ready, for the Son of Man is coming at an hour you do not expect."	5:2, 4-7, 8, 10 "For you yourselves know perfectly that the day of the Lord so comes as a thief in the night...But you, brethren, are not in darkness, so that this day should overtake you as a thief. You are all sons of light and sons of the day. We are not of the night nor of darkness. Therefore, let us not sleep, as others do, but let us watch and be sober. For those who sleep, sleep at night . . . . But let us who are of the day . . . whether we wake or sleep."
24:49 "drinks with the drunkards"	5:7-8 "[T]hose who get drunk are drunk at night. . . . be sober."
25:6 "[A] cry was heard . . .'go out to meet him.' "	4:16-17 "with a shout . . . to meet the Lord."

The apostle Paul revealed a mystery ("Behold, I tell you a mystery" 1 Cor. 15:51), which provides the answer to a question that had puzzled Jewish rabbis, specifically, what will happen to living followers of the Lord when the dead are raised. The answer is that Christ will glorify and gather the living saints when He resurrects the dead saints:

Behold, I tell you a mystery: We shall not all sleep, but we shall all be changed—in a moment, in the twinkling of an eye, at the last trumpet. For the trumpet will sound, and the dead will be raised incorruptible, and we shall be changed. For this corruptible must put on incorruption, and this mortal must put on immortality. So when this corruptible has put on incorruption, and this mortal has put on immortality, then shall be brought to pass the saying that is written: "Death is swallowed up in victory." "O Death, where is your sting? O Hades, where is your victory?" (1 Cor. 15:51-55)

This Olivet Discourse and this prophecy closely agree with Paul's rapture passage to the Thessalonians. All three passages reveal that the heavenly trumpet will signal the Son of God's return (Matt. 24:30; 1 Cor. 15:23; 1 Thess. 4:16-17) and the gathering of His saints (Matt. 24:31; 1 Thess. 4:16; 1 Cor. 15:52). Furthermore, while Jesus taught that the elect will include the righteous in heaven and on earth (Mark 13:27), the apostle taught that the Christians "who are alive and remain" (1 Thess. 4:17) will be changed and transformed at that time, receiving incorruption and immortality (1 Cor. 15:53-54). So while we may conceptualize of two distinct stages for the resurrection of the dead and the rapture of the living respectively, they will essentially occur together, nearly instantaneously ("in the twinkling [or blink] of an eye") at the last trumpet (1 Cor. 15:52).

Consistent with these motifs, the beginning of the seventh trumpet will signify that "the mystery of God would be finished, as He declared to His servants the prophets" (Rev. 10:7; cf. 1 Cor. 15:51). Elsewhere, the apostle taught that the result of this final trumpet will be that the kingdom of Christ will subsume the kingdoms of the world (Rev. 11:15; cf. v. 17). In other words, the last trumpet will usher in the hope of all the prophets—the consummation of Christ's kingdom.

This final trumpet will signal "the time of the dead, that they should be judged and that You should reward Your servants the prophets and the saints and those who fear Your name small and great" (Rev. 11:18). At the sounding of this trumpet, God will also pour out His eternal wrath so as to "destroy those who destroy the earth" (Rev. 11:18). Jesus explained that if He were to allow the unprecedented tribulation to continue unabated, instead of returning to terminate it, the entire human race would be destroyed ("no flesh would be saved" Matt. 24:22). He will not allow sinful humanity to annihilate itself! However, when Christ returns, He will gather all the nations together in order to punish the wicked with everlasting destruction and to reward the righteous with eternal life (Matt. 25:29-46).

In the Olivet Discourse, Jesus explained that the rapture will gather only those who have followed Him: "I tell you, in that night there will be two men in one bed: the one will be taken and the other will be left. Two women will be grinding together: the one will be taken and the other left. Two men will be in the field: the one will be taken and the other left" (Luke 17:34-35; cf. Matt. 24:40-41). In other words, when Christ returns in the clouds, He will instantaneously translate and rapture the living Christians to accompany Him ("taken" Luke 17:34). As Noah and his family entered the ark (Luke 17:27) and the angels removed the man Lot from Sodom (Luke 17:28-29), the angels will take the righteous away, while leaving the wicked on the earth to be destroyed.

The concept of a rapture is found throughout the Scriptures. For example, the righteous man Enoch was miraculously "taken away" so that he did not experience death (Gen. 5:24; Heb. 11:5). Similarly, God sent a whirlwind to remove the prophet Elijah into heaven (2 Kings 2:11-12). Furthermore, the Holy Spirit "caught Philip away" and transported him to another town so the Ethiopian eunuch no longer saw him (Acts 8:39). Finally, at the sound of the heavenly voice, the two witnesses will be resurrected and will ascend into heaven in a cloud (Rev. 11:11-14).

In the context of his teachings about the resurrection, the apostle Paul taught that Christians are not appointed to divine wrath: "For God did not appoint us to wrath, but to obtain salvation through our Lord Jesus Christ, who died for us, that whether we wake or sleep, we should live together with Him. Therefore comfort each other and edify one another, just as you also are doing" (1 Thess. 5:9-11). When Jesus returns (1 Thess. 4:14), the living and the dead will be glorified and brought into His presence ("whether we wake or sleep" 1 Thess. 5:10), instead of experiencing His eternal wrath (1 Thess. 1:10; cf. Rom. 5:9).

The immediate context reveals that God's wrath will be poured out upon the living and the dead (1 Thess. 5:9-10; 2 Thess. 1:6-10; cf. Rom. 2:5), thus indicating that the wrath of the great tribulation as such is not in view, but the eternal wrath which will begin at the day of Jesus Christ.

In Paul's first epistle to Christians in Corinth, he explained that the resurrection of the dead will fulfill two prophecies, one from Isaiah ("Death is swallowed up in victory" cf. Isa. 25:8) and the other from Hosea ("O Death, where is your sting? O Hades, where is your victory?" cf. Hosea 13:14). The immediate context of Isaiah's prophecy reveals that God has promised to "swallow up death forever" and to "wipe away tears from all faces" (Isa. 25:6-8; cf. 2 Cor. 5:4; Rev. 7:17; 21:4). In Hosea's prophecy, He promised to ransom and redeem Israel from "the power of the grave," that is, from death itself. Conflating these two prophecies, the apostle taught that Christ will return to destroy death through the resurrection.

The larger context of Isaiah's prophecy reveals that the birth pains of the tribulation (Isa. 26:16-18) will lead to the resurrection of the dead:

> Your dead shall live; together with my dead body they shall arise. Awake and sing, you who dwell in dust; for your dew is like the dew of herbs, and the earth shall cast out the dead. Come, my people, enter your chambers and shut your doors behind you; hide yourself, as it were for a little moment, until the indignation is past. For behold, the Lord comes out of His place to punish the inhabitants of the earth for their Iniquity; the earth will also disclose her blood and will no more cover her slain. (Isa. 26:19-21)

During the final tribulation, the Lord's people are instructed to flee for protection ("enter your chambers and shut your doors behind you" Isa. 26:20; cf. Job 14:13). His indignation upon the earth will last only "for a little moment" (Isa. 26:20) because He will return from heaven ("out of His place" Isa. 26:21) to punish the earth dwellers and to resurrect the dead. The prophet stressed that the resurrection will include the resuscitation of corpses from the earth ("with my dead body," "who dwell in dust," "the earth shall cast out the dead," and "the earth will also disclose her blood and will no more cover her slain" Isa. 26:19-21).

The resurrection will happen when God slays the Antichrist ("Leviathan the fleeing serpent" Isa. 27:1) with His sword and when "a great trumpet will be blown" to gather the holy people to worship the Lord in "the holy mountain at Jerusalem" (Isa. 27:12-13). When the trumpet sounds, the Lord will "glean" His people Israel by gathering them like one gathers grain: "In that day from the river Euphrates to the Brook of Egypt the Lord will thresh out the grain, and you will be gleaned one by one, O people of Israel" (Isa. 27:12-13). The final gathering at the sound of this "great trumpet" provides the primary backdrop for Christ's teaching that "the great sound of a trumpet" will signal the gathering of His elect (Matt. 24:31). In chapter 16, I will discuss whether this trumpet will also signal the gathering of the surviving Jews to Jerusalem.

In this passage, Isaiah provides us with prima fascia evidence that "the dead in Christ" (1 Thess. 4:16) will include the saints and prophets of the Old Testament. He prophesied that this resurrection of the dead will include his own resurrection ("together with my dead body they shall arise" Isa. 26:19). The prophet Job made a similar declaration about his own resurrection: "For I know that my Redeemer lives, and He shall stand at last on the earth; And after my skin is destroyed, this I know, that in my flesh I shall see God, whom I shall see for myself, and my eyes shall behold, and not another. How my heart yearns within me!" (Job 19:25-27). To restate this, the living Redeemer—the resurrected Christ—will stand upon the earth on the last day (cf. Zech. 14:4; Acts 1:9-11). When this takes place, Job will regain his flesh, which will be rescued from corruption, so that he can look upon Him ("I shall see for myself, and my eyes shall behold" Job 19:27). Similarly, King David held this conviction: "As for me, I will see Your face in righteousness; I shall be satisfied when I awake in Your likeness" (Ps. 17:15). We will be resurrected with the Old Testament saints so that "they should not be made perfect apart from us" (Heb. 11:40).

During his sufferings, Job cried out to God to hide him in burial until His wrath has been completed: "Oh, that You would hide me in the grave, that You would conceal me until Your wrath is past, that You would appoint me a set time, and remember me! If a man dies, shall he live again? All the days of my hard service I will wait, till my change comes. You shall call, and I will answer You; You shall desire the work of Your hands" (Job 14:13-15). In this statement, Job prophetically foretold of the resurrection, after a period of divine wrath. He concluded that dead men will "live again," and he declared that God will desire them—the work of His hands—and summon them again at the resurrection. Job declared that he will wait in the grave until his "change" occurs, a statement echoed by the apostle Paul, who wrote that "we shall all be changed" at the return of Jesus Christ (1 Cor. 15:51).

In addition, Ezekiel's Vision of the Valley of Dry Bones provides a unique glimpse into the bodily nature of the resurrection (Ezek. 37:1-14). In this vision, the prophet saw an open valley littered with parched human skeletons (Ezek. 37:1-2). Once he prophesied over the bones, that they should "hear" the Lord's message, they became reanimated as living persons, an "exceedingly great army" (Ezek. 37:3-10). He portrayed their resurrection in graphic terms:

> As I prophesied, there was a noise, and suddenly a rattling; and the bones came together, bone to bone. Indeed, as I looked, the sinews and the flesh came upon them, and the skin covered them over; but there was no breath in them. . . So I prophesied as He commanded me, and breath came into them, and they lived, and stood upon their feet, an exceedingly great army. (Ezek. 37:7-8, 10)

As a postlude to Ezekiel's vision, the Lord promised to resurrect the people of Israel and to bring them into the Promised Land:

> Behold, O My people, I will open your graves and cause you to come up from your graves, and bring you into the land of Israel. Then

you shall know that I am the Lord, when I have opened your graves,
O My people, and brought you up from your graves. I will put My
Spirit in you, and you shall live, and I will place you in your own land.
Then you shall know that I, the Lord, have spoken it and performed
it. (Ezek. 37:12-14)

While the vision itself likely contains symbolic elements, the Lord's
proclamation about its larger meaning reveals that a literal resurrection
is in view. First, like this prophecy, other prophets have forwarded the
concept that Israel's dead bodies will be resuscitated from the graves at
the time of the end (Isa. 26:19-21; Dan. 12:1-3). Second, Ezekiel's vision
detailed a resurrection of reanimated bodies containing bones, ligaments,
muscles, skin, and breath, an ontological similarity to Jesus' resurrected
body, which departed His tomb on resurrection Sunday (John 20:1-18).
Christ's body also contained "flesh and bones" (Luke 24:39; cf. Ezek.
37:7-10), and He demonstrated this by eating meals and allowing His
disciples to handle His scarred body (Luke 24:39-42; John 20:25-28;
21:10-13). Third, as we will see in chapter 16, the Lord will pour out His
Spirit upon the people of Israel and literally gather them to the Promised
Land, as Ezekiel's prophecy indicates ("bring you into the land of Israel. .
. put My Spirit in you, and you shall live" Ezek. 37:12, 14).

Consistent with the teachings of the prophets Job, David, and Isaiah,
who believed that they would be resurrected at the time of the end, "the
man clothed in linen" taught Daniel about the resurrection of the dead:

And at that time [of trouble] your people shall be delivered, every
one who is found written in the book. And many of those who sleep
in the dust of the earth shall awake, some to everlasting life, some
to shame and everlasting contempt. Those who are wise shall shine
like the brightness of the firmament, and those who turn many to
righteousness like the stars forever and ever. (Dan. 12:1-3)

The people of Israel, whose names are inscribed in the Lamb's scroll of life (Dan. 12:1; cf. Rev. 3:5; 13:8; 17:8; 20:12, 15; 21:27; 22:19), will be delivered from the unprecedented tribulation by the resurrection of the dead. The resurrection will include the resuscitation of dead bodies ("many of those who sleep in the dust of the earth shall awake" Dan. 12:2), with the righteous attaining eternal life ("some to everlasting life" Dan. 12:2) and the wicked receiving everlasting destruction ("shame and everlasting contempt" Dan. 12:2). The apostle Paul confirmed this interpretation when he taught that he fully expected "a resurrection of the dead, both of the just and the unjust" (Acts 24:15; cf. Luke 14:14).

Likewise, in the Gospels Jesus alluded to Daniel's resurrection prophecy. For example, in the parable of the tares, He taught that "the righteous will shine like the sun in the kingdom of their Father" at the end of the age (Matt. 13:43 with Dan. 12:3). This will be accomplished by the angelic gathering of "the wheat" (i.e., the righteous) into the barn, a symbol for God's kingdom (Matt. 13:30; cf. Matt. 24:31). Consistent with Daniel's prophecy, the Savior also promised that everyone who trusts in Him will be resurrected to receive everlasting life "at the last day" (John 6:39-40, 44, 54; 11:23-26). Additionally, Christ specifically referenced Daniel's passage when He taught the resurrection of the dead:

> Most assuredly, I say to you, the hour is coming, and now is, when the dead will hear the voice of the Son of God; and those who hear will live . . . Do not marvel at this; for the hour is coming in which all who are in the graves will hear His voice and come forth—those who have done good, to the resurrection of life, and those who have done evil, to the resurrection of condemnation. (John 5:25, 28)

Jesus spoke about two resurrections in this passage. The first resurrection is the spiritual regeneration accomplished by the Holy Spirit, which occurs when Christ initially forgives our sins ("now is" John 5:25; cf. Rom. 6:3-11; Rev. 20:5). The second resurrection is the one that will take place on the day of Jesus Christ, in other words, at the coming "hour" when the dead will hear His voice and will come forth from their graves (John 5:25, 28-29). At the resurrection, those who have performed righteousness will be raised to receive eternal life, and those who have done evil will receive a resurrection resulting in everlasting condemnation (John 5:29; cf. Dan. 12:2; Acts 24:15). The statement "all who are in their graves" (John 5:28) qualifies the meaning of Daniel's "many" who will be resurrected (Dan. 12:2), demonstrating that the "many" are all the dead.[6]

The apostles frequently communicated that Christ's resurrection provided the template for the resurrection of His people. As the second Adam,[7] Jesus is the firstfruits of those who will be resurrected by Him at His return (1 Cor. 15:20-23), and He is called the firstborn from among the dead (Rev. 1:5). As such, the same Spirit who raised Him from the dead will give immortality to our mortal bodies (Rom. 8:11; 1 Cor. 6:14). Saint Paul declared, "For our citizenship is in heaven, from which we also eagerly wait for the Savior, the Lord Jesus Christ, who will transform our lowly body that it may be conformed to His glorious body" (Phil. 3:20-21). Consequently, the answer to the apostle's question "Who will deliver me from this body of death?" (Rom. 7:24-25) is Jesus Himself.

Since the Father has predestined Christians "to be conformed to the image of His Son" (Rom. 8:29-30), we will share "in the likeness" of His resurrection through our own (Rom. 6:5; cf. 2 Cor. 4:14). The apostle John explained, "It has not yet been revealed what we shall be, but we know that when He is revealed, we shall be like Him, for we shall see Him as He is" (1 John 3:2). Despite a certain level of mystery that shrouds the nature of our resurrected bodies, we know that they will be like His resurrected body. Paul reminded us that after our resurrection, we will see Christ "face to face" and intimately know Him like He already knows us (1 Cor. 13:12; cf. Deut. 34:10; 1 John 3:2). In this manner, we will bear the incorruptible image

---

6   This verse may hint that Christ the firstfruits would be resurrected *prior to* the general resurrection.

7   For more on this topic, see Saint Irenaeus' Recapitulation Theory in *Against Heresies*.

of Jesus, the heavenly Man, and so, we will inherit God's glorious kingdom, an impossibility for mere mortal man ("flesh and blood") (1 Cor. 15:49-50; cf. Gen. 1:26-27).

In the resurrection, we will share in the glorious appearance of Jesus, which the apostle John described in the book of Revelation:

> One like the Son of Man, clothed with a garment down to the feet and girded about the chest with a golden band. His head and hair were white like wool, as white as snow, and His eyes like a flame of fire; His feet were like fine brass, as if refined in a furnace, and His voice as the sound of many waters. . . His countenance was like the sun shining in its strength. And when I saw Him, I fell at His feet as dead. (Rev. 1:13-15, 16-17)

This is why Paul described our resurrection glory as far exceeding the degree of sufferings in the present age (Rom. 8:18). Yet as Christians, we presently "groan within ourselves," while persevering and expectantly waiting for the redemption of our bodies—the resurrection (Rom. 8:23-25). As Christians groan for the addition of immortality, we inwardly desire to be "clothed" with our heavenly habitation, so that we will not be found "naked" and suffer shame in Christ's presence (2 Cor. 5:2-4; cf. Gen. 3:7-11; 1 Pet. 1:4; Rev. 16:15). We should not desire to depart from our physical bodies ("to be unclothed" 2 Cor. 5:4) but ultimately to recover our bodies of flesh, which will be perfectly transformed for glory and immortality ("further clothed" 2 Cor. 5:4).

The apostle Paul desired for every believer to learn obedience so that they can present themselves blameless and complete on the day of Jesus Christ (1 Cor. 1:7-8; 2 Cor. 4:14; Col. 1:28; Phil 1:10; 1 Thess. 3:13; 5:23-24; cf. 1 Tim. 6:14; Jude 1:24). Paul fully expected to rejoice upon seeing Christians in the presence of Christ (1 Thess. 2:19; cf. 2 Cor. 1:14). Echoing the prophet Zechariah (Zech. 14:5), the apostle taught that this will occur when Jesus returns with "all His saints" (1 Thess. 3:13; cf. 1 Thess. 2:19; "with ten thousands of His saints" Jude

1:14). Similarly, the apostle John wrote, "And now, little children, abide in Him, that when He appears, we may have confidence and not be ashamed before Him at His coming" (1 John 2:28).

God summoned us to obey the apostolic gospel so that we share the glory that belongs to Jesus (2 Thess. 2:14; cf. Col. 3:4; 1 Thess. 5:23; Heb. 2:10; 1 Pet. 5:1, 4). Because of our persevering faith, we will receive "praise, honor, and glory" when Christ is revealed (1 Pet. 1:7). He is committed to presenting us to Himself as "a glorious church, not having spot or wrinkle or any such thing, but that she should be holy and without blemish" (Eph. 5:27).

Paul emphasized that the same God who began a good work[8] of sanctification among His saints will complete their salvation on the day of Christ (Phil. 1:6; cf. 1 Cor. 1:7-8; 1 Thess. 3:13; 5:23-24; Titus 2:13-14; Jude 1:24). The result will be that every faithful Christian, in his entirety ("spirit, soul, and body"), will be presented blameless at the Lord's return (1 Thess. 5:23). The apostle declared, "He [the Lord] who calls you is faithful, who also will do it" (1 Thess. 5:24). Such promises demonstrate God's sovereign protection and preservation of His Church.

The blessed hope, our Lord's return, will bring about the final stage of our salvation—our glorification. This is the grace which will be given to us when Jesus Christ is revealed (1 Pet. 1:13; cf. 1 Pet. 1:3-5, 9). Isaiah foresaw this salvation: "And it will be said in that day: 'Behold, this is our God; we have waited for Him, and He will save us. This is the Lord; we have waited for Him; we will be glad and rejoice in His salvation' " (Isa. 25:9). On that day, Christ will bring vengeance and recompense to His enemies and will deliver His people (Isa. 35:4). Consequently, we must patiently wait for the Son of God to return from heaven (Phil. 1:10) and "hold fast" to the works of Christ until He comes (Rev. 2:25). Together with His apostles, we continue to earnestly pray, "O Lord, come!" (1 Cor. 16:22).

---

8   This primary meaning of this Greek word (ἔργων) is "battle." The backdrop for this imagery is the two battles of Philippi.

14

ALL ISRAEL WILL BE SAVED

COMMENTATORS VARY WIDELY as to whether the Scriptures guarantee a prophetic destiny for the Jewish nation. This chapter will demonstrate that the modern State of Israel will play a critical role in the end-time redemptive drama.

The corporate Jewish nation and its leaders were responsible for rejecting God and His law, as demonstrated most poignantly by their perpetual persecution and martyrdom of the prophets (e.g., 1 Kings 19:10, 14; 2 Chron. 36:16; Neh. 9:26; Jer. 26:20-24; Matt. 21:33-22:14; 23:29-38; Mark 12:1-12; Luke 14:15-24; 20:9-19). The nation was also responsible for rejecting and crucifying the Son of God (Matt. 21:37-39; 26:4; Mark 12:6-8; Luke 20:13-15; Acts 2:23; 3:15; 1 Thess. 2:15). Furthermore, the prophet Isaiah foresaw that the Jewish nation would continue to reject the message of the prophets and to lack spiritual understanding and insight. This spiritual hardening would continue until the land of Israel became completely desolate:

And He said, "Go, and tell this people: 'Keep on hearing, but do not understand; keep on seeing, but do not perceive.' Make the heart of this people dull, and their ears heavy, and shut their eyes; lest they see with their eyes, and hear with their ears, and understand with their heart, and return and be healed." Then I said, "Lord, how long?" And He answered: "Until the cities are laid waste and without inhabitant, the houses are without a man, the land is utterly desolate, the Lord has removed men far away, and the forsaken places are many in the midst of the land." (Isa. 6:9-12)

This prophecy has never been fulfilled. Although the two houses of Israel were taken into exile,[1] the Jews who returned under Ezra and Nehemiah did not experience national repentance as prophesied in this passage. Rather, the majority of the nation remained in a state of spiritual blindness, deafness, and imperceptiveness regarding the divine oracles and prophecies ("lest they see with their eyes, and hear with their ears, and understand with their heart" Isa. 6:10; cf. Isa. 28:12; 30:9; Jer. 5:21). Even as late as the first century AD, Jesus and His apostles taught that the Jews remained in this same spiritually impoverished condition (Matt. 13:14; Mark 4:12; Luke 8:10; John 12:37, 39-40; Acts 28:25-28; Rom. 11:8). Since this time, the majority of Jews, even those living in the modern State of Israel, have continued to reject the message of Isaiah and the prophets.

Curiously, Isaiah explained that the nation ("this people") will not repent until the people are taken away into foreign exile ("the Lord has removed men far away" Isa. 6:12) and their land becomes utterly desolate ("Until the cities are laid waste and without inhabitant, the houses are without a man, the land is utterly desolate" Isa. 6:11). Clearly then, these references ultimately point to the final desolation of the land and the final

---

[1] The northern kingdom of Israel was taken into captivity by the Assyrians in the late eighth century BC, and the southern kingdom of Judah was removed by King Nebuchadnezzar of Babylon in 587-86 BC.

captivity which will occur during the unprecedented tribulation (Zech. 14:2; Luke 21:24; cf. Matt. 24:15-28; Isa. 6:13). Only then will the Jews "return and be healed" (Isa. 6:10) and see, hear, and understand the message of the Prophets. This tribulation will ultimately "give birth" to the final redemption, Christ's answer to the age-enduring question "How long?" (Isa. 6:11; cf. Ps. 90:13; Dan. 8:13; 12:6; Hab. 1:2; Rev. 6:10).

Consistent with this theme, the prophet later described the message of the prophets and seers as a sealed scroll ("a book that is sealed" Isa. 29:11). He explained that illiterate people will not be able to read the scroll, and literate people will not properly decipher it, because it will remain "sealed" off to their understanding:

> Pause and wonder! Blind yourselves and be blind! They are drunk, but not with wine; they stagger, but not with intoxicating drink. For the Lord has poured out on you the spirit of deep sleep, and has closed your eyes, namely, the prophets; and He has covered your heads, namely, the seers. The whole vision has become to you like the words of a book that is sealed, which men deliver to one who is literate, saying, "Read this, please." And he says, "I cannot, for it is sealed." Then the book is delivered to one who is illiterate, saying, "Read this, please." And he says, "I am not literate." (Isa. 29:9-12)

In this passage, the prophet warned that God would bring this judgment of hardening to the Jewish people (Isa. 29:10; cf. Rom. 11:25). Jesus echoed this passage, explaining that God has blinded their eyes and hardened their hearts in order that they should not understand, convert, and so receive healing (John 12:37-41). According to Isaiah, the nation brought about their own impoverished, spiritual condition because they would "draw near with their mouths and honor Me with their lips, but have removed their hearts far from Me, and their fear toward Me is taught by the commandment of men" (Isa. 29:13). The larger part of the nation will remain in this spiritually hardened condition until the consummation of God's kingdom:

Therefore, behold, I will again do a marvelous work among this people, a marvelous work and a wonder; for the wisdom of their wise men shall perish, and the understanding of their prudent men shall be hidden . . . Is it not yet a very little while till Lebanon shall be turned into a fruitful field, and the fruitful field be esteemed as a forest? In that day the deaf shall hear the words of the book, and the eyes of the blind shall see out of obscurity and out of darkness. The humble also shall increase their joy in the Lord, and the poor among men shall rejoice in the Holy One of Israel . . . These also who erred in spirit will come to understanding, and those who complained will learn doctrine. (Isa. 29:9-14, 17-19, 24)

The "marvelous work" and "a wonder" which the Lord will do among the Jewish people is that those who are spiritually deaf will finally "hear the words of the book, and the eyes of the blind shall see out of obscurity and out of darkness" (Isa. 29:18; cf. Ps. 146:8; Hab. 1:5). Those who had previously "erred in spirit will come to understanding, and those who complained will learn doctrine" (Isa. 29:24). In other words, God will reveal to the Jews the hidden meaning of Isaiah's prophecies through the revelation of the crucified and risen Christ (cf. 1 Cor. 1:18-19)! This will take place at the day of Jesus Christ, when the proud will be humbled, and the humble will be exalted ("Lebanon shall be turned into a fruitful field, and the fruitful field be esteemed as a forest" Isa. 29:17; cf. Isa. 29:19; 32:15; 35:4-5).

In the meantime, the prophetic message of the Prophets will continue to be understood by only a smaller number of disciples, that is, a remnant of the larger nation.[2] In Isaiah's time, this inner circle included the prophet's own disciples, as he explained, "Bind up the testimony, seal the law among my disciples. And I will wait on the Lord, who hides His face from the house of Jacob; and I will hope in Him" (Isa.

---

[2] By extension, the illumined now includes Gentiles who trust in Jesus Christ. As such, the holy Church is comprised of believing Jews and Gentiles.

8:16-17). The Lord's teaching ("the testimony . . . the law" Isa. 8:16), especially as articulated and expounded upon by the prophets, points to Christ but remains a hidden mystery to outsiders. In the meantime, faithful disciples should expectantly wait for the Lord ("I will wait on the Lord . . . I will hope in Him" Isa. 8:17; 45:15), while He continues to "hide His face" from the larger house of Jacob, even until He reveals Himself to the nation.

The sealed scroll of the Prophets remained a hidden mystery during Jesus' earthly ministry. To demonstrate, Christ taught that the purpose of His parables is to reveal the mysteries of God's kingdom to His disciples while hiding them from outsiders (Matt. 13:10-12; Mark 4:9-12; Luke 8:9-10; cf. Num. 12:8; Matt. 11:25-30; 13:34-35; Mark 4:33-34). This is an act of divine mercy to those who reject the words of the Lord. According to Jesus, these parables enable only His people to see, hear, and understand the sealed scroll of the Prophets:

> Therefore I speak to them in parables, because seeing they do not see, and hearing they do not hear, nor do they understand. And in them the prophecy of Isaiah is fulfilled, which says: "Hearing you will hear and shall not understand, and seeing you will see and not perceive; for the hearts of this people have grown dull. Their ears are hard of hearing, and their eyes they have closed, lest they should see with their eyes and hear with their ears, lest they should understand with their hearts and turn, so that I should heal them." But blessed are your eyes for they see, and your ears for they hear; for assuredly, I say to you that many prophets and righteous men desired to see what you see, and did not see it, and to hear what you hear, and did not hear it. (Matt. 13:13-17)

The Lord gave His apostles and their subsequent disciples the grace to see, hear, and understand the fuller meaning of the "sealed scroll" of the Prophets—the gospel of Christ. The enduring foundation of the holy Church begins with the revelation that Jesus Christ is the Son of

God (Matt. 16:16-19; cf. Luke 10:21-24; John 10:3-4; Gal. 1:15). The Holy Spirit gives this revelation, enabling us to believe and understand the message which "many prophets and righteous men desired to see what you see, and did not see it, and to hear what you hear, and did not hear it" (Matt. 13:17).

Jesus taught that God consistently hides His mysteries from the proud but reveals them to the humble (Matt. 11:25-30). Christ prayed, "I thank You, Father, Lord of heaven and earth, that You have hidden these things from the wise and prudent and revealed them to babes. Even so, Father, for so it seemed good in Your sight" (Luke 10:21). The Lord initially prevented His disciples from comprehending His impending betrayal (Luke 9:43-45), and He temporarily concealed His own identity to some after His resurrection from the dead (Luke 24:15-16). He asked His disciples, "Do you not yet perceive nor understand? Is your heart still hardened? Having eyes, do you not see? And having ears, do you not hear?" (Mark 8:17-18; cf. John 8:43-47; 9:39). Similarly, God hid the mystery of Christ's crucifixion from the principalities and powers so that their earthly agents did not avoid crucifying him (1 Cor. 2:6-9).

Admittedly, Christ's gospel was not fully revealed to anyone until the Spirit was poured out, beginning at the day of Pentecost. The apostle Paul understood that the gospel had previously been a secret, hidden since the beginning of the world; nevertheless, he taught that this "revelation of the mystery" is the Christological message of the Prophets—the gospel—which is now being proclaimed to all nations (Rom. 16:25-26; 1 Cor. 2:6-9).

Saint Paul taught that a veil of unbelief covers the minds of unbelieving Jews when they hear the synagogue readings from the Old Testament, a veil which is taken away only when they turn to Christ by the Spirit's enablement by grace (2 Cor. 3:12-17; 4:3-6). He further explained that Satan has spiritually blinded them so that they cannot see the glory of the gospel (2 Cor. 4:3-4, 6). On the other hand, those who trust in Christ are unveiled in such a manner that they can behold His glory "as in a mirror" (2 Cor. 3:18).

God promised in Isaiah's prophecy that the "sealed scroll" of the Prophets will one day be understood by the recalcitrant nation of Israel: "The eyes of those who see will not be dim, and the ears of those who hear will listen. Also the heart of the rash will understand knowledge, and the tongue of the stammerers will be ready to speak plainly" (Isa. 32:3-4). A few chapters later, the prophet concluded, "They shall see the glory of the Lord. . . Behold, your God will come with vengeance. . . He will come and save you. Then the eyes of the blind shall be opened, and the ears of the deaf shall be unstopped. Then the lame shall leap like a deer, and the tongue of the dumb sing" (Isa. 35:2, 4-6; cf. Isa. 6:1-8; 33:17; 42:16). When Christ arrives in glory to save them, the Jewish nation will finally see, hear, and receive the Christological message of the Prophets (i.e., the gospel).

In contrast to Isaiah's "sealed scroll," God instructed Habakkuk to write his end-time prophetic vision upon clay tablets and elucidate its meaning: "Write the vision and make it plain on tablets, that he may run who reads it. For the vision is yet for an appointed time; but at the end it will speak, and it will not lie. Though it tarries, wait for it; because it will surely come, it will not tarry" (Hab. 2:2-3). The fulfillment of the vision would initially be delayed ("though it tarries" Hab. 2:3) but its contents are certain ("it will speak . . . it will surely come" Hab. 2:3). The writer of Hebrews reworded the prophecy to read "for yet a little while, and He who is coming will come and will not tarry" (Heb. 10:37).[3] In other words, Christians patiently "wait for" the coming of Jesus Christ, who will be revealed at the appointed time of the end ("appointed time . . . at the end" Hab. 2:3).

Reminiscent of Isaiah's prophecy, the larger context of Habakkuk's end-time vision shows that he also predicted a wondrous "work" intended for unbelieving Israel: "Look among the nations and watch— be utterly astounded! For I will work a work in your days which you

---

3   This prophecy conflated Habakkuk 2:3 with Isaiah 26:20 ("Hide yourself, as it were, for a little moment, until the indignation is past").

would not believe, though it were told you" (Hab. 1:5). Although this "work" could be interpreted as the arrival of King Nebuchadnezzar's armies, the plenary fulfillment will be the arrival of the military forces of the Antichrist ("For indeed I am raising up the Chaldeans" Hab. 1:6; cf. "the king of Babylon" Isa. 14:4ff). A future fulfillment is supported by the fact that the apostle Paul quoted this exact verse: "Beware therefore, lest what has been spoken in the prophets come upon you: 'Behold, you despisers, Marvel and perish! For I work a work in your days, a work which you will by no means believe, though one were to declare it to you' " (Acts 13:40-41). The context of the apostle's statement indicates that his Jewish audience was rejecting the proclamation of the gospel, placing them at risk of this divine judgment. The apostle's reference to "the scoffers" ("the despisers" NKJV), who also appear in Isaiah's prophecy of the "sealed scroll" (Isa. 28:14, 22; cf. 2 Pet. 3:3), lends credence to this end-time interpretation.

Reminiscent of Isaiah's sealed scroll motif, the prophet Daniel was instructed to "shut up" and "seal" the scroll of his final prophecy so that the nation would not understand its contents until the salvation and resurrection of his "people" at the time of the unprecedented tribulation (Dan. 12:1-4). This instruction reads as follows: "But you, Daniel, shut up the words, and seal the book until the time of the end; many shall run to and fro, and knowledge shall increase" (Dan. 12:4). Like the Lord's statement to Habakkuk ("that he may run who reads it" Hab. 2:2), Daniel was told that many people will "run to and fro" (Dan. 12:4), in other words, they will hastily go forth to proclaim the prophetic message of the eschatological gospel. It may also indicate that people will desperately seek to understand this message (cf. "They shall run to and fro, seeking the word of the Lord" Amos 8:12), with the result that their understanding of it will increase ("and knowledge shall increase" Dan. 12:4).

An angel asked how much time would elapse before Daniel's prophetic vision is fulfilled ("the fulfillment of these wonders" Dan. 12:6). The Angel answered that the vision will be completed after a tribulation period of three and a half years ("for a time, times, and half a time" Dan. 12:7). He then provided the reason for the unprecedented tribulation:

> And when the power of the holy people has been completely shattered, all these things shall be finished. . . Go your way, Daniel, for the words are closed up and sealed till the time of the end. Many shall be purified, made white, and refined, but the wicked shall do wickedly; and none of the wicked shall understand, but the wise shall understand. (Dan. 12:7, 9-10)

All the end-time events contained in this vision ("all these things" Dan. 12:7) will be finished once "the power of the holy people has been completely shattered" (Dan. 12:7). This verse restates the expectation contained in the book of Deuteronomy that the *power* of the Jewish nation will be removed during the period of their final distress in the last days (Deut. 31:29 with Deut. 4:30; cf. Deut. 32:20, 29; Jer. 23:20). The Song of Moses continues this concept: "For the Lord will judge His people and have compassion on His servants, when He sees that their power is gone, and there is no one remaining, bond or free" (Deut. 32:36). To restate, the purpose of the unprecedented tribulation, at least as it pertains to the Jewish people ("the holy people" Dan. 12:7), will be to remove their reliance on the arm of flesh, that is, their own strength ("their power is gone" Deut. 32:36; "the power . . . has been completely shattered" Dan. 12:7; cf. Zech. 4:6). However, God will display His power, resulting in the voluntarily obedience of His people at the day of Christ ("in the day of Your power" Ps. 110:3; cf. Judg. 5:2; Zech. 4:6).

One of the purposes of the great tribulation will be to purify and refine God's people ("Many should be purified, made white, and refined" Dan. 12:10; cf. Dan. 11:35; Zech. 13:9; 1 Pet. 1:7, 18; Rev. 3:4-5, 18; 7:14). The wicked will not understand the prophetic vision of the sealed scroll but "the wise" will comprehend it and will be saved and glorified at the end of the tribulation (Dan. 12:3, 10). The angel told the apostle John "Do not seal the words of the prophecy of this book, for the time is at hand. He who is unjust, let him be unjust still; he who is filthy, let him be filthy still; he who is righteous, let him be righteous still; he who is holy, let him be holy still" (Rev. 22:10-11; cf. Rev. 10:4). In other words, the purification of the righteous will not extend to the rebellious, those who will receive eternal condemnation (e.g., Rev. 9:20-21; 16:9, 11).

The prophet Zechariah also described the tribulation in terms of God testing the Jewish nation as a smelter refines gold and silver:

> Strike the Shepherd, and the sheep will be scattered; then I will turn My hand against the little ones. And it shall come to pass in all the land . . . That two-thirds in it shall be cut off and die, but one-third shall be left . . . I will bring the one-third through the fire, will refine them as silver is refined, and test them as gold is tested. They will call on My name, and I will answer them. I will say, "This is My people"; and each one will say, "The Lord is my God." (Zech. 13:7-8, 9)

This prophecy reveals that many Jews will survive the tribulation and will be numbered among the holy Church. The Jewish nation, after their rejection of Christ ("Strike the Shepherd" Zech. 13:7), became a scattered people "without a shepherd" (Zech. 13:7; Matt. 26:31; Mark 14:27). The "little ones," a term that elsewhere designates Christians (Matt. 10:42; 18:6, 10, 14; cf. Luke 12:32), will also be persecuted and martyred during the tribulation (Zech. 13:7). In addition, a staggering two-thirds of the people living in Israel will be killed during this time ("two-thirds in it shall be cut off and die" Zech. 13:8; cf. Ezek. 5:12); this fatality rate likely includes some of the Jews who will be displaced and exiled throughout the surrounding nations (cf. Zech. 14:2; Luke 21:24). However, the remaining one-third of the Jews who remain in the land ("one-third shall be left in it" Zech. 13:8) will be refined in the fires of persecution (Zech. 13:9), and as a result they will call upon the Lord's name and receive divine favor (Zech. 13:9). In short, they will become Christians. In the book of Revelation, a heavenly voice echoed the final promise of Zechariah's prophecy: "They shall be His people. God Himself will be with them and be their God" (Rev. 21:3; cf. "This is My people. . . The Lord is my God" Zech. 13:9).

In the final analysis, all the Jews who survive the great tribulation will become holy:

> In that day the Branch of the Lord shall be beautiful and glorious; and the fruit of the earth shall be excellent and appealing for those of Israel who have escaped. And it shall come to pass that he who is left in Zion and remains in Jerusalem will be called holy—everyone who is recorded among the living in Jerusalem. When the Lord has washed away the filth of the daughters of Zion, and purged the blood of Jerusalem from her midst, by the spirit of judgment and by the spirit of burning. (Isa. 4:2-4)

The fiery trial of the unprecedented tribulation ("the spirit of judgment and by the spirit of burning" Isa. 4:4) will result in Christ "washing away" the sins of pride and bloodshed from Jerusalem so that the nation becomes holy (Isa. 4:4; cf. Job 23:10; Isa. 1:25; Dan. 12:10; Zech. 13:9; Mal. 3:2-3; 1 Pet. 1:6-7; 4:12). On that day, the Branch of the Lord (i.e., Jesus Christ) will appear in all His beauty and brilliance (Isa. 4:2). Elsewhere, Zechariah picked up this motif: "For behold, I am bringing forth My Servant the Branch . . . and I will remove the iniquity of that land in one day. In that day . . . everyone will invite his neighbor under his vine and under his fig tree" (Zech. 3:8, 9-10; cf. Isa. 1:18; 29:23). At that time, the earth will bring forth abundant fruit[4] for the remnant of Jews who survived the final tribulation ("those of Israel who have escaped" Isa. 4:2; "he who is left . . . and remains in Jerusalem" Isa. 4:3). In other words, everyone who remains alive in Jerusalem ("everyone who is recorded among the living in Jerusalem"

---

4   Elsewhere, fruit is a symbol for good deeds produced by the Holy Spirit (e.g. Matt. 3:8; Gal. 5:22; Eph. 5:9).

Isa. 4:3; cf. Dan. 12:1; Rev. 13:8; 20:15) will receive forgiveness of sins and will inherit the blessings of Christ's kingdom.

The heavenly registry in Isaiah's prophecy presupposes that the entire remnant of Jews who survive the tribulation will also receive eternal life ("will be called holy" Isa. 4:3) on the day of Jesus Christ. The rabbis of the Second Temple period taught that the name of each Jew destined to live throughout the entire year was inscribed in the "scroll of life," the heavenly register, on the festival of trumpets (cf. Exod. 32:32-33). The book of Revelation further recognizes that the Lamb's Book of Life records the names of everyone who will receive eternal life, as a benefit of His death on the cross (Rev. 13:8; 17:8; 20:12, 15; 21:27; 22:19; cf. Phil. 4:3). Based on the context of Isaiah's prophecy, we can deduce that the prophet has in mind physical survival and eternal salvation. At His glorious return, Christ will reveal Himself to the Jewish nation in such a manner that every Jew who survives the great tribulation will receive eternal life!

One of the purposes of the great tribulation is to bring the Jewish nation to faith in Jesus Christ. The prophet Moses warned that before this occurs, Israel would commit great evil and turn their back on God (Deut. 31:18; 32:5, 20-29). As a result, God would forsake the nation and "hide His face" from the people "in the latter days" so that they experience many evils and troubles (Deut. 31:17-18, 29; 32:20; cf. Lev. 26:14-39; Deut. 28:15-68; 31:29; Ezek. 39:23). Moses yearned for them to wisely consider "their latter end," that is, the time of calamity when their "foot slips" (Deut. 32:29, 35; cf. Jer. 30:24). Nevertheless, the Lord will mercifully remember His covenant with their fathers and preserve the nation, but only "when you are in distress, and all these things come upon you in the latter days, when you turn to the Lord your God and obey His voice" (Deut. 4:30-31; cf. Deut. 30:1-10). As a result, the Lord will answer by saving them "in the day of trouble" (cf. 2 Sam. 22:7; Ps. 20:1, 9).

Elsewhere, Isaiah predicted that God will mercifully answer the prayers of Jerusalem's inhabitants when they cry out to Him for deliverance (Isa. 30:19). For example, Joel prophesied that on the day of the Lord, God will deliver everyone in Jerusalem who calls upon His name, and he identifies those who repent as the Jewish remnant (Joel 2:32; cf. Isa. 11:11; Jer. 31:7; Acts 2:21; Rom. 9:27). The repentance of the remnant will signal Christ's arrival: "The Redeemer will come to Zion, and to those who turn from transgression in Jacob" (Isa. 59:20).[5] As a result, they will be called "The Holy People, the Redeemed of the Lord" and "Sought Out, a City Not Forsaken" (Isa. 62:12).

The Lord promised to deliver the nation, the surviving remnant of Jacob, from the great tribulation: "Alas! For that day is great, so that none is like it; and it is the time of Jacob's trouble, but he shall be saved out of it" (Jer. 30:7; cf. vv. 5-6).[6] While in distress during "the latter days," the nation will finally "consider" God's redemptive purposes (Jer. 30:24). This is because the Antichrist ("a cruel one" Jer. 30:14) will be an instrument of divine wrath to recompense the Jewish nation for seeking after other "lovers" (i.e., foreign deities), but even then, God will not "make a complete end" of the people but will correct their waywardness (Jer. 30:11, 14-15; 46:28). Consequently, Israel will serve their resurrected Christ: "But they shall serve the Lord their God and David their king, whom I will raise up for them" (Jer. 30:9). The Lord has promised, "I will be the God of all the families of Israel, and they shall be My people. . . Yes, I have loved you with an everlasting love; therefore with lovingkindness I have drawn you" (Jer. 31:1, 3; cf. Isa. 54:9-10; John 6:44).

When the Lord delivers Jacob's descendants from the Antichrist and his armies ("I will save your children" Isa. 49:25), everyone on earth will know that He is their Savior and Redeemer (Isa. 49:26; cf. Deut. 32:43). He pledged, "the house of Israel shall know that I am the

---

5   The apostle Paul quoted this verse, while amending it slightly, in Romans 11:26. He saw the Redeemer as coming *out of* Zion, presumably, from the heavenly Jerusalem.

6   After the time of the patriarch Jacob's "trouble," Christ gave Him the name Israel, and He no longer hid His face from him, as Jacob declared, "For I have seen God face to face, and my life is preserved" (Gen. 32:30).

Lord their God from that day forward" (Ezek. 39:22). Similarly, the Gentiles will forever understand that the former disobedience of Israel had resulted in their captivity and in God "hiding His face from them" (Ezek. 39:23-24). However, He will no longer hide His face from the house of Israel once He has "poured out" His Spirit upon them (Ezek. 39:29). As we will see in chapter 16, the pouring out of the Spirit on the nation demands an eschatological setting.

Continuing this theme, the prophet Zechariah depicted the Lord pouring out the Holy Spirit upon the surviving remnant of Israel:

> And I will pour on the house of David and on the inhabitants of Jerusalem the Spirit of grace and supplication; then they will look on Me whom they pierced. Yes, they will mourn for Him as one mourns for his only son, and grieve for Him as one grieves for a firstborn. In that day there shall be a great mourning in Jerusalem, like the mourning at Hadad Rimmon in the plain of Megiddo. And the land shall mourn, every family by itself: the family of the house of David by itself, and their wives by themselves; the family of the house of Nathan by itself, and their wives by themselves; the family of the house of Levi by itself, and their wives by themselves; the family of Shimei by itself, and their wives by themselves; all the families that remain, every family by itself, and their wives by themselves. (Zech. 12:10-14)

A careful reading of the passage reveals that Yahweh is the One whom the people of Jerusalem will have pierced and killed ("they will look on Me whom they pierced" Zech. 12:10; cf. Gen. 3:15; Zech. 13:3; Matt. 24:30; John 19:37; 20:20; Rev. 1:7). The concept here is that God holds David's royal descendants and the people of Jerusalem ("the house of David and on the inhabitants of Jerusalem" Zech. 12:10) perpetually responsible for His Son's crucifixion, and they will look upon Christ when He returns to "pour out" His Spirit upon them ("I will pour . . . the Spirit of grace and supplication" Zech. 12:10; cf. John 20:20, 22). Their outpouring of the Holy Spirit will result in national repentance because divine grace will enable them to supplicate to Christ for forgiveness ("the Spirit of grace and supplication" Zech. 12:10; cf. Jer. 3:21; 31:9; 50:4-5; Heb. 4:16; 5:7).

The context demonstrates that this will occur when the returning Christ delivers and protects the remaining inhabitants of Jerusalem from the multinational military force which will have threatened to destroy the beloved people (Zech. 12:1-9; cf. Ezek. 38-39; Zech. 14:1-5). As we have seen, the Lord Jesus will return in glory to put an abrupt end to the battle of Armageddon ("the mourning at Hadad Rimmon in the plain of Megiddo" Zech. 12:11). He will save the surviving remnant of Jews from imminent physical death but most importantly from everlasting destruction.

When the Jewish nation "looks upon" the returning Christ, the people will weep profusely ("great mourning") (Zech. 12:10-14; cf. Jer. 31:9; 50:4-5). The grief of the inhabitants of Jerusalem will be like the bitter lamentation of a parent who weeps over the death of a firstborn son ("as one mourns for his only son, and grieve for Him as one grieves for a firstborn" Zech. 12:10). The description of this national lamentation echoes the weeping of the Egyptian families on the first Passover, when each family looked upon the slain body of its firstborn child (Exod. 12:29-30; cf. "each family by itself" Zech. 12:14).[7] Likewise, each family within the Jewish nation will mourn over the Father's only begotten Son, the firstborn, the true Passover Lamb, who died for transgressions. Christ explained that this mourning will extend to "all the tribes of the earth" when He returns (Matt. 24:30). The apostle John recorded, "Behold, He is coming with clouds, and every eye will see Him, even they who pierced Him. And all the tribes of the earth will mourn because of Him" (Rev. 1:7).

---

[7] The plagues of the exodus will be recapitulated during the unprecedented tribulation. For example, the ninth plague, thick darkness, appeared throughout the land of Egypt (Exod. 10:21-23), which will be mirrored by the cosmic darkness at the day of Jesus Christ. In the Exodus narrative, the plague of darkness was followed by the atonement of the slain Passover lambs, which protected the firstborn among the children of Israel from the angel of death.

Other biblical narratives highlight the transformative power of looking upon the crucified Christ, resulting in godly sorrow unto repentance. For example, the Roman soldiers acquired the revelation concerning "the Son of God" once they witnessed the great earthquake and saw the pierced Christ upon the cross (Matt. 27:54; cf. Matt. 16:17).[8] In addition, Thomas and the other disciples believed in Christ as their Lord and God when they saw and handled His pierced hands, feet, and side (John 20:24-29; cf. Acts 9:3-8; 22:6-11; 26:13-19; 1 Cor. 9:1; 15:8).

The prophet Isaiah also received an instantaneous conversion the moment he saw the glorious Son of God seated upon the throne of His temple (Isa. 6:1-13; cf. "Isaiah . . . saw His glory and spoke of Him" John 12:41). The careful reader should consider the prophet's three actions:

1. Hearing—He heard the angels crying, "Holy, holy, holy is the Lord of hosts; the whole earth is full of His glory!" (Isa. 6:3).

2. Vision—He saw the Second Person of the Holy Trinity reigning in His glory ("For my eyes have seen the King" Isa. 6:5; cf. Isa. 30:20).

3. Comprehension—He came to understand that he was sinfully unworthy, and He knew that Christ had instantaneously removed his iniquities and sins (Isa. 6:5-7).

The immediate context leaves no doubt that the unbelieving nation will be converted in the same fashion as Isaiah. At the conclusion of the unprecedented tribulation, the surviving remnant will receive spiritual hearing, vision, and understanding, in other words, instantaneous conversion resulting in repentance (Isa. 6:9-12).

Furthermore, Jesus also taught that the Jewish nation will welcome Him at His return. For instance, He told the Pharisees and scribes, "For I say to you, you shall see Me no more till you say, 'Blessed is He who comes

---

8   Notably, an earthquake will also signal the Second Coming of Jesus Christ.

in the name of the Lord!' " (Matt. 23:39; cf. Ps. 118:26; Luke 13:35). This statement was a well-known verse of a Hallel psalm (Ps. 118), which the Jews liturgically sang at their festivals. The psalm extols Yahweh for His mercy and covenant fidelity toward the Jewish nation (Ps. 118), and the context reveals that the nation will gratefully praise the Lord from His temple ("from the house of the Lord" Ps. 118:26). The context of Jesus' prophecy shows that the people of Jerusalem who murdered the prophets and crucified the Son of God would experience the divine judgment of the temple's destruction, an event which occurred in AD 70, and will faithfully welcome Him when He returns to the Holy City ("Blessed is He who comes" Matt. 23:39; cf. Matt. 23:37-39).

The Genesis narrative of the patriarch Joseph foreshadows Jesus Christ, initially hiding His face from the Jewish nation and later revealing Himself to them.[9] The narrative relays that Jacob's sons thought that Joseph was dead but he was alive (Gen. 37:32ff; 42:13, 32, 36, 38; cf. Matt. 28:11-15; Luke 24:13-49). Afterward, the brothers did not realize that the king had elevated Joseph to receive the right hand of his own authority (Gen. 41:37-42; cf. Acts 2:32-33; 1 Cor. 15:25-28). Although he knew his brothers, he spoke to them in a foreign language (Gen. 42:23; cf. Deut. 28:49; 1 Cor. 14:21), and they did not recognize him (Gen. 42:7-8; cf. John 1:10). Although he had been the reason for their distress (Gen. 42:21-22; cf. Matt. 27:25; 2 Thess. 2:14-16), his brothers finally recognized that they had caused "the anguish of his soul" and were responsible for his presumed death (Gen. 42:21-22; cf. Isa. 53:11; Mark 14:33; Luke 22:41-44; 23:32-49).

The narrative concludes with Joseph holding a banquet for his brothers at the time that he revealed his true identity (Gen. 43:16; cf. Matt. 22:2; 25:10; Luke 12:36; Rev. 19:6-21). They bowed down to him (Gen. 43:26, 28; 44:14; cf. Gen. 42:6; Rom. 11:25-27) once he revealed himself to them as their brother and "savior" (Gen. 45:1;

---

9   The concept that Joseph prophetically foreshadows Christ is well established, and the numerous details are documented in my book *Moshiach Now*.

48:11; cf. Zech. 12:10-14), and he no longer hid his face from them (Gen. 45:12; 47:25; cf. Matt. 24:30; Rev. 1:7). The evil that his brothers initially intended against him was sovereignly designed so that they would be saved (Gen. 45:5-8; 50:20; cf. Acts 2:23-24, 36-38; 3:12-18). Finally, his brothers wept when he revealed himself to them (Gen. 45:14-15; cf. Zech. 12:10-14). In this manner, the Joseph narrative divinely foreshadows the revelation of Jesus Christ and the mercy that He will extend to all the tribes of Jacob.

Like the other prophets, Hosea prophesied that the divine judgments against the Jewish nation will end once the Davidic kingdom has been consummated. The prophet taught that the children of Israel would "abide many days without king or prince, without sacrifice or sacred pillar, without ephod or teraphim" but would finally "return and seek the Lord their God and David their King . . . in the latter days" (Hosea 3:4-5). To paraphrase, the end result of the nation's long exile will be for the people to repent and to welcome Christ, the Davidic King. Continuing this theme, the prophet depicted God as a raging Lion, which would mangle and carry off the nation of Israel, presumably through exile (Hosea 5:14). This judgment would continue until the Lord returned from His heavenly abode ("My place" Hosea 5:15) and the nation repented ("return to the Lord" Hosea 6:1):

> "I will return again to My place till they acknowledge their offense. Then they will seek My face; in their affliction they will earnestly seek Me. Come, and let us return to the Lord; for He has torn, but He will heal us; He has stricken, but He will bind us up. After two days He will revive us; on the third day He will raise us up that we may live in His sight." (Hosea 5:15-6:2)

In this prophecy, God would return to heaven until the Jewish people "acknowledge their offense" and earnestly seek His face during their "affliction" (Hosea 5:15). The prophet did not specify their singular offense but their rejection of the Lord is implicit. This prophecy is consistent with other prophecies which predict an unprecedented tribulation at the end of days, after which time the nation will passionately seek the Lord's face (e.g., Deut. 4:29-31; 30:1-10). The Lord promised to descend from His heavenly place in order to "heal," "bind up," "revive," and "raise up" the nation "on the third day," so that they can live in His presence (Hosea 6:2-3; cf. Isa. 30:26). This is the language of resurrection! As we have seen, this resurrection has already begun in Christ's own resurrection, who also was raised up on the third day, becoming the firstfruits' offering of the larger harvest!

The Lord's return to His place in heaven points to Christ's ascension, an event which occurred just days after the Jewish nation rejected and crucified Him. His crucifixion was the nation's ultimate "offense" (Hosea 5:15), for which God allowed the nation to be "afflicted," "torn," and "stricken" (Hosea 5:15; 6:1; cf. Mic. 5:1). A similar passage provides confirming evidence for this interpretation:

> They will strike the judge of Israel with a rod on the cheek. "But you, Bethlehem Ephrathah, though you are little among the thousands of Judah, yet out of you shall come forth to Me the One to be Ruler in Israel, Whose goings forth are from of old, from everlasting." Therefore He shall give them up, until the time that she who is in labor has given birth; then the remnant of His brethren shall return to the children of Israel. (Mic. 5:1-3)

Micah's prophecy conveys the idea that the everlasting Ruler from Bethlehem, the Lord Jesus, will "give them up" *until* the woman in labor gives birth. The idea is that Christ would deliver the people of Judah over to covenantal judgment until the end of the unprecedented tribulation, or in eschatological parlance, until Jerusalem labors and gives birth to her children ("until the time that she who is in labor has given birth" Mic. 5:3; cf. Mic. 4:9-10). The cause[10] of this divine judgment is the

---

10   "Therefore" (Mic. 5:3) denotes a relationship of logical consequence between verses 1-2 (i.e., the cause) and verse 3 that immediately follows (i.e., the effect).

Jewish nation delivering the Judge of Israel over to be struck "with a rod [or scepter] on the cheek" (Mic. 5:1; cf. Mic. 6:9, 13; Matt. 27:30; Mark 15:19),[11] a metonym for Jesus' crucifixion. However, once this judgment ends, the remnant of Christ's brothers will return to join the remainder of their brethren (Mic. 5:3), implicitly, in the Promised Land.

As we return to Hosea's prophecy, we can identify Israel's specific "offense" as the crucifixion of Jesus Christ (Hosea 5:15), which resulted in the nation's long exile, beginning with the Roman destruction of Jerusalem in AD 70. The time indicators "after two days" and "on the third day" (Hosea 6:2) reveal that two days would elapse between Christ's ascension ("I will return again to My place, till they acknowledge their offence, and seek my face: in their affliction they will seek me early (Hosea 5:15) and His return to resurrect the dead ("He will revive us . . . He will raise us up that we may live in His sight" Hosea 6:2). Based on the apostle Peter's statement that "with the Lord one day is as a thousand years, and a thousand years as one day" (2 Pet. 3:8; cf. Ps. 90:4), a few commentators think that the two completed "days" is an enigmatic way of saying that Christ would remain in heaven for two thousand years before His return.[12]

Because Jesus fulfilled many of the prophetic expectations about the Messiah, His disciples understood Him to be the King of the Jews (Matt. 2:2; 27:11; Mark 15:12, 26; John 18:33; 19:19), the King of Israel (John 12:13), the King of Zion (John 12:15), the Consolation of Israel (Luke 2:25), and the One who will redeem Israel (Luke 24:21; cf. Luke 2:38). Consequently, the disciples correctly expected that the Davidic kingdom would be restored to Israel. After His resurrection, Jesus spent an additional forty days with them, teaching them about His kingdom (Acts 1:3), and they asked Him the following question:

---

11 The prophet asked, "Is there no king in your midst? Has your counselor perished?" (Mic. 5:9).

12 Such interpreters argue that since the exact year and date of Christ's ascension is debated, the modern reader is left with only an approximate date for His return. Significantly, a few of the holy Church fathers taught that Christ would return six thousand years after creation.

"Lord, will You at this time restore the kingdom to Israel?" And He said to them, "It is not for you to know times or seasons which the Father has put in His own authority. But you shall receive power when the Holy Spirit has come upon you; and you shall be witnesses to Me in Jerusalem, and in all Judea and Samaria, and to the end of the earth." (Acts 1:6-8)

The Lord did not rebuke the disciples for asking this question about the timing of Israel's restoration. Rather, He qualified their expectations by explaining that the gospel must first go forth from Jerusalem into all the world ("to the end of the earth" Acts 1:8; cf. Isa. 2:3). Their question already betrayed the concern that He might delay the restoration of His kingdom to the Jewish nation ("will You at this time restore the kingdom to Israel?" Acts 1:6; cf. Luke 19:11). His answer began to prepare them to consider the purposes for this mysterious inter-advent delay. One primary purpose has been for the apostolic Church to present the testimony of the gospel before all the nations ("you shall be witnesses to Me" Acts 1:8; cf. Isa. 52:10; Matt. 28:19; Luke 24:47). The disciples had not yet understood the apostolic mystery, namely, that the Gentiles would be grafted into His kingdom prior to the day of Christ (Rom. 11:25-26; Eph. 3:6; Col. 1:27).

The apostle Paul desired and earnestly prayed for the salvation of the Jewish nation: "Brethren, my heart's desire and prayer to God for Israel is that they may be saved" (Rom. 10:1). While Paul expressed tremendous grief regarding their recalcitrance to God, he expressed the intercessory heart of Christ, so that he would have, if possible, suffered God's curse in order for them to attain salvation:

I tell the truth in Christ, I am not lying, my conscience also bearing me witness in the Holy Spirit, that I have great sorrow and continual grief in my heart. For I could wish that I myself were accursed from Christ for my brethren, my countrymen according to the flesh, who are Israelites, to whom pertain the adoption, the glory, the covenants, the giving of the law, the service of God, and the promises. (Rom. 9:1-4)

The above passage is found in a section of the epistle (Rom. 9-11) wherein Paul often employed the term "Israel" to denote the ethnic descendants of Jacob who largely continued in an obstinate, disobedient, reprobate condition (Rom. 9:6, 27, 31; 10:19, 21; 11:2, 7, 11, 25, 26). He variously called them "my brethren, my countrymen according to the flesh, who are Israelites" and "my flesh" (Rom. 9:3; 11:14; cf. Rom. 11:1). Furthermore, the apostle taught that God's covenants and promises continued to belong to these ethnic Israelites (Rom. 9:4), and he called them "His [God's] people" (Rom. 11:1). Throughout Romans 11 he contrasted these unbelieving Israelites (they/them) with the Gentiles and the remnant of Jews who had trusted in Christ.[13]

In this passage, Saint Paul taught the future certainty of Israel's national redemption. The Jewish nation had rejected the Lord and His prophets, had failed to obtain salvation because they pursued it on the basis of the works of the law of Moses, and had rejected the gospel due to their hardened hearts (Rom. 11:3-10). On the other hand, many of the Gentiles had accepted the gospel of salvation, after Israel rejected it, in order that the Gentiles might make Israel jealous unto salvation (Rom. 11:11-12, 14, 31; cf. Deut. 32:21). The apostle contrasted the nation's ongoing failure to obtain the promises, a rejection that had resulted in reconciliation for the nations (Rom. 11:15), to its future acceptance and full inclusion into those promises: "Now if their [Israel's] fall is riches for the world, and their failure riches for the Gentiles, how much more their fullness" (Rom. 11:12). This future acceptance will result in resurrection life ("what will their acceptance be but life from the dead?" Rom. 11:15; cf. Rom. 11:2).

Paul continued to contrast unbelieving Israel with the largely Gentile Church with the analogy of the olive tree (Rom. 11:16-24). Gentile Christians were being grafted into the olive tree, a symbol for the nation of Israel, whereas many of the "natural branches" (i.e., ethnic Jews) had

---

13   The apostle consistently employed the pronouns "they," "them," "their," and "those" to describe this unbelieving Jewish nation.

been broken off because of their unbelief (Rom. 11:16-24). The apostle warned these Gentiles not to be arrogant toward ethnic Israel because they were being grafted into their promises because the unbelieving Jews had been broken off (Rom. 11:18-20), and in like manner, the Gentiles could be broken off through unbelief (Rom. 11:22). Paul then discussed the concept of the Lord grafting ethnic Jews back into the promises through faith in Jesus Christ (Rom. 11:23-24). He concluded with the following synopsis of Israel's future, national redemption:

> For I do not desire, brethren, that you should be ignorant of this mystery, lest you should be wise in your own opinion, that blindness in part has happened to Israel until the fullness of the Gentiles has come in. And so all Israel will be saved, as it is written: "The Deliverer will come out of Zion, and He will turn away ungodliness from Jacob; for this is My covenant with them, when I take away their sins." Concerning the gospel they are enemies for your sake, but concerning the election they are beloved for the sake of the fathers. For the gifts and the calling of God are irrevocable. (Rom. 11:25-29)

In this passage, the apostle Paul taught the mystery of the national restoration of Israel ("all Israel will be saved" Rom. 11:25, 26). The "partial hardening" of the Jewish nation will continue "until the fullness of the Gentiles has come" (Rom. 11:25). The larger context indicates that this "fullness" will include the believing Gentiles' provocation of Israel so that the surviving remnant of the nation finds salvation when Jesus returns from heaven ("The Deliverer will come from Zion" Rom. 11:26 from Isa. 59:20-21; cf. Deut. 32:43) and eradicates sin and ungodliness from the descendants of Jacob (Rom. 11:26-27; cf. Isa. 27:9). This restoration of Israel is intrinsically bound up with the consummation of the new covenant ("my covenant with them when I take away their sins" Rom. 11:27; cf. Isa. 27:9) and the irrevocable gifts and election of the nation that God promised to the patriarchs ("concerning the election they are beloved for the sake of the fathers. For the gifts and the calling of God are irrevocable" Rom. 11:28-29).

By saving the entire remnant of surviving Jews, Christ will once again demonstrate that He "will have mercy on whomever I will have mercy, and I will have compassion on whomever I will have compassion" (Rom. 9:15). In summary fashion, the apostle declared the following doxology: "Oh, the depth of the riches both of the wisdom and knowledge of God! How unsearchable are His judgments and His ways past finding out!" (Rom. 11:33). What a sobering assessment about the unsearchable riches of God's kindnesses toward the Jewish nation and toward all the nations.

15

THE JUDGMENT SEAT OF CHRIST

THE HOLY SCRIPTURES reveal that God will judge the world on judgment day (Matt. 12:36, 41-42; Rom. 3:6; Heb. 6:2). This judgment will take place on the day of Jesus Christ (2 Tim. 4:8; cf. John 12:48; Phil. 2:16; cf. 1 Cor. 3:13; 1 Pet. 2:12), the day "appointed" by the Father (Acts 17:31) when Jesus will return in glory.[1] Jesus will judge the living and the dead (Acts 10:42; 1 Pet. 4:5) because the Father has given Him the authority to execute judgment (John 5:22, 27; Acts 17:31; Jude 1:14-15). The apostle Paul wrote about the honor Christ will receive at the judgment: "At the name of Jesus every knee should bow, of those in heaven, and of those on earth, and of those under the earth, and that every tongue should confess that Jesus Christ is Lord, to the glory of God the Father" (Phil. 2:10-11).

At the judgment, the Lord will reward each person according to his

---

[1] Matt. 16:27; 19:28; Jude 1:14-15; cf. Isa. 40:10; 62:11; Luke 9:26; 1 Cor. 4:5; 2 Tim. 4:1.

deeds (Job. 34:11; Ps. 62:12; Isa. 40:10; 62:11; Rom. 2:6; 1 Cor. 3:14; Rev. 22:12). Christ taught, "For the Son of Man will come in the glory of His Father with His angels, and then He will reward each according to his works" (Matt. 16:27). The apostle Paul concluded, "For we must all appear before the judgment seat of Christ, that each one may receive the things done in the body, according to what he has done, whether good or bad" (2 Cor. 5:9-10).

On judgment day, everyone will give an account of his or her life before God (Matt. 12:36; Rom. 14:12; Heb. 4:13; 1 Pet. 4:5). While the Lord is merciful in judgment (Ps. 62:12; 2 Tim. 1:18), He will consider every deed people have done, including their secrets (Eccles. 12:14; Rom. 2:16; cf. Matt. 10:26; Heb. 4:13) and motives (1 Cor. 4:5). He will also evaluate every word that each person has spoken, which by itself, will be sufficient evidence to acquit or condemn them (Matt. 12:36-37). The risen Christ declared, "All the churches shall know that I am He who searches the minds and hearts. And I will give to each one of you according to your works" (Rev. 2:23).

A person's response to Jesus during his lifetime will play a decisive role in his eternal destiny. At His return, Christ will be ashamed of the person who has been ashamed of Him (Luke 9:26). The person who has rejected Jesus and His words will be judged by those words (John 12:48). Those who do not abide in Christ will be destroyed (John 15:6). On the other hand, Christ will confess before the angels the one who has confessed Him before people (Luke 12:8-9; Rev. 3:5). In addition, those who have accepted the prophetic message of those sent by God will receive the rewards given to such men, and those who have shown kindness to the Lord's disciples will be rewarded accordingly (Matt. 10:41-42).

God will proportionately require from each person according to the measure that He has given to him (Luke 12:48). To illustrate, in the parable of the talents, Jesus portrayed a man who entrusted his servants with various amounts of talents (measures of coinage) corresponding to their abilities while he traveled to a distant country for "a long time" (Matt. 25:14-15, 19). Those stewards who earned interest by investing his master's talents, whether few or many, were rewarded when he returned (Matt. 25:16-17, 20-23). However, the master severely punished the wicked, lazy servant because he excused himself from investing the money (Matt. 25:18, 24-26, 30; cf. Luke 19:24-27). On the other hand, the returning master promoted those who were faithful with the amount entrusted to them by making them rulers "over many things" so that they entered into their master's "joy" (Matt. 25:21-23, 27). Similarly, in the parable of the faithful servant, the master greatly punished ("beaten with many stripes" Luke 12:47) the servant who understood his will but did not do it but lightly punished ("beaten with few" Luke 12:48) the servant who did not understand his will but committed ignorant transgressions.

Likewise, God will save the righteous from divine wrath (Rom. 5:9; cf. 1 Cor. 5:5; 2 Tim. 1:18), and He will reward them with eternal life (2 Tim. 4:8; Rev. 3:4-5; cf. Phil 4:3). Christ stated, "Most assuredly, I say to you, he who hears My word and believes in Him who sent Me has everlasting life, and shall not come into judgment, but has passed from death into life" (John 5:24); in other words, those who trust in Him will not receive condemnation but have received eternal life, even in the present life. Obedience, not the performance of miracles, is the hallmark characteristic of those who inherit God's kingdom (Matt. 7:21-23).

On the other hand, the wicked will experience fear and torment on the day of judgment (1 John 4:18), having been "reserved" for doom and divine wrath (Job 21:30; Prov. 16:4; cf. Rom. 2:5, 8-9; Col. 3:6; 2 Thess. 1:8; Heb. 10:27; Rev. 14:10). The testimony of the righteous will condemn the wicked (Matt. 12:41-42; Luke 11:31-32). The resurrected Christ, who holds the keys to the Davidic kingdom (Rev. 3:7), and even to hades and death (Rev. 1:18), will shut the door to His kingdom (Luke 13:25; cf. Rev. 3:7). Then some of the unsaved will desire to enter but will be denied by Jesus, who will reply, "I tell you I do not know you, where you are from. Depart from Me, all you workers of iniquity" (Luke 13:27).

The apostle Paul often wrote about the day of judgment:

You are treasuring up for yourself wrath in the day of wrath and revelation of the righteous judgment of God, who "will render to each one according to his deeds": eternal life to those who by patient continuance in doing good seek for glory, honor, and immortality; but to those who are self-seeking and do not obey the truth, but obey unrighteousness—indignation and wrath, tribulation and anguish, on every soul of man who does evil. (Rom. 2:5-9)

When Christ returns, He will destroy the transgressors in fiery judgment (Isa. 1:25, 28; 2 Thess. 1:6-9). Those who had not produced good fruit will be condemned and thrown into hellfire.[2] According to Jesus' descriptions of hell, it will be a place of "outer darkness" (Matt. 22:13; 25:30), where the wicked will weep and "gnash their teeth" (Matt. 22:13; 24:51; 25:30; Luke 13:28). Paradoxically, it will also be a place where flames torment their bodies and souls (Matt. 5:29-30; 10:28; 18:8-9; Mark 9:43-49; Luke 16:23-26; cf. 2 Thess. 1:6; Rev. 18:10, 15), implying that they will have been resurrected prior to the judgment. The fires of hell will be everlasting (Matt. 18:8; 25:41; Jude 1:7; Rev. 19:3) and unquenchable (Isa. 66:24; Matt. 3:12; Mark 9:43, 45, 48), so the wicked will "go away into everlasting punishment" (Matt. 25:46) where their "worm" never dies (Isa. 66:24; Mark 9:44, 46, 48). In this manner, Christ will bring vengeance upon the wicked and will punish them with everlasting destruction:

[W]hen the Lord Jesus is revealed from heaven with His mighty angels, in flaming fire taking vengeance on those who do not know God, and on those who do not obey the gospel of our Lord Jesus Christ. These shall be punished with everlasting destruction from the presence of the Lord and from the glory of His power, when He comes, in that day, to be glorified in His saints and to be admired among all those who believe. (2 Thess. 1:7-10)

---

2   Matt. 3:10-11; 5:22; 7:19; 23:33; Luke 3:9, 16; John 15:6; Heb. 6:8; 10:27.

The apostle John's description of the destruction of the great city Babylon symbolizes the fate of the wicked on the day of Jesus Christ. The city will be "utterly burned with fire" (Rev. 18:8), and fearing her "torment" (Rev. 18:10, 15), those who had traded with her will "weep" and "wail" when they see her burning (Rev. 18:15; cf. v. 9). The smoke from her destruction will rise up "forever and ever!" (Rev. 19:3; cf. Rev. 18:9, 18) Those who will have taken the mark of the Antichrist or worshipped his image will experience eternal torment:

> "If anyone worships the beast and his image, and receives his mark on his forehead or on his hand, he himself shall also drink of the wine of the wrath of God, which is poured out full strength into the cup of His indignation. He shall be tormented with fire and brimstone in the presence of the holy angels and in the presence of the Lamb. And the smoke of their torment ascends forever and ever; and they have no rest day or night, who worship the beast and his image, and whoever receives the mark of his name." Here is the patience of the saints. (Rev. 14:9-12)

Everyone must flee this divine wrath by repenting and producing the fruit of righteousness (Matt. 3:7-8; Luke 3:7-8). John the Baptizer warned, "His [Christ's] winnowing fan is in His hand, and He will thoroughly clean out His threshing floor, and gather His wheat into the barn;[3] but He will burn up the chaff with unquenchable fire" (Matt. 3:12; cf. Luke 3:17). The judgment upon the people of Sodom and Gomorrah will be more tolerable than for those who refuse to repent when they hear the gospel (Matt. 10:15; 11:22-24; Luke 10:12-15).

At judgment day, God will separate the righteous from the wicked. Jesus illustrated this in the parable of the tares, in which a farmer grows wheat in his field and allows the wheat and "look alike" tares to grow together until the harvest, at which time his reapers will gather the tares

---

3   The barn is a symbol for God's kingdom (cf. Matt. 13:30, 43).

for burning and gather the wheat into his barn (Matt. 13:30; cf. Mal. 3:18; Matt. 3:12; Luke 3:17). The Lord provided His disciples with a proper understanding of the parable:

> He who sows the good seed is the Son of Man. The field is the world, the good seeds are the sons of the kingdom, but the tares are the sons of the wicked one. The enemy who sowed them is the devil, the harvest is the end of the age, and the reapers are the angels. Therefore as the tares are gathered and burned in the fire, so it will be at the end of this age. The Son of Man will send out His angels, and they will gather out of His kingdom all things that offend, and those who practice lawlessness, and will cast them into the furnace of fire. There will be wailing and gnashing of teeth. Then the righteous will shine forth as the sun in the kingdom of their Father. He who has ears to hear, let him hear! (Matt. 13:37-43)

The parable communicates that Christ will allow the righteous and the wicked to live together in the world until the harvest—the end of the age (Matt. 13:37-39). At that time, His angels will separate the two groups by throwing the wicked ("those who practice lawlessness" Matt. 13:41) into hellfire ("the furnace of fire" Matt. 13:42; cf. v. 50) to experience "wailing and gnashing of teeth" (Matt. 13:42; cf. v. 50) and gathering the righteous to "shine forth as the sun" in God's kingdom (Matt. 13:43). This latter statement echoes the prophet Daniel ("those who are wise shall shine. . . like the stars forever and ever" Dan. 12:3). This parable of Christ is closely followed by another statement of Jesus that the angels will separate the wicked from the righteous, casting the evildoers into the fiery furnace to experience "wailing and gnashing of teeth" (Matt. 13:49-50).

Many of Jesus' other parables highlight the final division between the righteous and the wicked at the end of the age. For example, the parable of the sheep and the goats aptly demonstrates this division:

When the Son of Man comes in His glory, and all the holy angels with Him, then He will sit on the throne of His glory. All the nations will be gathered before Him, and He will separate them one from another, as a shepherd divides his sheep from the goats. And He will set the sheep on His right hand, but the goats on the left. Then the King will say to those on His right hand, "Come, you blessed of My Father, inherit the kingdom prepared for you from the foundation of the world." . . . Then He will also say to those on the left hand, "Depart from Me, you cursed, into the everlasting fire prepared for the devil and his angels." . . . And these will go away into everlasting punishment, but the righteous into eternal life. (Matt. 25:31-34, 41, 46)

The Chief Shepherd will divide the sheep ("you blessed . . . the righteous" Matt. 25:34, 46) from the goats ("you cursed" Matt. 25:41) when He, the Son of Man, returns in glory accompanied by all His holy angels (Matt. 25:31-32; cf. Ezek. 34:17, 20-22; Matt. 16:27). At that time, the Son of Man will sit upon His glorious throne ("*when* the Son of Man comes in His glory . . . *then* He will sit on the throne of His glory" Matt. 25:31, emphasis added; cf. Dan. 7:9, 13; Matt. 19:28) to gather the peoples of the nations to Himself in order to pronounce judgment upon them (Matt. 25:32).[4]

Then the King will reward those who had assisted God's persecuted flock, His Church ("the least of these My brethren" Matt. 25:40, 45), by providing food and drink, clothing, and visitation, as if they had done these deeds to Him personally (Matt. 25:35-40; cf. Matt. 10:41-42). Then they will inherit God's kingdom and eternal life (Matt. 25:34, 46). Conversely, the wicked will be condemned as those who refused to do these deeds (Matt. 25:42-45), and they will be sent into the punishment of everlasting hellfire, which has been sovereignly "prepared" for the devil and his demons (Matt. 25:41, 46; cf. Matt. 8:29). As an aside, the demons will remain bound by the everlasting "chains of darkness" of

---

4   While nations may also be judged as nations on judgment day, the nations here likely serve as a synecdoche for the individuals throughout the nations.

hell until they are formally condemned on judgment day (2 Pet. 2:4-9; Jude 1:6; Rev. 20:10).

The prophetic backdrop for the Son of Man's throne judgment (Matt. 25:31-46) is found in Daniel 7. The primary portion of the prophet's vision reads as follows:

> I watched till thrones were put in place, and the Ancient of Days was seated; His garment was white as snow, and the hair of His head was like pure wool. His throne was a fiery flame, its wheels a burning fire; a fiery stream issued and came forth from before Him. A thousand thousands ministered to Him; ten thousand times ten thousand stood before Him. The court was seated, and the books were opened. (Dan. 7:9-10)

Several features in Matthew's throne passage mirrors the larger vision of Daniel: First, like Matthew's account, Daniel portrayed "the Son of Man, coming with the clouds of heaven" (Dan. 7:13; cf. "when the Son of Man comes in His glory" Matt. 25:31; cf. Matt. 24:30). Second, God is seated on His throne of glory (Dan. 7:9; Matt. 25:31). Third, the Son of Man is accompanied by all the holy angels ("thousand thousands ministered to Him; ten thousand times ten thousand" Dan. 7:10; Matt. 25:31). Fourth, the righteous from all nations receive the everlasting kingdom ("a kingdom that all peoples, nations, and languages . . . an everlasting dominion" Dan. 7:14; "all the nations . . . inherit the kingdom" Matt. 25:32, 34). Fifth, the wicked are destroyed by fire ("a fiery stream issued and came forth" Dan. 7:10; "into the everlasting fire prepared for the devil" Matt. 25:41). While Jesus taught that hellfire has been "prepared for the devil" (Matt. 25:41; cf. Rev. 20:10), Daniel's vision portrays the fiery destruction of the Antichrist ("the beast was slain, and its body destroyed and given to the burning flame" Dan. 7:11; cf. Rev. 19:20; 20:10), an event which will occur at Christ's return.

Earlier in Matthew's Gospel, Jesus explained that He will sit upon His glorious throne to give eternal rewards to those who have abandoned their lives for the sake of His kingdom:

Assuredly, I say to you, that in the regeneration, when the Son of Man sits on the throne of His glory, you who have followed Me will also sit on twelve thrones, judging the twelve tribes of Israel. And everyone who has left houses or brothers or sisters or father or mother or wife or children or lands, for My name's sake, shall receive a hundredfold, and inherit eternal life. But many who are first will be last, and the last first. (Matt. 19:28-30)

The Son of Man sitting on His throne "in the regeneration" (Matt. 19:28) refers to His Second Advent, when the faithful will inherit everlasting life in His kingdom. Although Jesus reigns as the primary Judge, the twelve apostles will sit with Him on twelve thrones (Matt. 19:28; cf. "till thrones were put in place" Dan. 7:9; Rev. 20:4), exerting a secondary authority of judgment and reign in the consummated kingdom, to judge Israel's twelve tribes. As part of the penetration ("already and not yet") of God's kingdom, the holy apostles, ten of whom experienced martyrdom, have begun their heavenly reign with Christ in His kingdom (see chapter 20).

The judgment scene in Revelation 20, like Matthew 19:28, envisions the thrones of judgment which we encountered in Daniel 7. The apostle John saw multiple thrones ("I saw thrones, and they sat on them, and judgment was committed to them" Rev. 20:4; cf. Rev. 4:4; 11:16), synonymous with the thrones in Daniel's vision ("I watched till thrones were put in place" Dan. 7:9), which undoubtedly will include the twelve thrones of the apostles ("you who have followed Me will also sit on twelve thrones" Matt. 19:28). In the same chapter of the Apocalypse, John continued to borrow the imagery of Daniel's vision:

Then I saw a great white throne and Him who sat on it, from whose face the earth and the heaven fled away. And there was found no place for them. And I saw the dead, small and great, standing before God, and books were opened. And another book was opened, which is the Book of Life. And the dead were judged according to their works, by the things which were written in the books. The sea gave up the dead who were in it, and Death and Hades delivered up the dead who were in them. And they were judged, each one according to his works. Then Death and Hades were cast into the lake of fire. This is the second death. And anyone not found written in the Book of Life was cast into the lake of fire. (Rev. 20:11-15)

When Christ returns, heaven and earth will "flee away" before His presence (Rev. 20:11; cf. "heaven and earth will pass away" Matt. 24:35; cf. v. 29), and He will sit upon His "great white throne" to judge the living and the dead (Rev. 20:11, 12). As we saw in chapter 10, the destruction of the present heaven and earth will occur on the day of Jesus Christ. And according to Daniel 7, the heavenly books will be opened at the Son of Man's return with clouds ("the court was seated, and the books were opened" Dan. 7:10; cf. "and books were opened" Rev. 20:12), in other words, when Christ descends from heaven to kill the Antichrist (Rev. 19:11-21; cf. Dan. 7:11, 26). Finally, the other references to people being judged "according to their works" (Rev. 20:12-13) refer to the time of Christ's return (e.g., Matt. 16:27; Rom. 2:6). Consequently, all the dead will be resurrected at this time (cf. Dan. 12:1-4; John 5:25, 28; Acts 24:15); however, only the wicked, whose names are not written in the Lamb's Book of Life (Rev. 20:15), will be thrown into the fiery "lake" (Rev. 20:14-15; cf. Dan. 7:10) to experience the "second death" of everlasting destruction (Rev. 2:11; 20:14; cf. "to consume and destroy it forever" Dan. 7:26).

Satan will be cast into hellfire at the same time that Christ devours the Antichrist and his armies, that is, at the battle of Gog and Magog (Rev. 20:8-9). John wrote, "The devil, who deceived them, was cast into the lake of fire and brimstone where the beast and the false prophet are. And they will be tormented day and night forever and ever" (Rev. 20:10). The verse does not indicate that the devil will be cast into hellfire long after the Antichrist and the false prophet have been cast there. Rather, it communicates that Satan will receive the same fate, the eternal torment that these two men will receive, as the apostle saw in his previous vision (Rev. 19:20), so that the unholy trinity will receive eternal destruction on judgment day (see chapter 18).

TABLE 6: THE THRONES OF JUDGMENT

	Daniel 7	Revelation	Matthew
The Son of Man coming with clouds	behold, One like the Son of Man, coming with the clouds of heaven (Dan. 7:13)	behold, a white cloud, and on the cloud sat One like the Son of Man (Rev. 14:14)	When the Son of Man comes in His glory (Matt. 25:31); on the clouds of heaven (Matt. 24:30)
Accompanied by myriads of holy angels	Ten thousand times ten thousand stood before Him (Dan. 7:10)	many angels . . . ten thousand times ten thousand (Rev. 5:11)	all the holy angels with Him (Matt. 25:31)
The Lord seated on a glorious throne	the Ancient of Days was seated [on His throne]; His garment was white as snow (Dan. 7:9)	Then I saw a great white throne and Him who sat on it (Rev. 20:11)	then He will sit on the throne of His glory. (Matt. 25:31)

All nations gathered before Him	all peoples, nations, and languages (Dan. 7:27)	You . . . have redeemed us to God by Your blood out of every tribe and tongue and people and nation and have made us kings and priests (Rev. 5:9-10) And I saw the dead, small and great, standing before God (Rev. 20:12)	all the nations will be gathered before Him (Matt. 25:32)
Thrones established	I watched till thrones were put in place . . . the court was seated (Dan. 7:9-10)	Around the throne were twenty-four thrones, and on the thrones I saw twenty-four elders sitting . . . and they had crowns of gold (Rev. 4:4; cf. Rev. 5:8) And I saw thrones, and they sat on them, and judgment was committed to them (Rev. 20:4)	when the Son of Man sits on the throne of His glory, you . . . will also sit on twelve thrones, judging (Matt. 19:28)
Books opened	and the books were opened (Dan. 7:10; cf. Dan. 12:1)	and books were opened (Rev. 20:12)	

The wicked thrown into everlasting hellfire	The beast was slain, and its body destroyed and given to the burning flame. (Dan. 7:11) some to shame and everlasting contempt (Dan. 12:2)	Then the beast . . . and with him the false prophet . . . were cast alive into the lake of fire burning with brimstone (Rev. 19:20) The devil, who deceived them, was cast into the lake of fire and brimstone . . . and they will be tormented day and night forever and ever. (Rev. 20:10)	Depart from Me, you cursed, into the everlasting fire prepared for the devil and his angels (Matt. 25:41) And these will go away into everlasting punishment (Matt. 25:46)
The righteous inherit the kingdom	Then the kingdom . . . shall be given to the people, the saints of the Most High. His kingdom is an everlasting kingdom (Dan. 7:27; cf. Dan. 7:22; 12:2)	He who overcomes shall inherit all things, and I will be his God and he shall be My son (Rev. 21:7; cf. Rev. 5:9-10; 21:1-22:5)	"Come, you blessed of My Father, inherit the kingdom prepared for you" (Matt. 25:34) but the righteous into eternal life (Matt. 25:46)

16

THE NEW AND EVERLASTING COVENANT

THE LORD MADE AN EVERLASTING COVENANT with the patriarch Abraham and his posterity which includes giving them "all the land of Canaan, as an everlasting possession" (Gen. 17:8; cf. Gen. 12:1-3, 12; 13:5, 14-17; 15:18-21; 17:1-14; 26:3-4; 28:4). The land of the Canaanites has always belonged to Abraham and his offspring (Gen. 13:15; cf. Gen. 17:7-8), and this covenant will continue as long as the nation exists "throughout their generations" (Gen. 17:9). Moses utilized the strongest Hebrew words available to communicate the eternal perpetuity of these land promises.[1] In addition, the Lord promised to remember this covenant for a thousand generations: "He remembers His covenant forever, the word which He commanded, for a thousand generations, the covenant which He made with Abraham . . . to Israel as an everlasting

---

[1] This same language is used for God's everlasting covenant with Noah, which specifies that He would never again ("for perpetual generations") destroy the earth with a flood (Gen. 9:12-16).

covenant, saying, 'To you I will give the land of Canaan as the allot-
ment of your inheritance' " (Ps. 105:8-9, 10-11; cf. 1 Chron. 16:15-22).

In addition to the Promised Land, the Lord pledged to exponentially
increase Abraham's offspring (Gen. 13:16; 15:5; 17:2, 6; 22:17; 26:4;
28:3, 14). He also promised that the patriarch and his wife would have
a son, whom they named Isaac, who would become his heir and would
bring forth the promised nation, as well as fathering other nations and
kingdoms (Gen. 15:4; 17:16, 19; cf. Gen. 17:3-11; Rom. 4:16-17). The
Lord established the Abrahamic covenant with Isaac "for an everlasting
covenant, and with his descendants after him" (Gen. 17:19; cf. Gen.
17:7-8; 21:12); this demonstrates that the covenant was not limited to
the patriarchs but was also purposed for their descendants in perpetuity
(Gen. 17:7, 19; cf. Gen. 26:3-5; 28:13-15).

As the sign of the everlasting covenant, the nation of Israel circumcised each male child "in the flesh" of his foreskin (Gen. 17:11). This
ordinance ultimately pointed to the permanent sign of God's people
circumcising "the foreskins of their hearts," in other words, repenting
from their stubborn disobedience (Deut. 10:16; Jer. 4:4; cf. Gen. 17:11;
Jer. 9:25). The apostle Paul explained, "For he is not a Jew who is one
outwardly, nor is circumcision that which is outward in the flesh; but
he is a Jew who is one inwardly; and circumcision is that of the heart,
in the Spirit" (Rom. 2:28; cf. Rom. 8:4).

The vast majority of the nation, however, has always had uncircumcised hearts (cf. Lev. 26:41-42; Deut. 31:26-29) and has refused to love
the God of Israel with all their heart, soul, and mind (Deut. 6:5-6; cf.
Deut. 10:12-13; 26:16). While God has not yet given the nation "a heart"
to perceive the truth (Deut. 29:4), He promised to circumcise their heart:

> When all these things come upon you . . . and you return to the Lord
> your God and obey His voice, according to all that I command you
> today, you and your children, with all your heart and with all your
> soul, that the Lord your God will bring you back from captivity, and
> have compassion on you, and gather you again from all the nations

where the Lord your God has scattered you. If any of you are driven out to the farthest parts under heaven, from there the Lord your God will gather you, and from there He will bring you. Then the Lord your God will bring you to the land which your fathers possessed, and you shall possess it. He will prosper you and multiply you more than your fathers. And the Lord your God will circumcise your heart and the heart of your descendants, to love the Lord your God with all your heart and with all your soul that you may live. (Deut. 30:1, 2-6)

In this prophecy, Moses outlined the promises of what later prophets and the holy apostles called the new covenant. These promises include the Lord having compassion on the nation (Deut. 30:3; cf. Deut. 32:36) and gathering the people from the lands of their captivity, that is, all the nations where He had scattered them (Deut. 30:3). In addition, He pledged to give them the Promised Land (Deut. 30:5). In point of fact, He promised to regather the nation, even if the people will have been scattered to "the farthest parts under heaven" (Deut. 30:4). This demonstrates that no obstacle, not even nearly two thousand years of exile, will prevent God from bringing His people back to the land. He will also make them more prosperous and numerous than their fathers (Deut. 30:5), and most importantly, He will "circumcise" the nation's heart so that they thoroughly and completely love Him. These new covenant blessings would fulfill the expectations of the Abrahamic covenant (cf. Deut. 4:31; 30:6; Ezek. 16:60).

The apostle Paul taught that those baptized into Jesus Christ, whether Jews or Gentiles, have already received this inward circumcision: "You were also circumcised with the circumcision made without hands, by putting off the body of the sins of the flesh, by the circumcision of Christ, buried with Him in baptism, in which you also were raised with Him through faith in the working of God" (Col. 2:11-12; cf. Rom. 6:3-9). However, the miraculous circumcision of the nation of Israel, promised in Deuteronomy, will include national repentance ("and you return to the Lord your God and obey His voice . . . with all your heart and with all your soul" Deut. 30:2; cf. Deut. 4:29; "when you turn to the Lord" Deut. 4:30).

> But from there [throughout all the nations] you will seek the Lord your God, and you will find Him if you seek Him with all your heart and with all your soul. When you are in distress, and all these things come upon you in the latter days, when you turn to the Lord your God and obey His voice (for the Lord your God is a merciful God), He will not forsake you nor destroy you, nor forget the covenant of your fathers which He swore to them. (Deut. 4:29-31)

This national repentance and the subsequent regathering of the Jewish people to the Promised Land will take place "in the latter days" (Deut. 4:30), more specifically, when the nation has experienced intense tribulation ("when you are in distress, and all these things come upon you" Deut. 4:30; "when all these things come upon you" Deut. 30:1; Jer. 30:6-7). Consequently, any setting prior to the great tribulation does not fulfill the primary scope of this prophecy.

The prophet Jeremiah referred to God making a "new covenant" with the nation, the houses of Israel and Judah:

> Behold, the days are coming, says the Lord, when I will make a new covenant with the house of Israel and with the house of Judah . . . But this is the covenant that I will make with the house of Israel after those days, says the Lord: I will put My law in their minds, and write it on their hearts; and I will be their God, and they shall be My people. No more shall every man teach his neighbor, and every man his brother, saying, "Know the Lord," for they all shall know Me, from the least of them to the greatest of them, says the Lord. For I will forgive their iniquity, and their sin I will remember no more. (Jer. 31:31, 33-34; cf. Heb. 8:8-12)

As the Lord previously wrote His commandments upon stone tablets at Mount Sinai (Exod. 34:1-4; Deut. 10:1-4), His new covenant includes the promise that He will write His law on the tablet of the minds and hearts of the people ("I will put My law in their minds, and write it on their hearts" Jer. 31:33; cf. Ezek. 37:24). This heart transplant will involve God removing their stony heart and replacing it with a compliant heart of flesh so that they wholeheartedly trust in Him (Ezek. 11:19; 36:26-27; cf. Jer. 24:7).[2] Those belonging to the holy apostolic Church have already received the gift of the Holy Spirit: "You are an epistle of Christ . . . written not with ink but by the Spirit of the living God, not on tablets of stone but on tablets of flesh, that is, of the heart . . . the new covenant" (2 Cor. 3:3, 6; cf. vv. 7-11). When the Jewish nation receives the new covenant, they will be included among God's people (i.e., the holy Church), and the Lord will become their God (Jer. 24:7; 30:22; 31:33; cf. Jer. 32:38; Ezek. 11:20; 34:30-31; 36:28; 37:27; Zech. 8:8; Heb. 8:13).

Jesus Christ inaugurated the new covenant with His sacrificial death on the cross. Jesus Himself testified to this when, after He blessed the cup of wine at the Last Supper (Matt. 26:27; Mark 14:23; Luke 22:20), He declared, "For this is My blood of the new covenant, which is shed for many for the remission of sins" (Matt. 26:28). This covenant will be consummated at the time the nation receives Christ's sacrificial blood: "I will remember My covenant with you in the days of your youth, and I will establish an everlasting covenant with you . . . when I provide you an atonement for all you have done" (Ezek. 16:60, 63; cf. Deut. 32:43; Dan. 9:24). Furthermore, the Father sent His Suffering Servant (i.e., Jesus Christ), whom He "raised up" (i.e., exalted through resurrection), to be an everlasting covenant for Israel and to restore and "raise up" (i.e., resurrect) the tribes of Jacob (Isa. 42:6 with 49:6).

The Almighty pledged the Promised Land to the nation of Israel as an everlasting possession, but only when all the people receive His everlasting righteousness. To demonstrate, He promised, "Your people

---

2   The *stone* tablets of the law and the *flesh* of Jesus Christ are fitting corollaries to these two conditions of the heart.

shall all be righteous; they shall inherit the land forever . . . that I may be glorified" (Isa. 60:21; cf. Dan. 9:24). Similarly, He promised, "I will bring back Israel to his home, and he shall feed on Carmel and Bashan; his soul shall be satisfied on Mount Ephraim and Gilead . . . The iniquity of Israel shall be sought, but there shall be none; and the sins of Judah, but they shall not be found; for I will pardon those whom I preserve" (Jer. 50:19, 20; cf. "I will forgive their iniquity, and their sin I will remember no more" Jer. 31:34; cf. Ezek. 36:25, 29; 37:23). In other words, the Lord will forgive all the sins of all Israel's people. When the people return to the land, they will remove all remnants of idolatry (Ezek. 11:18; 36:25).

No longer will anyone need to evangelize the people of Israel ("no more shall every man teach his neighbor . . . saying, 'Know the Lord,'" because they will all know the Lord "from the least of them to the greatest of them" Jer. 31:34; cf. Jer. 32:37; Ezek. 39:22). The nation will be established in righteousness and all its children "shall be taught by the Lord" (Isa. 54:13-14; cf. v. 17), and the Holy Spirit will speak behind them so to speak, saying, "This is the way, walk in it" (Isa. 30:21). They will never depart from Him because they will have the fear of the Lord (Jer. 32:40); there will be no defectors! The remnant will be completely righteous, honest, and without deceit (Zeph. 3:13). These prophecies were not fulfilled in the nation's history but await a future fulfillment.

Because of their righteousness, the descendants of Israel will never again be "cast off" for their iniquities (Jer. 31:37). The nation is permanent, like the fixed orders of the solar system and oceanic currents: "If those ordinances depart from before Me, says the Lord, then the seed of Israel shall also cease from being a nation before Me forever" (Jer. 31:36; cf. Isa. 66:22; Jer. 31:35; 33:23-26). As God promised to never again cover the Earth with a flood, He promised an everlasting "covenant of peace" to mercifully preserve the nation (Isa. 54:9-10).

The prophet Ezekiel also wrote about these features of the new covenant. He often connected the nation's acceptance of it with the final ingathering of its people to the land of Israel:

I will gather you from the peoples, assemble you from the countries where you have been scattered, and I will give you the land of Israel. And they will go there, and they will take away all its detestable things and all its abominations from there. Then I will give them one heart, and I will put a new spirit within them, and take the stony heart out of their flesh, and give them a heart of flesh, that they may walk in My statutes and keep My judgments and do them; and they shall be My people, and I will be their God. (Ezek. 11:17-20; cf. Jer. 32:37-41; Ezek. 36:24-27)

As this passage demonstrates, the national reception of the ever-lasting covenant cannot be divorced from the reception of the Promised Land (cf. Isa. 60:21; Jer. 50:19-20). The land is the same land of the Canaanites which God promised to the patriarchs (Ezek. 36:28; cf. Ps. 105:8-11). Furthermore, the Promised Land cannot be allegorized to refer to a non-earthly place in heaven, without causing violence to the sacred text. The following passage illustrates the importance of a literal interpretation:

On the day that I cleanse you from all your iniquities, I will also enable you to dwell in the cities, and the ruins shall be rebuilt. The desolate land shall be tilled instead of lying desolate in the sight of all who pass by. So they will say, "This land that was desolate has become like the garden of Eden; and the wasted, desolate, and ruined cities are now fortified and inhabited." Then the nations which are left all around you shall know that I, the Lord, have rebuilt the ruined places and planted what was desolate. I, the Lord, have spoken it, and I will do it. (Ezek. 36:33-36)

The immediate context reveals that this prophecy pertains to the new covenant (Ezek. 36:24-27). The prophet taught that this will take place when God has completely purified the nation of Israel ("on the day that I cleanse you from all your iniquities" Ezek. 36:33). The phrase "the nations which are left" (Ezek. 36:36) refers to the peoples of the surrounding nations who will remain alive after the unprecedented tribulation and the war of Gog and Magog. They will also understand that the Lord has restored the fortunes of Israel (Ezek. 36:36).

In the next chapter, the prophet specified that the everlasting covenant will include the children of Israel returning to their ancestral homeland and fully accepting Christ Jesus:

Surely I will take the children of Israel from among the nations, wherever they have gone, and will gather them from every side and bring them into their own land; and I will make them one nation in the land, on the mountains of Israel; and one king shall be king over them all . . . I will deliver them from all their dwelling places in which they have sinned and will cleanse them. Then they shall be My people, and I will be their God. David My servant shall be king over them, and they shall all have one shepherd; they shall also walk in My judgments and observe My statutes and do them. Then they shall dwell in the land that I have given to Jacob My servant, where your fathers dwelt; and they shall dwell there, they, their children, and their children's children, forever; and My servant David shall be their prince forever. Moreover I will make a covenant of peace with them, and it shall be an everlasting covenant with them; I will establish them and multiply them. (Ezek. 37:21-22, 23-26; cf. vv. 15-21)

This new and everlasting covenant ("a covenant of peace . . . an everlasting covenant" Ezek. 37:26; cf. Jer. 32:37; Ezek. 34:25) will include the eternal reign of the Davidic Messiah, Jesus Christ, over the nation of Israel ("David My Servant shall be King over them, and they shall all have one Shepherd" Ezek. 37:24; "My servant David shall be their [P]rince forever" Ezek. 37:25[3]; cf. Isa. 55:3-4; Ezek. 34:23-24; Hosea 1:11). This reign will occur in the land of Israel after the children

---

[3] Capitalization added for clarity.

of Israel have regathered from their dispersion throughout the nations (Ezek. 37:21-22, 25; cf. Jer. 32:37; Ezek. 11:17; 34:23-25, 31). In addition, they will live there in eternal perpetuity ("they shall dwell there, they, their children, and their children's children, forever" Ezek. 37:25).[4] This prophecy emphasizes that the Promised Land is the same geographical region where the patriarchs once lived ("in the land that I have given to Jacob My servant, where your fathers dwelt" Ezek. 37:25).

One purpose of Jesus Christ coming to redeem His people was to fulfill the covenantal promises given to the patriarchs. The priest Zechariah, the father of John the Baptizer, delivered the following prophecy:

> "Blessed is the Lord God of Israel, For He has visited and redeemed His people, and has raised up a horn of salvation for us in the house of His servant David, as He spoke by the mouth of His holy prophets, who have been since the world began, that we should be saved from our enemies and from the hand of all who hate us, to perform the mercy promised to our fathers and to remember His holy covenant, the oath which He swore to our father Abraham: To grant us that we, being delivered from the hand of our enemies, might serve Him without fear, in holiness and righteousness before Him all the days of our life." (Luke 1:68-75)

The Lord promised to assemble the entire nation of Israel back to their land (Jer. 23:3; Ezek. 28:25; Mic. 2:12; Zech. 10:9). Isaiah taught, "The Lord will have mercy on Jacob, and will still choose Israel, and settle them in their own land" (Isa. 14:1; cf. Jer. 24:6). The people will be firmly "planted" in the land and will never again be "plucked up" or oppressed by their enemies (2 Sam. 7:10; Jer. 24:6; Amos 9:15; cf. Jer. 24:6; 32:41). The Lord has spoken, "For a mere moment I have forsaken you, but with great mercies I will gather you. With a little wrath I hid

---

4   cf. Jer. 32:37, 41; Ezek. 11:17; 34:25-29; 36:24, 28; 37:25-26; 39:26-28.

My face from you for a moment; but with everlasting kindness I will have mercy on you" (Isa. 54:7-8).

As we have seen, the Jews will be removed and dispersed throughout the nations by one final, short captivity, which will begin with the Antichrist's invasion of the Promised Land (Zech. 14:2; Luke 21:24). Nevertheless, the Lord will not allow all the descendants of Jacob and Judah to be destroyed by their enemies, but He will save a remnant to inherit the land (Isa. 65:8-9; Jer. 31:7; cf. Isa. 49:19). Only this "meek and humble" remnant of surviving Jews will come to trust in the Lord (Zeph. 3:12-13). Isaiah declared, "For though your people, O Israel, be as the sand of the sea, a remnant of them will return" (Isa. 10:22; cf. Jer. 23:3; Mic. 2:12). The people of Israel and Judah will be called the "children of the living God" when they come up from throughout the earth, some through resurrection, on the great day of Jezreel (Hosea 1:10-11), after the battle of Armageddon (see chapter 9). Elsewhere, Isaiah wrote, "In that day that the Lord shall set His hand again the second time to recover the remnant of His people who are left. . . He will set up a banner for the nations, and will assemble the outcasts of Israel, and gather together the dispersed of Judah from the four corners of the earth" (Isa. 11:11, 12). He also prophesied that "the remnant of Israel, and such as have escaped" will no longer lean upon the Antichrist ("never again depend on him who defeated them" Isa. 10:20) but only upon the Lord; consequently, "the remnant of Jacob" will return to their God (Isa. 10:20-21).

The Lord will break the yoke from Israel's neck and deliver them from their captors so that they live in perpetual safety in their own land (Ezek. 34:27). He promised, "I will cause their captives to return, and will have mercy on them" (Jer. 33:26). At this time, Christ will proclaim liberty to the captives, open the prisons to release those bound in chains (Isa. 61:1), and escort prisoners from their dark prisons ("bring out prisoners from the prison, those who sit in darkness from the prison house" Isa. 42:7). Long before these prophecies, King David exclaimed, "Oh, that the salvation of Israel would come out of Zion! When the Lord brings back the captivity of His people, let Jacob rejoice and Israel be glad" (Ps. 14:7). Consistent with this theme, one of the Songs of Ascent describes the joyful reaction of the returning Jews:

> When the Lord brought back the captivity of Zion, we were like those who dream. Then our mouth was filled with laughter, and our tongue with singing. Then they said among the nations, "The Lord has done great things for them." The Lord has done great things for us, and we are glad. Bring back our captivity, O Lord, as the streams in the South. Those who sow in tears shall reap in joy. He who continually goes forth weeping, bearing seed for sowing, shall doubtless come again with rejoicing, bringing his sheaves with him. (Ps. 126:1-6)

The Lord promised to bring back the Jewish captives from all the nations of their dispersion.[5] When He "roars like a lion," the remnant of Israel will fearfully leave the nations, so they can live in their own homes (Hosea 11:10-11; cf. Joel 3:16); in addition to other nations, these will include Egypt, Iraq, Turkey, Syria, Ethiopia, the islands, and the nations of the West (Isa. 11:11; 43:5-8; 49:12; Hosea 11:10-22; Zech. 8:7; 10:10-11). During this return in "the latter days," the Jewish captives will also leave Jordan and Iran (Jer. 48:47; 49:6; 49:39). Then God will disgrace the nations which had afflicted Israel but will then cause the nations to praise His people (Zeph. 3:19).

One theme of the final regathering of the nation is that they will be gathered together like a massive flock of sheep brought to their folds (Jer. 23:3; Ezek. 36:37-38; Mic. 2:12; Zeph. 2:6-7). Like such flocks are offered as holy sacrifices during a Jewish festival, "so shall the ruined cities be filled with flocks of men" (Ezek. 36:37-38). The Good Shepherd, the Davidic Christ, will lead them home ("He will gather the lambs with His arm, and carry them in His bosom, and gently lead

---

5   Jer. 30:10, 18; 31:23; 39:28; 46:27; Ezek. 39:25, 28; Joel 3:1, 7; Amos 9:14; Zeph. 2:7; 3:20; cf. Isa. 49:21.

those who are with young" Isa. 40:11; cf. Jer. 31:10; Mic. 2:13; 5:4; John 10:11). The prophet Ezekiel discussed that the Lord will seek out the lost sheep of the house of Israel after the "cloudy and dark day," that is, at the day of the Lord:

> I Myself will search for My sheep and seek them out. As a shepherd seeks out his flock on the day he is among his scattered sheep, so will I seek out My sheep and deliver them from all the places where they were scattered on a cloudy and dark day. And I will bring them out from the peoples and gather them from the countries, and will bring them to their own land; I will feed them on the mountains of Israel, in the valleys and in all the inhabited places of the country. I will feed them in good pasture, and their fold shall be on the high mountains of Israel. There they shall lie down in a good fold and feed in rich pasture on the mountains of Israel. I will feed My flock, and I will make them lie down . . . I will seek what was lost and bring back what was driven away, bind up the broken and strengthen what was sick. (Ezek. 34:11-15, 16)

The Lord will provide for His sheep during their return home:

> They shall feed along the roads, and their pastures shall be on all desolate heights. They shall neither hunger nor thirst, neither heat nor sun shall strike them; for He who has mercy on them will lead them, even by the springs of water He will guide them. I will make each of My mountains a road, and My highways shall be elevated. Surely these shall come from afar; look! Those from the north and the west and these from the land of Sinim. (Isa. 49:9-12)

The prophets understood the final regathering of the children of Israel to be a new and greater exodus, which will greatly eclipse the former one (Jer. 16:14-16; 23:7-8). In this exodus, God will fulfill His oath to the patriarchs by delivering Israel out of all the nations "with a mighty hand, with an outstretched arm, and with fury poured out" (Ezek. 20:33-34; cf. Deut. 4:34). Unlike the first exodus, the people "shall not go out with haste, nor go by flight" because the Lord will always be before and behind them (Isa. 52:11-12; cf. Exod. 12:11, 33; 14:19).

As the people under Moses were fed with heavenly manna, quail, and water from the rock which followed them throughout the desert, the Lord will once again provide for those who return to their land ("They shall neither hunger nor thirst" Isa. 49:10). The desert will feature new rivers so that His chosen people may drink (Isa. 43:19-20; cf. Jer. 31:9) as God provided for them during the desert wanderings of the first exodus. He will dry up the Sea of Egypt and strike "the River" into seven streams, so the people can cross over on dry land, as during the Red Sea crossing (Isa. 11:15-16; Zech. 10:11; cf. Isa. 27:12; 51:10-11).

The great earthquake on the day of the Lord will radically distort the topography of the Middle East, including elevating highways into the mountain tops, enabling the people to travel upon them to the land of Israel (Isa. 11:16; 40:3-5; 49:11; 57:14; 62:10). They will travel by these highways from the north, the West, and the land of Sinim[6] (Isa. 49:12). One new highway in the desert will enable the people of Israel to leave Iraq, as when they "came up from the land of Egypt" (Isa. 11:16; cf. Isa. 19:23-25; 43:19; 51:10-11):

> A highway shall be there, and a road, and it shall be called the Highway of Holiness. The unclean shall not pass over it, but it shall be for others. Whoever walks the road, although a fool, shall not go astray. No lion shall be there, nor shall any ravenous beast go up on it; it shall not be found there. But the redeemed shall walk there, and the ransomed of the Lord shall return and come to Zion with singing, with everlasting joy on their heads. They shall obtain joy and gladness, and sorrow and sighing shall flee away. (Isa. 35:8-10; cf. Isa. 51:10-11)

---

6   Some commentators suggest that this is an ancient toponym for China.

This final exodus will take place at the sounding of the last trumpet that also signals Christ's return and the resurrection of the dead. Isaiah declared, "You will be gathered one by one, O you children of Israel. So it shall be in that day: The great trumpet will be blown; they will come, who are about to perish in the land of Assyria and they who are outcasts in the land of Egypt, and shall worship the Lord in the holy mount at Jerusalem" (Isa. 27:12-13; cf. Isa. 19:23-25). Jeremiah also depicted this return from exile:

> "O Lord, save Your people, the remnant of Israel!" Behold, I will bring them from the north country and gather them from the ends of the earth, among them the blind and the lame, the woman with child and the one who labors with child, together; a great throng shall return there. They shall come with weeping, and with supplications I will lead them. I will cause them to walk by the rivers of waters, in a straight way in which they shall not stumble. (Jer. 31:7-9)

The Lord will save the remnant of Israel by bringing them out from all the nations of their captivity. The Jews will travel back to the land with "weeping" and "supplications" (Jer. 31:9), which will result because He will pour out "the Spirit of grace and supplication" upon them so that they "mourn" when they look upon the pierced and returning Christ (Zech. 12:10; cf. Matt. 24:30). Nevertheless, they will no longer weep once they have come back from all the lands of their enemies (Jer. 31:7-11, 16-17).

When the Lord pours out His Spirit upon the house of Israel, He will no longer hide His face from them (Ezek. 39:29; cf. Isa. 32:15). In addition, He promised, "This is My covenant with them: My Spirit who is upon you, and My words which I have put in your mouth, shall not depart from your mouth, nor from the mouth of your descendants . . . from this time and forevermore" (Isa. 59:21). The Lord will pour the water of regeneration and the Holy Spirit upon Jacob's children (Isa. 44:3-4). In this manner, the nation will receive the heavenly birth, a necessary requirement for anyone to see God's kingdom (Mark 1:8; John 3:3). Isaiah described this new birth:

> Sing, O barren, you who have not borne! Break forth into singing, and cry aloud, you who have not labored with child! For more are the children of the desolate than the children of the married woman . . . Enlarge the place of your tent, and let them stretch out the curtains of your dwellings; do not spare; lengthen your cords and strengthen your stakes. For you shall expand to the right and to the left, and your descendants will inherit the nations, and make the desolate cities inhabited. (Isa. 54:1, 2-3)

As the barren matriarchs[7] of the nation miraculously conceived, the holy nation, which will be bereft of children through exile and death, will suddenly give birth to many children (Isa. 54:1). This new birth, the resurrection life of the Spirit, will be given to Israel's exiles, who will return to their ancestral land, which will only recently have become desolate (Isa. 54:1, 3; cf. Isa. 26:17-21; Hosea 13:13-14). The exiles will stream into this wasted land until "no more room is found for them" (Zech. 10:10) and it becomes "too small" for the inhabitants so to speak (Isa. 49:19-20). Because the Lord will exponentially increase the nation of Israel, they will expand all their borders into the surrounding nations ("Enlarge the place of your tent, and let them stretch out the curtains of your dwellings; do not spare; lengthen your cords and strengthen your stakes" Isa. 26:15; cf. Isa. 54:2; Zech. 10:8).

Isaiah asked, "Who has heard such a thing? Who has seen such things? Shall the earth be made to give birth in one day? Or shall a nation be born at once? For as soon as Zion was in labor, she gave birth to her children" (Isa. 66:8). After Jerusalem experiences the short tribulation ("for as soon as Zion was in labor" Isa. 66:8), the entire nation will be born from heaven "in one day"—the day of the Lord Jesus Christ

---

7   Sarah, Rebekah, Rachel, and Hannah, the mother of Samuel.

(Isa. 66:8; cf. Mic. 4:9-10; 5:3). The Spirit who resurrected the male Child—Jesus Christ—will also give the nation the heavenly "birth" of regeneration (cf. Isa. 66:7).

Some argue that the aforementioned prophecies only describe the return of the Jewish exiles during the postexilic period. One difficulty with this interpretation is that many of these land prophecies specify that they will be fulfilled at the day of the Lord. Other passages describe realities which have not yet been fulfilled, such as every descendant of Jacob regathering to the land, obtaining permanent security and peace there, and receiving the everlasting righteousness under Christ's reign. A further problem of that interpretation is that the postexilic prophets also prophesied the return of the Jews to the land:

> Peoples shall yet come, inhabitants of many cities; the inhabitants of one city shall go to another, saying, "Let us continue to go and pray before the Lord, and seek the Lord of hosts. I myself will go also." Yes, many peoples and strong nations shall come to seek the Lord of hosts in Jerusalem, and to pray before the Lord. . . In those days ten men from every language of the nations shall grasp the sleeve of a Jewish man, saying, "Let us go with you, for we have heard that God is with you." (Zech. 8:20-22, 23)

Every nation on the planet will send a delegation of ten men[8] to accompany a Jewish man as he journeys back to the Holy City (Zech. 8:23; cf. Isa. 45:14, 24; 60:14). These representatives will entreat favor from the Lord and pray to Him in Jerusalem on behalf of their nations ("to pray before the Lord" Zech. 8:22). The imagery is that each group of Gentiles will cling to the corner of their Jewish man's sleeve in order to accompany him to the Holy City (Zech. 8:23; cf. Matt. 14:35-36;

---

8   In Jewish law, a quorum of ten Jewish men (i.e., *minyan*) is required to perform many legal actions, such as removing the Torah scrolls from a synagogue ark. In this prophecy, each of the nations sends a delegation of their own.

Mark 5:27-28; 6:56). Reminiscent of the name Immanuel ("God is with us" Isa. 7:14), these representatives will speak to the Jew, "We have heard that that God is with you" (Zech. 8:23).

Isaiah also wrote about the Gentiles assisting the Jews in returning to their homeland:

> Behold, I will lift My hand in an oath to the nations, and set up My standard for the peoples; they shall bring your sons in their arms, and your daughters shall be carried on their shoulders; kings shall be your foster fathers, and their queens your nursing mothers; they shall bow down to you with their faces to the earth, and lick up the dust of your feet. Then you will know that I am the Lord, for they shall not be ashamed who wait for Me. (Isa. 49:22-23)

As the Jews brought the gospel to the nations, the Gentiles will assist in bringing their newly converted Jewish brethren back to their ancestral land. They will bring the remnant of Israel back to the land by planes ("like doves to their roosts") and by ships (Isa. 60:8-9). Others will transport them upon "horses and in chariots and in litters, on mules and on camels, to My holy mountain Jerusalem" (Isa. 66:20). Some Gentiles will even carry their Jewish friends in their arms and upon their shoulders (Isa. 49:22; cf. Isa. 14:1-2). Leaders of nations ("kings shall be your foster fathers, and their queens your nursing mothers" Isa. 49:23) will even bow down to them in veneration and to honor God's favor over them ("they shall bow down to you with their faces to the earth, and lick up the dust of your feet" Isa. 49:23; cf. Rev. 3:9). The everlasting covenant includes the nations knowing the descendants of Jacob as "the posterity whom the Lord has blessed" (Isa. 61:8-9).

After the Lord gathers Israel back to the land, their "wasted, desolate, and ruined cities" will be rebuilt so they look like the garden of Eden (Ezek. 36:35; cf. Jer. 31:4; Amos 9:14). Elsewhere, the Lord declares, "And they will dwell safely there, build houses, and plant vineyards; yes, they will dwell securely," which will occur when He brings judgments on "all those around them who despise them" (Ezek. 28:26). The former desolations, along with the house building and vineyard planting, demonstrate beyond all reasonable doubt that the land of Israel, not heaven per se, is in view. They will dwell safely in the land with no fear (Jer. 30:10; 46:27; Ezek. 39:26).

Mount Zion will be the epicenter for the gathering of Israel's descendants (Jer. 3:14, 18; Zech. 8:8, 22). God will gather together Jerusalem's sons, and the armies of the nations will no longer bring desolation and destruction upon the Promised Land (Isa. 49:17-19; cf. Isa. 60:4, 17-18). In those days

> the children of Israel shall come, they and the children of Judah together; with continual weeping they shall come and seek the Lord their God. They shall ask the way to Zion, with their faces toward it, saying, "Come and let us join ourselves to the Lord in a perpetual covenant that will not be forgotten." (Jer. 50:4-5)

As we have perceived, Christ inaugurated the new covenant by His death (Luke 22:20; 1 Cor. 11:25), and the Holy Spirit seals the members of the holy Church, whether Jews or Gentiles, into this everlasting covenant (2 Cor. 3:1-6). And yet, when this covenant is consummated, the entirety of Jacob's descendants will receive permanent holiness and security in the Promised Land. The ultimate Son-Seed of the patriarchs—Jesus Christ—is the nation's only hope of receiving the Abrahamic promises (Gal. 3:16, 19; cf. Gal. 3:29), so by His grace, the Jews will receive His everlasting righteousness and become joint heirs with the patriarchs of these eternal promises (cf. Rom. 4:16-17).[9] Nothing will fulfill the expectations of the covenant except a permanent and complete salvation of Israel's surviving children under the headship of Christ.

The Old Testament prophets expected a literal fulfillment of the

---

9   The Gentiles who trust in Christ are also heirs of the everlasting covenant. Together, the two groups comprise the one holy Church.

very land which God had promised to the patriarchs. Furthermore, Christ and His apostles did not teach in depth about these land promises because they assumed the correctness of the traditional Jewish interpretations of those promises. If the land promises, in some manner, had found their fulfillment in the Person of Christ or in His apostolic Church, we would expect the New Testament to provide abundant evidence of how these promises have been modified, reinterpreted, or superseded; however, the canonical texts do not communicate any supposed fulfillment. Neither the prophets, the apostles, nor Christ Himself taught an allegorical fulfillment of the land promises.

To the contrary, the exhaustive fulfillment of the land promises requires that the entire Jewish nation receives the everlasting righteousness under the headship of Jesus Christ, thereby acquiring the entire Promised Land as a permanent inheritance. During a few brief periods of history, the nation possessed almost all the land that had been sworn to the patriarchs (cf. Gen. 15:18-21; cf. Gen. 13:14-18). Nevertheless, the Israelites never completely drove out the foreign nations from the land (Josh. 23:4-13; 1 Kings 4:21), despite the fact that their territory extended throughout most of these boundaries after the conquest under the prophet Joshua (Josh. 21:43) and during the reign of King Solomon (1 Kings 4:21). In addition, the nation was unable to retain the land due to national disobedience.

Current estimates reveal that roughly 21.7 million Jews live in the world, 6.3 million of whom reside in the modern State of Israel. However, the preliminary regathering of Jews to the land, which began in earnest during and after its nationhood in 1947-48, does not constitute the final, permanent regathering of the nation, as prophesied throughout the Prophets. The largely secular State of Israel does not reflect the gloriously transformed remnant of Jews who will receive the new birth of regeneration when they return to the land following the day of the Lord. This final gathering cannot occur until the nation welcomes the returning Christ and prayerfully repents of her iniquities.

17

THE NEW JERUSALEM

THIS CREATED UNIVERSE will continue to experience the "labor pains" of tribulation until the promised redemption:

> For the earnest expectation of the creation eagerly waits for the revealing of the sons of God. For the creation was subjected to futility, not willingly, but because of Him who subjected it in hope; because the creation itself also will be delivered from the bondage of corruption into the glorious liberty of the children of God. For we know that the whole creation groans and labors with birth pangs together until now. (Rom. 8:19-22)

The book of Revelation confirms that the entire created cosmos, not just humanity, will experience a radical intensification of travail in the final years preceding Christ's return. However, the Pauline passage above emphasizes that the heavens and earth have suffered the "futile" conditions of tribulation since the fall (cf. Gen. 3:16-19). Since that time, the entire created order has eagerly anticipated (Rom. 8:19), through its "groans and labors," its future liberation from sin, entropy, decay, and death ("the bondage of corruption" Rom. 8:21). This liberty will take place when the earth gives birth to its dead through resurrection (Isa. 26:18-19 with Isa. 66:7-9), and God's children are glorified ("the revealing of the sons of God" Rom. 8:19). In other words, the created world will be renewed when Jesus returns to consummate His kingdom and to resurrect the dead.

The Lord will gloriously renew the present heavens and earth after their destruction on the day of Christ. The apostle Peter longed, "Nevertheless we, according to His promise, look for new heavens and a new earth in which righteousness dwells" (2 Pet. 3:13; cf. Isa. 66:22). The present heavens and earth (Gen. 2:1) will not undergo a complete disintegration nor will the creation of a new heavens and earth introduce an altogether separate planet (see chapter 10). Rather, the Earth will exist forever (Eccles. 1:4).

To take this a step further, the psalmist compared the transition from the old to the new cosmos to a person changing his outer attire: "Of old You laid the foundation of the earth, and the heavens are the work of Your hands. They will perish, but You will endure; yes, they will all grow old like a garment; like a cloak You will change them, and they will be changed" (Ps. 102:25-26; cf. Isa. 51:6; Matt. 5:18; 24:35). In other words, many of the ontological properties of the original creation will continue into the new creation, in the same way that our present bodies will have continuity with our resurrection bodies, despite them being "further clothed" with glory (2 Cor. 5:4; cf. Isa. 52:1; 1 Cor. 15:53). This illustrates the continuity which exists between anthropology and cosmology, both of which emerge from a proper Christology.

The arrival of the new creation will correspond to the appearance of the new Jerusalem. The prophet Isaiah depicted the future conditions in Jerusalem, which will exist at the creation of the new heavens and earth:

Because the former troubles are forgotten, and because they are hidden from My eyes. For behold, I create new heavens and a new earth; and the former shall not be remembered or come to mind. But be glad and rejoice forever in what I create; for behold, I create Jerusalem as a rejoicing and her people a joy. I will rejoice in Jerusalem, and joy in My people; the voice of weeping shall no longer be heard in her, nor the voice of crying. (Isa. 65:16-19)

Likewise, when the apostle John saw the new heaven and earth (Rev. 21:1), he immediately saw the descent of the new Jerusalem ("Then I, John, saw the holy city, New Jerusalem, coming down out of heaven from God" Rev. 21:2). Regarding the new creation, he wrote, "Now I saw a new heaven and a new earth, *for* the first heaven and the first earth had passed away" (Rev. 21:1, emphasis added). This verse demonstrates that the removal of the original creation is the reason for the arrival of the new creation. In other words, the new creation and new Jerusalem will arrive concurrently with the expiration of the old creation, specifically, at the day of Jesus Christ.

The prophets taught that Jerusalem will serve as the eternal capital of God's kingdom (Mic. 4:7), the throne for Christ's eternal reign, and the quintessential glory of Israel and the world. The Lord promised to make Jerusalem the eternal place of His rest (Ps. 132:13-14), the city where His name will remain forever (1 Kings 9:3; 2 Kings 21:7; 2 Chron. 7:16; 33:7). Consequently, after the Lord returns, He will make Judah His inheritance and "will again choose Jerusalem" (Zech. 2:12; cf. Zech. 8:2). Mount Zion will be sanctified as the place for the nation's final salvation (Obad. 1:17). Isaiah declared, "Look upon Zion, the city of our appointed feasts; your eyes will see Jerusalem, a quiet home, a tabernacle that will not be taken down; not one of its stakes will ever be removed, nor will any of its cords be broken" (Isa. 33:20). The Lord asked, "Can a woman forget her nursing child and not have compassion on the son of her womb? Surely they may forget, yet I will not forget you [Zion]. See, I have inscribed you on the palms of My hands; your walls are continually before Me" (Isa. 49:15-16).

The prophet Zechariah expounded that the topography of Jerusalem and its surrounding region will be greatly transformed. The unprecedented earthquake on the day of Jesus Christ will significantly elevate the Holy City (Zech. 14:4-11; cf. Isa. 40:3-4). Consequently, Jerusalem will be elevated to become part of a mountain plain, which will include Geba to the north and Rimmon to the south:

> All the land shall be turned into a plain from Geba to Rimmon south of Jerusalem. Jerusalem shall be raised up and inhabited in her place from Benjamin's Gate to the place of the First Gate and the Corner Gate, and from the Tower of Hananel to the king's winepresses. The people shall dwell in it; and no longer shall there be utter destruction, but Jerusalem shall be safely inhabited. (Zech. 14:10-11)

Before the ministry of Zechariah, Jeremiah prophesied that Jerusalem will be built "upon its own mound" to provide a perpetual location for the royal palace (Jer. 30:18; cf. Ps. 48:3; Isa. 2:1-5). His description of the city is similar to Zechariah's description:

> Behold, the days are coming, says the Lord, that the city shall be built for the Lord from the Tower of Hananel to the Corner Gate. The surveyor's line shall again extend straight forward over the hill Gareb; then it shall turn toward Goath. And the whole valley of the dead bodies and of the ashes, and all the fields as far as the Brook Kidron, to the corner of the Horse Gate toward the east, shall be holy to the Lord. It shall not be plucked up or thrown down anymore forever. (Jer. 31:38-40)

This prophecy further adds that the corpses and ashes will be strewn throughout the entire valley ("the whole valley of the dead bodies and of the ashes" Jer. 31:40), and the valley will become holy to the Lord (Jer. 31:40; cf. Zech. 14:20-21). This does not allude to the ancient sacrifices offered up to the god Moloch, as some commentators suppose, but to the carnage in the Valley of Jehoshaphat, resulting from the battle of Armageddon.

Micah also prophesied about the great elevation of the Holy City and its temple:

> Now it shall come to pass in the latter days that the mountain of the Lord's house shall be established on the top of the mountains and shall be exalted above the hills; and peoples shall flow to it. Many nations shall come and say, "Come, and let us go up to the mountain of the Lord, to the house of the God of Jacob; He will teach us His ways, and we shall walk in His paths." For out of Zion the law shall go forth and the word of the Lord from Jerusalem. (Mic. 4:1-2; cf. Isa. 2:2-3)

Based on the other prophetic witnesses of Scripture, we understand that the temple in Jerusalem ("the mountain of the Lord's house" Mic. 4:1) will be topographically elevated above all mountains ("the top of the mountains and shall be exalted above the hills" Mic. 4:1; cf. Isa. 2:2-3; 40:9). Everyone will see its glory, consistent with the teaching of Jesus that "a city set on a hill [mountain] cannot be hidden" (Matt. 5:14). Many Gentiles will ascend the mountain ("let us go up" Mic. 4:2) and will flow into its temple to learn Christ's ways, while His teachings will proceed from this place to the nations (cf. Acts 1:8). The sons of Korah dedicated a psalm to the Lord and to the terrifying glory of His holy mountain:

> Great is the Lord, and greatly to be praised in the city of our God, in His holy mountain. Beautiful in elevation, the joy of the whole earth, is Mount Zion on the sides of the north, the city of the great King. God is in her palaces; He is known as her refuge. For behold, the kings assembled, they passed by together. They saw it, and so they marveled; they were troubled, they hastened away. (Ps. 48:1-5)

King David depicted the other mountain peaks as "fuming with envy" over the mountain of Jerusalem because God has chosen to dwell in Mount Zion forever (Ps. 68:16). He Himself will "build up" the Holy City and will "appear in His glory" (Ps. 102:16; cf. Isa. 40:9; Jer. 31:23). The city will be called "the City of Truth, the Mountain of the Lord of hosts, the Holy Mountain" (Zech. 8:3; cf. Jer. 31:23) and "the City of the Lord, Zion of the Holy One of Israel" (Isa. 60:14). In the land of Israel, Ezekiel saw a vision of the future Jerusalem, which appeared as "something like the structure of a city" upon "a very high mountain" (Ezek. 40:2). The entire area surrounding the mountaintop, which will include the holy temple, will be of the upmost holiness (Ezek. 43:12). The Lord has chosen the temple in Jerusalem as the place where He will put His name forever (2 Chron. 7:16).

An underground fountain will spring forth from within the holy temple, creating rivers and streams, sustaining life within the Holy City and its surrounding areas. The prophet Joel predicted, "A fountain shall flow from the house of the Lord and water the Valley of Acacias" (Joel 3:18). Because of the elevation of Jerusalem, rivers will flow down the eastern and western sides of the mountain: "And in that day it shall be that living waters shall flow from Jerusalem, half of them toward the eastern sea and half of them toward the western sea; in both summer and winter it shall occur" (Zech. 14:8; cf. John 4:14; 7:38). Ezekiel saw that this water will flow from under the threshold of the temple, beginning as a small trickle but quickly becoming a river too deep for a man to cross (Ezek. 47:1-6). He also provided details about the eastern flow of this river:

> This water flows toward the eastern region, goes down into the valley, and enters the sea. When it reaches the sea, its waters are healed. And it shall be that every living thing that moves, wherever the rivers go, will live. There will be a very great multitude of fish, because these waters go there; for they will be healed, and everything will live wherever the river goes. It shall be that fishermen will stand by it from En

Gedi to En Eglaim; they will be places for spreading their nets. Their fish will be of the same kinds as the fish of the Great Sea, exceedingly many. But its swamps and marshes will not be healed; they will be given over to salt. (Ezek. 47:8-11)

This life-giving river will flow toward the east, "healing" the salinous waters of the Dead Sea, one of the saltiest places on Earth. Currently, the extreme conditions of this sea are not conducive to sustain fish, but after this miracle, the sea will teem with marine life so that fishermen take to their nets. Nevertheless, the marshes and swamps near the Dead Sea will remain salty (Ezek. 47:11; cf. Gen. 19:24-26).

The life-giving fountain will also be for purification from sin. Zechariah wrote, "In that day a fountain shall be opened for the house of David and for the inhabitants of Jerusalem, for sin and for uncleanness" (Zech. 13:1; cf. Ezek. 36:25; Zech. 12:7-12). In other words, the surviving remnant of Jews, and likely, the surviving Gentiles, will be baptized into the Holy Trinity for the remission of their sins. Consistent with this theme, the apostles baptized three thousand Jews at the temple on the day of Pentecost (Acts 2:38-41); this first-century event illustrates the concept of *inaugurated* eschatology, the "already and not yet" principle of God's kingdom (see chapter 20).

The Lord promised to "comfort" Zion's waste places and to make her desert "like Eden" and "like the garden of the Lord" (Isa. 51:3; cf. Ezek. 41:18-25). The sons of Korah declared, "There is a river whose streams shall make glad the city of God, the holy place of the tabernacle of the Most High. God is in the midst of her, she shall not be moved" (Ps. 46:4-5). Such imagery recollects the Genesis narrative concerning Eden and the river which left it to water the garden of Eden—Paradise (Gen. 2:10). Jerusalem will become "a place of broad rivers and streams, in which no galley with oars will sail, nor majestic ships pass by" (Isa. 33:21).

In Ezekiel's vision, he saw various trees, with incorruptible leaves and fruit, on each side of the life-giving river (Ezek. 47:7, 12). On a monthly basis, these trees will bear fruit for food and leaves for medicine because the water nourishing them will flow from the holy temple sanctuary (Ezek. 47:7, 12; cf. Rev. 22:1-2). Those who keep Christ's commandments will have the right to eat from the fruit of the tree of life, which is "in the midst" of Paradise (Rev. 2:7; 22:14; cf. Gen. 2:9; 3:22-24). The apostle John also saw that the tree of life is on both sides of the river of life:

> And he showed me a pure river of water of life, clear as crystal, proceeding from the throne of God and of the Lamb. In the middle of its street, and on either side of the river, was the tree of life, which bore twelve fruits, each tree yielding its fruit every month. The leaves of the tree were for the healing of the nations. (Rev. 22:1-2)

Although the river of life will flow through the new Jerusalem, John prophesied that the sea from the first heaven and earth will cease to exist ("Also there was no more sea" Rev. 21:1; cf. Isa. 33:21). Some commentators have speculated that this sea refers to the "sea of glass" (i.e., the laver) in the heavenly temple (cf. Rev. 4:6; 15:2), but this interpretation ignores the fact that the immediate context of 21:1 is concerned with the created world, not with heaven. Others have suggested that the sea in this verse refers to the evil underworld of the sea Beast, or to the chaos, dangers, and evil of the seas more generally (cf. Rev. 13:1). However, in the Apocalypse, "the sea" nearly always denotes a large body of water, and most of these occurrences (including Rev. 21:1) reveal this literalness by its juxtaposition with the actual heaven and earth.[1] As such, "the sea" in 21:1 denotes a large body of water, and most likely refers only to the Mediterranean Sea. If this reading is correct, the verse does not presume that all seas and oceans will be absent from the new creation, only that the Mediterranean will be displaced from its current location due to the topographical changes of the land. To further demonstrate this concept, the prophets predicted that the Dead Sea will continue to exist, albeit with abundant life, after the day of Christ (Ezek. 47:8-11; cf.

---

[1] Rev. 5:13; 7:1-3; 8:8-9; 10:2, 5-6, 8; 12:12; 14:7; 16:3; 18:17, 19, 21; 20:8, 13.

Ezek. 47:15-20; Zech. 14:8). Finally, the Greek grammar of Revelation 21:1 directly connects the absence of the sea with the old creation, and not the new creation, to refer to the dissolution of "the sea" at the day of the Lord. Even if the oceans instantaneously vaporize at that time, Christ may recreate them anew with the new heaven and new earth ("Behold, I make all things new" Rev. 21:5).

The inhabitants of the Holy City will live in complete safety, without manmade walls, because God will be "a wall of fire all around her . . . the glory in her midst" (Zech. 2:4-5; cf. Isa. 26:1; 60:18). As the cloud of smoke by day and fire by night led the Israelites in their journey to the Promised Land, His cloud of glory will cover every dwelling place in Jerusalem: "Then the Lord will create above every dwelling place of Mount Zion, and above her assemblies, a cloud and smoke by day and the shining of a flaming fire by night. For over all the glory there will be a covering. And there will be a tabernacle for shade in the daytime from the heat, for a place of refuge, and for a shelter from storm and rain" (Isa. 4:5-6). This phenomenon was seen, as a partial installment, when tongues of fire dwelt upon each Christian on the day of Pentecost (Acts 2:3-4).

In his elaborate depictions of the new Jerusalem, the apostle John borrowed heavily from the prophecies of Ezekiel. For example, Ezekiel prophesied that each of the four walls of the new Jerusalem will have three gates, so that the twelve gates can be dedicated to the twelve tribes of Israel (Ezek. 48:30-35; cf. Isa. 49:16). The apostle John provided the same description of the heavenly city:

> Also she had a great and high wall with twelve gates, and twelve angels at the gates, and names written on them, which are the names of the twelve tribes of the children of Israel: three gates on the east, three gates on the north, three gates on the south, and three gates on the west. Now the wall of the city had twelve foundations, and on them were the names of the twelve apostles of the Lamb. And he who talked with me had a gold reed to measure the city, its gates, and its wall. The city is laid out as a square; its length is as great as its breadth. (Rev. 21:12-16)

The Lord addressed Jerusalem, promising, "Behold, I will lay your stones with colorful gems and lay your foundations with sapphires. I will make your pinnacles of rubies, your gates of crystal, and all your walls of precious stones" (Isa. 54:11-12; cf. Zech. 9:16-17). As we would expect, John also saw these precious stones in his vision of the new Jerusalem:

> The construction of its wall was of jasper; and the city was pure gold, like clear glass. The foundations of the wall of the city were adorned with all kinds of precious stones: the first foundation was jasper, the second sapphire, the third chalcedony, the fourth emerald, the fifth sardonyx, the sixth sardius, the seventh chrysolite, the eighth beryl, the ninth topaz, the tenth chrysoprase, the eleventh jacinth, and the twelfth amethyst. The twelve gates were twelve pearls: each individual gate was of one pearl. And the street of the city was pure gold, like transparent glass. (Rev. 21:16-21)

Isaiah prophesied that Jerusalem will be called "the city of righteousness, the faithful city" (Isa. 1:26). Only those who trust in the Lord will possess the land and inherit the holy mountain (Isa. 26:1-3; 57:13) and enter the gates of the new Jerusalem to eat from the tree of life (Rev. 22:14; cf. Isa. 26:1). Saint John taught, "But there shall by no means enter it anything that defiles, or causes an abomination or a lie, but only those who are written in the Lamb's Book of Life" (Rev. 21:27). Likewise, David described the behavior of the people who will enter Jerusalem:

> Lord, who may abide in Your tabernacle? Who may dwell in Your holy hill? He who walks uprightly, and works righteousness, and speaks the truth in his heart; he who does not backbite with his tongue, nor does evil to his neighbor, nor does he take up a reproach against his friend; in whose eyes a vile person is despised, but he honors those who fear the Lord; he who swears to his own hurt and does not change; he who does not put out his money at usury, nor does he take a bribe against

the innocent. He who does these things shall never be moved. . . . Who may ascend into the hill of the Lord? Or who may stand in His holy place? He who has clean hands and a pure heart, who has not lifted up his soul to an idol, nor sworn deceitfully. He shall receive blessing from the Lord, and righteousness from the God of his salvation. This is Jacob, the generation of those who seek Him, who seek Your face. Selah (Ps. 15:1-5; cf. Ps. 24:3-6)

On the other hand, the wicked will remain outside the city walls. John wrote, "But outside are dogs and sorcerers and sexually immoral and murderers and idolaters, and whoever loves and practices a lie" (Rev. 22:14-15). Hell will be outside the city gates, where evildoers will experience "the second death" in the fiery lake which "burns with fire and brimstone" (Rev. 21:8; cf. Isa. 66:24; Mal. 3:5; Rev. 14:10-11). Isaiah spoke about this second death, elaborating, "And they [the worshippers of the nations] shall go forth and look upon the corpses of the men who have transgressed against Me. For their worm does not die, and their fire is not quenched. They shall be an abhorrence to all flesh" (Isa. 66:24; Mark 9:44, 46, 48).

The book of Hebrews explains that the new Jerusalem is the heavenly city, which has foundations, but "whose builder and maker is God" (Heb. 11:10; cf. Heb. 10:34). Abraham and the other righteous people of antiquity longed to inherit Jerusalem, and they will receive it as their everlasting inheritance (Heb. 11:8, 10, 16; 13:14). In addition, as the Israelites arrived at the foot of Mount Sinai, Christians have arrived at the new Jerusalem: "But you have come to Mount Zion and to the city of the living God, the heavenly Jerusalem, to an innumerable company of angels" (Heb. 12:22; cf. "to an inheritance incorruptible . . . reserved in heaven for you" 1 Pet. 1:4). The idea is not that Christians presently dwell in the heavenly city but that we have already tasted "the powers of the age to come" and have the promise of this future inheritance (Heb. 6:5).

The apostle John saw the Holy City, the new Jerusalem, "coming down out of heaven from God, prepared as a bride adorned for her husband" (Rev. 21:2; cf. Rev. 3:12). Just verses later, he described this descent: "And he [the angel] carried me away in the Spirit to a great and high mountain, and showed me the great city, the holy Jerusalem, descending out of heaven from God, having the glory of God. Her light was like a most precious stone, like a jasper stone, clear as crystal" (Rev. 21:10-11). As we saw previously, this "great and high mountain" will be created by the unprecedented earthquake on the day of Christ. Then the heavenly Jerusalem will descend to earth, signifying the miraculous transformation of God endowing the city with heavenly glory, consistent with the new and everlasting covenant (cf. Gal. 4:26). John's prophecies, coupled with those in the book of Hebrews, demonstrate that the Holy City's descent from heaven will be the work of God Himself, and it will transcend any human attempt to rebuild the fallen capital of Israel. Nevertheless, this heavenly transformation is not inconsistent with the fact that the Holy City "shall be inhabited *again* in her own place—Jerusalem" (Zech. 12:6, emphasis added).

The apostle John identified the new Jerusalem as "the bride, the Lamb's wife" (Rev. 21:9). This adheres with the teaching of Isaiah, who described the inhabitants of the city as being bound to her like bridal ornaments to their bride (Isa. 49:18). In that day, Jerusalem will no longer be termed Forsaken and Desolate but will be called Married because her sons will be married to her (Isa. 62:4-5). According to the book of Revelation, the descent of the heavenly Jerusalem will be concurrent with the Lamb's wedding supper ("New Jerusalem, coming down . . . prepared as a bride adorned for her husband" Rev. 21:2; cf. Rev. 19:7-9), and both events, as we have seen, will take place at the Second Advent of Jesus Christ (Rev. 19:11-16).

In the book of Revelation, the new Jerusalem sometimes refers to the city's inhabitants, and not to its edifice or location per se. For instance, the apostle John heard the statement "The marriage of the Lamb has come, and His wife has made herself ready," and then he saw the bride "arrayed in fine linen, clean and bright, for the fine linen is the righteous acts of the saints" (Rev. 19:7-8). This will fulfill the Lord's promise to

Israel, wherein He vowed, "I will betroth you to Me forever; yes, I will betroth you to Me in righteousness and justice, in lovingkindness and mercy; I will betroth you to Me in faithfulness, and you shall know the Lord" (Hosea 2:19-20). Concluding the Apocalypse, the Holy Spirit and "the bride" (i.e., the holy Church) summon everyone who thirsts to drink the free waters from the fountain of everlasting life (Rev. 22:17; cf. "Ho! Everyone who thirsts, come to the waters; and you who have no money" Isa. 55:1; cf. Rev. 21:6). Those who are willing can already ingest the life-giving waters of the Spirit, which belong to the future Jerusalem (cf. John 4:13-14; Isa. 55:1-3).

Along these lines, the Lord Jesus employed wedding imagery to speak about His return:

> Let not your heart be troubled; you believe in God, believe also in Me. In My Father's house are many mansions; if it were not so, I would have told you. I go to prepare a place for you. And if I go and prepare a place for you, I will come again and receive you to Myself; that where I am, there you may be also. And where I go you know, and the way you know. (John 14:1-4)

A typical first-century Jewish groom would build ("prepare") a house for his bride, often adjacent to his father's house, and later arrive at her house to escort her to their new home—but only at a time which he alone knew. Likewise, the Father's heavenly temple ("house") contains many "mansions" (variously translated "rooms" or "dwelling places"; cf. John 14:23), and Christ promised to "prepare a place" in this house for Christians so that He could return to take His bride, the sacred Church, to live with Him there (John 14:2).

The unknowability of "the day and hour" of Christ's return is implicit in the associated wedding imagery of this passage (cf. Zech. 14:7; Matt. 24:36, 50; Mark 13:32). These verses also connect the timing of His return ("I will come again" John 14:3) with the rapture of the church ("and receive you to Myself" John 14:3) and their entrance into the Father's house—the new Jerusalem ("that where I am, there you may be also" John 14:3). As a result, Christians will dwell forever in the new Jerusalem, in a state of holy matrimony with Christ. As we have seen, the new Jerusalem will descend from heaven in glory precisely when He descends from heaven in glory.

Jesus will descend to the Mount of Olives (see chapter 13) to abide in Jerusalem forever. The Lord stated, "Sing and rejoice, O daughter of Zion! For behold, I am coming and I will dwell in your midst" (Zech. 2:10). Later in the same book, He promised, "I will return to Zion, and dwell in the midst of Jerusalem" (Zech. 8:3). As a result, people will see the King "in His beauty" and the glorious city from very far away (Isa. 33:17). At that time, the new name for the new Jerusalem will be "The Lord is there" (Yahweh Shammah) (Ezek. 48:35; cf. Isa. 62:2) because Christ will reside there. He even promised to write the name of the Holy City and of His Father upon His people (Rev. 3:12).

King David foretold that Jesus Christ, the King of glory, will enter the gates of the Holy City:

> Lift up your heads, O you gates! And be lifted up, you everlasting doors! And the King of glory shall come in. Who is this King of glory? The Lord strong and mighty, the Lord mighty in battle. Lift up your heads, O you gates! Lift up, you everlasting doors! And the King of glory shall come in. Who is this King of glory? The Lord of hosts, He is the King of glory. Selah (Ps. 24:7-10)

Malachi described Christ as returning in glory and suddenly arriving to His holy temple: "And the Lord, whom you seek, will suddenly come to His temple, even the Messenger of the covenant, in whom you delight. Behold, He is coming" (Mal. 3:1; cf. Hab. 2:20). Then Jesus, the "Desire of All Nations," will fill the temple with His glory (Hag. 2:7-9). In all probability, this verse does not refer to the remnants of the Third Temple, upon which the Antichrist will bring desolation at the beginning of the final forty-two months, but to the new covenant temple. Corroborating this event, the prophet Ezekiel saw a vision of God gloriously entering the temple of the new Jerusalem:

> Afterward he brought me to the gate, the gate that faces toward the east. And behold, the glory of the God of Israel came from the way of the east. His voice was like the sound of many waters; and the earth shone with His glory . . . And the glory of the Lord came into the temple by way of the gate which faces toward the east. The Spirit lifted me up and brought me into the inner court; and behold, the glory of the Lord filled the temple. Then I heard Him speaking to me from the temple, while a man stood beside me. And He said to me, "Son of man, this is the place of My throne and the place of the soles of My feet, where I will dwell in the midst of the children of Israel forever. No more shall the house of Israel defile My holy name." (Ezek. 43:1-2, 4-7; cf. Ezek. 44:4)[2]

The heavenly temple also appears throughout the Apocalypse (e.g. Rev. 14:15, 17), and God's throne was seen there (Rev. 4:2-6; 5:1, 6; 16:17). Furthermore, the Lord promised to make each victorious Christian "a pillar in the temple of My God, and he shall go out no more" (Rev. 3:12). In other words, every faithful disciple will enjoy a permanent place in God's temple (cf. Isa. 56:3-5). Finally, the apostle John explained that the saints will approach God's throne to serve Him day and night "in His temple" (Rev. 7:15). In each of these verses, the heavenly temple is presented as the eternal abode of Christians.

People will not build the heavenly temple. To illustrate, the writer of the book of Hebrews referred to Christ as the High Priest of "the sanctuary and of the true tabernacle which the Lord erected, and not man" (Heb. 8:2; cf. Heb. 8:5; 9:11). For theological purposes, the

---

2   Similarly, Ezekiel saw that the Eastern Gate of the temple will be closed after the glory of Christ enters it (Ezek. 44:1-2). This prophecy is followed by the Trinitarian statement by God, saying, "O house of Israel, let *Us* have no more of all your abominations" (Ezek. 44:6, emphasis added).

writer substituted the term "tabernacle" in place of the more frequently utilized term "temple," but the concept is essentially the same. He further elucidated that while human hands previously constructed these holy edifices, they only served as earthly copies of the true tabernacle in heaven (Heb. 9:24; cf. Heb. 8:5). The heavenly tabernacle is "greater and more perfect" precisely because it was "not made with hands, that is, not of this creation" (Heb. 9:11). Christ Himself will build this eternal temple (2 Chron. 6:9).

The Apocalypse also mentions the heavenly tabernacle on two occasions: First, the apostle saw "the temple of the tabernacle of the testimony" opened in heaven, and he learned that no one could enter it until the day of Jesus Christ (Rev. 15:5, 8). Grammatically, the phrase "the temple of the tabernacle" likely functions as a genitive of apposition, which identifies the tabernacle as the temple. Second, when John saw the arrival of the new heaven and new earth and the descent of the new Jerusalem from heaven, a heavenly voice proclaimed, "Behold, the tabernacle of God is with men, and He will dwell with them, and they shall be His people. God Himself will be with them and be their God" (Rev. 21:3; cf. Exod. 29:45; Lev. 26:11-12). In other words, God's heavenly city is itself His "tabernacle" and "dwelling place" among His people. We will revisit this concept momentarily.

As part of the new and everlasting covenant, God promised the people of Israel that He would put His dwelling place and sanctuary "in their midst forevermore" (Ezek. 37:26-27; cf. 2 Chron. 2:6; 6:18). The prophet Ezekiel provided us extensive details regarding the temple of the new Jerusalem. He outlined nine chapters of meticulous architectural blueprints for the city and the temple complex, including the dimensions of its walls, chambers, gates, courtyards, dining rooms, staircases, walkways, columns, windows, and altars (Ezek. 40-48, esp. 40:5-37, 44-49; 41:1-26; 42:1-20; 43:11-17; 48:30-35). As part of this large section of prophecy, God commanded the house of Israel to "keep its [the temple's] whole design and all its ordinances, and perform them" (Ezek. 43:11; cf. Ezek. 44:5).

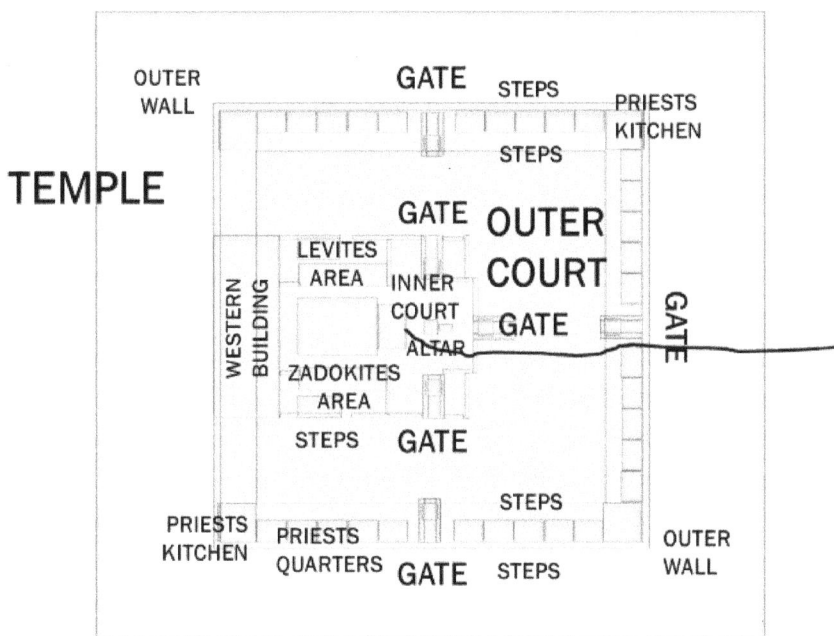

This final section of the book of Ezekiel (Ezek. 40-48) is extremely difficult to interpret, and it serves to highlight multiple interpretive difficulties, many of which appear insurmountable, which have been discussed in detail by rabbinic and Christian commentators. In the next several paragraphs, I will discuss some of these difficulties and offer some possible solutions.

The most significant interpretive difficulty is that Ezekiel prophesied that the Levitical priesthood will perform sacrifices in the new covenant temple. The prophet foretold that after God regathers the people of Israel to the land, they will bring the required firstfruits offerings and sacrifices: "For on My holy mountain, on the mountain height of Israel . . . all the house of Israel, all of them in the land, shall serve Me;

there I will accept them, and there I will require your offerings and the firstfruits of your sacrifices, together with all your holy things" (Ezek. 20:40). He later predicted that the Zadokites, a smaller group within the Levitical order of priests, will minister within the holy temple (Ezek. 40:46; 43:19; 44:10-31; 45:5).

Levitical priests again offering sacrifices at the holy temple has precedent in the Prophets. For example, Malachi prophesied that the Lord will return in fiery judgment on the day of the Lord and will purify the priests by a fiery trial so they once again make acceptable offerings before Him:

> And the Lord, whom you seek will suddenly come to His temple, even the Messenger of the covenant in whom you delight. Behold, He is coming . . . But who can endure the day of His coming? And who can stand when He appears? . . . He will sit as a refiner and a purifier of silver; He will purify the sons of Levi and purge them as gold and silver that they may offer to the Lord an offering in righteousness. Then the offering of Judah and Jerusalem will be pleasant to the Lord, as in the days of old, as in former years. (Mal. 3:1-2, 3-4)

Consistent with this theme, Jeremiah prophesied that the priests and Levites will never "lack a man to offer burnt offerings before Me, to kindle grain offerings, and to sacrifice continually" (Jer. 33:18; cf. Isa. 19:19-21; Joel 2:14). Even Gentiles will offer burnt offerings and sacrifices upon the altar in Jerusalem (Isa. 56:7). Jeremiah went even further, teaching that the Levitical priesthood is as permanent as the Davidic covenant and the perpetual cycle of day and night (Jer. 33:18-24).

The Levitical priesthood offering sacrifices again, especially as part of the new and greater covenant, as these prophecies convey, presents at least two interpretive difficulties: First, the writer of Hebrews explained that since the Levitical priesthood could never bring perfection, God changed it, even superseding it, by the greater priesthood of Christ, our High Priest "according to the order of Melchizedek" (Heb. 7:11-17; cf. Ps. 110:4; Heb. 5:6, 10; 6:20; 7:21). This New Testament statement appears to contradict the prophets' anticipation that the Levitical priests will again offer sacrifices. To reconcile this apparent discrepancy, we should not imagine that God has abrogated His promise to eternally maintain the Levitical priesthood. Rather, the greater priesthood of the new covenant (the order of Melchizedek) incorporated and subsumed many of the Levitical priests. This began when many descendants of Levi, Aaron, and Zadok first became obedient to Jesus Christ and became part of the holy apostolic Church ("a great many of the priests were obedient to the faith" Acts 6:7).

Second, the prospect of Levitical priests offering sacrifices in the new covenant temple appears to be unnecessary, sinful, and even a non sequitur, chiefly because Christ offered Himself on the cross as the perfect sacrifice for sins ("once for all" Heb. 7:27; cf. Heb. 10:10). Answering this objection requires a thorough investigation of the related Scriptures, which I will now endeavor to do. To begin, we should recognize that Ezekiel specified many details regarding this sacrificial system, and he prescribed a reinstitution of sin offerings, grain offerings, burnt offerings, and peace offerings (Ezek. 40:38-43, 47; 42:13; 43:18-27; 44:11, 15-16, 27; 45:13-25; 46:1-24). Even more astonishing is his explanation that some of these offerings will "make atonement" for the house of Israel (Ezek. 45:17; cf. v. 15). It is difficult to imagine how this concept could be consistent with accepted Christian doctrine.

Some Christian commentators attempt to avoid these interpretive challenges by contending that Israel's reception of the promises of Ezekiel 40-48, including the temple and sacrifices, was conditioned upon the nation's response, and since the prophet's contemporaries refused to repent, these promises will never find fulfillment. This interpretation emphasizes the conditions of God's instruction: "And if they are ashamed of all that they have done, make known to them the design of the temple and its arrangement . . . Write it down in their sight, so that they may keep its whole design and all its ordinances, and perform them" (Ezek. 43:11). While Israel's reception of these promises may have been temporarily withheld due to disobedience, the remainder of Ezekiel's book outlines the absolute certainty of the nation's future repentance and salvation. Consequently, the interpretation of these commentators is unsatisfying because it assumes only a theoretical fulfillment of these nine chapters and implicitly denies the actual fulfillment of Israel's ultimate redemption.

Ezekiel's visions can be properly interpreted by putting together several observations from the text: First, the prophet explained, "One lamb shall be given from a flock of two hundred, from the rich pastures of Israel . . . for grain offerings, burnt offerings, and peace offerings, to make atonement for them [the people]" (Ezek. 45:15). The grammatical construction of this verse may indicate that a particular lamb ("one lamb shall be given") will be offered in place of or as a substitute "for" the other offerings specified in the verse, which were prescribed for the purpose of making atonement for the transgressions of the people of Israel. As such, this verse may point to the sacrificial offering of the Lamb of God, Jesus Christ, for the atonement of sins.

Second, Ezekiel revealed that the figure known as the "prince" will be responsible for providing or presiding over these offerings (Ezek. 45:17). As commentators have noted, the man's functions will include those of a king and a high priest, and as such, he should be identified as the Messiah, the Prince, and the King-Priest of Jerusalem. This demonstrates that Jesus Christ, the great High Priest, will preside over the priests who will offer these sacrifices, including the offerings which atone for sins and transgressions.

A common objection to our identification of Christ as "the prince" is that this high priest was commanded to make the sin offering "for himself and for all the people" (Ezek. 45:22; cf. "offer the bull as a sin offering . . . and make atonement for himself and for his house" Lev. 16:6), whereas Jesus never sinned. But suffice it to say that Christ presented this required sacrifice when He offered Himself on the cross, although His death effected only the removal of the sins of His people because He never committed any transgression (2 Cor. 5:21; Heb. 4:15; 1 Pet. 2:22; 1 John 3:5).

Third, the new Passover laws revealed to Ezekiel specify that "the prince" must present specific offerings, including a bull "for a sin offering" on the fourteenth day of the month of Nisan (Ezek. 45:21-22). The law of Moses specified that the Levitical high priest must offer this sin offering annually on the day of Atonement (Lev. 16:6), but in stark contrast, Ezekiel's prophecy commands the prince to bring this sin offering on the fourteenth of Nisan (i.e., Passover), the day the paschal lambs were slaughtered (Exod. 12:1-28). As such, this prophecy foresaw a significant change in the law, appropriate for a new covenant context (cf. Heb. 7:12). As we would expect, Christ our High Priest fulfilled the prophetic requirements of the atonement when He presented Himself as a sin offering upon the cross (Heb. 9:7-28), which He accomplished on the fourteenth of Nisan! Therefore, He became our Passover Lamb ("Behold, the Lamb of God who takes away the sin of the world" John 1:29; cf. 1 Cor. 5:7-8).[3]

Fourth, the prophet did not mention many of the utensils and vessels used in the Mosaic priestly service. It is possible that he deemed it unnecessary to mention these implements; however, the reader is left to wonder how the priests can prepare the sacrifices without them. However, this omission likely hints to a greater truth, specifically, that Jesus Christ already presented these new covenant offerings through His sacrificial death.

Fifth, despite his detailed descriptions of the temple furniture, Ezekiel did not mention a golden altar of incense, as prescribed by the law (Exod. 30:1-10), but he replaced it with a similarly shaped wooden structure called "the table that is before the Lord" (Ezek. 41:21-22).[4] This altar will likely memorialize His sacrificial death, which took place upon a wooden cross. Also, Ezekiel did not mention the priestly offering

---

[3] Consistent with this theme, the apostle Paul taught Christians to observe the new Passover "with the unleavened bread of sincerity and truth" (1 Cor. 5:7-8).

[4] The golden altar of incense was comprised of acacia wood and overlaid with gold. This prophecy does not mention gold.

of incense, likely because the altar points us to the greater reality in Christ, who has "given Himself for us, an offering and a sacrifice to God for a sweet-smelling aroma" (Eph. 5:2).

Consequently, this temple altar will function like church altars, from which Christians regularly ingest the sacrificial body and blood of Christ. Through the mystery of the Eucharist, the holy Church regularly consumes this singular sacrifice of Christ Himself, which the presbyters perpetually offer upon the holy altar. The writer of Hebrews testified that believers partake of the new covenant sacrifice offered upon the altar of the heavenly tabernacle (Heb. 13:10; cf. Ezek. 43:13-27).[5] In addition, Isaiah prophesied that the Gentiles will become His servants and will make sacrifices and offerings to Him: "Even them I will bring to My holy mountain and make them joyful in My house of prayer. Their burnt offerings and their sacrifices will be accepted on My altar; for My house shall be called a house of prayer for all nations" (Isa. 56:7). These kingdom offerings are not Mosaic sacrifices but Eucharistic offerings consistent with the new covenant.

Further evidence of this concept is Ezekiel's holy altar, which appears to be a deliberate conflation of two pieces of tabernacle furniture: the altar of incense and the table of showbread ("the table that is before the Lord" Ezek. 41:21-22). The Levitical priests presented showbread as a perpetual offering before the Lord (Exod. 25:23-30). However, bringing this image into a sacrificial context, Jesus identified Himself as the living bread from heaven, and He further identified this bread as His flesh, promising eternal life for everyone who eats His flesh and drinks His blood:

> I am the living bread which came down from heaven. If anyone eats of this bread, he will live forever; and the bread that I shall give is My

---

5   In addition, Christians continually offer "the sacrifice of praise" with "the fruit of our lips" (Heb. 13:15; cf. Isa. 57:19; Hosea 14:2; Heb. 9:23) and other sacrifices shared with other believers (Heb. 13:16; cf. Phil. 4:18).

flesh, which I shall give for the life of the world . . . Most assuredly, I say to you, unless you eat the flesh of the Son of Man and drink His blood, you have no life in you. Whoever eats My flesh and drinks My blood has eternal life, and I will raise him up at the last day. For My flesh is food indeed, and My blood is drink indeed. He who eats My flesh and drinks My blood abides in Me, and I in him. (John 6:51, 53-56)

Additionally, Malachi prophesied that the Gentiles living throughout the world will offer incense to God: "From the rising of the sun, even to its going down, My name shall be great among the Gentiles; in every place incense shall be offered to My name and a pure offering; for My name shall be great among the nations" (Mal. 1:11). This priestly offering of incense has already begun, and has continued unabatedly throughout the centuries of Christianity, in the practice of Christian presbyters offering holy incense "in every place" to Jesus Christ.

Sixth, the prophet Ezekiel did not mention the golden lampstand, which the law mandated for the temple sanctuary (Exod. 25:31-40). This exclusion points us to the fact that the temple of the new Jerusalem will not need this light because Jesus Christ, the substance to which the lampstand pointed ("I am the light of the world. He who follows Me shall not walk in darkness" John 8:12), will illuminate the city. The apostle John explained, "The throne of God and of the Lamb shall be in it [the new Jerusalem], and His servants shall serve Him. They shall see His face . . . There shall be no night there: They need no lamp nor light of the sun, for the Lord God gives them light. And they shall reign forever and ever" (Rev. 22:3-4, 5; cf. Rev. 21:23, 25). Consequently, the Sun and Moon will no longer be needed for light, and night as such will no longer exist, because "the Lord will be to you an everlasting light and your God your glory" (Isa. 60:19-20; cf. Isa. 62:1; Rev. 21:23, 25). The contrast between the brilliance of His uncreated light will cause these luminary bodies to feel "ashamed" so to speak (Isa. 24:23), and the intensity of the Lord's light will make the Moon appear to emanate sunlight and cause the Sun to radiate light seven times more brilliant than before (Isa. 30:25-26; cf. Isa. 60:19-20; 62:1).

Seventh, Ezekiel did not even mention in his temple visions the ark of the covenant with its mercy seat, which the law prescribed to be placed before the Lord (Exod. 25:10-22). The prophet Jeremiah provided the reason for this omission:

> They will say no more, "The ark of the covenant of the Lord." It shall not come to mind, nor shall they remember it, nor shall they visit it, nor shall it be made anymore. At that time Jerusalem shall be called The Throne of the Lord, and all the nations shall be gathered to it, to the name of the Lord, to Jerusalem. No more shall they follow the dictates of their evil hearts. (Jer. 3:16-17)

The Son of Man's throne ("The Throne of the Lord" Jer. 3:17) will replace the mere shadow of the ark of the covenant and its mercy seat (cf. Rev. 22:3). After Jesus, our great High Priest, offered Himself before the Father as an eternal sacrifice, He entered the holy of holies within the heavenly tabernacle ("with His own blood He entered the Most Holy Place" Heb. 9:12; cf. Heb. 7:27; 9:11-28) and sat down upon His throne, at the Father's right hand (Heb. 10:12). Based on this fulfillment, we can deduce that the incarnate God also fulfills the contents of the ark, including Aaron's rod that budded, the golden pot with manna, and the tablets of the covenant (Heb. 9:4). As such, Christ has become our life-giving High Priest, provision from heaven, and fulfillment of the law. Since the ark of the covenant signifies Christ's throne, this may explain why the apostle John saw the ark in the heavenly temple only once he heard the last trumpet, the signal for the Second Coming (Rev. 11:19).

In the temple visions of Ezekiel, the reader encounters some obscurity between the features presented by the prophet and the Christological realities to which they point. Based on the above considerations, we understand that the new covenant priesthood will offer the actual presence of Christ in Eucharistic worship. While Paul wrote, "For as often as you eat this bread and drink this cup, you proclaim the Lord's death till He comes" (1 Cor. 11:26), Ezekiel's visions evidence that Israel will continue to feast upon Christ, our eternal sacrifice before the Father, in the consummated kingdom. We can deduce that these sacrifices will find fulfillment in the marriage banquet of the Lamb, which Christians already receive in the sacrament of the Eucharist.

Furthermore, Ezekiel prophesied that the term "holy of holies" will no longer describe only the innermost chamber of the sanctuary but will characterize the entire temple complex (Ezek. 43:12). This illustrates the superiority of the greater and more enduring covenant in Christ Jesus. In the everlasting kingdom, the greater holiness of the temple will extend outward to the places which were once inferior in holiness; for example, Zechariah prophesied that it will be transferred to the entirety of the new Jerusalem:

> In that day "HOLINESS TO THE LORD" shall be engraved on the bells of the horses. The pots in the Lord's house shall be like the bowls before the altar. Yes, every pot in Jerusalem and Judah shall be holiness to the Lord of hosts. Everyone who sacrifices shall come and take them and cook in them. In that day there shall no longer be a Canaanite in the house of the Lord of hosts. (Zech. 14:20-22)

Even common objects, such as ornamental bells upon horses, will become as holy as the metal plate upon the high priest's forehead, which was engraved with "HOLINESS TO THE LORD" (Zech. 14:20; cf. Exod. 39:30). Likewise, the holiness of the gold and silver temple bowls will extend to the common vessels throughout Jerusalem and its vicinity (Zech. 14:21). In the same verse, the prophet mentioned that Canaanites will not be allowed to enter the temple (Zech. 14:21), implying that the Gentiles will no longer be "strangers and foreigners" (Eph. 2:19) but will be transformed by the same power of Christ that transforms profane vessels into holy ones.

The people of Israel will return to the land, as incense is offered to the Lord ("I will accept you as a sweet aroma" Ezek. 20:41). For example, Zephaniah prophesied, "From beyond the rivers of Ethiopia My worshipers, the daughter of My dispersed ones, shall bring My offering" (Zeph. 3:10). In other words, the believing Gentiles will bring the dispersed Jews back to the land as an offering to God. This accords with Isaiah's prophecy that Gentiles will "bring all your brethren for an offering to the Lord out of all nations . . . to My holy mountain Jerusalem . . . as the children of Israel bring an offering in a clean vessel into the house of the Lord. And I will also take some of them for priests and Levites" (Isa. 66:20, 20, 21). While the immediate context may support the idea that these priests and Levites will be descendants of Israel, the grammatical ambiguity allows the possibility that some of these priests will be Gentiles.[6]

At that time, the nations and their kings will see the glory and righteousness of the new Jerusalem (Isa. 62:2-3). The prophet Joel taught that the holiness of the city will prohibit "aliens" from passing through it again (Joel 3:17).[7] Likewise, Ezekiel prophesied, "No foreigner, uncircumcised in heart or uncircumcised in flesh, shall enter My sanctuary" (Ezek. 44:9; cf. v. 5). But such statements must be understood in light of the mystery of the Gentiles, which was revealed to the holy apostles:

> Now, therefore, you [believing Gentiles] are no longer strangers and foreigners, but fellow citizens with the saints and members of the household of God, having been built on the foundation of the apostles and prophets, Jesus Christ Himself being the chief cornerstone, in whom the whole building, being fitted together, grows into a holy temple in the Lord, in whom you also are being built together for a dwelling place of God in the Spirit. (Eph. 2:19-22)

---

[6]   This double entendre is an example of Gentile inclusion into Israel, a mystery which remained concealed until the apostolic period.

[7]   The fact that strangers once passed through the Holy City reinforces the concept that the city will be on Earth.

The apostle taught that Gentiles who trust in Christ have been grafted into Israel (Rom. 11:17), and as a result are "no longer strangers and foreigners" but fellow citizens! In addition, Paul also received an orthodox understanding of the new covenant temple, wherein the holy Church, comprised of Jews and Gentiles, is growing up into one holy temple for the dwelling place of God's Spirit (Eph. 2:21-22; cf. Amos 9:11). This apostolic revelation helps us to identify the new Jerusalem temple.

The prophets foresaw the large-scale inclusion of the Gentiles, which has already begun, at the day of Christ. Zechariah prophesied, "Many nations shall be joined to the Lord in that day, and they shall become My people. And I will dwell in your midst" (Zech. 2:11). Believing Gentiles will travel "from the ends of the earth" to the new Jerusalem, declaring, "Surely our fathers have inherited lies, worthlessness and unprofitable things [idolatry]" (Jer. 16:19; cf. vv. 20-21). Then they will enter the Holy City: "And the nations of those who are saved shall walk in its light, and the kings of the earth bring their glory and honor into it. Its gates shall not be shut at all by day. . . And they shall bring the glory and the honor of the nations into it" (Rev. 21:24-25, 26; cf. Isa. 60:3, 11; Hag. 2:7). The Lord will give them a "pure language" so that they can serve Him in unity (Zeph. 3:9); while this could refer to a heavenly language, Isaiah referred to it as "the language of Canaan" (Isa. 19:18), that is, the language of the Jews.

Some people will observe new moons, Sabbaths, and festivals in the consummated kingdom (Ezek. 45:17; 46:1-6; cf. Isa. 66:22-23); however, the apostle Paul taught that such observances are merely "a shadow of things to come, but the substance is of Christ" (Col. 2:17). To illustrate how the interpreter can reconcile this seeming contradiction, we will evaluate Zechariah's prophecy regarding the future observance of the Feast of Tabernacles:

> And it shall come to pass that everyone who is left of all the nations which came against Jerusalem shall go up from year to year to worship the King, the Lord of hosts, and to keep the Feast of Tabernacles. And

it shall be that whichever of the families of the earth do not come up to Jerusalem to worship the King, the Lord of hosts, on them there will be no rain. If the family of Egypt will not come up and enter in, they shall have no rain; they shall receive the plague with which the Lord strikes the nations who do not come up to keep the Feast of Tabernacles. This shall be the punishment of Egypt and the punishment of all the nations that do not come up to keep the Feast of Tabernacles. (Zech. 14:16-19)

This passage reveals that the believing Gentiles will make pilgrimage to Jerusalem to observe the Feast of Tabernacles. The phrase "everyone who is left of all the nations which came against Jerusalem" likely refers to the survivors among the nations, most particularly, the soldiers of the international forces who will have invaded the Holy Land prior to the day of the Lord (Zech. 14:1-2). The idea is that these Gentiles will make pilgrimage to the new Jerusalem to worship Christ who tabernacled among us ("dwelt among us" John 1:14; cf. Matt. 17:4-7; Mark 9:5-8; Luke 9:33-36). The families of the earth will be welcomed into the new Jerusalem ("come up and enter in" Zech. 14:18) and will worship continually ("from year to year") at this tabernacle (Zech. 14:16-18), whereas those who do not go to Him will be punished with drought and ruin (cf. Isa. 60:12). In the light of New Testament revelation, the plague of water scarcity likely refers to hellfire ("dip the tip of his finger in water and cool my tongue" Luke 16:24; cf. "lest you receive of her plagues" Rev. 18:4, 8), especially since the wicked in hell will be prohibited from entering the new Jerusalem (Rev. 22:15; cf. Rev. 21:8).

The believing Gentiles who attain victory over the Antichrist and his image, mark, and name, will worship Christ, declaring, "For all nations shall come and worship before You, for Your judgments have been manifested" (Rev. 15:4; cf. vv.2-4). Many Gentiles will receive the promises made to the patriarchs, including the Promised Land, while the unbelieving Jews will be cast out of the kingdom:

There will be weeping and gnashing of teeth, when you see Abraham and Isaac and Jacob and all the prophets in the kingdom of God, and yourselves thrust out. They [Gentiles] will come from the east and the west, from the north and the south, and sit down in the kingdom of God. And indeed there are last who will be first, and there are first who will be last. (Luke 13:28-30)

Furthermore, Ezekiel prophesied that the Promised Land will be divided after Christ's glorious return so that each of the twelve tribes will receive equal allotments of territory (Ezek. 47:13-23; 48:1-29). As we should expect, the believing Gentiles will receive their inheritance among the various tribal allotments (Ezek. 47:22-23), which is consistent with apostolic expectations that they are included within the commonwealth of Israel (Eph. 2:12) and are coheirs of God's promises to the patriarchs and their descendants (Rom. 10:12; Gal. 3:14, 28-29; Eph. 2:11-19; 3:6). Consequently, all believing Jews and Gentiles will be unified in the land under the headship of Christ, completing the mystery of the "one new man"—the holy Church (Eph. 2:15), as He assured through Moses, "Rejoice, O Gentiles, with His people; for He will avenge the blood of His servants and render vengeance to His adversaries; He will provide atonement for His land and His people" (Deut. 32:43).

TRIBES
ORDERED

Cyprus

Syria

Lebanon

DAN
ASHER
NAPHTALI
MANASSEH
EPHRAIM
RUBEN
JUDAH
HOLY
DISTRICT
BENJAMIN
SIMEON
ISSACHAR
ZEBULUN
GAD

Jordan

Egypt

The Promised Land will include allotments for the priests, the Levites, and the Holy City and its surrounding territory (Ezek. 45:1-8). The temple will be located within the inheritance belonging to the messianic Prince, and He will dwell in the midst of His people (Ezek. 46:10; cf. Rev. 21:3). As we should expect, His district will be provided "for the Lord, a holy section of the land" (Ezek. 45:1; cf. vv. 7-8).

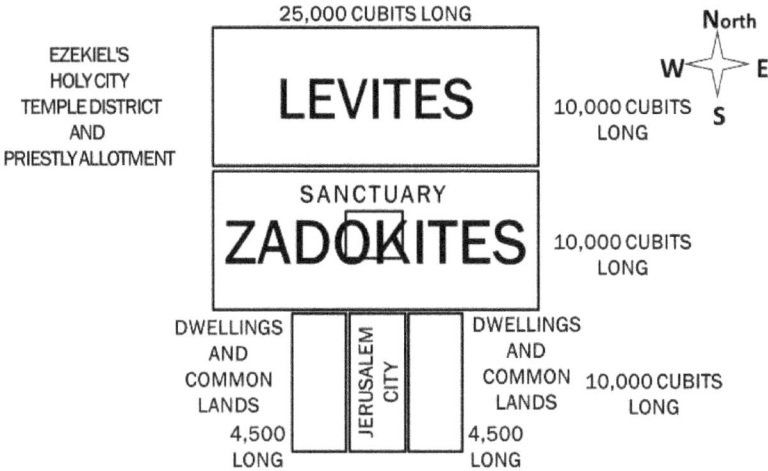

A peculiar feature of Ezekiel's vision is that he saw the holy temple outside the new Jerusalem. The apostle John did not see a physical temple in the Holy City: "But I saw no temple in it, for the Lord God Almighty and the Lamb are its temple" (Rev. 21:22; cf. Matt. 12:6). However, any attempt to syncretize Ezekiel and John's visions creates another interpretive difficulty. If these visions are to be taken at face value, we would expect two new covenant temples, specifically, the temple outside the Holy City, which will be the place of the Prince's throne (according to Ezekiel), and Christ Himself (according to John). I confess that I am unable to reconcile this discrepancy using a literal hermeneutic. Nonetheless, John's statement is an absolute indication that the new earth will not contain a physical temple. This reinforces the concept that Ezekiel's visions (Ezek. 40-48) also contain symbolic elements, including the temple itself, which point to the Person and energies of Jesus Christ (cf. John 4:21).

At any rate, according to Ezekiel, the temple complex will be a square plot with each of its four walls measuring 500 rods (8,250 feet) in length (Ezek. 40:3; 42:15-20; 45:2-3).[8] Each of the four walls of the

---

8   Each rod equals six cubits (Ezek. 40:5) or 122 feet.

new Jerusalem will be 4,500 cubits in length (Ezek. 48:30-35). The apostle John also recorded the measurements for the new Jerusalem with divergent results (Rev. 21:16-17), although it is uncertain whether the first measurement of 12,000 furlongs for "the city" is the wall length (cf. Ezek. 48:30-35), diameter (cf. Ezek. 48:35), surface area, or cubic volume (cf. "its length, breadth, and height" Rev. 21:16). According to the apostle, the Holy City will have equal dimensions of breadth, length, and height, reminiscent of the cubic nature of the holy of holies (1 Kings 6:20) and conveying the idea that the entire city will be the most holy place. In addition, the square dimensions of the city are roughly equivalent to the surface area of the entire Promised Land!

As we have seen, Ezekiel's prophetic visions of Jerusalem and its temple present a complex and mysterious interplay between the visible realities of our present age and the radically transformed Jerusalem with its heavenly glory. While we should contend for a literal hermeneutic, we are constrained by the biblical texts to resist interpreting his visions in an overly literal manner. We must allow for some accommodation as we interpret such Old Testament prophecies. To demonstrate this truth, the prophet also depicted the future battle of Gog and Magog using the imagery of horses and their riders, shields, swords, bows, arrows, javelins, and spears (Ezek. 38:4; 39:9, see chapter 4). Failing to recognize this hermeneutical principle of accommodation, or overworking it by denying its future fulfillment, will lead to error.

One final consideration regarding Ezekiel's visions of Jerusalem and its temple may provide the key to proper interpretation. The prophet was instructed to lay their architectural blueprints before the Jewish leaders so that the people could construct these holy edifices (Ezek. 43:11; 44:5), and this was decisively during the administration of the Mosaic law. This explains why he cast the visions in Mosaic terms that his sixth-century BC audience could implement. However, since this generation of Jews refused to complete the necessary conditions to fulfill the content of these visions, their prophetic fulfillment awaited until after Christ had ushered in the new covenant. Consequently, we should recognize that if Ezekiel's original audience had built Jerusalem and its temple in the manner that he prescribed, the Holy City would have functioned only as a prophetic foreshadowing of the final, glorified new Jerusalem as revealed in the book of Revelation. Consequently, the content of the apostle's vision fulfills the prophetic visions of Ezekiel.

While it may be tempting to see the discrepancies between Ezekiel and John's visions as actual contradictions, examples of non-fulfillment, or prophecies awaiting fulfillment at two different "end times," I have presented what I believe to be a preferable interpretative approach. In addition, we should readily admit our need for caution as we interpret Ezekiel's prophecies (Ezek. 40-48), especially since many professing Christians have unwittingly adopted the heresy of Cerinthus, who purportedly taught the future necessity of Jews returning to the sacrificial practices of the Mosaic law!

To summarize, the composite picture of Ezekiel and John's visions conflates the new heavens and earth with the new Jerusalem, the temple with its furnishings, the tabernacle, the Church comprised of believing Jews and Gentiles, and the land of Israel. This eternal state of glorification and oneness, properly known as theosis, is the ultimate goal for mankind. The apostle Paul summarized:

> Having made known to us the mystery of His will, according to His good pleasure which He purposed in Himself, that in the dispensation of the fullness of the times He might gather together in one all things in Christ, both which are in heaven and which are on earth—in Him. In Him also we have obtained an inheritance. (Eph. 1:9-11)

The end of redemptive history is also depicted as the wedding of the bride of Christ to our heavenly Bridegroom, the Lamb of God—Jesus Christ. Zechariah summarized: "And the Lord shall be King over all the earth. In that day it shall be—'The Lord is one,' and His name one" (Zech. 14:9). The apostle John summarized the spiritual conditions of the new creation:

And God will wipe away every tear from their eyes; there shall be no more death, nor sorrow, nor crying. There shall be no more pain, for the former things have passed away. Then He who sat on the throne said, "Behold, I make all things new." And He said to me, "Write, for these words are true and faithful." And He said to me, "It is done! I am the Alpha and the Omega, the Beginning and the End. I will give of the fountain of the water of life freely to him who thirsts. He who overcomes shall inherit all things, and I will be his God and he shall be My son." (Rev. 21:4-7)

The prophetic Church is called to be like watchmen standing upon the city walls who "never hold their peace day or night" until Christ establishes Jerusalem and makes her "a praise in the earth" (Isa. 62:6-7; cf. v. 1; Jer. 31:6). The Holy City will be "redeemed without money" (Isa. 52:3; cf. Isa. 55:1; 62:1; Rev. 21:6; 22:17) but with the sacrificial blood of Christ, and the watchmen must continue to proclaim His gospel (good news) of eternal peace and salvation until that time:

How beautiful upon the mountains are the feet of him who brings good news, who proclaims peace, who brings glad tidings of good things, who proclaims salvation, who says to Zion, "Your God reigns!" Your watchmen shall lift up their voices, with their voices they shall sing together; for they shall see eye to eye when the Lord brings back Zion. Break forth into joy, sing together, you waste places of Jerusalem! For the Lord has comforted His people, He has redeemed Jerusalem. (Isa. 52:7-9)

The Church militant must continue to proclaim to Jerusalem and to the Jewish people that they should repent and believe in the gospel because Christ has come to save them, to still their hearts, and to rejoice over them "with singing" (Zeph. 3:16-17).

18

THE KINGDOM OF GOD

A PLETHORA OF SCRIPTURES describe the kingdom of Jesus Christ. One foundational theme is that His dominion is everlasting, and His kingdom will never come to an end (Dan. 4:3; 6:26; Luke 1:33; 2 Pet. 1:11). Consistent with the biblical testimony, the Nicene-Constantinopolitan Creed of the holy Church reads that Christ's kingdom "shall have no end."

Jesus taught that His kingdom is heavenly and "not of this world" (John 18:36; 2 Tim. 4:18). Such statements must be understood as describing the origin or source of the kingdom because the domain of Christ's reign will include heaven and earth, as conveyed by His statement "on earth as it is in heaven" (Matt. 6:10; Luke 11:2). To demonstrate, the Scriptures express that those who have humbly submitted to Christ's reign will inherit the Earth when He consummates His kingdom (Matt. 5:5; 1 Cor. 6:9-10; 2 Tim. 4:18; cf. Eccles. 1:4). This is why the apostle Paul taught that God will give His saints "all things" (Rom. 8:32), including the world (1 Cor. 3:21-22).

After He returns in glory, Jesus will be King over the entire Earth (Zech. 14:9). King Solomon summarized, "He shall have dominion also from sea to sea, and from the River to the ends of the earth" (Ps. 72:8). At that time, everyone on the planet, from the west to "the rising of the sun," will fear the Lord's holy name (Isa. 59:19). The Father has decreed that His only begotten Son will acquire the nations, even "the ends of the earth," as His eternal inheritance (Ps. 1:6-8; cf. Ps. 67:7). Consequently, "the earth shall be full of the knowledge of the Lord as the waters cover the sea" (Isa. 11:9; cf. Hab. 2:14).

In addition, Isaiah prophesied the Davidic Messiah's birth and His eternal reign over the kingdom:

> For unto us a Child is born, unto us a Son is given; and the government will be upon His shoulder. And His name will be called Wonderful, Counselor, Mighty God, Everlasting Father, Prince of Peace. Of the increase of His government and peace there will be no end, upon the throne of David and over His kingdom, to order it and establish it with judgment and justice from that time forward, even forever. The zeal of the Lord of hosts will perform this. (Isa. 9:6-7)

The government of God's eternal kingdom will be "upon His [Christ's] shoulder,"[1] and He will continue to sit on David's throne forever (Isa. 9:6-7; "no end . . . from that time forward, even forever" Isa. 9:7; cf. Luke 1:32). Jesus Christ is "very God of very God" ("Mighty God" Isa. 9:6; cf. Isa. 10:21), the pristine revelation of the Father ("Everlasting Father" Isa. 9:6; cf. John 1:18; 14:9), the leading attorney ("Wonderful Counselor" Isa. 9:6; cf. Judg. 13:18; Isa. 11:2; 28:29), and God's Son who will bring everlasting peace ("Prince of Peace . . . peace there will be no end" Isa. 9:6).

We should not imagine that the God-Man will begin to reign from David's throne only at His future return (cf. Matt. 19:28; 25:31-32). Rather, His heavenly reign over His kingdom began when He ascended

---

[1] Likely a double entendre which conveys the idea that Christ carried the cross upon His shoulders (cf. Gen. 22:6).

to sit at the Father's right hand (Acts 2:29-36; cf. Matt. 28:18), and He will continue to reign until the time that His enemies become His footstool (Ps. 110:1-2; 1 Cor. 15:24-26; Heb. 10:12-13). In the meantime, He mysteriously reigns "in the midst" of His enemies (Ps. 110:2) in an "already and not yet" manner (see chapter 20).

Using this theological parlance, the apostle Paul distinguished between the Lord's present inter-advent reign and the future consummation of His reign. For example, the apostle Paul wrote this way about the Second Coming ("His coming" 1 Cor. 15:23): "Then comes the end, when He delivers the kingdom to God the Father, when He puts an end to all rule and all authority and power. For He must reign till He has put all enemies under His feet. The last enemy that will be destroyed is death" (1 Cor. 15:24-26; cf. Ps. 8:6). In other words, God will put all His enemies ("all rule and all authority and power" 1 Cor. 15:24) under Christ's feet, an image of military subjugation. This will include the destruction of death itself ("the last enemy" 1 Cor. 15:26) through the resurrection of the dead "at the end" of the age (1 Cor. 15:22-24). At this time, Jesus will complete His work of redemption, delivering up the kingdom to His Father (1 Cor. 15:24), and as a result, God will become "all in all" (1 Cor. 15:28). In other words, the Holy Trinity will fill all things and all His people with His divine grace.

Concerning Christ's return and kingdom reign, the psalmist declared, "He is coming to judge the earth. He shall judge the world with righteousness, and the peoples with His truth" (Ps. 96:13; cf. Ps. 98:9). Jesus, upon whom the Holy Spirit eternally rests and indwells, will judge the world:

The Spirit of the Lord shall rest upon Him, the Spirit of wisdom and understanding, the Spirit of counsel and might, the Spirit of knowledge and of the fear of the Lord. His delight is in the fear of the Lord, and He shall not judge by the sight of His eyes, nor decide by the hearing of His ears; but with righteousness He shall judge the poor, and decide with equity for the meek of the earth. (Isa. 11:2-4)

Christ will not judge the world by mere appearances or based on hearsay testimony ("not judge by the sight of His eyes, nor decide by the hearing of His ears" Isa. 11:3) but with perfect righteousness forever. The resurrected King's reign will prosper, and He will "execute judgment and righteousness in the earth" (Jer. 23:5; cf. Jer. 33:14-16).[2] The righteous will flourish, and Christ will rescue the poor who cry out to Him, granting them equity and justice for the violence and oppression they had endured (Ps. 72:1-2, 4-5, 7, 12-15; Isa. 11:4). People will praise the Lord and pray to Him continually (Ps. 72:15), and He will immediately hear and answer these prayers, even before the people utter them (Isa. 65:24). King Solomon lauded the glory of His name and kingdom:

> His name shall endure forever; His name shall continue as long as the sun. And men shall be blessed in Him; all nations shall call Him blessed. Blessed be the Lord God, the God of Israel, who only does wondrous things! And blessed be His glorious name forever! And let the whole earth be filled with His glory. Amen and Amen. (Ps. 72:17-19)

Jesus Christ will become a glorious crown and beautiful diadem for the surviving remnant of the nation of Israel (Isa. 28:5), eternally reigning over the house of Jacob (Luke 1:32). As we saw in previous chapters, He will save Jerusalem and Judah so that the people live in security (Jer. 23:6; 33:16; cf. Zech. 9:16). Then the nation will prostrate itself before the Lord and obey Him (Gen. 49:8, 10; "in the latter days" v. 1). Consequently, the Lord will show mercy unto salvation to the remnant of Israel ("You are My people . . . You are my God" Hosea 2:23), who prior to that time, because of their largely unregenerate condition, will not be considered God's people ("not My people" Hosea 2:23), at least not in the strictest sense of the term.

---

2   Jeremiah prophesied that the Messiah's name will be "THE LORD OUR RIGHTEOUSNESS" (Jer. 23:6; 33:16).

At this point, I will digress to discuss an important interpretive issue. The holy apostles revealed a new covenant mystery, specifically, that Gentiles who follow Jesus Christ are now "grafted into" Israel (Rom. 9:24-26). The apostolic Church, consisting of believing Jews and Gentiles, is the "one new man" (Eph. 2:15) and the "manifold wisdom of God" (Eph. 3:10). Through His prophets, God foretold this mystery in the Old Testament, but intentionally concealed and preserved it. Nevertheless, the New Testament clearly reveals that believing Gentiles receive the true circumcision made without hands (Phil. 3:3; Col. 2:11; cf. Deut. 10:16; Gal. 6:15), partake of the commonwealth of Israel (Eph. 2:12), and become heirs of the promises given to the patriarchs (Gal. 3:14, 29; cf. Rom. 8:17). In short, none of the promises given to Israel's descendants will be withheld from believing Gentiles because they too are "the Israel of God" (Gal. 6:16)—the Church.

This raises afresh the question of Israel's identity as a nation and a people. More than the Old Testament expectation that the nations will worship Israel's God in the kingdom, this means that through Jesus Christ, the nations have received the very promises belonging to Israel and that they will receive the full benefits of being His nation! While the believing Gentiles remain ethnically separate from believing Jews, they are indistinguishable in their new corporate identity in Christ (Gal. 3:28).

Based on these critical observations, the biblical interpreter is justified in reading the believing Gentiles back into Israel's promises. Many scholars object to this manner of interpreting the Prophets, accusing those who do of eisegesis[3] and revisionism. However, the New Testament requires us to deduce that the apostolic Church, not just the surviving remnant of Jews, will inherit the Promised Land and the new Jerusalem. It is the Church which receives Israel's glorious promise of Christ and the resurrection of glory. And if we can receive it, the Church is the true Israel, even the holy nation and kingdom of priests (Exod. 19:5-6 with 1 Pet. 2:5, 9; Rev. 1:6; 5:10). The implication is that New

---

3 Reading foreign ideas and personal biases into a text.

Testament revelation about the Church does not contradict the Old Testament prophecies and promises regarding Israel, but it expands and elucidates them.

As you might have deduced by now, I am careful to consistently interpret the prophetic Scriptures in a literal manner. This method of interpretation keeps one within important guardrails: First, it follows the literal, grammatical, historical interpretation, consistent with apostolic tradition. Second, it gives room for figurative language and other literary devices, such as the symbolism inherit within Ezekiel's visions. Third, it allows for the Christological interpretation of the Prophets, as illumined by later apostolic revelation, such as reading the inclusion of the Gentiles back into Israel's promises.

On the one hand, this hermeneutical method will be unpopular among those who deny any prophetic destiny for the Jews as a nation or collective people because of their supposition that the predominantly Gentile Church has entirely and permanently replaced them. On the other hand, this method will also be rejected by those who embrace an overly literal interpretive system which generates false dichotomies, such as a harsh distinction between Israel and the holy Church. Contrary to both systems, we should understand that the Jewish nation and the holy Church are distinct but ultimately inseparable, largely because the entire surviving nation will share the same prophetic destiny as the holy Church. God is daily adding people to His Church, Jews and Gentiles alike, and the surviving Jewish remnant will receive Christ and join the Church during the unprecedented tribulation and on the day of Jesus Christ.

As a result of the miraculous deliverance of Israel, the nation will be known throughout the earth, and all peoples will joyfully praise God (Ps. 67:1-5, 7). The surviving remnant will be famous among the nations, and everyone who sees them will recognize them as "the posterity whom the Lord has blessed" (Isa. 61:9). They will be among the Lord's priests and servants (Isa. 61:6; cf. Exod. 19:5-6). Furthermore, the small number of the Antichrist's soldiers who survive ("those among them who escape" Isa. 66:19) will return to their homelands to declare the good tidings of Christ's return ("they shall declare My glory among the Gentiles" Isa. 66:19). Then all those who had previously despised and afflicted Israel will prostrate themselves at the soles of their feet (Isa. 60:14; Rev. 3:9; cf. Ps. 72:9).

When they see the brightness of Christ's presence, the peoples of all nations and languages will begin making pilgrimage to the new Jerusalem (Isa. 60:3 with 66:18; cf. Isa. 11:10; 66:23; Matt. 25:32). In addition, Jesus will bring salvation to all the peoples of the world and will illuminate them with His law of justice, righteousness, and salvation (Isa. 42:6 with 49:6; 50:4-5). The saved nations will walk in His light (Rev. 21:23-24), and His fame will extend to "the ends of the earth" (Mic. 5:4; cf. Ps. 67:7). At that time, Israel will summon other nations, which will not yet know Him, and they will "run" to her and to her God (Isa. 55:5; 56:8).

Gentile kings and their entourages will bring great wealth, including gold and silver, to Jerusalem (Isa. 60:5, 9, 11, 17; Rev. 21:24; cf. Isa. 18:7). King Solomon prophesied, "Yes, all kings shall fall down before Him; all nations shall serve Him" (Ps. 72:11). As a metaphor for these abundant gifts, Isaiah portrayed Israel as drinking milk from the breast of Gentile kings (Isa. 60:16; 66:11; cf. Isa. 61:6). He also prophesied, "Behold, I will extend peace to her [Jerusalem] like a river, and the glory of the Gentiles like a flowing stream. Then you shall feed; on her sides shall you be carried and be dandled on her knees" (Isa. 66:10-13). The Arabs will praise the Lord and bring Him gifts of camels, dromedaries, gold, and incense (Isa. 60:6; cf. Ps. 72:9-11, 15; Matt. 2:11). Also, Christ will glorify "the house of His glory" with flocks of sheep and rams which the Gentiles bring to His altar (Isa. 60:7), and He will beautify the "place for His feet," His sanctuary, with cypress, pine, and box trees brought from Lebanon (Isa. 60:13; cf. Isa. 11:10; 66:1).

Five cities in the land of Egypt will trust Christ, speak "the language of Canaan" (Hebrew?), and worship and perform vows to Him at His altar in Egypt (Isa. 19:18-19, 21). Although God will have used the instrumentality of the Antichrist to strike Egypt, their land will be healed after they return to Him in repentance (Isa. 19:22), presumably at the day of Jesus Christ. A memorial pillar will be erected at Egypt's border, serving as a sign and witness that the nation cried to the Lord during the invasion by the Antichrist's forces ("the oppressors" Isa. 19:20) and that He delivered them by sending "a Savior and a Mighty One"—the Lord Jesus Christ (Isa. 19:19-20; cf. Isa. 60:16). One Egyptian city will be called the City of Destruction (Isa. 19:18), presumably because the Antichrist destroyed or threatened to destroy most of the city.

The surviving Gentiles will join the surviving remnant of Israel in their pilgrimage to Jerusalem, and they will travel along a massive highway system created by the unprecedented earthquake on the day of the Lord:

> In that day there will be a highway from Egypt to Assyria, and the Assyrian will come into Egypt and the Egyptian into Assyria, and the Egyptians will serve with the Assyrians. In that day Israel will be one of three with Egypt and Assyria—a blessing in the midst of the land, whom the Lord of hosts shall bless, saying, "Blessed is Egypt My people, and Assyria the work of My hands, and Israel My inheritance." (Isa. 19:23-25)

Jesus Christ will bring unprecedented peace to all the peoples of the world (Ps. 72:7-8). The nations where Israel was formerly in captivity, such as Egypt and Assyria, will unify to worship the Lord together (Isa. 19:23-25). The apostle John heard the redeemed singing, "All nations shall come and worship before You, for Your judgments have been manifested" (Rev. 15:4; cf. Ps. 86:9; Isa. 66:23).

Christ's kingdom will be characterized by comfort and joy. For example, Isaiah personified the created things as jubilantly singing when the remnant of Israel returns to their land: "Sing, O heavens! Be joyful, O earth! And break out in singing, O mountains! For the Lord has comforted His people and will have mercy on His afflicted" (Isa. 49:13). Later, the prophet declared, "For you [the remnant] shall go out with joy and be led out with peace; the mountains and the hills shall break forth into singing before you, and all the trees of the field shall clap their hands" (Isa. 55:12). Furthermore, Israel's "warfare" will cease and her iniquities will be "pardoned," and the Lord will comfort the nation and give the people everlasting joy; they will receive double honor, the inheritance of a firstborn (Isa. 40:2; cf. Isa. 61:7; 66:13).

The Lord will increase the nation's joy, and the people will rejoice like those at harvest (Isa. 9:3). They will joyfully celebrate and give thanks to Him (Jer. 30:19). They will no longer experience sorrow, and they will arrive with joyful singing at the mountain height of Zion (Jer. 31:12). God will "console those who mourn in Zion, to give them beauty for ashes, the oil of joy for mourning, the garment of praise for the spirit of heaviness; that they may be called trees of righteousness, the planting of the Lord, that He may be glorified" (Isa. 61:1-3). Similarly, Jeremiah prophesied, "Then shall the virgin rejoice in the dance, and the young men and the old, together; for I will turn their mourning to joy, will comfort them, and make them rejoice rather than sorrow. . . and My people shall be satisfied with My goodness" (Jer. 31:13-14). In addition, those who had loved and mourned for Jerusalem will rejoice with her (Isa. 66:10).

The Lord also promised to give rest and peace to His people, and He Himself will be peace (Mic. 5:5). The prophet Micah depicted the conditions of peace during the reign of Jesus Christ:

He shall judge between many peoples and rebuke strong nations afar off; they shall beat their swords into plowshares and their spears into pruning hooks; nation shall not lift up sword against nation, neither shall they learn war anymore. But everyone shall sit under his vine and under his fig tree, and no one shall make them afraid; for the mouth of the Lord of hosts has spoken. (Mic. 4:3-4; cf. Isa. 2:4)

The result of God's righteous reign over the Earth will be that people live in eternal peace, security, quietness, and rest (Isa. 32:16-18; cf. Jer.

23:6). The Lord promised, "Bow and sword of battle I will shatter from the earth, to make them lie down safely" (Hosea 2:18; cf. Ezek. 34:28), and as a result, His people will never again experience fear, terror, or bondage but will experience unprecedented rest and peace (Isa. 14:3; "great shall be the peace of your children" Isa. 54:13-14). As Ezekiel recorded, "They shall dwell safely, and no one shall make them afraid" (Ezek. 34:28; cf. Mal. 3:12). Instead of sorrow, they will live in joy and peace (Isa. 14:3; 65:24-25; 66:12).

God will make a covenant of peace with nature so that people can sleep safely in the forest with beasts, birds, and creeping things (Ezek. 35:23-25, 28; Hosea 2:18; cf. Ezek. 34:28). Like the conditions that existed before the fall, the wild beasts and livestock will live harmoniously with each other and with people, so that even small infants will safely play around them:

> The wolf also shall dwell with the lamb, the leopard shall lie down with the young goat, the calf and the young lion and the fatling together; and a little child shall lead them. The cow and the bear shall graze; their young ones shall lie down together; and the lion shall eat straw like the ox. The nursing child shall play by the cobra's hole, and the weaned child shall put his hand in the viper's den. They shall not hurt nor destroy in all My holy mountain. (Isa. 11:6-9; cf. Isa. 65:25)

The returning Lord will also bring abundant rainfall, "the former rain and the latter rain in the first month," to Jerusalem (Joel 2:23; cf. Ps. 72:6; Ezek. 34:26; Hosea 6:3; Zech. 10:1). As a result, the brooks of Judah will flood (Joel 3:18), while rivers and streams will flow on every high mountain and hill (Isa. 30:25; cf. Isa. 41:18). The deserts will produce springs, streams, and pools, sustaining new grasses, reeds, and rushes (Isa. 35:6-7; 41:18; cf. Zech. 10:1), so they abundantly "blossom as the rose" and praise the Lord "with joy and singing" so to speak (Isa. 35:1-2; cf. 1 Chron. 16:31-32).

At this time, the Holy Spirit will be poured out from heaven so that Israel's "wilderness becomes a fruitful field, and the fruitful field is counted as a forest" (Isa. 32:15). Instead of the curse of thorns and briers (cf. Gen. 3:18), the Earth will produce cypress and myrtle trees forever (Isa. 55:13). Cedar, acacia, myrtle, cypress, olive, pine, and box trees will also flourish (Isa. 41:19; 60:13).

Plants will produce buds and blossoms throughout Israel, and the world will be filled with its fruit (Isa. 27:6).[4] No one will experience hunger because of the nourishment from the Lord's "garden of renown," a reference to the garden of Eden (Ezek. 34:29). After the battle in the Valley of Jezreel, the land will produce abundant grain in open pastures, lush vineyards, fruit-bearing trees, and olive oil (Hosea 2:15, 21-22; Joel 2:18-19, 22; cf. Ps. 67:6; 72:16; Isa. 30:23; Jer. 31:12; Ezek. 34:27; 36:29-30; Zech. 8:12; 9:17). The abundant rain will lead to threshing floors being filled with wheat and vats overflowing with wine and oil (Joel 2:24; cf. Ezek. 34:27). The prophet Joel asked, "Who knows if He will turn and relent and leave a blessing behind Him—a grain offering and a drink offering for the Lord your God?" (Joel 2:14). He also prophesied, "And it will come to pass in that day that the mountains shall drip with new wine, the hills shall flow with milk" (Joel 3:18). The prophet Amos also depicted the abundant bounty of the harvests:

> Behold, the days are coming . . . when the plowman shall overtake the reaper and the treader of grapes him who sows seed; the mountains shall drip with sweet wine and all the hills shall flow with it. . . They shall plant vineyards and drink wine from them; they shall also make gardens and eat fruit from them. (Amos 9:13, 14)

The land of Israel will also be filled with flocks and herds (Isa. 65:10; Jer. 31:12). Jeremiah explained, "And there shall dwell in Judah itself, and in all its cities together, farmers and those going out with flocks. For I have satiated the weary soul, and I have replenished every

---

4   This could be a double entendre referring also to the fruit of the Spirit.

sorrowful soul" (Jer. 31:24-25; cf. v. 27). The oxen will feed in large pastures (Isa. 30:23-24), and Gentiles will participate in feeding animals, plowing fields, and dressing vineyards (Isa. 61:5-7). The Lord's people, like stall-fed calves, will eat plentifully (Mal. 4:2) while praising His name (Joel 2:26).

Meanwhile, the forsaken land of Israel will become "an eternal excellence, a joy of many generations" (Isa. 60:15). Her people will rebuild and repair the ruined, desolate cities "of many generations" (Isa. 61:4; cf. Jer. 31:28; Ezek. 38:8), and Gentiles will help with the construction (Isa. 60:10). In the new Jerusalem, people will toil with their hands to construct houses, engage in agricultural endeavors, and eat: "Behold, I create new heavens and a new earth. . . They shall build houses and inhabit them; they shall plant vineyards and eat their fruit. They shall not build and another inhabit; they shall not plant and another eat . . . and My elect shall long enjoy the work of their hands. They shall not labor in vain" (Isa. 65:17, 21–23; cf. Jer. 31:28).

A proper interpretation of the prophecies pertaining to the arrival of the new Jerusalem reconciles the passages depicting the descent of the heavenly Jerusalem with those predicting that the redeemed people of Israel will rebuild the desolated places within the post-Armageddon land. This reconciliation recognizes that some passages highlight the absolute necessity of divine provision, while others focus on the subsequent human endeavors and the permanence of divine blessings. These different emphases do not exclude each other nor do the prophecies contain incompatible details. For example, God will cause the glorified Jerusalem, the tabernacle "not made with hands" (Heb. 9:11), to descend to the Earth, and subsequently, the city's inhabitants will voluntarily restore and rebuild their fallen waste places.

Isaiah provided additional details about the marriage supper of the Lamb, which will take place in Jerusalem: "And in this mountain the Lord of hosts will make for all people a feast of choice pieces, a feast of wines on the lees, of fat things full of marrow, of well-refined wines on the lees" (Isa. 25:6). As such, when Christ's kingdom arrives, He

Himself will partake of the Passover meal with His people (Matt. 26:29; Mark 14:25; Luke 22:16, 18). Christians frequently memorialize His death in the Eucharist (1 Cor. 11:26), and many of them celebrate the annual Pascha, the new covenant Passover. These kingdom blessings do not consist of merely consuming food and drink but of receiving grace resulting in "righteousness and peace and joy in the Holy Spirit" (Rom. 14:17). In the verse immediately following his description of the wedding supper, Isaiah connected the supper with the time of the resurrection of the dead:

> And He will destroy on this mountain the surface of the covering cast over all people and the veil that is spread over all nations. He will swallow up death forever, and the Lord God will wipe away tears from all faces; the rebuke of His people He will take away from all the earth; for the Lord has spoken. (Isa. 25:7-8)

When Christ returns to Jerusalem ("on this mountain" Isa. 25:7), He will resurrect the dead, destroying death itself ("He will swallow up death forever" Isa. 25:8 in 1 Cor. 15:54; see chapter 13). Simultaneously, He will destroy the "veil" that separates humanity ("all people . . . all nations" Isa. 25:7) from His glorious presence (Heb. 6:19; 9:3; Rev. 11:19; cf. Matt. 27:51; "the veil" of unbelief in 2 Cor. 3:14-16; 4:3) that everyone who sees Him may believe. As a bridal veil is removed, our heavenly Groom will remove this veil, revealing both Himself and His glorified bride to the world.

Like the resurrected body of Jesus (Luke 24:36-43), the resurrected bodies of the saints will retain their corporeality, enabling us to participate in human activities, such as eating, in the consummated kingdom. However, we will no longer engage in many activities, such as marriage and sex, because our immortality will make us ontologically equal to angels (Matt. 22:29-30; Mark 12:24-25; Luke 20:34-36). In other words, our resurrected bodies will retain their material properties but will receive transcendent properties fit for eternal life on Earth. This reinforces the concept that the created universe will be redeemed, not discarded.

In the new Jerusalem, no one will experience premature death: "The voice of weeping shall no longer be heard in her [Jerusalem], nor the voice of crying. No more shall an infant from there live but a few days, nor an old man who has not fulfilled his days; for the child shall die one hundred years old, but the sinner being one hundred years old shall be accursed" (Isa. 65:19-20). To restate, if anyone were to die at the age of one hundred, others would consider him to have died as a mere child and as the consequence of sin ("the sinner . . . accursed"), whereas the righteous will have extremely long lifespans ("as the days of a tree" Isa. 65:22). Taken together, these descriptions hint that the righteous will receive everlasting life and will avoid the accursed fate of the wicked (cf. Isa. 25:8; Dan. 12:2). This interpretation is buttressed by the apostle John's allusion to this prophecy, which he used refer to the eternal, resurrection life in the new Jerusalem ("there shall be no more death, nor sorrow, nor crying" Rev. 21:4 from Isa. 65:19; cf. Isa. 25:8).

The postexilic prophet Zechariah also vividly depicted the future conditions of Jerusalem: "Old men and old women shall again sit in the streets of Jerusalem, each one with his staff in his hand because of great age. The streets of the city shall be full of boys and girls playing in its streets" (Zech. 8:4). We should not assume that old men and women sitting with staffs indicates that the human aging process will continue into the new Jerusalem. Rather, the old people in this verse points to the new realities of eternal life ("old . . . great age"), experiential wisdom, restfulness, and peace. The image of boys and girls playing in the streets evokes the idea of youthfulness and carefree fun which all God's children will enjoy. The Lord will be satisfied when Israel's remnant ("the remnant of this people" Zech. 8:6) experiences these conditions.

The righteous will no longer sin (cf. Jer. 31:31-34), yet the wicked will experience death in hell as a result of their willful iniquities (cf. "shall die for his own iniquity" Jer. 31:30). In addition, humanity will no longer inherit ancestral sin from their fathers: "In those days they shall say no more: 'The fathers have eaten sour grapes, and the children's teeth are set on edge.' But every one shall die for his own iniquity" (Jer. 31:29-30; cf. Ezek. 18:2).

At His return, Christ will eliminate physical and emotional infirmities. As during His earthly ministry, He will perform miracles, such as healing the blind and deaf and enabling the non-verbal to sing and paraplegic to "leap like a deer" (Isa. 35:5-6; cf. Isa. 42:7, 16; Acts 3:8; Rev. 22:2). He will also heal the brokenhearted (Isa. 61:1). Likewise, the prophet Malachi taught that "the Sun of Righteousness shall arise with healing in His wings" (Mal. 4:2); the rising Sun is a metaphor for Christ. Without coincidence, Jesus' garment ("His wings") also provided healing during His earthly ministry (Matt. 9:20-22; 14:35-36; Mark 6:56).[5]

Idolatry will be abolished when the kingdom arrives (Isa. 1:28-29; 27:9; 30:22; Hosea 2:16-17; Zech. 13:2), and prophecy will no longer be needed. Zechariah predicted the consequences for prophesying after the day of the Lord:

> It shall be in that day . . . that I will cut off the names of the idols from the land, and they shall no longer be remembered. I will also cause the prophets and the unclean spirit to depart from the land. It shall come to pass that if anyone still prophesies, then his father and mother who begot him will say to him, "You shall not live, because you have spoken lies in the name of the Lord." And his father and mother who begot him shall thrust him through when he prophesies. And it shall be in that day that every prophet will be ashamed of his vision when he prophesies; they will not wear a robe of coarse hair to deceive. (Zech. 13:2-4)

It is unclear whether this prohibition will apply only to false prophets (and therefore not to true prophets) or whether it will extend to anyone who prophesies. The latter would imply that prophecy itself

---

5   The term "wings" likely alludes to the tassels of a tallit, a Jewish prayer garment.

will become obsolete, as the apostle Paul indicated, "For we know in part and we prophesy in part. But when that which is perfect has come, then that which is in part will be done away" (1 Cor. 13:9-10). At any rate, the idea of a deceptive prophet speaking lies will be so offensive and intolerable to the people that his own parents will slay him ("thrust him through" Zech. 13:3), reminiscent of the high priest Phineas who thrust a javelin through a couple engaged in idolatrous coitus (Num. 25:6-8). The conditional statement "if anyone still prophesies" (Zech. 13:3) reveals the hyperbolic nature of the statement, implying that such prophets will not be found in Christ's kingdom.

19

MILLENNIAL CONSIDERATIONS

AFTER HIS KINGDOM HAS BEEN CONSUMMATED, Jesus Christ will reign over all the nations "with a rod of iron" (Rev. 12:5; 19:15; cf. Ps. 2:9; Rev. 2:27). In other words, He will impose and enforce His inviolable reign over the righteous and the wicked. He will establish righteous judges for His administration: "I will restore your judges as at the first and your counselors as at the beginning" (Isa. 1:26; cf. Jer. 30:21). The twelve apostles will reign, and in one sense are already reigning, in heaven as the judges of Israel (see chapter 20). Christ promised, "But you are those who have continued with Me in My trials. And I bestow upon you a kingdom, just as My Father bestowed one upon Me, that you may eat and drink at My table in My kingdom, and sit on thrones judging the twelve tribes of Israel" (Luke 22:28-30; cf. Matt. 19:28). In addition, His holy bishops will "shepherd" the saints with apostolic authority, according to His own heart, and will feed them with "knowledge and understanding" so that they no longer fear or lack anything (Jer. 3:15; 23:4; cf. Ps. 23).

In addition, Christ's kingdom authority will be distributed to all faithful Christians. The resurrected Lord promised that those who overcome "the world" will sit with Him on His throne, as He overcame and sat down with His Father on His throne (Rev. 3:21; cf. 2 Tim. 2:12). As Christ overcame the world through His death on the cross (John 16:33), Christians will receive authority to reign with Him because of their faithfulness unto death: "And he who overcomes, and keeps My works until the end, to him I will give power over the nations—'He shall rule them with a rod of iron; they shall be dashed to pieces like the potter's vessels'—as I also have received from My Father" (Rev. 2:26-27; cf. Rev. 3:21). The apostle Paul taught that the saints will judge the world and even angels (1 Cor. 6:2-3; cf. Heb. 2:5-6).

Furthermore, by His blood Christ has redeemed people from "every tribe and tongue and people and nation" and has made us "kings and priests" (Rev. 1:5-6; 5:9-10; cf. Exod. 19:5-6; Isa. 61:6; 1 Pet. 2:5, 9-10). By virtue of this royal priesthood, Christians will reign upon the earth (Rev. 5:10). The Apocalypse continues this theme:

> And I saw thrones, and they sat on them, and judgment was committed to them. Then I saw the souls of those who had been beheaded for their witness to Jesus and for the word of God, who had not worshiped the beast or his image, and had not received his mark on their foreheads or on their hands. And they lived and reigned with Christ for a thousand years. But the rest of the dead did not live again until the thousand years were finished. This is the first resurrection. Blessed and holy is he who has part in the first resurrection. Over such the second death has no power, but they shall be priests of God and of Christ, and shall reign with Him a thousand years. (Rev. 20:4-6)

The apostle John saw "the souls" of Christians who were beheaded for their testimony about Christ, including those who will refuse to worship the Antichrist or his image and do not take his mark (Rev.

20:4; cf. Rev. 13:7-8, 14-17; 15:1-4).[1] These martyrs would sit on thrones and receive judicial authority ("judgment was committed to them" Rev. 20:4; cf. Dan. 7:9) and would live and reign as kings and priests with Christ for "a thousand years" (Rev. 20:4, 6). The phrase "the first resurrection" points to them being resurrected before or during the "thousand years" (Rev. 20:4-6). In addition, these Christian martyrs will never experience "the second death," that is, eternal hellfire (Rev. 2:11; 20:6, 14; 21:8).

One early eschatological interpretation of this passage is known as chiliasm (i.e., premillennialism). This position is predominantly based upon a literal interpretation of the phrase "thousand years." According to this view, Jesus Christ will return to establish His kingdom on Earth for exactly one thousand years before the general resurrection and final judgment. Premillennialists interpret Revelation 20:4-6 as referring exclusively to the future reign of the martyrs, and contend that "the first resurrection" refers to the bodily resurrection of the righteous at the return of Jesus Christ (cf. 1 Cor. 15:22-23, 50-58; 1 Thess. 4:13-17). The wicked will not participate in this first resurrection (Rev. 20:5-6; cf. Isa. 26:14, 19, 21).

Several ante-Nicene Fathers taught chiliasm. One early proponent of this view was Bishop Papias of Hierapolis, a disciple of the apostle John. Others who likely held this view included Theophilus of Antioch, Saint Irenaeus of Lyons, Tertullian, Saint Hippolytus of Rome, Saint Methodius of Olympus, and Lactantius. In addition, Justin Martyr taught that "right-minded Christians" were convinced of the veracity of this interpretation, but he admitted that "many who belong to the pure and pious faith, and are true Christians, think otherwise."[2]

Premillennialism offers a plausible explanation for how God will glorify the Jewish remnant and the Gentiles who come to faith during

---

1   The apostle previously saw the righteous departed, who were *victorious* over the Beast and his image, mark, and name, *in heaven* (Rev. 15:1-4).

2   Schaff, Philip. The Complete Ante-Nicene Fathers Collection: with linked footnotes (p. 814). Kindle Edition.

and after seeing the returning Jesus. Advocates argue that the wicked will be resurrected at the final resurrection, which they teach will occur one thousand years after Christ's return (cf. "But the rest of the dead did not live again until the thousand years were finished" Rev. 20:5). However, it is plausible that those who come to faith after Christ's return will be immediately glorified when they arrive to the new Jerusalem. Premillennialists may object that such an assertion epitomizes an argument from silence, but they share this difficulty since they are unable to produce biblical verses demonstrating many of their assertions about the millennium. For example, consider the following questions which flow out of an assessment of premillennialism:

- After Christ's return, how will sin, deception, war, sorrow, corruption, and death, which result from the fall, continue to exist in the world (cf. Rom. 8:19-22)? Since Christ will defeat and "swallow up death in victory" at that time (Isa. 25:7-9; 1 Cor. 15:54; Rev. 21:1-4), how will anyone, especially Christians, continue to die? What immediate state will mortals and their offspring, whether righteous or wicked, experience at death? Where will their spirits and bodies go?

- Since it is impossible for a mortal ("flesh and blood") to inherit Christ's kingdom (1 Cor. 15:50-57), how will the righteous Jews inhabit an earthly new Jerusalem that is separate from the heavenly new Jerusalem which Christ has prepared for His resurrected saints, those who will be with Him forever, after His heavenly descent to earth?

- The reason for Christ's patience and long-suffering before He returns is to provide time for people to repent (2 Pet. 3:9, 15), so how does this agree with the premillennial concept that people will continue to accept or reject the gospel during the subsequent thousand years?

- How would a fully regenerate Jewish nation lead the nations, partially comprised of unregenerate Gentiles, without negating the unity and impartiality of the "one new man"—the holy Church? Would this restored Jewish kingdom be a partially glorified, partially consummated kingdom?

- If the righteous Jews will reestablish animal sacrifices in the millennium, how will they avoid "crucifying the Son of God afresh" by returning to the inferior covenant of Moses (Heb. 6:6)?

Many other early Christians embraced the interpretative model known as amillennialism.[3] This position teaches that the phrase "thousand years" in Revelation 20:1-10 is a symbol for the present reign of Christians, most especially, the Church triumphant reigning in heaven. As such, it represents the apostolic period from Christ's ascension until His glorious return. Adherents of this position point out that the qualifier "thousand," when used elsewhere in Scripture, usually confers the sense of totality upon the noun it modifies (Job 9:3). For example, God stated that He owns "the cattle on a thousand hills" (Ps. 50:10), which is a poetic manner of saying that He lays claim to everything. Similarly, the phrase "thousand years" is used elsewhere to refer to a long period of time, at least as people count time (Ps. 90:4; 2 Pet. 3:8).

During the first two centuries of Christianity, amillennialism emerged to predominate the theological landscape and became the established eschatology of the holy Church. The Catholicity of this interpretation was recognized during the period of the ecumenical councils. Early proponents of this view included Clement of Alexandria, Origen, and Saint Cyprian. With great theological acumen, Saint Augustine of Hippo further articulated this position. Amillennialism has remained the accepted eschatological position of the Orthodox Church, the Roman Catholic Church, and nearly all the Protestant Reformers and other early Protestants.

---

3   meaning "no millennium"

The strongest premillennial argument against amillennialism is that it contains a glaring chronological anachronism. They point out that the apostle John taught that "the first resurrection" occurs no later than the "thousand years" (Rev. 20:4-5), and it includes the resurrection of the martyrs who will refuse to take the Antichrist's mark during the future unprecedented tribulation (Rev. 20:4; cf. Rev. 13:5-18). Amillennialism equates the unprecedented tribulation with the "little while" after the thousand years (Rev. 20:3, 7-9). Premillennialists argue that logic would require amillennialism to place the resurrection of the tribulation martyrs *before* their own deaths! However, amillennialists reject this argument as a non-sequitur because they reject the premise that "the first resurrection" refers to the bodily resurrection of the martyrs.

Based on two primary considerations, amillennialism posits that the first resurrection refers to Christians' participation in Jesus Christ's own resurrection: First, the apostle Paul taught that Christ was "the first to rise from the dead" (Acts 26:23), so He became "the firstborn from the dead" (Col. 1:18; Rev. 1:5) and "the firstfruits of those who have fallen asleep" (1 Cor. 15:20; cf. 1 Cor. 15:23). Second, Christians share in Christ's resurrection through baptism ("raised with Christ" Rom. 6:4; Col. 2:12; 3:1),[4] a sacrament which precedes physical death. To further illustrate, John recorded that the spiritually "dead" who hear Christ's voice and trust in Him in the present age have already "passed from death into life" (John 5:24-26). Furthermore, when others spoke about the resurrection on the last day, Jesus responded, "I am the resurrection and the life. He who believes in Me, though he may die, he shall live" (John 11:24-25). As a result, those who participate in His death and resurrection will not experience "the second death" in hell (cf. Rev. 2:11; 20:6).

The book of Revelation conveys that Christ has already made Christians into "kings and priests," particularly, by washing away our

---

4   After regeneration, we continue to participate in Christ's death ("died with Christ") through the daily mortification of "the flesh" (Rom. 6:3-14; Col. 2:20; 3:3; cf. Matt. 10:38-39; Luke 14:27; Gal. 2:20; 5:24), the greatest expression of which is martyrdom.

sins "in His own blood" (Rev. 1:5-6; cf. 1 Pet. 3:21). Furthermore, the apostle John saw twenty-four presbyters in heaven, and they sat on thrones and wore crowns (Rev. 4:4, 10). These presbyters sang about how Christ redeemed them so that they serve as "kings and priests" before God, and their reign began before they witnessed the resurrected Lamb breaking the seven seals (Rev. 5:8-10, 14; cf. 1 Cor. 3:22; 4:8; Eph. 2:6; Rev. 2:10; 20:4). This vision demonstrates that the kingly reign of these priests coincides with Christ's present reign at the Father's right hand. Furthermore, Christ also promised the faithful martyrs "the crown of life" after death (Rev. 2:10).

Consistent with John's teaching, the apostle Paul taught the Ephesian Christians that God "raised us up together, and made us sit together in the heavenly places in Christ Jesus" (Eph. 2:6), and he told the Corinthians that they already reigned as kings (1 Cor. 4:8; cf. 1 Cor. 3:22). Clearly then, Christians have already been resurrected with Christ and have ascended to sit with Him in heavenly places, and we have already received authority with Him to reign as kings and priests. This heavenly reign will undoubtedly continue after we die because we will enter the presence of the reigning Christ (cf. 2 Cor. 5:8; Phil. 1:23). The present reign of the Church militant, and the heavenly reign of the Church triumphant, whether now or after the glorious return of Jesus, exemplifies the "already and not yet" principle of His kingdom (see chapter 20).

John wrote that the judicial reign of the martyrs for a "thousand years" (Rev. 20:4-6) corresponds with the period of Satan being sealed in the Abyss (ἀβύσσου; translated "the bottomless pit"):

> Then I saw an angel coming down from heaven, having the key to the bottomless pit and a great chain in his hand. He laid hold of the dragon, that serpent of old, who is the Devil and Satan, and bound him for a thousand years; and he cast him into the bottomless pit, and shut him up, and set a seal on him, so that he should deceive the nations no more till the thousand years were finished. But after these things he must be released for a little while . . . Now when the

thousand years have expired, Satan will be released from his prison and will go out to deceive the nations. (Rev. 20:1-3, 7-8)

Premillennialists argue that the apostle's vision of the archangel Michael casting Satan from heaven (Rev. 12:7-12) and his vision of the angel descending in order to bind the devil and to seal him in the Abyss (Rev. 20:1-3) depict two, progressive stages of Satan's demise. They correctly teach that Satan will be cast from heaven forty-two months before Christ's return, and they contend that His return will be the cause for his binding for the thousand years. They also argue that the devil's inability to "deceive the nations" (Rev. 20:3) must be nearly absolute, as evidenced by his being bound with "a great chain" and being "shut up" and "sealed" in the Abyss.

On the other hand, amillennialists argue that the portrait of Satan being sealed in the Abyss symbolizes his present inability to prevent the gospel from reaching the nations (Acts 26:18; cf. Mark 3:27; John 12:31-32). They emphasize that the Gentiles were largely unable to receive the gospel prior to Christ's ascension and subsequent outpouring of the Holy Spirit. After this binding, however, people throughout the Roman Empire accepted the faith of Christ. According to this view, the devil will be released from the Abyss for "a little while" (Rev. 20:3; cf. Rev. 17:10), during the period of unprecedented tribulation when the Antichrist greatly deceives all the nations (Matt. 24:5, 11, 24; 2 Thess. 2:3, 10-12; Rev. 12:9; 13:14; 18:23; 19:20).

Jesus Christ gave His Church the apostolic authority to bind and loose: "And I will give you the keys of the kingdom of heaven, and whatever you bind on earth will be bound in heaven, and whatever you loose on earth will be loosed in heaven" (Matt. 16:19; cf. Matt. 18:18). This includes the grace bestowed by the Holy Spirit to forgive sins. Christ promised, "If you forgive the sins of any, they are forgiven them; if you retain the sins of any, they are retained" (John 20:23; cf. Matt. 18:18). In addition, when Christians unite with Him in baptism, the power of Christ's cross "disarms," makes a "public spectacle" of, and "triumphs over" the demonic "principalities and powers" (Col. 2:11-15).

The Apostle's Creed and the Athanasian Creed relate that Christ "descended into hell" between His death and resurrection. Afterward, He defeated death and despoiled hell so that He could escort the saints with Him into Paradise (1 Pet. 3:18-19; 4:6; cf. Matt. 12:40; Eph. 4:8-9). According to amillennialism, Jesus "bound the strong man" (i.e., Satan) through His death, burial, resurrection, and ascension, and thereafter more earnestly "plundered" his kingdom: "But if I cast out demons by the Spirit of God, surely the kingdom of God has come upon you. Or how can one enter a strong man's house and plunder his goods, unless he first binds the strong man? And then he will plunder his house" (Matt. 12:28-29).

Premillennialists reject this amillennial interpretation based on several considerations. For example, they argue that the Scriptures do not define a thousand years as an indeterminate period of time, such as the New Testament period. They also contend that Satan cannot be bound so that he "no longer deceives the nations" because he continues to prevent most of the world from receiving the Gospel. For example, under the leadership of the Islamic caliphates, Muslim armies forcefully conquered many Christian lands, including North Africa and the Middle East. Furthermore, Satan's evil designs continue to advance unabatedly throughout the world, as evidenced by two World Wars, the Holocaust, Communism, terrorism, genocide, secularism, poverty, abortion, racism, dictatorships, pandemics, widespread apostasy, and so forth.

Some amillennial interpretations display another potential weakness by requiring two falls of Satan. For example, many amillennialists teach that Christ's passion resulted in Satan being "cast out" (John 12:31), presumably from heaven, to be incarcerated in the Abyss (Rev. 20:1-3, 7-8). Some of these interpreters also teach that the devil will attempt to usurp heaven again, after his release from the Abyss, resulting in Michael casting him out so that Satan initiates the great tribulation on Earth (Rev. 12:7-12). In addition, any amillennialist position which places Satan's final ousting from heaven immediately prior to the future tribulation must envision him as "accusing" Christians before God while sealed in the Abyss (compare Rev. 12:7-12 with 20:1-3).

At any rate, amillennialism maintains that the internal evidence of the Apocalypse supports the identification of "a little while [season]" (μικρόν χρόνον Rev. 20:3) as the future period of unprecedented tribulation. The phrase appears in one other place in the book, specifically, at the breaking of the fifth seal, and in response to the martyrs' prayers for vindication. There, the martyrs are instructed to "rest a little while longer, until both the number of their fellow servants and their brethren, who would be killed as they were, was completed" (Rev. 6:10-11; cf. Rev. 12:12). In other words, God will vindicate the martyrs after they have continued to rest for "a little while," that is, after the unprecedented tribulation, during which tribulation their fellow Christians will be martyred (cf. Rev. 13:10)! If this connection was intentional, it indicates that the thousand years before the "little while" is the present reign of the martyrs.

We previously discovered, based on the analogy of Scripture, that the Antichrist's war of Gog and Magog (Ezek. 38-39) will take place concurrently with the forty-two months of unprecedented tribulation. We also saw that the Antichrist will begin this war by invading Jerusalem and that Christ will abruptly end the battle of Armageddon by His glorious return (see chapters 4 and 9). In Revelation 20, the apostle John concluded that this war will take place during the "little while" of great tribulation, immediately after Satan is released from the Abyss:

> Now when the thousand years have expired, Satan will be released from his prison and will go out to deceive the nations which are in the four corners of the earth, Gog and Magog, to gather them together to battle, whose number is as the sand of the sea. They went up on the breadth of the earth and surrounded the camp of the saints and the beloved city. And fire came down from God out of heaven and devoured them. (Rev. 20:7-9)

In the preceding chapter, John portrayed the Antichrist's war as ending when Christ returns to slay him with the sword of His mouth (Rev. 19:11-21), and in this very portrayal, he provided an allusion to Ezekiel's Gog and Magog prophecy, specifically, to the sacrificial banquet at which the beasts and birds will feast upon the corpses of the Antichrist's soldiers (Ezek. 39:1-20 in Rev. 19:17-18). This evidence strongly suggests that the war of Gog and Magog in Revelation 19 is the same war which appears under the same name only verses later (Rev. 20:7-9).

The apostle also employed the same Greek phrase ("to gather them unto the war/battle")[5] to describe the battle of Armageddon (Rev. 16:14; cf. Rev. 19:19) and the postmillennial war of Gog and Magog (Rev. 20:8-9). As with this latter description, John depicted the unprecedented tribulation as the time for the mobilization of the international forces against the beloved city (Rev. 11:2; 16:14; cf. Ezek. 38:9; Luke 21:20-24) and for Satan's persecution of the saints (Rev. 13:7; cf. Dan. 7:25; Rev. 12:17). Finally, the apostle described both the armies of the Antichrist and those of Satan as being devoured by fire from heaven at the time of this final war (Rev. 19:19-20 with 20:9; cf. Ezek. 38:22; 39:6, 9-10; Dan. 7:11). These similarities further buttress the importance of equating the postmillennial events with these previously described events.

On the other hand, premillennialism postulates that the apostle John predicted two wars of Gog and Mogog, one during the tribulation (Rev. 19:11-21) and another one thousand years later (Rev. 20:8-9). Advocates admit that the devil will gather the international armies together to wage a post-tribulation battle, but they argue that John did not depict an actual battle as taking place because God will prevent it by instantaneously incinerating the devil and his armies. Nevertheless, amillennialists dismiss this on the basis that it represents an argument from silence.

Amillennialists highlight that the apostle always connected the largescale deception of the nations with the Antichrist's unprecedented tribulation (Rev. 12:9; 13:14; 18:23; 19:20; cf. Matt. 24:5, 11, 24;

---

5   συναγαγεῖν αὐτοὺς εἰς τὸν πόλεμον

2 Thess. 2:3, 10-12). To further illustrate this connection, the same Greek word group (translated "to deceive") appears five times outside of Revelation 20, and with the exception of Christ's warning to the church of Thyatira (Rev. 2:20), it always refers to the Antichrist's deception of the nations during the great tribulation. Consequently, they argue that Satan's deception during the "little while" following his release from the Abyss (Rev. 20:3; cf. Rev. 17:10) refers to this same tribulation.

Further supporting this interpretation, John depicted three ascensions of demonic spirits from the Abyss: First, at the sounding of the fifth trumpet, he saw an angel, the "star fallen from heaven to the earth," who will open the Abyss with "the key," immediately resulting in the ascension of a multitude of demons, who will wage a largescale war against humanity (Rev. 9:1-2, 11). Their king is Satan, whom the text calls "the angel of the bottomless pit [the Abyss]" and "the destroyer" (Rev. 9:11; cf. Exod. 12:23; 1 Cor. 10:10). Second, he mentioned that the Antichrist will ascend from the Abyss to become the full incarnation of Satan and to initiate the great tribulation (Rev. 17:8; cf. Rev. 11:7); this is the time when his deadly head wound will be healed through resurrection (Rev. 13:3, 12; cf. Gen. 3:15). Third, he saw Satan ascending from the Abyss to begin the war of Gog and Magog (Rev. 20:7). The composite portrait of these thematically related prophecies illustrates that Satan himself will be released from the Abyss to incarnate the Antichrist at the midpoint of the final seven years. In mock parody of the resurrected Christ (cf. Rev. 1:4, 8; 4:8; 11:17), the Beast is called the one who "was, is not [presumably, at the time John wrote], and will ascend out of the bottomless pit [the Abyss] and go to perdition" (Rev. 17:8).

The Apocalypse reveals that the Antichrist will "deceive the whole world" for the entirety of the unprecedented tribulation (Rev. 12:9; cf. Rev. 18:23), which will be concurrent with the dragon's persecution of the heavenly woman and her children (Rev. 12:6, 13-17). During this same forty-two months, the false prophet will "deceive those who dwell on the earth" (Rev. 13:14; cf. Rev. 19:20). It stands to reason, then, that this will also be when the dragon will "deceive the nations . . . of the earth" to wage the war of Gog and Magog (Rev. 20:8). The apostle summarized that the three unclean spirits of the unholy trinity will work collectively to deceive the nations and to gather them together for the battle of the day of God (Rev. 16:13-14).

The primary Old Testament backdrop for Satan's binding is found in the Isaiah Apocalypse (Isa. 24:21-23). This prophecy reveals that God will punish "the kings of the earth" and the army of exalted demons ("on high the host of exalted ones" Isa. 24:21; cf. Rev. 19:19-21).

> It shall come to pass in that day that the Lord will punish on high the host of exalted ones and on the earth the kings of the earth. They will be gathered together, as prisoners are gathered in the pit, and will be shut up in the prison; after many days they will be punished. Then the moon will be disgraced and the sun ashamed; for the Lord of hosts will reign on Mount Zion and in Jerusalem and before His elders, gloriously. (Isa. 24:21-23)

The prophet foretold that the Lord's heavenly and earthly enemies would be incarcerated in the Abyss ("gathered in the pit . . . shut up in the prison") for a long time, only to be punished much later.[6] Premillennialist interpreters see the twice-mentioned "punishment" as an indication of two separate retributions: one at the day of the Lord followed by a second one "after many days" ("after many generations" LXX). On the other hand, amillennialists understand this passage as describing the solitary punishment of these enemies at the same time, at the day of Jesus Christ ("in that day" Isa. 24:21-22; cf. Dan. 7:12). In the latter interpretation, verse 22 explains the punishment of the preceding verse.

Three primary observations support the amillennial interpretation: First, the prophet mentioned that the punishment of verse 21 will occur on the day of the Lord ("in that day" Isa. 24:21), and he communicated that the punishment of verse 22 will take place at the time

---

6   The terms "pit," "prison," and "shut up" occur in Isaiah 24:22 and Revelation 20:1-8.

of the cosmic darkness ("*Then* the moon will be disgraced and the sun ashamed" Isa. 24:23, emphasis added). Second, the prophet previously communicated that "the kings of the nations" will "rise up" to greet Lucifer, the king of Babylon (i.e., the Antichrist), when he arrives in hell on the day of the Lord (Isa. 14:9-11, 15-16). Clearly then, Isaiah portrayed the dead kings of the earth as having been gathered together in hell ("the Pit" Isa. 14:15) prior to the day of Jesus Christ. Third, elsewhere, Isaiah's expression "many days" means "many generations" which will terminate at the day of the Lord ("after many days they will be punished" Isa. 24:22 LXX; Dan. 8:26; 10:14), and Ezekiel alluded to this verse to describe the Antichrist's final punishment ("after many days you will be visited" Ezek. 38:8)!

Other Scriptures communicate the idea that many demons are currently bound with everlasting "chains of darkness" in hell until they are punished on judgment day (2 Pet. 2:4-9; Jude 1:6; Rev. 20:10). At that time, they will be sent into the everlasting punishment of hellfire, which God has sovereignly "prepared" for the devil and his demons (Matt. 25:41, 46; cf. Matt. 8:29; Luke 8:31). The apostle John also wrote about this: "The devil, who deceived them, was cast into the lake of fire and brimstone where the beast and the false prophet are. And they will be tormented day and night forever and ever" (Rev. 20:10). Premillennialists correctly argue that the grammar of this verse could indicate that the Antichrist and the false prophet will be thrown into hell before the devil joins them; however, amillennialists contend that this statement invites the reader to thematically connect the devil's fate with that of these two wicked men, as described in the previous vision (Rev. 19:19-21).

Another premillennial argument is that the apostle John attempted to establish a cause-and-effect relationship between these events by placing his visions about Christ's return to kill the Antichrist and false prophet (Rev. 19:11-21) immediately before his visions concerning the millennium (Rev. 20:1-10). Yet admittedly, as amillennialism maintains, the order of these visions could also be explained as an example of recapitulation, a technique which John frequently employed throughout the book. Recapitulation means to repeat and summarize events mentioned previously in the book, often to reveal their deeper meaning. If this interpretation is correct, then the binding of Satan in the Abyss provides the reason for the reign of the martyrs, and his loosing for a "little while" explains the sudden emergence and destruction of the Antichrist and his kingdom.

Finally, the apostle John concluded his chapter on the "thousand years" by providing a description of judgment day (Rev. 20:11-15). This section begins with the statement "Then I saw a great white throne and Him who sat on it, from whose face the earth and the heaven fled away. And there was found no place for them" (Rev. 20:11). The purpose for Christ sitting on His "great white throne" will be to judge the living and the dead (Rev. 20:11-12), an event which we have previously seen will occur at His return. Furthermore, the Holy Scriptures reveal that the dissolution and destruction of the first creation and the arrival of the new creation will occur in tandem at the day of Jesus Christ (2 Pet. 3:10-13; Rev. 20:11; 21:1; cf. Isa. 65:17-20; Matt. 24:35; Heb. 12:26-28). Based on such passages, it seems improbable that the destruction of the present cosmos will be separated from the arrival of the new heavens and earth by a thousand years, as premillennialists argue.

John continued with his depiction of the judgment: "And I saw the dead, small and great, standing before God, and books were opened. And another book was opened, which is the Book of Life. And the dead were judged according to their works, by the things which were written in the books" (Rev. 20:12). According to the prophet Daniel, these heavenly books will be opened ("the court was seated, and the books were opened" Dan. 7:10) when Christ descends from heaven to kill the Antichrist and to throw him into hellfire (Dan. 7:11, 13; Rev. 19:11-21). When mentioned elsewhere, the concept of people being judged "according to their works" (Rev. 20:12-13) refers to the time of Christ's Second Coming (Matt. 16:27; Rom. 2:6).

Another amillennial argument is that Jesus and His apostles taught that all the dead, the righteous and the wicked, will be resurrected at the last day. For example, Jesus taught, "Do not marvel at this; for the hour is coming in which all who are in the graves will hear His voice and come forth—those who have done good, to the resurrection of life, and those who have done evil, to the resurrection of condemnation" (John 5:28-29). To summarize, there will be a solitary moment ("the hour" John 5:28) when both groups will be resurrected to receive different eternal destinies. The apostle Paul also taught that there will be one resurrection for the two groups ("there will be a resurrection of the dead, both of the just and the unjust" Acts 24:15). Both these prophecies allude to Daniel's prophecy about the resurrection: "And at that time [of unprecedented trouble] your people shall be delivered, every one who is found written in the book. And many of those who sleep in the dust of the earth shall awake, some to everlasting life, some to shame and everlasting contempt" (Dan. 12:1-2).

Furthermore, Revelation 20 ends with a depiction of the wicked being judged and thrown into hellfire (Rev. 20:13-15). Every related passage of Scripture places the everlasting destruction of the wicked at Christ's glorious return (Matt. 25:31-33, 41, 46; 2 Thess. 1:7-10; 2 Pet. 3:7, 10-12). All these facts appear to militate against premillennialism, a view which separates the solitary resurrection into two resurrections by interposing the thousand years (cf. Rev. 20:4-5, 13-15).

More to the point, amillennialism posits that *all* the detailed events that John described as taking place after the thousand years are depicted elsewhere in the Scriptures as taking place at the day of Jesus Christ. Consequently, proponents argue that Revelation 20 should not be regarded as the solitary exception.

20

THE ALREADY AND NOT YET

MANY PROFESSING CHRISTIANS incorrectly think that God's kingdom is entirely future, while others adhere to an overrealized eschatology in which the kingdom is fully equated with the apostolic Church. Those who embrace the former view often minimize the relevance and power of the gospel in the life of the Church, while those holding to the latter have largely abandoned the Christian hope. In this chapter, I will expound the "already and not yet" concept I touched upon earlier in this book.

The New Testament first presents this concept with the proclamation of John the Forerunner. John emerged from the desert, baptizing and preaching, "Repent, for the kingdom of heaven is at hand!" (Matt. 3:2). Likewise, Jesus Himself preached, "The time is fulfilled, and the kingdom of God is at hand. Repent, and believe in the gospel" (Mark 1:15), and He commissioned His apostles and seventy evangelists to proclaim this message of kingdom nearness (Matt. 10:7; "The kingdom of God has come near to you" Luke 10:9; cf. v. 11). As they went throughout the country, they proclaimed the gospel (meaning "good news"), that is, the message concerning God's kingdom (Mark 1:14; Luke 8:1; cf. Acts 20:25).

This declaration shocked Jewish ears because it meant that the messianic kingdom had become accessible in a different way than before, specifically, through the visitation of the incarnate Son of God. The Forerunner proclaimed that judgment day was imminent and that everyone should immediately flee from divine wrath by receiving baptism and the repentance that produces good fruit. He proclaimed, "*Even now* the ax is laid to the root of the trees. Therefore every tree which does not bear good fruit is cut down and thrown into the fire" (Matt. 3:10-12, emphasis added; cf. Luke 3:17). Whereas God had previously overlooked many transgressions which people committed through ignorance, He was now commanding everyone to repent (cf. Acts 17:30). In short, the arrival of God's Son demands repentance from everyone.

Fundamentally, Christ's kingdom is about His dynamic reign in the lives of people. As we may surmise, then, the kingdom is not just imminent (i.e., "at hand" or near) but accessibly present. He evidenced His kingdom authority through the power of His words and deeds for people, as He proclaimed in the Capernaum synagogue:

The Spirit of the Lord is upon Me because He has anointed Me to preach the gospel to the poor; He has sent Me to heal the brokenhearted, to proclaim liberty to the captives and recovery of sight to the blind, to set at liberty those who are oppressed; To proclaim the acceptable year of the Lord . . . Today this Scripture is fulfilled in your hearing. (Luke 4:18-19, 21)

In this message, Jesus quoted the promises about the kingdom found in Isaiah 61:1-2, declaring its fulfillment to be in Himself. These promises were no longer only a future hope but they were finding their actualization in the Person and energies of Christ. To further demonstrate, after He performed great miracles, Jesus conflated several prophecies about the day of the Lord into one statement: "the blind see and the lame walk; the lepers are cleansed and the deaf hear; the dead are raised up and the poor have the gospel preached to them" (Matt. 11:5 from Ps. 22:26; Isa. 29:18; 35:4-6; 61:1). By doing this, He demonstrated that the blessings of the messianic redemption, such as His miracles of healings, had mysteriously arrived before the day of Jesus Christ.

Jesus fulfilled many prophecies about the kingdom, thus, He inaugurated it before its consummation. Therefore, the kingdom is not simply waiting for the age to come, but it has already penetrated this present evil age. Christ taught about this mysterious breaking in: "But if I cast out demons with the finger of God, surely the kingdom of God has come upon you" (Luke 11:20; cf. Matt. 12:28). If His kingdom was reaching people ("come upon you" Luke 11:20), then it was present. This verse does not indicate that the kingdom was near but that it had already arrived. Similarly, the text does not demonstrate that only the signs and powers of the kingdom were present, but the kingdom itself was there. Jesus was invading Satan's kingdom and binding this "strong man" in order to overcome him and plunder his goods (Matt. 12:29; cf. Rev. 20:1-3). The eschatological Spirit of the age to come had arrived in advance of the day of the Lord.

Jesus taught that people enter the kingdom of God in the present age (Matt. 21:31; 23:13): "The law and the prophets were until John. Since that time the kingdom of God has been preached, and everyone is pressing into it" (Luke 16:16; cf. Matt. 11:11-12; John 18:36). This is why people must receive Christ's kingdom now (Mark 10:15). This present aspect of the kingdom is seen in the parable of the hidden treasure and the parable of the pearl (Matt. 13:44-46); the idea is that people must give up everything now for Christ. This includes the promise of eternal life in the present (1 John 5:13).

Christ answered the Pharisees about when His kingdom will come: "The kingdom of God does not come with observation; nor will they say, 'See here!' or 'See there!' For indeed, the kingdom of God is within you" (Luke 17:20-21). This verse reveals that the kingdom's arrival occurs before its consummation, and it has arrived in Christ and in His apostolic Church. As such, God is the agent who brings the kingdom to men, which is why the Scriptures do not communicate that people build the kingdom or cause it to arrive.

The parables of Jesus also show us that the kingdom is a present reality. For example, the parable of the growing seed begins as follows:

> The kingdom of God is as if a man should scatter seed on the ground, and should sleep by night and rise by day, and the seed should sprout and grow, he himself does not know how. For the earth yields crops by itself: first the blade, then the head, after that the full grain in the head. But when the grain ripens, immediately he puts in the sickle, because the harvest has come. (Mark 4:26-29)

In this parable, the sower does not understand how his crops sprout and grow, but he notices that they arrive in stages: the blade, the head, the full grain, and the ripened grain at the harvest.[1] The meaning is that God's kingdom appears in progressive stages: First, it arrived in the earthly ministry of Christ. Second, Jesus, with all kingdom authority, ascended to sit and reign at God's right hand (Matt. 28:18). As a result, the Holy Spirit was poured out beginning at the day of Pentecost, resulting in the gospel advance throughout the nations. Third, Jesus will return "with great power and glory." This "harvest" is the consummation of His kingdom—the day of Christ.

The stepwise, progressive stages of Christ's kingdom brought an unexpected twist to traditional Jewish eschatology, but it was foreshadowed by the establishment of King David's dynasty. To illustrate, the prophet Samuel did not anoint David to be king until after he had crushed the giant's forehead. And during the early years of his reign,

---

[1] Jesus also taught, "The wind blows where it wishes, and you hear the sound of it, but cannot tell where it comes from and where it goes" (John 3:8); the Greek word here can be translated Spirit, spirit, wind, or breath, illustrating that the Spirit's movements are unpredictable, like wind currents (cf. Gen. 1:2).

David remained a contested king, a "rejected stone" (Ps. 118:22). After many years, the Lord established his kingdom at Hebron, and later, throughout the regions of Judah and then throughout Israel.

In the parable of the tares, Jesus illustrated that His kingdom would include the righteous and the wicked living together until the end of the age (Matt. 13:24-43). The parable portrays "an enemy" planting tares (i.e., darnel, a ryegrass) in a farmer's wheat field. These "look alike" plants appear similar to wheat during their early growth stages. The servants allow both to grow together until the harvest, at which time the reapers separate out the darnel to be burned and gather the wheat into a barn. The meaning of the parable is that Jesus "plants" the children of the kingdom, while Satan also "plants" his children. They exist together in the world until the harvest, revealing in a mystery that the kingdom is operative before the end of the age. On judgment day, the angelic reapers will divide the two groups, throwing Satan and his children into hellfire and gathering the righteous into the kingdom.

The parable of the mustard seed (Matt. 13:31-32; Mark 4:30-32; Luke 13:18-19) and the parable of the leaven (Matt. 13:33; Luke 13:20-21) reveal that God's kingdom begins small but progressively grows until it becomes a great, worldwide kingdom. These parables also reveal that the kingdom would exist long before its consummation. These parables reveal that the "already and not yet" of Christ's kingdom is the mystery which He "kept secret from the foundation of the world" (Matt. 13:35). This is why Jesus ended some parables with the statement "He who has ears to hear, let him hear." Not all people receive the grace to understand.

Christ's parables are a double-edged sword: They further demonstrate the revealed mystery of the kingdom to His disciples while ratifying the spiritual resistance that outsiders have toward the truth. He explained this purpose: "To you [the disciples] it has been given to know the mystery of the kingdom of God; but to those who are outside, all things come in parables, so that 'seeing they may see and not perceive, and hearing they may hear and not understand; lest they should turn, and their sins be forgiven them' " (Mark 4:11-12). Having entered the world in a hidden form, the kingdom secretly belongs to Christians. This mystery was concealed in ages past but Christ has revealed it to the apostles; therefore, those who receive the apostolic gospel see, hear, and understand the things that even "many prophets and righteous men" could not (Matt. 13:17). This "already and not yet" mystery elucidates, but does not replace the eschatology of the prophets.

Consequently, the mystery of the kingdom is that it has penetrated into the present age in advance of its final expression at the day of the Lord. This represents a kingdom inauguration apart from its consummation. This revealed mystery is best understood as an extension of Christ's two advents. Although the Jews understood that the Messiah's arrival would signal the kingdom's arrival, Jesus appeared millennia before the day of the Lord. This confused the demons, who then feared whether He would torment them "before the appointed time" (Matt. 8:29, translation mine). Furthermore, during Christ's earthly ministry, He prevented outsiders from understanding the messianic secret, namely that He is the incarnate Son of God who came to destroy sin through His death. "The rulers of this age," which included the demonic principalities, would not have "crucified the Lord of glory" had they understood this mystery (1 Cor. 2:8).

The scribes and Pharisees "shut up" the kingdom, preventing the people from entering it (Matt. 23:13), so God removed it from them (Matt. 21:43) and give it to a "foolish nation"—the holy apostolic Church. This is why Jesus gave the apostles "the keys" to this kingdom (Matt. 16:19). He also commanded them to transform this hidden secret about His identity into a proclaimed secret ("Whatever I tell you in the dark, speak in the light" Matt. 10:27). On Pentecost, it became a revealed secret. The Spirit enabled the apostle Peter to proclaim Christ's session at God's right hand (Acts 2:29-36; cf. Ps. 110:1; Matt. 22:43-44; Mark 16:19; Luke 22:69; Eph. 1:20-22; Heb. 1:3; 2:8; 12:2; 1 Pet. 3:22). At the Lord's return, the mystery of Christ will become a fully manifested secret because He will visibly reveal His glory to everyone (Matt. 24:27).

Christ's heavenly session during the inter-advent period demonstrates the "already and not yet" interim of the kingdom. When Jesus ascended, He traveled to a distant country, so to speak, in order "to receive for himself a kingdom and to return" (Luke 19:12; cf. Matt. 28:18). Consistent with this theme, Peter's sermon reveals that Christ is currently seated on His heavenly throne, that is, the throne of His father David (Acts 2:29-35; cf. Rev. 3:7, 21). He will continue to reign from the Father's right hand "until He has put all His enemies under His feet" (1 Cor. 15:25), and in the meantime, He has "made us a kingdom" of priests in which we participate (Rev. 1:6, 9; 5:10).

The events of Christ's crucifixion also display the "already and not yet" principle. In the divine irony of kingdom fulfillment, Jesus was raised up on a Roman cross ("exalted and lifted up" Isa. 52:13, translation mine) instead of being exalted and installed as king on a throne (cf. Isa. 6:1). Soldiers dressed Him in a royal robe of purple and scarlet and stripped Him naked (Mark 15:17, 20; John 19:2, 5; cf. Gen. 3:7, 10). They also forced Him to wear a crown of thorns (Matt. 27:29; Mark 15:17; John 19:2, 5; cf. Gen. 3:18) instead of a traditional gold or silver one. They mockingly struck Him with a makeshift scepter made of reed (Matt. 27:48), and they bowed before Him, declaring, "Hail, King of the Jews" (Matt. 27:29). At His crucifixion, a mighty earthquake shook the land and thick darkness appeared over it (Matt. 27:45, 51-54; Mark 15:33; Luke 23:44)—the first installments of some of the eschatological features of the day of the Lord.

Many other examples demonstrate that the powers of the coming age had invaded the present age as a first installment. For example, before Christ's resurrection, Jews believed that the resurrection would occur only on the last day (cf. Dan. 12:1-4). But He rose from the dead as a first installment, the firstfruits' offering of the greater harvest of the righteous (1 Cor. 15:20, 23). In this manner, the resurrection began with His resurrection, and Christians have received the Spirit as a firstfruits' deposit or guarantee of their own resurrection (Rom. 8:23). To take this a step further, the faithful have already been "raised with Christ" before the resurrection on the last day (see chapter 19).

Christians participate in the kingdom in an "already and not yet" manner. For example, in this present age, Christians have already "tasted the heavenly gift" and "the powers of the age to come" (Heb. 6:4-5). Though not having entered it yet, Christians have already arrived at the heavenly Jerusalem (Heb. 9:22-24). Furthermore, the apostle Peter proclaimed that the gift of the Holy Spirit was the very event that Joel had prophesied would happen in the latter days (Acts 2:16-21 with Joel 2:28-32; cf. "the fields . . . are already white for harvest" John 4:35). Finally, although the prophets had foretold that the nations will come to faith in Israel's God and in her Messiah after the day of the Lord, God is already grafting in the Gentiles before the day.

The kingdom's "already and not yet" helps us to recognize how the apostles understood that the last days had already arrived:

- "the time is short . . . the form of this world is passing away" (1 Cor. 7:29; cf. v. 31)

- "the ends of the ages have come" (1 Cor. 10:11)

- "in these last days" (Heb. 1:2; James 5:3)

- "at the end of the ages" (Heb. 9:26)

- "in these last times" (1 Pet. 1:20)

- "it is the last hour" (1 John 2:18)

As the prophets had portrayed the day of the Lord as near, the apostles taught that Christ's return is a proximate event:

- "the Lord is at hand" (Phil. 4:5; James 5:8)

- "the Judge is standing at the door" (James 5:9)

- "the end of all things is at hand" (1 Pet. 4:7)

- "the true light is already shining" (1 John 2:8)

- "the time is near" (Rev. 1:3; cf. v. 1)

- "the time is at hand" (Rev. 22:10)

- "I am coming quickly" (Rev. 22:12, 20)

The apostles did not teach that the Lord's return was imminent, at least not in the sense that He could return at any moment, without signs and portents. Rather, they taught the nearness of His return as the primary reason for immediate repentance.

In point of fact, many eschatological events that will occur during the years leading up to the return of Jesus have penetrated the present age. For example, the apostle Paul believed that the Antichrist's "mystery of lawlessness" was "already at work" (2 Thess. 2:7). Likewise, the arrival of antichrists in the first century ("even now" 1 John 2:18; "now it is already" 1 John 4:3) meant that the last hour had arrived (1 John 2:18). Similarly, while Christ did not deny that the prophet Elijah will arrive during the great tribulation (read "not yet"; cf. Rev. 11:1-14), He identified John the Forerunner as Elijah ("has come already" Matt. 17:12; cf. Matt. 11:14; 17:11-13; Mark 9:12-13; Luke 7:27). To summarize, Jesus and His apostles saw the eschaton as breaking into the then present.

The archangel Michael casting Satan from heaven also highlights the "already and not yet" of the eschaton. For example, the crucifixion of our Lord serves as the ground and basis for the devil's ousting, although he will be cast out at the beginning of the unprecedented tribulation (Rev. 12:7, 9-10). When Jesus spoke about His imminent crucifixion, He declared, "Now is the judgment of this world; now the ruler of this world will be cast out" (John 12:31). To take this further, Satan's casting out had begun prior to this in the apostolic ministry of the seventy (Luke 10:18). Such passages illustrate the fact that the progressive stages of redemption, such as Christ's death on the cross and the advancement of His gospel, progressively dismantle Satan's kingdom. Ultimately, the mysterious transcendence of space and time that characterizes non-corporeal, spiritual beings, may best explain the devil's downfall.

Many other prophecies evidence that the day of Jesus Christ has invaded the present age. For example, Isaiah prophesied the appearing of the light of Christ's presence at the Second Coming: "The people who walked in darkness have seen a great light; those who dwelt in the land of the shadow of death, upon them a light has shined" (Isa. 9:2). Matthew recognized Jesus as having fulfilled this passage during His earthly ministry because He brought His light to the people of the Galilee (Matt. 4:13-16; cf. Isa. 9:1). The idea is that they already saw Christ's presence and power because God revealed His Son in advance of the day. As a result, the kingdom of heaven was "at hand," that is, present and accessible to the people to whom He ministered (Matt. 4:17). This was a divine summons (Matt. 4:18-20).

In addition, Christ's glorious arrival has already penetrated the present age. To demonstrate, He prophesied, "For the Son of Man will come in the glory of His Father with His angels, and then He will reward each according to his works. Assuredly, I say to you, there are some standing here who shall not taste death till they see the Son of Man coming in His kingdom" (Matt. 16:27-28; cf. Mark 8:38; Luke 9:26). The theme of the glorious coming of Christ with angels to bring rewards always refers to the Second Coming (Dan. 7:13-14; Matt. 24:30-31; 25:31-46; Rom. 2:6; 2 Cor. 5:10; Rev. 20:12-13). Nevertheless, the careful reader will notice that Jesus did not say that some of His first-century disciples would live long enough to see the Second Coming, accompanied by angels and rewards,[2] only that they would see Him coming "in His kingdom" (Matt. 16:28).[3]

Three of the apostles, Peter, James, and John, saw Christ transfigured in resplendent glory upon the Mount of Transfiguration, an event which Peter described as a "prophetic word" of certainty regarding the Lord's glorious coming (2 Pet. 1:19). Then the eleven apostles (Judas was dead) "heard," "saw with their eyes," "looked at," and "handled" the resurrected Jesus (1 John 1:1). Afterward, having become "eyewitnesses of His majesty," they made known to others "the power and coming of our Lord" (2 Pet. 1:16). Later, John saw the resurrected Jesus on the island of Patmos (Rev. 1:12-20), and he saw the Second Coming (Rev. 14:14-16; 19:11-21). All of the aforementioned first-century, eyewitness experiences consisted of the surviving disciples seeing Christ gloriously arriving "in His kingdom" (Matt. 16:28). In addition, the Holy Spirit was poured out upon the holy Church, and the kingdom came "with power" (Mark 9:1) so that the nations received the gospel. These events all prophetically foreshadowed the Lord's glorious return at the day of Christ.

Likewise, Jesus told the Sanhedrin that they would "see the Son of Man sitting at the right hand of the Power, and coming on the clouds of heaven" (Matt. 26:64). Presumably, none of the judges of the Great Assembly saw the glorified Christ sitting at God's right hand (cf. Acts 7:55-56).[4] However, they were eyewitnesses of Christ's kingdom authority, His reign at the Father's right hand, in the advancement of the apostolic gospel and the accompanying miraculous signs and wonders (cf. Acts 4:5-31). At any rate, these representatives of the nation

---

2   Contra preterism, which contends that the Son of Man's "coming" (e.g., Matt. 16:28) refers to the destruction of the Second Temple in AD 70. For a complete refutation, see my book *Debunking Preterism*.

3   Mark and Luke condensed Matthew's construction ("the Son of Man coming in His kingdom") to read "the kingdom of God present with power" (Mark 9:1) and "the kingdom of God" (Luke 9:27), respectively.

4   The first-century historical writings indicate that most of these men (likely, all of them), including the high priest Caiaphas, died *before* the destruction of the Second Temple in AD 70.

were responsible for the crucifixion of Christ (Acts 2:23; 3:13-15; 4:10; 1 Thess. 2:15), and they will see Him at God's right hand when He returns "on the clouds of heaven" (Matt. 24:30; Rev. 1:7).

Eternal life can be received now, not only in the age to come (John 3:36; 5:21, 24; 6:47, 54; 1 John 5:13). Those who trust in Christ have received His resurrection life by the Spirit, which is why Jesus taught that we have already "passed from death into life" and that "the hour is coming ['not yet'], and now is ['already']" when the dead will be resurrected (John 5:24-28; cf. John 4:23). The mystery is not the future resurrection but that this resurrection life is accessible now through Jesus Christ. The resurrection and ascension of Christ have been applied to Christians by the Spirit (cf. Eph. 2:5-6; Col. 2:13; 3:1) so that we now live and reign with Him (see chapter 18). In this manner, we have already received the new covenant that Israel will receive on the day of the Lord, and we already belong to the new creation that is coming: "Therefore if anyone is in Christ, he is a new creature; the old things passed away; behold, new things have come" (2 Cor. 5:17; cf. Gal. 6:15).

Judgment day has also penetrated the present. For example, Jesus explained that the wicked are already condemned and have begun to experience God's wrath (John 3:18-19, 36; Rom. 1:18). On the other hand, the righteous are already justified (i.e., legally "acquitted") before God through faith in the death and resurrection of Jesus Christ (Rom. 3:24; 5:1, 9; 8:30). Even the death of Christ is an expression of the judgment which has already come upon the world (John 12:31).

APPENDIX

THE MEANING OF "THIS GENERATION"

NOTE TO THE READER: This appendix is academic in nature and is not a necessary extension of the book. It is intended for those with an academic interest in the meaning of "this generation" (e.g., Matt. 24:34; Mark 13:30; Luke 21:32).

In the Olivet Discourse, Jesus Christ prophesied that the unprecedented tribulation (Matt. 24:15-28) will terminate with His glorious return on the day of the Lord (Matt. 24:29-33). Then He declared, "Assuredly, I say to you, this generation will by no means pass away till all these things take place" (Matt. 24:34; cf. Mark 13:30; Luke 21:32). Many commentators argue that the phrase "this generation" must refer to the period of Jesus' contemporaries because it always carries this meaning when it appears throughout the Synoptic Gospels. They contend that the term "generation" refers to all people living during a specific time frame, usually during a period of approximately forty years. I will demonstrate that this reasoning is incorrect and betrays an ignorance of the phrase's essential meaning and how Christ employed it throughout the Gospels. I will also show that "this generation" includes the contemporaries of Jesus but is not restricted to them.

The Greek word γενεά ("generation") refers to "children" or "offspring," and not to a group of individuals living during a specific time frame. Gerhard Kittel's *Theological Dictionary of the New Testament* correctly notes that in general usage "generation" means "birth" or "descent."[1] The word has a primary meaning of "sired, produced, brought out, or generated from."[2] English speakers sometimes use the word "generation" in this manner; for example, Christians speak of the eternal "generation" of the Son from the Father with reference to the Holy Trinity and of "regeneration" to speak of a person receiving new life in Jesus Christ.

The Greek word translated "generation" is roughly equivalent to the Hebrew word meaning "generation" (דּוֹר) which came over into the Septuagint (LXX) as γενεά. This Hebrew word is found throughout the Old Testament and often carries a qualitative meaning. In other words, the Hebrew word "generation" describes a general quality or character of people or children and is not primarily concerned with a specific time period. For example, the psalmist wrote about "the generation of the righteous" (Ps. 14:5), "the generation of his fathers" (Ps. 49:19), "the generation of Your [God's] children" (Ps. 73:15), and "the generation of the upright" (Ps. 112:2; cf. Ps. 12:7; 71:18).

Throughout the Synoptic Gospels, the expression "this generation" functions as a technical term (Matt. 11:16; 12:41-42; 23:36; 24:34; Mark 8:12; 13:30; Luke 7:31; 11:30-32, 50-51; 17:25; 21:32). As I will demonstrate, Jesus' frequent use of this expression is part of a larger thematic interweaving of Deuteronomic expressions (Deut. 1:35; 32:5, 20). In addition, Christ and His apostles developed this larger theme by modifying the word "generation" by adding adjectives:

---

[1] Kittel, Gerhard, Gerhard Friedrich, and Geoffrey William Bromiley. *Theological Dictionary of the New Testament*. Dallas, TX: CDWord Library, 1989.

[2] The holy Church fathers regularly used the word "generation" (γενεά) in this manner.

- O faithless generation (Mark 9:19)

- O faithless and perverse generation (Matt. 17:17; Luke 9:41)

- this wicked generation (Matt. 12:45)

- an evil and adulterous generation (Matt. 12:39; 16:4)

- an evil generation (Luke 11:29)

- this adulteress and sinful generation (Mark 8:38)

- this perverse generation (Acts 2:40)

- a crooked and perverse generation (Phil. 2:15)

We can discover how Christ and His apostles used these expressions once we properly understand what they meant in their original context in the book of Deuteronomy. The first expression, "this evil generation" (Deut. 1:35), refers to the Israelites who died because of their unbelief during the forty years of wandering in the desert (Deut. 1:34-39; cf. Heb. 3:7-19). As we will see, this expression in not primarily quantitative, referring to those people who lived at the time of the exodus, but qualitative, to the offspring or children produced with an evil disposition.

The other two Deuteronomic expressions, located in the Song of Moses, categorically convey a qualitative meaning. In the preamble to the song, Moses rebuked the children of Israel for their evil "inclination" toward rebellion and stubbornness (Deut. 31:21, 27). The song itself defines this wicked "generation" as the sired offspring of Israel, children brought forth with a sinful disposition: "They have corrupted themselves; they are not His children because of their blemish: A perverse and crooked generation" (Deut. 32:5; cf. Hosea 2:2-5). Verses later, God Himself warned, "I will see what their end will be, for they are a perverse generation, children in whom is no faith" (Deut. 32:20; cf. Deut. 31:17). The larger context characterizes the nation as a corporate offspring of "blemished" children who *perpetually* reject God and engage in idolatry. In point of fact, their corruption would continue long after Moses' death, reaching a crescendo in "the latter days" (Deut. 31:16-29; cf. Deut. 4:25-31). Therefore, the generation in question cannot be limited to a specific time period; it refers to offspring with a transhistorical inclination or disposition toward iniquity.

The prophet Isaiah borrowed from these themes in the Song of Moses for the introduction of his book: "I have nourished and brought up children, and they have rebelled against Me . . . Alas, sinful nation, a people laden with iniquity, a brood of evildoers, children who are corrupters! They have forsaken the Lord, they have provoked to anger the Holy One of Israel" (Isa. 1:2, 4; cf. Isa. 1:24). Once again, such passages emphasize that Israel's "children" are a corrupt, idolatrous "brood of evildoers," which have continued to rebel against God (cf. Num. 32:14; Isa. 14:20; Matt. 3:7-9; 12:34; 23:33; Luke 3:7-8). We may conclude, then, that the New Testament motif of "this generation" is faithful to its Old Testament usage as a description of the largely unregenerate Israelite nation.

This evil generation does not refer to ethnic descendants of Jacob as such but to those with a degenerate disposition toward sin. This definition is further qualified by the appearance of the phrase in Paul's epistle to the Philippians: "Do all things without complaining and disputing, that you may become blameless and harmless, *children* of God without fault in the midst of a crooked and perverse generation, among whom you shine as lights in the world, holding fast the word of life, so that I may rejoice in the day of Christ that I have not run in vain or labored in vain" (Phil. 2:14-16, emphasis added; cf. Deut. 32:5). The unique feature here is that the Philippians "among whom" these Christians lived were predominantly Gentiles. Therefore, we see that "this generation" was not a uniquely Jewish identity; it includes all unregenerate mankind since the introduction of ancestral sin (Rom. 3:9; cf. Ps. 14:2-5), wicked people who will inhabit the Earth until the return of Jesus Christ. In his seminal work, *Jesus and 'this Generation,'* Evald Lövestam painstakingly demonstrated that the concept of "this generation" should be understood qualitatively as referring to a character or type of people.[3] He demonstrates that the Synoptic Gospels include specific, repetitive themes to describe "this generation": First, the expression always has a negative tone and refers to people characterized by moral wickedness. In other words, "this generation" is decisively "evil" and "perverse." Consequently, Christ never included Himself in "this generation," and He generally excluded His disciples from this descriptor; furthermore, He frequently contrasted the people of the evil generation with the righteous. Second, God repeatedly sends preachers to "this generation" to proclaim a message of repentance. Third, while miraculous signs accompany this message, "this generation" reacts with doubt and disbelief. Fourth, "this generation" persecutes and often murders God's righteous messengers. Fifth, "this generation" will be condemned on judgment day, but the righteous messengers will be vindicated and receive rewards, having previously been rescued from "this perverse generation" (cf. Acts 2:40). Sixth, the New Testament links this pattern of rejecting "the sent ones" with similar narratives in the Old Testament. These consistent themes in Christ's teachings about "this generation" consistently highlight the Jewish nation's perpetual, consistent disposition of rejecting the message of salvation.

As Lövestam demonstrates, this salvific-historical pattern for "this generation" is evident in every pericope (i.e., section of material) where the expression appears. The repeated elements discussed above appear in the pericopes regarding the demand for a sign (Matt. 12:38-42; 16:1-4; Mark 8:11-13; Luke 11:16, 29-32), the parable of the playing children (Matt. 11:16-19; Luke 7:31-35), the epileptic boy (Matt. 17:14-20; Mark 9:14-29; Luke 9:37-43), the eschatological sayings about "this

---

3   Lövestam Evald. *Jesus and 'This Generation': A New Testament Study.* Stockholm: Almqvist & Wiksell International, 1995.

generation" (Mark 8:38; Luke 17:22-37), the judgment on "this generation" (Matt. 23:34-36; Luke 11:49-51), the Olivet Discourse (Matt. 24;
Mark 13; Luke 21), Peter's appeal on the day of Pentecost (Acts 2:40),
and the epistolary references (Phil. 2:12-16; Heb. 3:7-4:11). This is
conclusive evidence that the phrase "this generation" conveys a technical
meaning referring to the transhistorical offspring of wickedness, as it
does in the Song of Moses (Deut. 32:5, 20).

Clearly then, Christ's statement about "this generation" in Matthew
24:34 continues the theme established by Moses and the Prophets concerning this "perverse generation, children in whom is no faith" (Deut.
32:20; cf. Ps. 12:7). Furthermore, this statement and the similar expression in Matthew 23:36 together function as theological "bookends" for
the Olivet Discourse. Matthew 23:29-36 reads as follows:

> Woe to you, scribes and Pharisees, hypocrites! Because you build the
> tombs of the prophets and adorn the monuments of the righteous,
> and say, "If we had lived in the days of our fathers, we would not have
> been partakers with them in the blood of the prophets." Therefore
> you are witnesses against yourselves that you are sons of those who
> murdered the prophets. Fill up, then, the measure of your fathers'
> guilt. Serpents, brood of vipers! How can you escape the condemna-
> tion of hell? Therefore, indeed, I send you prophets, wise men, and
> scribes: some of them you will kill and crucify, and some of them you
> will scourge in your synagogues and persecute from city to city, that
> on you may come all the righteous blood shed on the earth, from the
> blood of righteous Abel to the blood of Zechariah, son of Berechiah,
> whom you murdered between the temple and the altar. Assuredly, I
> say to you, *all these things will come upon this generation.* (Matt. 23:29-
> 36, emphasis added; cf. Luke 11:47-51; 13:34-36)

Many commentators argue that the expression "this generation"
must be understood quantitatively, referring only to Christ's first-
century Jewish contemporaries. Certainly, the Lord's original audience,

whom He identified as the scribes and Pharisees (Matt. 23:29), belonged to the evil generation in question. In addition, God's judgment "upon this generation" certainly included the destruction of the Jerusalem temple in AD 70 ("Your house is left to you desolate" Matt. 23:38). However, although "this generation" included Christ's contemporary audience, it was not restricted to them.

The scribes and Pharisees comprised only part of this larger generation, specifically, the transhistorical offspring of wicked children, as depicted in the Song of Moses and alluded to by the prophets. The text specifies that God held "this generation" responsible for the rejection of all the righteous "from the blood of righteous Abel to the blood of Zechariah" (Matt. 23:35; cf. Gen. 4:8-11). In other words, these evil children will be condemned for the heinous sins of the entirety of Old Testament history. Although the scribes and Pharisees did not personally commit the transgressions of their biblical past, Jesus explained that they maintained a corporate solidarity of guilt with their "fathers" who persecuted and rejected "all the prophets" of the Old Testament, a solidarity evidenced by their continued ancestral pattern of wickedness (Matt. 23:29-31, 34-35; cf. Matt. 5:12; 21:33-41). Under their leadership, the covenant nation soon murdered the Son of God and persecuted His apostles (Luke 17:25; Acts 2:23; 5:30; 1 Thess. 2:14-15). For this reason, the apostle Peter also labeled them "this crooked generation" (Acts 2:40).

Christ taught that the scribes and Pharisees maintained culpability for their transgressions because they were children or offspring (read "the generation") of their fathers, who also committed these evil deeds (cf. Ps. 12:7; Jer. 2:30-31; Matt. 11:16-19; Luke 7:31-35). This is why He called them "sons of hell" (Matt. 23:15) and the "sons of those who murdered the prophets" (v. 31). He even labeled them "serpents, brood of vipers" (v. 33; cf. Deut. 32:33; Matt. 3:7; 12:34; John 8:44), and elsewhere He scolded them, saying, "You are of your father the devil, and the desires of your father you want to do" (John 8:44). In other words, Christ's contemporaries were the spiritual descendants of those who persecuted the prophets, and ultimately, of the devil himself! Thus, "this generation" refers to the qualitative, age-enduring offspring of the serpent (Gen. 3:15; cf. Deut. 32:33; Matt. 3:7; 12:34; John 8:44).

For this reason, these men deserved divine wrath including eternal damnation ("the condemnation of hell" Matt. 23:33). They soon filled up "the measure of [their] fathers' guilt" by persecuting the apostles, as their ancestors had rejected and murdered the prophets (Matt. 23:29-36). The Judean Jews as a collective whole deserved divine retribution, as seen in the Pauline phrase "*as always* to fill up the measure of their sins" (1 Thess. 2:16, emphasis added; cf. Matt. 23:32). They perpetually deserved divine wrath ("as always" 1 Thess. 2:16; cf. Matt. 3:7) because they refused to repent for how they responded to the Lord's messengers.

Stephen, the first Christian martyr, spoke about their persistent, ancestral pattern of rejecting God's messengers: "You stiff-necked and uncircumcised in heart and ears! *You always* resist the Holy Spirit; *as your fathers did, so do you.* Which of the prophets did your fathers not persecute? And they killed those who foretold the coming of the Just One, of whom you now have become the betrayers and murderers" (Acts 7:51-52, emphasis added). Similarly, the people of Jerusalem continued this pattern of wickedness: "I [Peter] know that you did it in ignorance, as did also your rulers" (Acts 3:17).

Christ borrowed the phrase "all these things" (Matt. 24:33-34; cf. Matt. 23:36) from a series of Old Testament eschatological passages regarding (1) the unprecedented tribulation and (2) the subsequent salvation of the nation of Israel. The primary source for this phrase is found in the covenantal "blessings and curses" listed in the book of Deuteronomy. In these prophetic portions of Scripture, Moses warned that the covenantal curses would ravage the nation (Deut. 32:21-30), most particularly at its "latter end" (Deut. 32:29; cf. Deut. 31:17-18; 32:20) and "in the latter days" (Deut. 31:29). The prophet connected this time period with Israel's tribulation and national repentance (Deut. 4:30-31; cf. Jer. 5:19). This new covenant promise is that the nation will return to God to mercifully receive a spiritual "circumcision," an event that will occur "when *all these things* come upon you [Israel], the blessing and the curse" (Deut. 30:1ff, emphasis added; cf. Ezek. 37:21-28; Jer. 31:33-40).

Consequently, the "all these things" will not be fulfilled until the return of Jesus Christ, as He Himself predicted (Matt. 24:34; Mark 13:30; Luke 21:32). Christ remarked that this transhistorical generation ("this generation") will remain until His glorious return. This is why His diatribe against the scribes and Pharisees in Matthew 23 ends with the statement, "See! Your house is left to you desolate; for I say to you, you shall see Me no more till you say, 'Blessed is He who comes in the name of the Lord!' " (Matt. 23:38-39). Then the persecutors of God's elect will come to a complete end.

To summarize, Jesus presented the Church with an enigma in Matthew 24:34. The interpreter who believes in the inspiration of Scripture is divinely hedged in by the biblical evidence to embrace the conclusion that the expression "this generation" points to the qualitative, transhistorical offspring or children of evildoers. We can further identify them as "the sons of the wicked one" (Matt. 13:38), that is, the spiritual offspring of Satan, the ruler and god of "this world" (John 12:31; 14:30; 16:11; 2 Cor. 4:4). They will continue to live in this world during "this present evil age" (Gal. 1:4). As such, "this generation" includes anyone who has not escaped the corruption of this age by trusting in our Lord Jesus Christ.

Christ's statement about "this generation" (Matt. 24:34) serves many purposes: First, the transhistorical nature of this phrase helps preserve the unknowability of the timing of Christ's return. It even allowed for the possibility, at least in their minds, that the first-century disciples could have lived to see His glorious return. Second, the expression allows the events surrounding the destruction of Jerusalem and its temple in AD 70 to function as a partial, typological fulfillment of the Olivet Discourse while demanding that the exhaustive, plenary fulfillment await the end of the age (see chapter 20). Eusebius of Caesarea illustrated this versatility of application by chronicling that the Judean

Christians heeded Christ's warnings to flee when they saw armies surrounding Jerusalem (Luke 21:20-21), enabling them to escape the Roman onslaught in AD 70. Nevertheless, this wicked generation, which persecutes Christ's disciples, will certainly not "pass away" until all the aforementioned eschatological events have occurred ("all these things" Matt. 24:34; cf. Matt. 24:4-33). Third, the modern ambiguity of this expression stumbles academic presumption, demanding that the reader humbly wrestle with the timing of the Lord's return and the age-enduring application of the prophecy.

TABLE 1: THE ABOMINATION OF DESOLATION
IN DANIEL 8, 9, AND 11-12

	Daniel 8	Daniel 9	Daniel 11-12
Time of Fulfillment	[17] the vision refers to the time of the end.	[27] Even until the consummation	[11:35] until the time of the end
	[19] what shall happen in the latter time of the indignation; for at the appointed time of the end		[11:35] because it is still for the appointed time.
	[26] Therefore seal up the vision, for it refers to many days in the future.		[12:9] the words are closed up and sealed till the time of the end.
Evil Agent	[9] a little horn [23] a king	[26] the prince who is to come	 [11:36] the king

Self-Exaltation	9 which grew exceedingly great. . . 10 And it grew up to the host of heaven; and it cast down some of the host and some of the stars to the ground, and trampled them. 11 He even exalted himself as high as the Prince of the host 25 And he shall exalt himself in his heart. ... He shall even rise against the Prince of princes	—	11:36 Then the king shall do according to his own will: he shall exalt and magnify himself above every god, shall speak blasphemies against the God of gods, and shall prosper. 37 ... for he shall exalt himself above them all.
His Military Destroys Jerusalem and its Temple Sanctuary	9 and toward the Glorious Land. 11 by him ... the place of His sanctuary was cast down. 12 an army was given over to the horn	26 the people of the prince who is to come shall destroy the city and the sanctuary. The end of it shall be with a flood, and till the end of the war desolations are determined.	11:41 He shall also enter the Glorious Land 11:31 And forces shall be mustered by him, and they shall defile the sanctuary fortress

Removes the Daily Sacrifice (tamid)	[11] and by him the daily sacrifices were taken away [12] Because of transgression, an army was given over to the horn to oppose the daily sacrifices;	[27] he shall bring an end to sacrifice and offering.	[11:31] then they shall take away the daily sacrifices,
Sets up the Abomination of Desolation	[13] and the transgression of desolation	[27] And on the wing of abominations shall be one who makes desolate	[11:31] and place there the abomination of desolation.
He Will Prosper Until the End	[12] and he cast truth down to the ground. He did all this and prospered. [24] And shall prosper and thrive [25] But he shall be broken without human means.	[27] Even until the consummation, which is determined, is poured out on the desolate.	[11:36] and shall prosper till the wrath has been accomplished; for what has been determined shall be done. [11:41] yet he shall come to his end, and no one will help him.

Length of the Fulfillment	[13] "How long will the vision be, concerning the daily sacrifices and the transgression of desolation, the giving of both the sanctuary and the host to be trampled underfoot?" [14] And he said to me, "For two thousand three hundred days; then the sanctuary shall be cleansed."	[27] Then he shall confirm a covenant with many for one week; but in the middle of the week he shall bring an end to sacrifice and offering. And on the wing of abominations shall be one who makes desolate, even until the consummation	[11:32] Those who do wickedly against the covenant he shall corrupt with flattery [12:11] "And from the time that the daily sacrifice is taken away, and the abomination of desolation is set up, there shall be one thousand two hundred and ninety days.

TABLE 2: COMMON ELEMENTS OF THE MAN OF SIN AND THE BEAST

The Man of Sin in 2 Thessalonians 2	The Beast in the Book of Revelation
the son of destruction (v. 3)	and go to destruction (Rev. 17:8) it goes to destruction (Rev. 17:11)
who opposes and exalts himself against every so-called god or object of worship, so that he takes his seat in the temple of God, proclaiming himself to be God. (v. 4)	they worshipped the beast . . . And the beast was given a mouth uttering haughty and blasphemous words, and it was allowed to exercise authority for forty-two months. It opened its mouth to utter blasphemies against God, blaspheming his name and his dwelling . . . and all who dwell on earth will worship it (Rev. 13:4, 5-6, 8; cf. Rev. 11:1-3)
the mystery of lawlessness is already at work. (v. 7)	the mystery . . . of the beast (Rev. 17:7)
And then the lawless one will be revealed, whom the Lord Jesus will kill with the breath of his mouth and bring to nothing by the appearance of his coming. The coming of the lawless one is by the activity of Satan with all power and false signs and wonders, (vv. 8-9)	From his mouth comes a sharp sword with which to strike down the nations . . . And the beast was captured, and with it the false prophet who in its presence had done the signs by which he deceived . . . These two were thrown alive into the lake of fire that burns with sulfur. And the rest were slain by the sword that came from the mouth of him who was sitting on the horse . . . (Rev. 19:15, 20, 20-21; cf. Rev. 17:14)

and with all wicked deception for those who are perishing, because they refused to love the truth and so be saved. Therefore God sends them a strong delusion, so that they may believe what is false, (vv. 10-11)	And to it the dragon gave his power . . . It performs great signs, even making fire come down from heaven to earth in front of people, and by the signs that it was allowed to work in the presence of the beast it deceives those who dwell on the earth (Rev. 13:2, 13-14)
in order that all may be condemned who did not believe the truth but had pleasure in unrighteousness. (v. 12)	If anyone worships the beast and its image and receives a mark . . . he also will drink the wine of God's wrath, poured full strength into the cup of his anger, and he will be tormented with fire and sulfur in the presence of the holy angels and in the presence of the Lamb. (Rev. 14:9-10)

TABLE 4: PARALLEL PASSAGES OF DANIEL 11

	Daniel 11	Parallel Passages
Ships of Cyprus Arrive	For ships from Cyprus shall come against him; therefore, he shall be grieved, and return in rage against the holy covenant, and do damage. (Dan. 11:30)	Come, I will advise you what this people will do to your people in the latter days. . . But ships shall come from the coasts of Cyprus, And they shall afflict Asshur and afflict Eber (Num. 24:14, 24)
King of the North Removes the Tamid and Sets Up the Abomination of Desolation	And forces shall be mustered by him, and they shall defile the sanctuary fortress; then they shall take away the daily sacrifices, and place there the abomination of desolation. (Dan. 11:31)	And from the time that the daily sacrifice is taken away, and the abomination of desolation is set up (Dan. 12:11)
The Wise Will Understand and Be Refined, Purified, and Made White	And those of the people who understand shall instruct many . . . And some of those of understanding shall fall, to refine them, purify them, and make them white, until the time of the end; because it is still for the appointed time. (Dan. 11:33, 35)	Many shall be purified, made white, and refined, but the wicked shall do wickedly; and none of the wicked shall understand, but the wise shall understand. (Dan. 12:10)

The Lawless One Will Exalt Himself Above Every Deity	Then the king shall do according to his own will: he shall exalt and magnify himself above every god, shall speak blasphemies against the God of gods (Dan. 11:36)	[T]he man of sin is revealed, the son of perdition, who opposes and exalts himself above all that is called God or that is worshiped, so that he sits as God in the temple of God, showing himself that he is God. (2 Thess. 2:3-4)

TABLE 7: COMMON ELEMENTS OF MATTHEW 24, 1 THESSALONIANS 4, AND 1 CORINTHIANS 15

	Matthew 24:30-31	1 Thessalonians 4:16 -17	1 Corinthians 15:22-23, 51-53
Jesus Christ Appearing in/ from Heaven	Then the sign of the Son of Man will appear in heaven . . . and they will see the Son of Man coming	For the Lord Himself will descend from heaven	[I]n Christ all shall be made alive . . . afterward those who are Christ's at His coming
Clouds	on the clouds of heaven	in the clouds . . . the Lord in the air	——
Angel(s)	And He will send His angels	with the voice of an archangel	——
A Trumpet	with a great sound of a trumpet	with the trumpet of God	in a moment, in the twinkling of an eye, at the last trumpet. For the trumpet will sound
Gathering of the Righteous	and they will gather together His elect from the four winds, from one end of heaven to the other. (cf. "from the farthest part of earth to the farthest part of heaven" Mark 13:27)	And the dead in Christ will rise first. Then we who are alive and remain shall be caught up together with them in the clouds to meet the Lord in the air.	Behold, I tell you a mystery: We shall not all sleep, but we shall all be changed . . . and the dead will be raised incorruptible, and we shall be changed.

SCRIPTURE INDEX